A *Swift* Guide

to Butterflies of North America

Second Edition

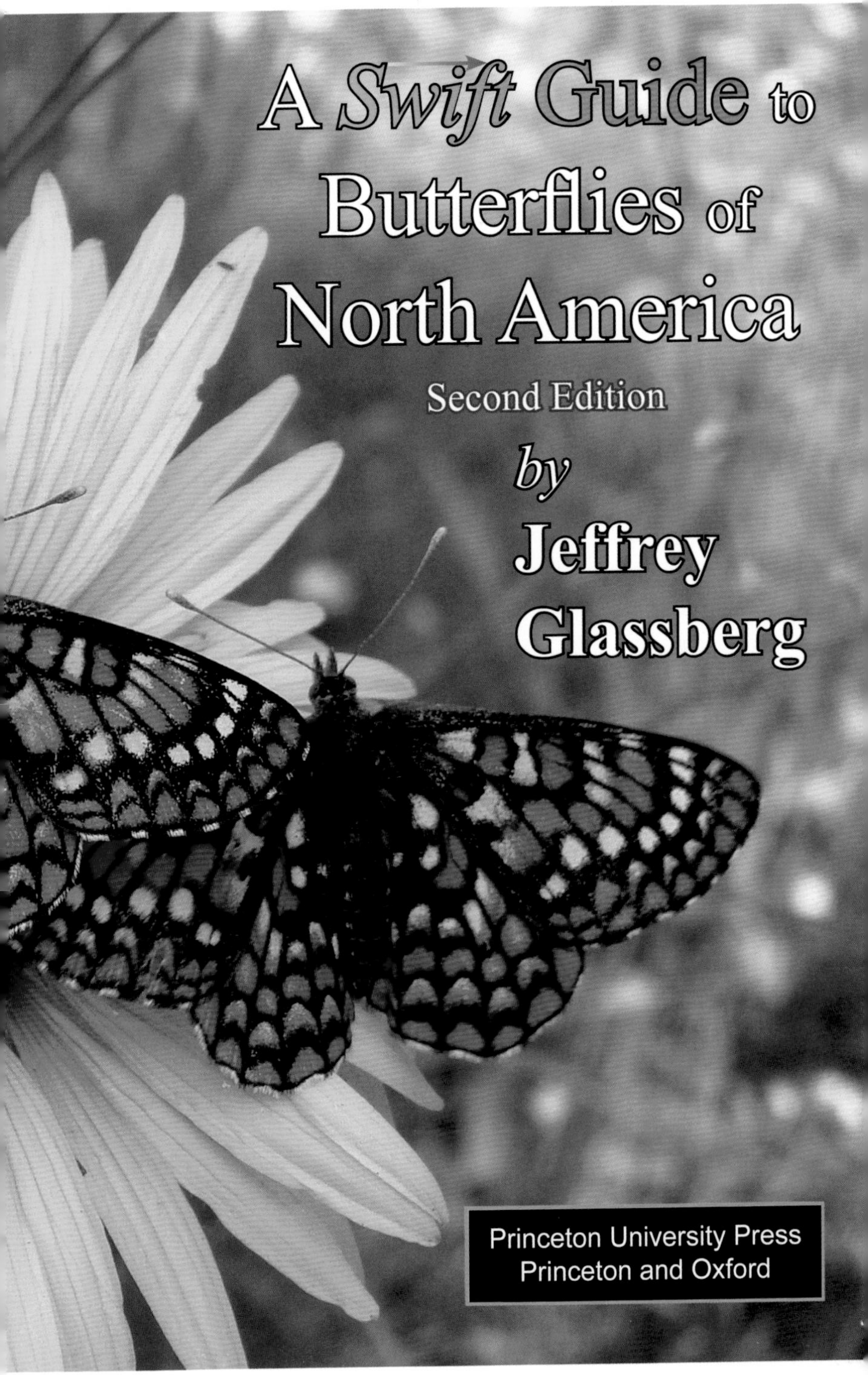

A *Swift* Guide to Butterflies of North America

Second Edition

by

Jeffrey Glassberg

Princeton University Press
Princeton and Oxford

Acknowledgements

This book would not have been possible without the help, support and love from my wife, Jane Vicroy Scott.

Over the past 30 years, hundreds of people have helped me learn about the butterflies of North America, by providing detailed local information and photographs. Please refer to the *Butterflies through Binoculars* books for a complete listing of all of these contributors.

Most of the approximately 3600 photographs in this book were taken by the author, but another one hundred photographers provided about 225 wonderful photographs that increase the usefulness of this guide. Thanks to them all for allowing their photographs to be used in this work.

Jane V. Scott's careful eyes found many typographical errors and looked over all of this work, making useful suggestions for its improvement.

Published by Princeton University Press, 41William Street, Princeton, New Jersey 08540

ISBN 978-0-691-17650-5
Library of Congress Control Number: 2016960487
Printed on acid-free paper. ∞

Printed in China

10 9 8 7 6 5 4 3 2 1

Half-title page: A Martial Scrub-Hairstreak (*Strymon martialis*)

Title page: Two Variable Checkerspots (*Euphydryas chalcedona*)

INTRODUCTION

Nets

Butterflies are fragile. Unless one is a scientist, or working at the behest of a scientist conducting legitimate scientific research, sweeping them into nets is inappropriate behavior. Netting a butterfly not infrequently injures the butterfly, and an injured butterfly is soon a dead butterfly. Besides, if you are interested in butterflies, netting butterflies defeats your interest because you don't get to see what they doing; how they are behaving. Actually, you don't get to see them well at all, because a butterfly wriggling around in a net is more difficult to see well than is a butterfly sitting on a flower, especially through the lenses of your binoculars or your camera.

Of course, while netting and then releasing butterflies is not the way to interact with butterflies, killing them as a hobby, so that one can possess boxes of dead butterflies, now makes no sense at all in the United States. Besides pointlessly killing wild butterflies, the majority of hobbyists who kill butterflies focus on rare butterflies, many of which they then "trade" or sell, as people trade or sell inanimate baseball cards. But butterflies are living animals, and each rare butterfly that is killed diminishes the genetic diversity of the species. In extreme cases, hobbyists who kill butterflies can extirpate a species or a population. This is what happened in New Jersey, when a small group of people came year after year to the same small habitat where the last Mitchell's Satyrs in New Jersey lived and killed each Mitchell's Satyr that they found. Although the destruction of a population or species of butterflies by hobbyists who kill them is a rare event, their activities frequently interfere with other people. When rare butterflies are killed by these hobbyists, then the much larger number of butterfliers are denied the opportunity to see the butterfly themselves.

Just to be clear, I am not saying that people who kill butterflies as a hobby are evil people – just that they are out of step with the needs of the modern world. Bird enthusiasts gave up "collecting" birds more than 60 years ago. The use of binoculars and cameras has led to a tremendous increase in the number of birders and thus directly to an explosion of knowledge about birds. Thus, those who are truly interested in advancing knowledge of butterflies will put away nets and embrace the future.

Commercially Raised Butterflies and Butterfly "Releases"

Dumping commercially raised butterflies into the environment at weddings or other events is a disaster for butterflies. "Releasing" isn't the right word for these events because it is the commercial breeder (and therefore the purchaser of the butterflies) who first imprisoned them in tiny envelopes. Often, when he unsuspecting bride dumps out the contents of the box, the butterflies simply tumble to the ground, unable to fly after their period of imprisonment. On the two occasions when I was present at such events, that is exactly what happened.

Once "released" they often find themselves in an environment in which they will die — either because they are already sick and dying, or because it's the wrong time of year for them, or because there is no suitable habitat for them in the vicinity. But the truly shocking conclusion is that, for the sake of our native wild butterflies, we must hope that these farm butterflies die quickly. Raised under unnatural conditions, farmed butterflies provide fertile ground for the spread of the many diseases that affect butterflies. By shipping them around the country and by placing them into the environment, we run the very real risk of decimating populations of our native butterflies by disease epidemics.

These farmed butterflies create other problems as well. Scientific studies have

INTRODUCTION

Focus on the World of Butterflies and Find Yourself

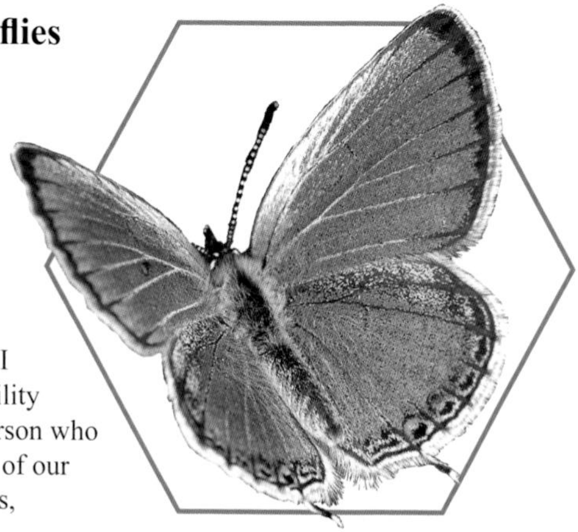

Beginning their lives as caterpillars (which, like humans, are earthbound), butterflies — fragile, ephemeral and ethereal — are connected to the human soul and to the possibility of transformation. Your involvement with butterflies will connect you to nature, allowing you to find your place within it. I hope that the beauty, intensity and tranquility of butterflies will transform you into a person who works to conserve the biological heritage of our planet. Because, if we can save butterflies, we can save ourselves®.

About This Book

The purpose of this book is to help you to identify adult North American butterflies. Very little information that is not directly related to this purpose is included. For a more expansive introduction to butterfly biology, butterfly gardening and other topics, see my book *Butterflies of North America* (Sterling Publishing).

The *Swift Guide* format places all text directly with the illustrations, allowing swift access to the information while you are in the field. In order to facilitate identification, images of butterflies are arranged so that similar species can be easily compared. This means rotating images to align the butterflies in similar orientations so that you don't need to perform mental gymnastics to compare them.

This book treats all of the species of butterflies found in North America and Hawaii. The order of presentation is based upon the *NABA Checklist and English Names of North American Butterflies*, slightly modified to compare similar species or to provide a more pleasing layout.

All photographs of live butterflies taken by the author are of wild, unrestrained butterflies.

Butterfly Identification

If you are new to butterflying, start by sorting the butterflies you see into one of the six families found in North America — swallowtails; whites and yellows; gossamerwings; metalmarks; brushfoots; and skippers. This is usually easy, because, in general, swallowtails are large with "tails," whites and yellows are white or yellow, gossamerwings are very small and delicate, brushfoots are medium-sized orange to brown and skippers have distinctive flight and large bodies. Soon you'll recognize subgroups, such as grass-skippers and then be able to identify species by using this book, noting the indicated field marks, range, habitat and foodplant. Of course, not every individual butterfly you see will be identifiable to species. Some, you might not see well enough. Some may be too

Contents

Contents

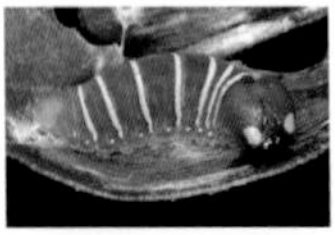

shown that mixing farmed organisms with wild populations lowered the genetic fitness of the wild populations. Two of the most widely used butterflies for these "releases" are Monarchs and Painted Ladies. Both of these species migrate. We really know very little about these migrations. Since, for example, it is not known how the Monarchs find their overwintering sites in central Mexico, it is entirely possible (not likely, but possible) that interactions with farm-raised Monarchs could interfere with the ability of wild Monarchs to migrate properly. Another obvious consequence of selling butterflies is that this creates a commercial market for butterflies. Even in our material society, this is aesthetically repugnant. It also has the potential to cause widespread killing of native wild butterflies. When a Monarch for a wedding is worth $10/individual, there is much incentive for people to gather up wild Monarchs from migrating or overwintering aggregations and sell them. I am told that there have already been incidents of this sort.

In the 1890s, people thought "wouldn't it be wonderful to have all the birds mentioned by Shakespeare, right here in North America." So they released European Starlings into Central Park, New York. These birds have caused billions of dollars in damage to crops and harmed native songbirds. Yet, if you had said, in 1890, "Where's your proof that this will damage the environment," one could not provide that proof. The proof can come only when it is too late and the environment has been severely damaged.

Conservation

Every day, there are fewer butterflies in North America. This is because, every day, an expanding population of human beings requires new housing, new roadways and new shopping malls. The loss of habitat necessary to support butterfly populations is, by far, the single largest factor decreasing butterfly populations. To some extent, you can help offset the loss of habitat by creating habitats for butterflies around your home. Visit the website, for NABA's Butterfly Gardens and Habitats program, www.naba.org, and learn what plants to use in your area.

A second factor affecting butterflies is the misuse and overuse of pesticides. Butterflies are not pests, but these toxic chemicals kill them as well. Besides killing millions of butterflies and driving some toward extinction, the main effect of continuous spraying for gypsy moths and for mosquito control is to pollute the environment with chemicals that are almost certainly toxic to humans.

The North American Butterfly Association

The North American Butterfly Association (NABA) is a non-profit, membership association that is the largest group of people in North America focused on butterflies. NABA's mission is to educate the public about the importance of conserving butterflies and their habitats. To this end, NABA publishes two full-color magazines, *American Butterflies* and *Butterfly Gardener*, conducts an extensive butterfly monitoring program throughout North America whose data are increasingly used by scientists, offers the Program for Butterfly Gardens and Habitats, works to conserve rare and endangered species such as Miami Blues, Regal Fritillaries and Poweshiek Skipperlings and operates the 100 acre National Butterfly Center in Mission, Texas, on the Rio Grande River.

Butterfly Wing Areas and Body Parts

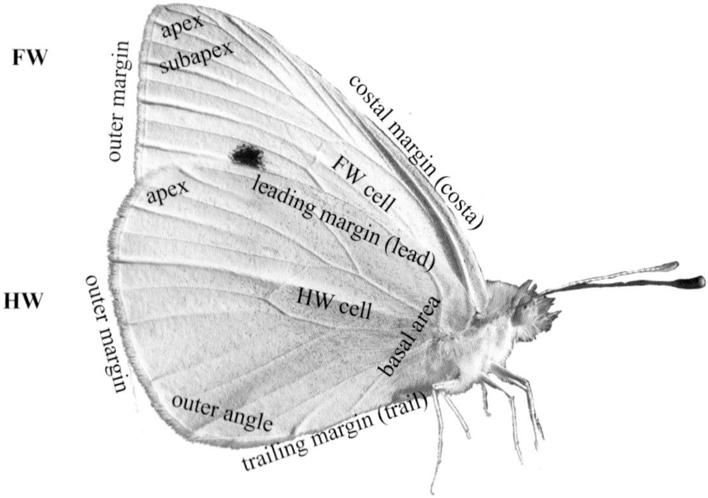

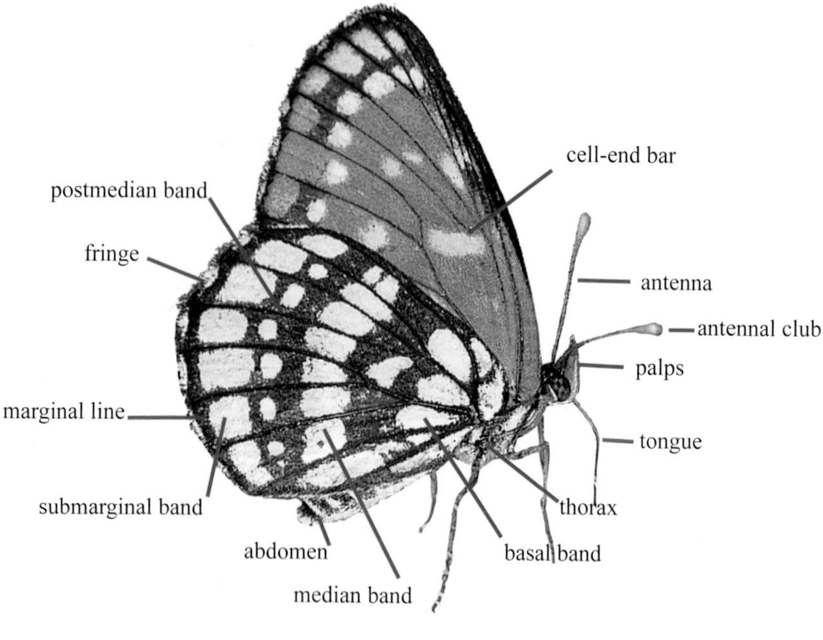

INTRODUCTION

About the Species Accounts

FIELD MARKS — A red line draws your attention to a feature that may be helpful in identifying this species.

SIZE — The length of the blue/white bar that is placed directly above the name of the species, is the actual length of the FW, measured from its base to its apex.

CATERPILLAR FOODPLANT — **citrus** — If all species on a page use the same group of foodplants, that information may be given at the top right of the page.

ABUNDANCE AND FLIGHT TIMES — **R-U Feb-Oct** — Because this guide covers such a large area, abundance and flight times are generalized and may vary at particular locations. In general, flight times will be later in the year and/or for shorter periods of time the farther north and/or the higher the elevation. With the advent of global warming, these flight times may change rapidly.

HABITAT — **desert and scrub** — Generalized habitat information helps in finding and identifiying the species.

COMMENTS — **hilltops** — Various comments about the species are placed here.

ADDITIONAL ID INFORMATION — large with slow flight

RANGE

Clodius Parnassian *Parnassius clodius* — A green color-wash over the species name indicates that the species is endemic to the United States and Canada.

Phoebus Parnassian *Parnassius phoebus* — A blue color-wash over the species name indicates that the species is primarily Holarctic, (found in northern Eurasia as well as in North America) although some of these species, such as Red Admiral, are even more widespread.

Black Swallowtail *Papilio polyxenes* — No color-wash over the species name indicates that the species also occurs in Mexico but is not primarily tropical.

Pipevine Swallowtail *Battus philenor* — A purple wash over the species name indicates that the species is primarily Neotropical, although it may occur in much of southern North America.

Schaus' Swallowtail *Papilio aristodemus* — An orange wash over the species name indicates that the species is primarily West Indian.

Montezuma's Cattleheart *Parides montezuma* — A red wash over the species name indicates that the species is a stray to the U.S., not seen each year.

Cabbage White *Pieris rapae* — A yellow color-wash over the species name indicates that this species is not native to North America and was introduced by the activities of humans.

INTRODUCTION

Abbreviations and Glossary

A	abundant (likely to see more than 20 individuals in the right habitat at the right time of year)
Bor.	borough
C	common (likely to see 3-20 individuals in the right habitat at the right time of year)
Co.	county
costa	the leading edge of the forewing
esp	especially
et al.	et alia (and others)
FW	forewing
ground	ground color of the wing (the main background color)
hilltops	males of this species often congregate at the top of the highest spot in the area where they perch and wait for unmated females
HW	hindwing
Keys	Florida Keys
L	local (absent from many areas in range, even in appropriate habitat)
lead	the leading edge of the hindwing
LRGV	the Lower Rio Grande Valley of Texas
m	median
mtn	mountain
mudpuddles	often congregates at damp sand to accumulate dissolved salts and other minerals
n	north
NP	national park
pg	page
pm	postmedian (past the middle of the wing, away from the body)
R	rare (unlikely to be seen, even in the right habitat at the right time of year)
RS	rare stray
R-S	roadside-skipper
s	south
scrophs	Scrophulariaceae
se AZ	southeastern Arizona
sm	submarginal (not actually at the wing margin, but a short way inward)
trail	the trailing edge of the hindwing
U	uncommon (likely to see 0-3 individuals in the right habitat at the right time of year)
w	west
w/	with
w/o	without

INTRODUCTION

About the Maps

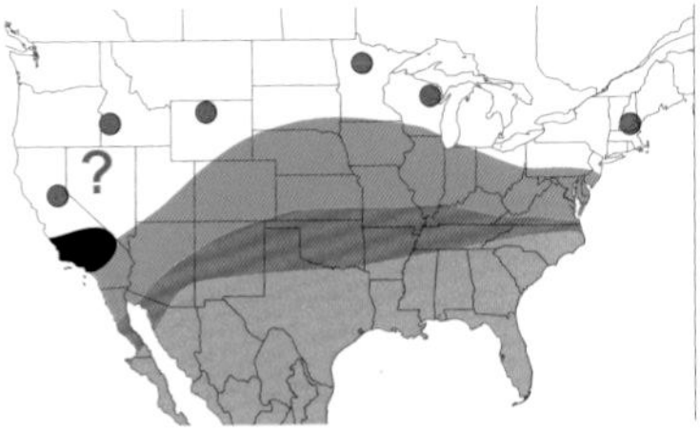

three broods
two broods
one brood
extirpated from this area
stray

? reports from this area (base of question mark) may be incorrect

? there are no reports from this area (base of question mark), but this species may occur here

Ranges of butterfly are not “facts” That is because the location(s) where a particular species of butterfly can be found is a moving target. It changes from year to year and it can change from month to month (for immigrant species). In addition, no butterfly species is found on every acre within its “range.” Where it may be found is influenced by habitat and by chance. So, how close together do two populations need to be to be shown as one? A mile, ten miles, twenty-five miles, a hundred miles? All of these considerations will affect how one draws a range “map”. Also bear in mind, that with the advent of global warming, the ranges of many species are rapidly changing! On the maps in this book, I have tried to indicate the general area where a species might be found most years, in the right habitat at the right time of year.

For species that range into southern Canada and the lower 48 states of the United States, maps similar to the one on this page, or of a portion of this area if the range is limited, are shown. For truly arctic species, maps of Canada and Alaska are shown.

For some species that only stray into the United States, into the Lower Rio Grande Valley of Texas, into southeastern Arizona, or the Florida Keys; or are resident only in the Lower Rio Grande Valley (LRGV), rather than a map, there is a small box indicating where the species has been found.

LRGV In the U.S., normally found only in the LRGV, where it is seen most years.

LRGV Rare stray to the LRGV, where it not seen in most years.

not yet LRGV Has not yet been reliably recorded in the United States, but occurs in northern Mexico and probably strays to the Lower Rio Grande Valley.

Swallowtails are our largest butterflies and, except for Monarchs, probably the butterflies most often noticed. Most swallowtails are easy to recognize as swallowtail, because they are large and do have "tails." However, the parnassians, large, red-spotted white or yellow butterflies associated with the far north or alpine peaks, lack tails, as do some other swallowtail species.

In North America, there are four broad groups of swallowtails — the parnassians (*Parnassius*), the pipevine-feeding swallowtails (*Battus* and *Parides*), the kite-swallowtails (*Eurytides*) and the true swallowtails (*Papilio*). While caterpillars of the parnassians feed on wildflowers and those of *Battus* and *Parides* on vines, caterpillars of most species of the kite-swallowtails and the true swallowtails feed on trees and shrubs.

Fewflower Fumewort

LR
June-July

mountain tundra

life cycle takes two years to complete

the only yellowish parnassian

females are white, or yellowish-white, and have yellow body rings

food plant

female

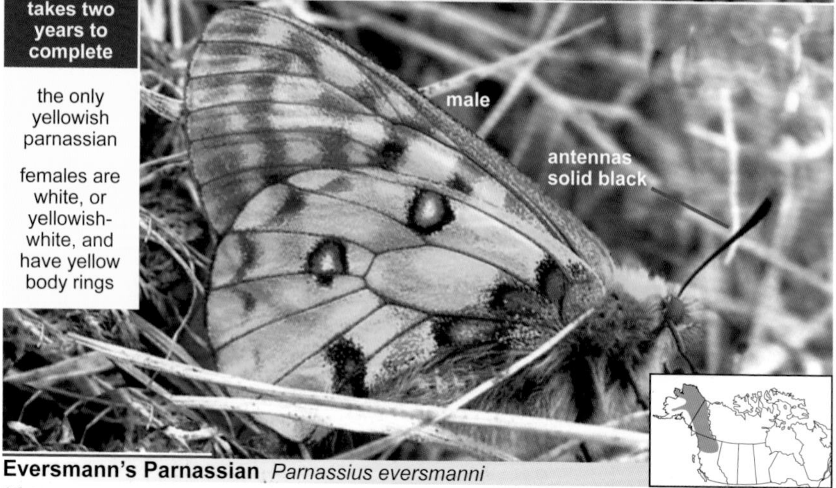
male
antennas solid black

Eversmann's Parnassian *Parnassius eversmanni*

stonecrops

Rockies C late May-Aug; Sierra Nevada, R July; Siskiyous, R July-Aug

open mountain areas, especially rocky hilltops

some treat *P. p. behrii* in the California Sierra Nevada and *P. p. smintheus* in the Rockies, as separate species

flight usually 1-2 ft. off the ground

female

black bar usually doesn't cross cell
large red spots
male

large red spots
antennas ringed black and white

Phoebus Parnassian *Parnassius phoebus*

bleeding hearts

C-A May-Sept, mostly June-Aug

woodland meadows

white and black with red spots

flight is slow and sailing, usually higher off the ground than Phoebus Parnassians

usually found at lower elevations than Phoebus Parnassians

female

black bar cross's cell
male

antennas solid black
large red spots

Clodius Parnassian *Parnassius clodius*

pipevines

LC, but R-U in much of range

South Feb-Oct

farther north Apr-Oct

gardens, woodland edges, open thorn-scrub

bright colors signal that this species is distasteful

Black Swallowtails, and Red-spotted Purples mimic its appearance

a black and blue swallowtail that averages slightly smaller than other dark swallowtails

blue iridescence depends upon the angle of light

our only dark swallowtail with a single row of very prominent orange postmedian spots on the HW below

red form caterpillar

male
pale spots
extensive iridescent blue

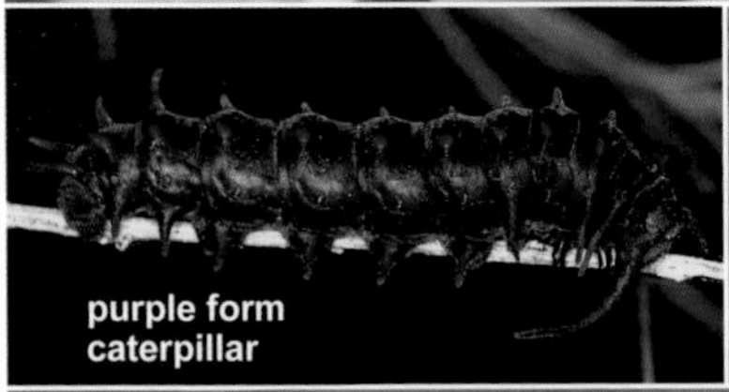
purple form caterpillar

single orange spotband
strongly iridescent blue

Pipevine Swallowtail *Battus philenor*

pipevines

LU where resident; RS elsewhere

gardens, woodland edges, open thorn-scrub

rarely stays still, even when nectaring

caterpillar

yellow submarginal band
no tail

black with a yellow submarginal band on the HW topside

below, note the marginal S-shaped red spots and the cream HW apex

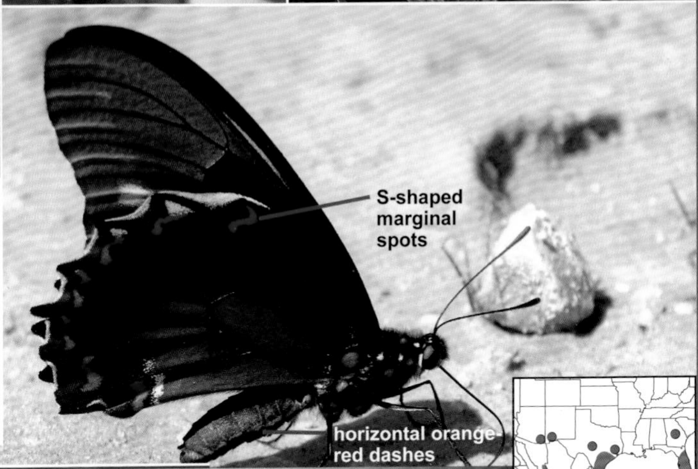
S-shaped marginal spots
horizontal orange-red dashes

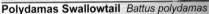

Polydamas Swallowtail *Battus polydamas*

pipevines

pm band of white dots
one row of red crescents
red bars on abdomen
pm band of white dots
red crescents

se AZ once

White-dotted Cattleheart *Parides alopius*

pipevines

one row of red crescents
vertical red bars on abdomen
one row of red crescents

not yet LRGV

Montezuma's Cattleheart *Parides montezuma*

citrus

R-U
all year, but most frequent in the fall

gardens, woodland edges, open thorn-scrub

there are no other large black butterflies w/ large bright red/pink spots in the middle of the HW

females with more white on FW

female
large spots

female

large red median spots, no marginal spots
male

Ruby-spotted Swallowtail *Papilio anchisiades*

citrus

as you can see, Pink-spotted Swallowtails are similar to resident Ruby-spotted Swallowtails, but with two narrow pm bands rather than one large one

Victorine Swallowtails, opposite page, also have two red spot bands below, but one of those is marginal

two pink spot bands; one complete, one partial
two pink/red median/pm spotbands

Pink-spotted Swallowtail *Papilio pharnaces*

two complete
red spot rows
three spot rows

Laredo
once

Victorine Swallowtail *Papilio victorinus*

red rectangles
female
male
blue or red
rectangles
red vertical lines

LRGV
twice

Red-sided Swallowtail *Mimoides phaon*

citrus

will be U-C

many

this Afro-Asian species was first reported from the Dominican Republic in 2004; it is now widespread on Puerto Rico, has reached Jamaica and is probably on Cuba; it will soon be in citrus groves in South Florida

yellow with rusty pm band

motled
black &
off-white
large
spot
black
lines

not yet
Keys

Lime Swallowtail *Papilio demoleus*

parsley family and some rue family

U-C; Florida all year; northward Apr/May - Sept

open areas, including, disturbed and even urban areas

hilltops

Ozark Sw., not shown, in woods glades in the Ozarks, is identical, and may not be a species distinct from Black Swallowtail

median
spotband
complete

female
females w/
yellow pm
band reduced
females w/
HW blue
extensive

caterpillar

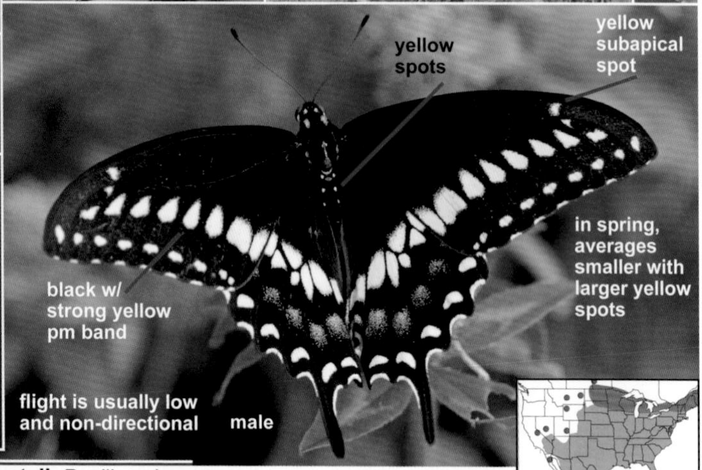
yellow
spots
yellow
subapical
spot
in spring,
averages
smaller with
larger yellow
spots
black w/
strong yellow
pm band
flight is usually low
and non-directional
male

Black Swallowtail *Papilio polyxenes*

no
orange
spot

female
large
marginal
spots

Florida
female

Sassafras and Northern Spicebush

U-A three broods Feb-Oct; two broods Apr-Sept

open woods and edges

caterpillar

no yellow
subapical spot
green-blue
cloud
flight is
usually direct
large marginal spots
male

Spicebush Swallowtail *Papilio troilus*

parsley family including Common Cowparsnip and Scottish Licorice-root

U

restricted to the Canadian Maritime provinces and adjacent Quebec June-July

gardens, grassy open areas

one of the few species that are endemic to Canada

long yellow shoulders
short tails

Short-tailed Swallowtail *Papilio brevicauda*

Black Cherry, Tuliptree

C-A Mar/Apr-Sept/Oct

deciduous woodlands and edges, including suburbia

black females comprise greater than 50 percent of females in the deep south, with decreasing frequency northward

they are R-U at the northern edge of their range

usually w/ a shadow of the tiger pattern

marginal spots narrow

Eastern Tiger Swallowtail, black form female *Papilio glaucus*

parsley family and some rue family

U-C

southward Feb-Oct

northward May-Sept

open areas, including disturbed areas

hilltops

spots
usually
w/ much
orange

two or three rows of
yellow spots
shoulders
usually
black
yellow spots
visible from
above
black spot
small and
centered
or reaching
inner margin

Black Swallowtail *Papilio polyxenes*

Tarragon

R-U
May-June,
mid July-Sept

dry hills, prairies, open woods

hilltops

map shows range of all southern Old World Swallowtail populations

black forms occur mainly south of central Utah-central Colorado

see page 26 for more information

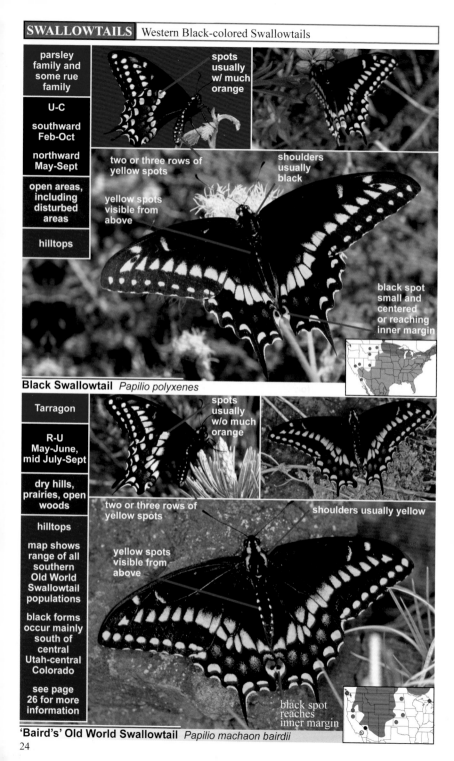

spots
usually
w/o much
orange

two or three rows of
yellow spots
shoulders usually yellow
yellow spots
visible from
above
black spot
reaches
inner margin

'Baird's' Old World Swallowtail *Papilio machaon bairdii*

parsley family

R-U
May-July

open areas including disturbed areas

hilltops

black form occurs mainly along the eastern edge of the Rockies; these may may be hybrids between Anise and Black Swallowtails

see page 27 for yellow form

spots usually w/o much orange
one row of yellow spots
shoulders yellow or black
yellow spots not visible from above
black spots small and centered

Anise Swallowtail (black form) *Papilio zelicaon*

desert parsleys and other parsley family

LR-LU
Mar-July

hilltops and arid slopes

usually lands on ground with wings spread, just below the top of hilltops

there are at least 13 named subspecies

some s California and n Arizona/ s Utah populations have longer tails (see right inset)

Josephine Co., OR

Emery Co., UT

abdomen black with yellow toward end
Jefferson Co., CO
no yellow
short tails
black spots large and reach margin

Indra Swallowtail *Papilio indra*

Tarragon

R-U southward May-June, mid July-Sept; northward, June-July

dry hills, prairies, open woods

hilltops

until the 1990s, Old World Swallowtail populations in North America were generally considered to consist of three species — Old World Swallowtail, Oregon Swallowtail (in eastern Oregon and Washington State and vicinity) and Baird's Swallowtail over most of the range (with yellow form Bairds generally north of central Utah-central Colorado and dark form Bairds (see page 24) generally south of Utah-central Colorado

top map shows range of northern populations; bottom map shows range of southern populations

abdomen
is yellow
w/ central
black stripe
Fairbanks
North Star
Bor., AK
(both photos)
large orange
spot ringed
with black

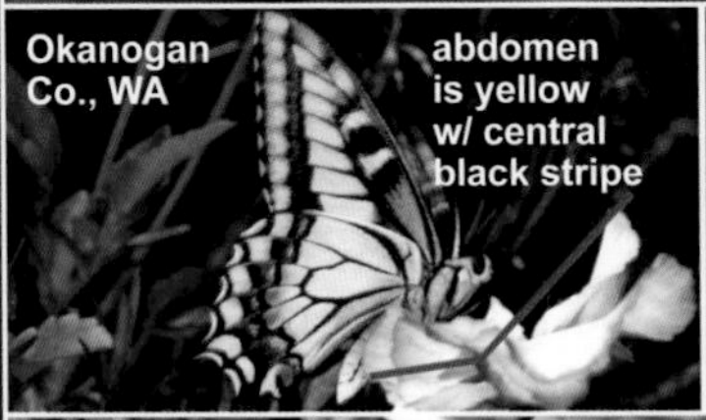
Okanogan
Co., WA
abdomen
is yellow
w/ central
black stripe

Okanogan
Co., WA

Fremont
Co., CO
black spot reaches
inner margin

Old World Swallowtail *Papilio machaon*

parsley family, especially Sweet Anise

U-C
Mar-Sept

open and disturbed areas

hilltops

the western counterpart of Black Swallowtail and the most common western "black" swallowtail

see page 25 for the rare black form

black spot centered
FW marginal spots flattened outwardly

Anise Swallowtail *Papilio zelicaon*

parsley family

R-U
Feb-Oct

desert and scrub

map shows all Black Swallowtails

yellow forms of Black Swallowtails are most common in southeastern California and western Arizona deserts, but also occur all along the U.S.-Mexican border

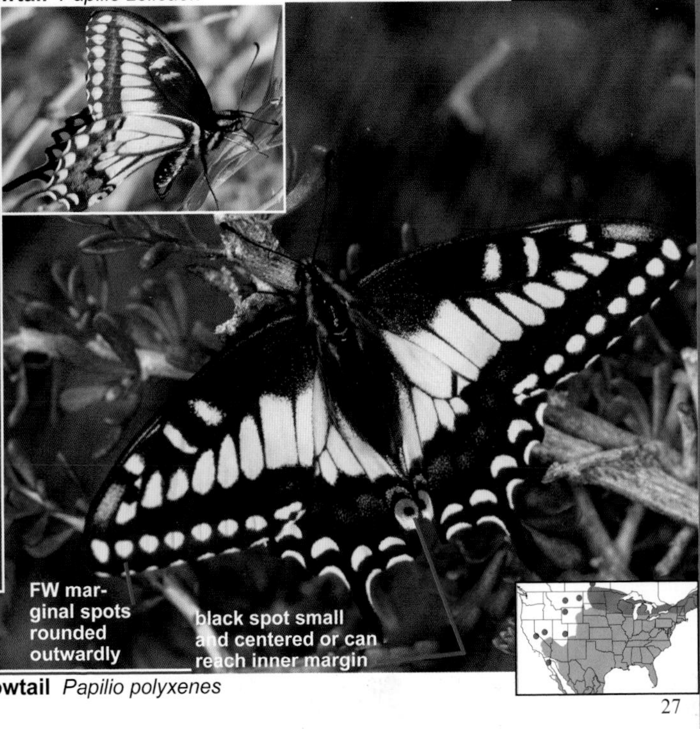
FW marginal spots rounded outwardly
black spot small and centered or can reach inner margin

Black Swallowtail *Papilio polyxenes*

Black Cherry, Tuliptree

C-A Mar/Apr-Sept/Oct

deciduous woods, including suburbia

often seen high in the trees although they readily descend for nectar and mudpuddling

in the high Appalachians occurs a large form that some treat as a separate species, Appalachian Tiger

sm band
of spots
black
stripe thin

female
females
w/ more
blue

caterpillar

yellow w/
black stripes
spot orange
(if present)
male

Eastern Tiger Swallowtail *Papilio glaucus*

birches, aspens et al.

C-A mostly late May-mid July

deciduous & mixed woods and edges

many early spring Eastern Tiger Swallowtails resemble Canadian Tigers and there appears to be a broad hybrid band where Canadian and Eastern meet, at least in New England

they might best be treated as one species

sm band
continuous

female

black stripe
thick
spot orange
(if present)
male

Canadian Tiger Swallowtail *Papilio canadensis*

willows, aspens et al.

C
mostly June-July

in two brood areas Mar/Apr-Sept/Oct

woods and woodland openings, especially near water; suburban gardens

females usually with more blue than on males, but blue not as extensive as on female Eastern Tiger Swallowtails

sm band
continuous

wide black bars
spot yellow
(if present)

Western Tiger Swallowtail *Papilio rutulus*

cherries, ashes et al.

C in south, R-U north
mostly Apr/May-Aug/Sept

woods, especially in canyons & ravines near water

this species is common throughout much of the Mexican highlands and was prominently featured in Aztec mythology

females with wider bars and more blue

female

males w/
black bars
narrow
male
second
"tail"

Two-tailed Swallowtail *Papilio multicaudata*

buckthorns, ceanothuses, et al.

U-C
May- July;
Apr-Sept along Pacific

moist montane deciduous woods or chaparral

a pale, off-white tiger swallowtail

some with enough yellow to resemble Western Tiger Swallowtails

black vertical bars usually wider, especially HW median bar near the lead

wide black bar
HW cell-end bar thick and connected to median band
wide black bar

Pale Swallowtail *Papilio eurymedon*

laurel family

RS to southeastern Arizona

occurs in nearby Mexico, but no confirmed Texas records

flight is slow and "heavy-bottomed"

chocolate brown stripes
three tails
se AZ

Three-tailed Swallowtail *Papilio pilumnus*

pawpaws

LC
Feb/Apr-Sept

moist open woods, brushy fields, gardens

small (for a swallowtail)

flight is low and rapid

spring individuals (right inset) are smaller with narrower bands and shorter tails

summer form

summer form

spring form

orange antennas
black-and-white w/ red
long white-tipped tail

Zebra Swallowtail *Eurytides marcellus*

Annonaceae

unlike most strays to the Lower Rio Grande Valley, this species is seen most frequently in the spring and summer

wide black bands
black antennas

Dark Kite-Swallowtail *Eurytides philolaus*

LRGV

rue family

LU-C
all year in Deep South, May-Sept northward

periodically expands and contracts its range

open woods, scrub, gardens

some treat population west and south of central TX as a separate species

in flight, dark topside contrasts w/ pale underside

paler
cream
band
outer edge
of spots
less angled
Thoas
Swallowtail
shown here
not yet
LRGV

caterpillar

yellow
bands
form an
X near
FW sub-
apex
usually w/ yellow
spot in tail

Giant Swallowtail *Papilio cresphontes*

Redbay and others in the laurel family

LC-A
mostly Mar-Oct

swamp edges and nearby open areas and gardens

can be reliably seen at Great Dismal Swamp NWR, VA, at the ne edge of its range, and at Aransas NWR, TX, at the sw edge of its range

almost black when fresh, color quickly fades to brown

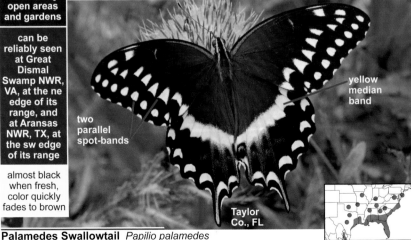

basal
yellow
stripe

Aransas
Co., TX

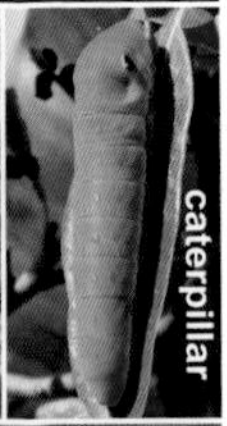
caterpillar

yellow
median
band
two
parallel
spot-bands
Taylor
Co., FL

Palamedes Swallowtail *Papilio palamedes*

Lime Pricklyash and Sea Torchwood

LR late Apr-early June

hardwood hammocks

listing this species as endangered, in 1984, has not led to its recovery — now only on North Key Largo and Elliott Key

habitat loss is the main cause of the decline, but anti-mosquito spraying also takes its toll

rusty
median
band

habitat

caterpillar

males w/ yellow clubs
yellow bands don't form an X near FW subapex
no yellow spot in tail

Schaus' Swallowtail *Papilio aristodemus*

Sea Torchwood

LR-LU on Elliott Key in Biscayne National Park

hardwood hammocks

individuals from the Cuban population occasionally stray to the Lower Keys

males w/ yellow clubs

food plant

yellow bar in FW cell
often w/ dark bar in yellow band

Bahamian Swallowtail *Papilio andraemon*

rue family

R
but regular, seen most years, in the LRGV

occasionally strays to the northwest in Webb and Zapata Counties, Texas

yellow paler than Giant Swallowtail
no yellow
yellow bands don't form an X

wide marginal spots
some females are black
female
long tail

Ornythion Swallowtail *Papilio ornythion*

rue family

RS
seen every few years in the LRGV

one report from Harding County, New Mexico

similar to Ornythion Swallowtail but FW band is wider and the HW below has a postmedian red spot band

cell spot
marginal spots

female
red pm spot band

short tail
male
red postmedian spot band

Broad-banded Swallowtail *Papilio astyalus*

rue family

a colony existed in southern Florida from 1976-1983

resident in the West Indies and Mexico, it may again stray to South Florida or to the LRGV

similar above to Broad-banded Swallowtail

FW lacks marginal spots

HW has longer tails

cell spot
no marginal spots
red pm spot band
no median band

not yet LRGV

Androgeus Swallowtail *Papilio androgeus*

many

in their native habitat these magnificent butterflies glide high over trees, circling and often remaining in an area for some time

see Palamedes Swallowtail, page 32

no sm spots
spiked median band
male

LRGV once

Magnificent Swallowtail *Papilio garamas*

female

Ponderosa Pine and others in the pine family

C-A
July-Aug/ early Sept

pine forests

flight is floating and graceful, often high in the pines

females have a red-orange ring of "lipstick" around the HW below

male and female, black costal bar curves across cell, both above and below
male

Pine White *Neophasia menapia*

Ponderosa Pine and others in the pine family

C-A
mid June-early Nov; peaks late June-early July, Oct

pine forests

unpredictably move, en masse, from high in the trees to ground level

similar to Pine Whites, but with the FW cell completely black

male

female

male

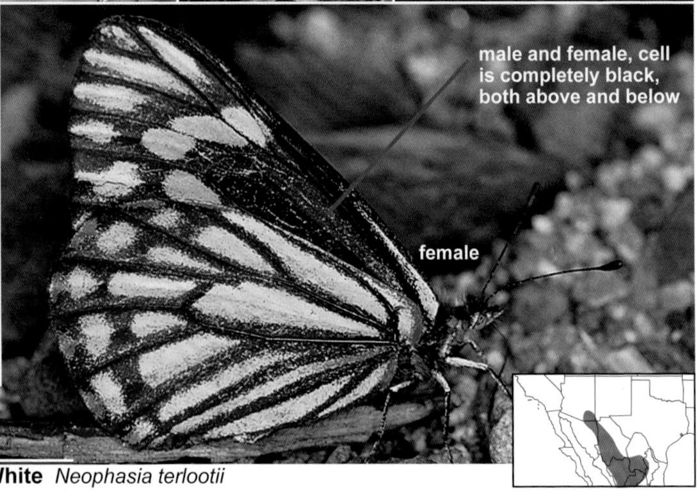
male and female, cell is completely black, both above and below
female

Chiricahua White *Neophasia terlootii*

mistletoes
black flecked w/ yellow w/ a white median band
Big Bend

Mexican Dartwhite *Catasticta nimbice*

unknown
white
pink
LRGV once

Painted White *Pieriballia viardi*

probably mistletoes
faded gray zigzag pattern
not yet LRGV

Pallid Tilewhite *Hesperocharis costaricensis*

female

usually w/o or w/ weak black here
male

bar slants out
female

caterpillar

mustards

mostly U-C, most common in the Southwest & FL, R-U at northern edges of range; flies throughout warm weather

open areas, especially disturbed lowland habitats and farmland

more common in the East 100 years ago when farmland was more extensive

bar slants out
marginal spots usually as black as pm band
strong black rectangle
male

Checkered White *Pontia protodice*

male

female

mustards

U-C
Apr-Sept but only 1 brood at high altitudes

open areas, especially at high altitudes

hilltops

usually with stronger markings than Checkered Whites, but current knowledge doesn't allow separation of many/most individuals

marginal spots usually grayer than pm band
usually w/ strong black here
male

Western White *Pontia occidentalis*

mustards

U-C
Feb-Apr
in the
Southwest;
Apr-June
in the
Northwest;
into Aug
at high
elevations

open areas
including
sagebrush,
desert
and open
coniferous
woods

hilltops

although
widespread
and not rare,
it isn’t easy
to get good
looks at this
butterfly

female

male

FW cell-
end bar is
notched
dark veining
w/ pm
interruption

Spring White *Pontia sisymbrii*

mustards

U-C
Mar-Aug,
mostly
May-June
and Aug

arid areas,
including
deserts,
sagebrush
and juniper

one of
our most
beautiful
whites

marbles and
orangetips
also have
green patches
below, but
their pattern is
more irregular
along the HW
trailing edge

bar
slants in
male

female

bar slants in
this broad and
greenish spot
doesn’t follow
the vein
veining
usually
yellow

Becker’s White *Pontia beckerii*

mustards

C-A
but R in Deep South; flying throughout warm weather

gardens, farmland, suburbia, but also in open woods and cities; less frequent in true native habitats

this gracefully flying European immigrant (first appearing in western Canada in the 1860s) adds life to areas that would otherwise be devoid of butterflies

HW unmarked below, often w/ a yellowish cast

female
male
two spots
one spot
gray/black is horizontal
some in spring w/o spots

Cabbage White *Pieris rapae*

toothworts

Appalachians LC

elsewhere LR-LU

Apr-May

rich deciduous woods, near streams and moist areas w/ the foodplant

appears to be declining in some areas

spring eastern Mustard Whites normally have much darker, sharper HW veining below

foodplant
foodplant
unmarked topside
soft gray veining

West Virginia White *Pieris virginiensis*

mustards

U-C
Feb-Aug,
mostly
June-July

open, moist woods, usually coniferous

some treat *marginalis* and *oleracea* as distinct species and as distinct from Old World *P. napi*

spring individuals usually strongly marked

summer individuals less marked, sometimes immaculate

some populations w/ yellow individuals

North Slope Bor., AK
Humboldt Co., CA
Teton Co., WY
North Star Fairbanks Bor., AK
rarely w/ black spot
San Mateo Co., CA
if present, gray/black is vertical
gray veining
Teton Co., WY
summer individual

'Margined' Mustard White *Pieris napi marginalis*

mustards

LR-U
late Apr-mid June;
early July-Aug

deciduous woods

some treat the eastern and western subspecies as distinct species and as distinct from Old World *P. napi*

spring individuals are usually strongly marked while summer individuals are often immaculate

Door Co., WI
summer
no gray/ black horizontal apex
strong gray veining (in spring)
Coos Co., NH

'Veined' Mustard White *Pieris napi oleracea*

mustards, saltworts, capers

south Florida C-A

south Texas C all year

northward, decreasing rapidly, occurring mostly in the fall

open coastal areas, but also thorn scrub, fields and gardens

some years this species becomes tremendously abundant on the Florida Keys and then moves northward

rarely, the turquoise blue antennal club color fades when old

below, males are usually off-white but some are distinctly yellowish (see top left inset).

Male jagged black FW border is sometimes not visible from below

females are normally more heavily marked than are males

females vary from white to dark smoky gray

male

male

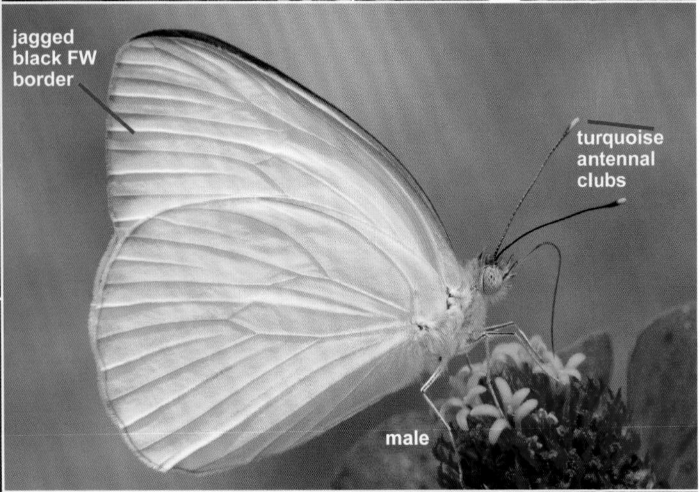
jagged black FW border
turquoise antennal clubs
male

female

female

jagged black FW border
female

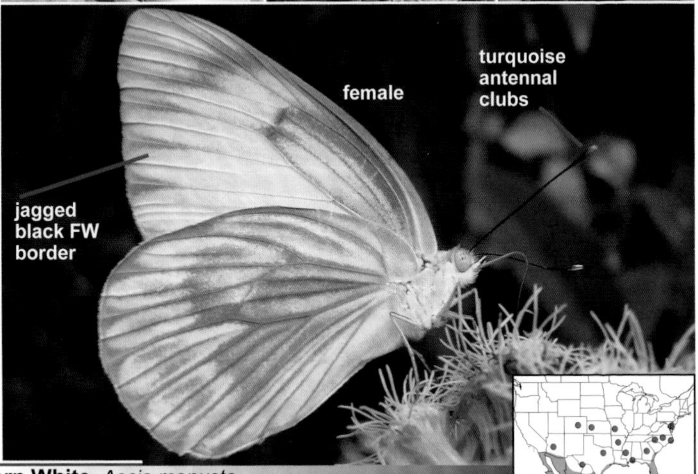
female
turquoise antennal clubs
jagged black FW border

Great Southern White *Ascia monuste*

capers

south Florida
LU-LC
all year

south Texas
R-U
all year

shaded tropical woods in south Florida

more general in south Texas

probably the most reliable spot in the U.S. to see this butterfly is at Matheson Hammock County Park, in Miami-Dade Co., Florida

when fresh, males are satiny white, without black markings

females vary from almost as white as males to having yellow HWs above and thick black borders

females in Texas often have black veining below and broad black borders above

male
often w/ a satiny sheen

male
unmarked above

gray-white antennal clubs
orange crescent
male

female
Hidalgo Co., TX

female
smooth black FW border

yellow base of FW
gray-white antennal clubs
Monroe Co., FL
orange crescent
female

Florida White *Appias drusilla*

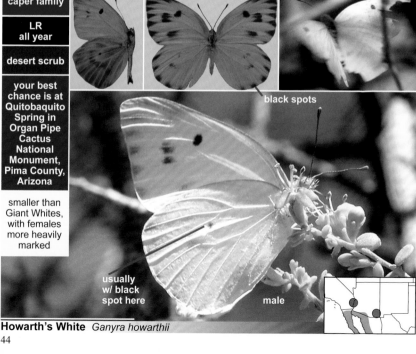

caper family

LRGV
R-U
all year, but most frequent in fall

abundance varies greatly – at times becomes common

mainly thorn scrub

large, with sailing flight that often takes it high into the trees

females w/ extra spots
female

female

male

large black spot
orange
male

Giant White *Ganyra josephina*

caper family

LR
all year

desert scrub

your best chance is at Quitobaquito Spring in Organ Pipe Cactus National Monument, Pima County, Arizona

smaller than Giant Whites, with females more heavily marked

female

female

male

black spots
usually w/ black spot here
male

Howarth's White *Ganyra howarthii*

mistletoes

first reported in the U.S. in 2004, this species has been seen a number of times since then

creamy overall, the yellowish FW apex contrasts with the white on the rest of the FW

FW apex is yellowish
entire HW is yellowish

LRGV

Common Melwhite *Melete lycimnia*

caper family

black-brown cross bar

LRGV once

Cross-barred White *Itaballia demophile*

unknown

as far as I can determine, all 20 species in the genus *Leptophobia* have bright green eyes

this is the only Mexican species in the genus

emerald green eye
black arrowhead

not yet LRGV

Common Greeneyed-White *Leptophobia aripa*

mustard family, especially rock cresses

East
LR-LU
mostly April-May

West
U
mostly Apr-June

prairies, barrens, dunes

hilltops

white with green marbling that is sparser than on other marbles

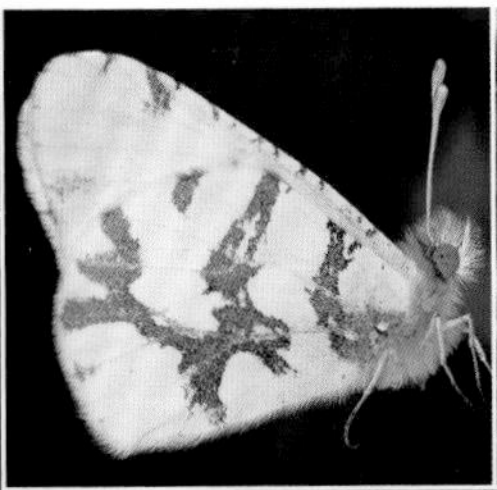

often w/ a rosy flush when fresh
white antennas
outer, lower portion of HW w/ little marbling

Olympia Marble *Euchloe olympia*

mustard family

U-LC
Mar-July, about 3 weeks at any given location

'desert' populations in dry open areas; California populations in chaparral and forest

some treat 'Desert' and California' populations as separate species – intermediates occur in the southern California Sierra

'Desert' usually w/ wide black bar

'California' w/ narrow black bar

ground color usually white
white costa
strong bar

Pearly Marble *Euchloe hyantis*

rock cresses and other mustards

C-A mostly Mar-Aug about 3 weeks at any given location

many types of open areas including roadsides, forest openings and meadows

similar to Pearly Marbles, but usually buffy or off-white, rather than white

ground color usually buffy or off-white
buffy costa
weak bar

Large Marble *Euchloe ausonides*

mustards

RS to southeastern Arizona (once)

flies Mar-Apr in Sonora, Mexico

hilltops

open
"horseshoe"

Sonoran Marble *Euchloe guaymasensis*

se AZ once

mustards

LC
June

limestone scree and gravel fields

green marbling is more extensive than on other marbles

co-occurring subspecies of Large Marble also has fairly extensive green, but the green is brighter

Northern Marble has brighter yellow veins and checked costa

extent of green marbling varies, as shown
unchecked, or weakly checked, costa

Green Marble *Euchloe naina*

rockcresses and other mustards

R
June-July

openings in subalpine coniferous woods

barely enters the United States lower 48 states in Glacier National Park

similar to Large Marble (page 47), which is sympatric in eastern Alaska, but with more extensive green and less white

green "dam" blocking white area
checked costa
yellow veins

Northern Marble *Euchloe creusa*

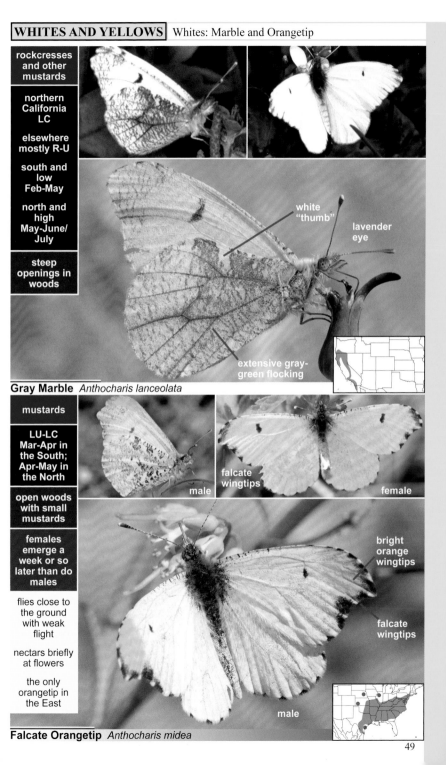

rockcresses and other mustards

northern California LC

elsewhere mostly R-U

south and low Feb-May

north and high May-June/July

steep openings in woods

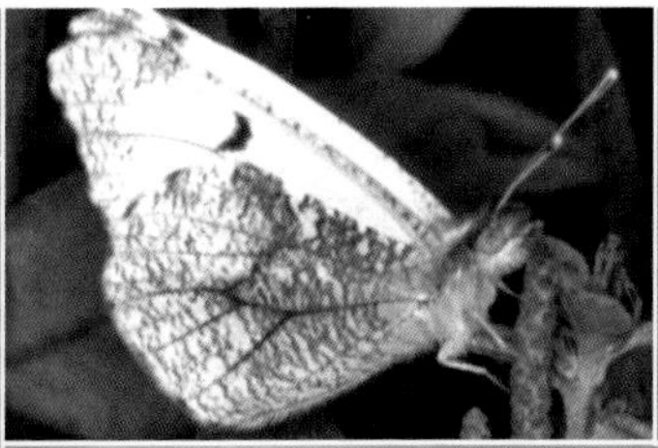

white "thumb"
lavender eye
extensive gray-green flocking

Gray Marble *Anthocharis lanceolata*

mustards

LU-LC Mar-Apr in the South; Apr-May in the North

open woods with small mustards

females emerge a week or so later than do males

flies close to the ground with weak flight

nectars briefly at flowers

the only orangetip in the East

male

falcate wingtips
female

bright orange wingtips
falcate wingtips
male

Falcate Orangetip *Anthocharis midea*

mustards

C

southern lowlands Feb-early Apr

Northwest Mar-mid July

high mountains mid July-mid Aug

many, from desert hills to conferous woods

not a hilltopper

females vary from white to cream to bright yellow

in its range, only Desert Orangetip is similar, but it has wider white FW apexes

at locations where both Sara and Desert Orangetips are found, the species usually segregate topographically, with most Sara Orangetips flying in canyons and most Desert Orangetips flying on hilltops

Alpine
Co., CA
female

San Bernardino
Co., CA
female

bright
orange
wingtips
Mono
Co., CA
female

San Diego
Co., CA
white ray
male

Orange
Co., CA
female

bright
orange
wingtips
black
spot
Los Angeles
Co., CA
male

Sara Orangetip *Anthocharis sara*

mustards

Sara Orangetips are quite variable and some have treated these populations as four distinct species

there is little in the way of data to support that treatment

ground color of females varies from white to cream to bright yellow

San Bernardino Co., CA
white ray

Bernallilo Co., NM
female

bright orange wingtips
black spot
male
San Diego Co., CA

Sara Orangetip *Anthocharis sara*

mustards

LU-LC Feb-Apr in the South, mid Apr-mid May in the North

desert hills

a strong hilltopper

ground color of both males and females varies from white to cream to bright yellow

flies with faster wingbeats than does Sara Orangetip

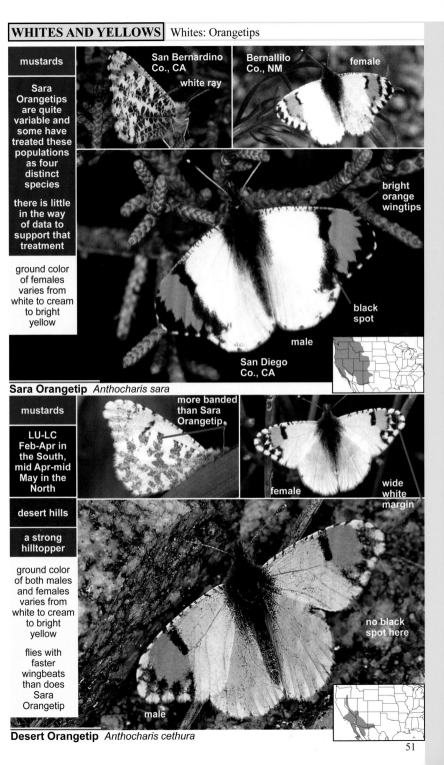

more banded than Sara Orangetip

female
wide white margin

no black spot here
male

Desert Orangetip *Anthocharis cethura*

Alfalfa and other legumes

C-A through all warm weather

all open areas

the most common, widespread orange sulphur

sometimes hybridizes with Clouded Sulphur

almost all sulphurs have some females white/off-white; the percentage varies with species, location and season

in most of the United States, a *Colias* sulphur with any orange above will be an Orange Sulphur; a sulphur that is pure yellow above will be a Clouded Sulphur; the other *Colias* sulphurs are mainly northern and/or at high elevation

both sexes usually have some black postmedian spots on the FW below

male

male

at least some orange on FW (topside visible in flight). Most individuals with strong and extensive orange.
male
both sexes usually w/ some black pm spots
spot is usually double
often w/ brown pm HW spots

female

female

female

some females are off-white & perhaps inseparable from Clouded Sulphur
at least some orange on FW
female w/ some pale spots in black border
both sexes usually w/ a dark smudge here
female

Orange Sulphur *Colias eurytheme*

clovers and other legumes

C-A through all warm weather

all open areas

the most common, widespread yellow sulphur

sometimes hybridizes w/ Orange Sulphur

some Orange Sulphurs have very little orange; in the East and South, it is probably best to call any sulphur w/ ANY orange an Orange Sulphur

some females are off-white and perhaps inseparable from off-white Orange Sulphurs

both sexes often w/ some FW black pm spots (see the three inset photos of undersides)

male

lemon-yellow topside w/ no orange
male

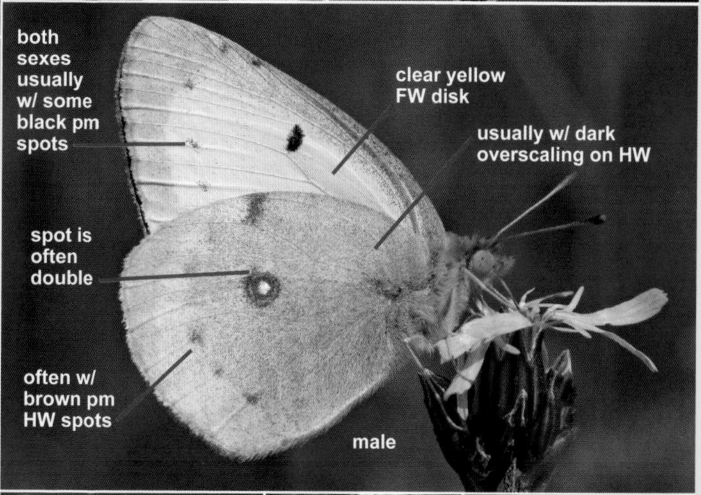
both sexes usually w/ some black pm spots
clear yellow FW disk
usually w/ dark overscaling on HW
spot is often double
often w/ brown pm HW spots
male

some females are off-white & may be inseparable from Orange Sulphur
female

female

female

female w/ some pale spots in black border
female
both sexes usually w/ a dark smudge here

Clouded Sulphur *Colias philodice*

peas in the genus *Lathyrus* and other legumes

LU-C
May-Sept
mostly
June-July

open coniferous woods

one of the few sulphurs regularly seen flying *within* a forest

yellow above (except for white females); HW with extensive faint black overscaling

some females are off-white
Crook Co., OR
female

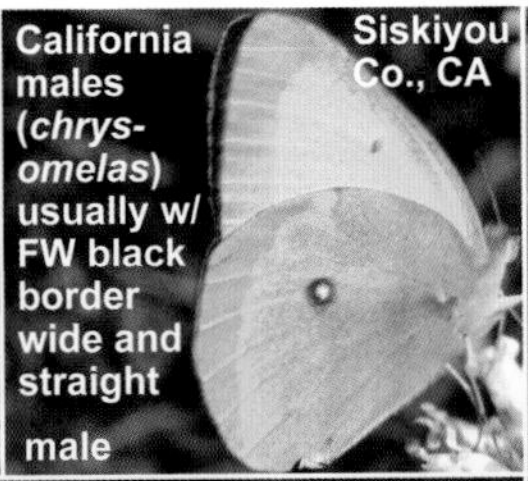
California males (*chrys-omelas*) usually w/ FW black border wide and straight
Siskiyou Co., CA
male

Wallowa Co., OR
female

Wallowa Co., OR
male

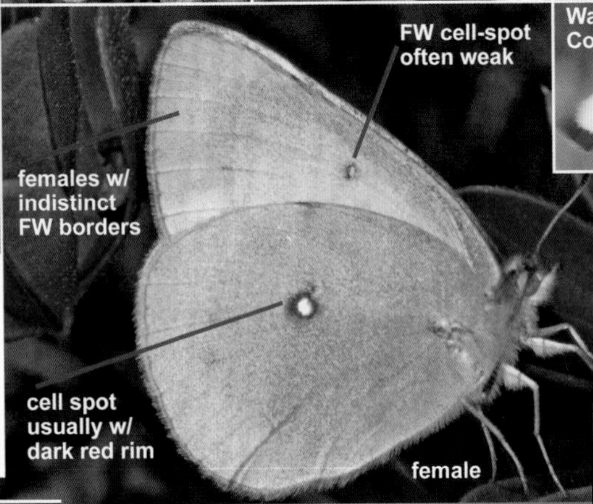
FW cell-spot often weak
females w/ indistinct FW borders
Clallam Co., WA
cell spot usually w/ dark red rim
female

Western Sulphur *Colias occidentalis*

milkvetches and other legumes

U-C
May-Aug

prairie, grasslands and meadows; *columbiensis* (one brood area) in open conifer woods

a very confusing group (see also Harford's Sulphur and Christina's Sulphur) some place *columbiensis* w/ Western Sulphur

yellow above (except for white females)

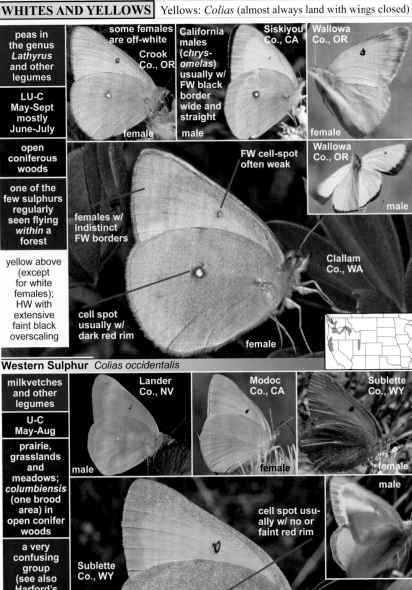

Lander Co., NV
male

Modoc Co., CA
female

Sublette Co., WY
female

male

Sublette Co., WY
cell spot usu-ally w/ no or faint red rim
HW pale to medium green
male

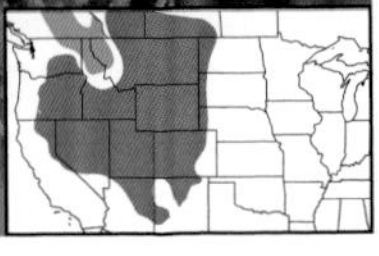

Queen Alexandra's Sulphur *Colias alexandra*

milkvetches

LU
Mar-May, mid June-Aug

dry canyons and hillsides

perhaps best considered to be a full species

yellow above

overlaps with Clouded Sulphur only at eastern edge of its range

usually flies more slowly and higher than does Clouded Sulphur

black border is narrow
female

female
black border eroded by yellow

black borders are narrow
male
usually w/ dark overscaling on HW

'Harford's' Queen Alexandra's Sulphur *Colias alexandra harfordii*

legumes

U-C
June-Aug

openings in coniferous woods

Christina's Sulphur is treated by some as a subspecies of Queen Alexander's Sulphur

shown at right is the subspecies *krauthii*, from the Black Hills of South Dakota

some females are off-white

female

orange w/ yellow wing bases
male

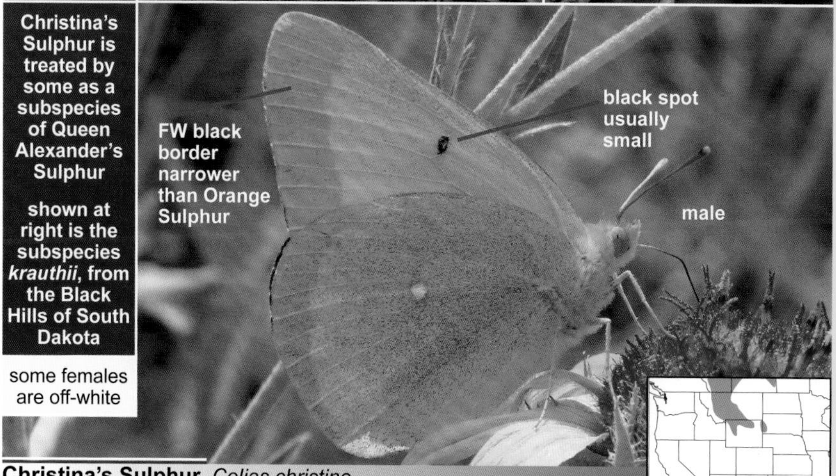
FW black border narrower than Orange Sulphur
black spot usually small
male

Christina's Sulphur *Colias christina*

blueberries

East R-LU w/ isolated populations in the mountains of Pennsylvania and West Virginia

West U June-Aug

blueberry barrens, openings w/ blueberries in coniferous woods

males are bright yellow above; females are either yellow or off-white above

female
male
black border (above) narrow and slightly curved
no black over-scaling on FW disk
male
cell spot single, usually round

Pink-edged Sulphur *Colias interior*

blueberries

R-U July-Aug

subalpine forest openings, – roadsides and powerline cuts

in Rockies, range extends north to Horn, Alberta, and is disjunct from the high Arctic tundra populations of nw Canada and Alaska and of ne Canada

yellow above (except for white females)

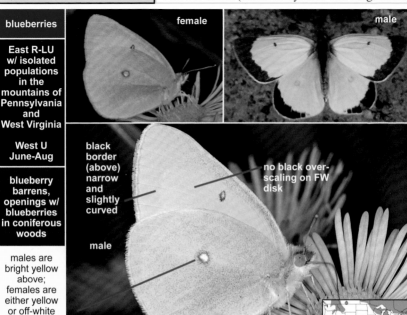

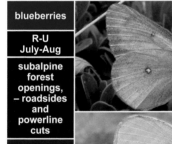

female
male
black border narrow and slightly curved
much black overscaling on FW disk
female

Pelidne Sulphur *Colias pelidne*

willows

R-U
July-Aug

willow bogs in boreal and mixed forests

this species and Scudder's Sulphur are very similar – probably inseparable except for range – and are possibly best treated as one species

males are yellow above; most females are pale yellow above, some are off-white

females w/o or w/ greatly reduced black borders (above)
female

Park Co., WY
female

male

Yukon Koyukuk Bor., AK
North Slope Bor., AK
black border (above) straight
note large size
male
Sublette Co., WY
cell spot usually large, often wider than high, and often w/ a small satellite spot

Giant Sulphur *Colias gigantea*

willows

R-U
July-Aug

9-12,000 ft in alpine willow bogs

this species and Giant Sulphur are very similar – probably inseparable except for range – and are possibly best treated as one species

males are yellow above

most females are off-white above

HW light green to olive green
outer portion of HW usually paler
female

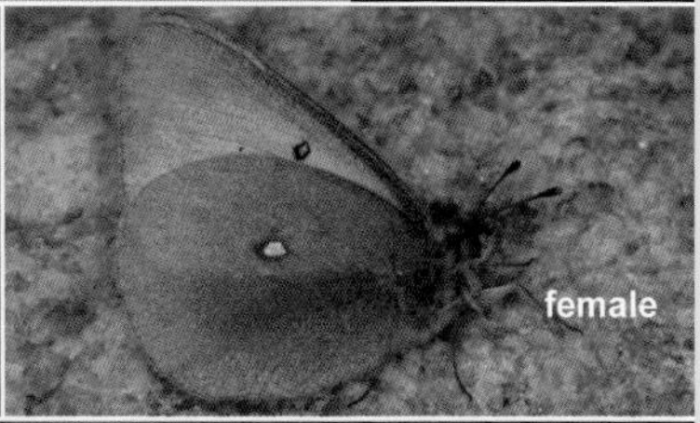
female

male
extensive green-gray overscaling

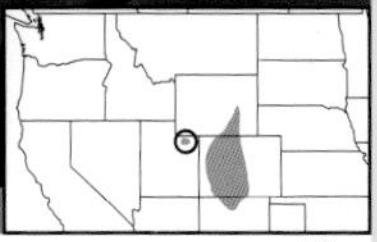

Scudder's Sulphur *Colias scudderi*

Dwarf Bilberry

LC
mid July-mid Aug

moist subalpine meadows

Tuolomne Meadows, in Yosemite National Park, is a classic location for this species

the only sulphur in its range that has a greenish topside

female
green topside
female w/ pink fringe
male w/ off-white fringe
cell spot w/o or w/ thin pink border
male
green ground color

Sierra Sulphur *Colias behrii*

blueberries

C
mid June-early Aug

tundra and boreal forest openings with blueberries

males are yellow above

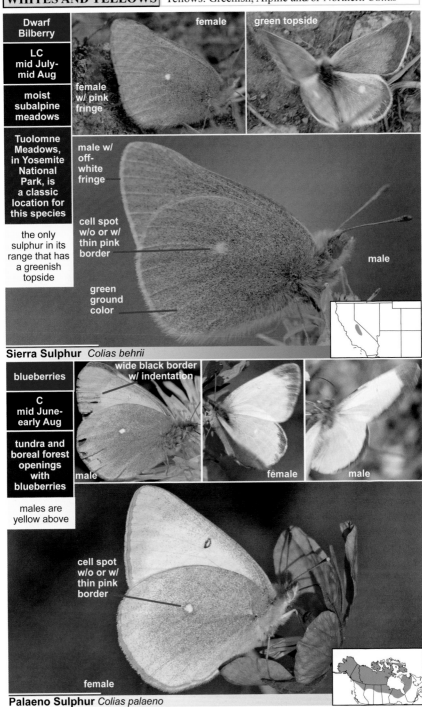

wide black border w/ indentation
male
female
male
cell spot w/o or w/ thin pink border
female

Palaeno Sulphur *Colias palaeno*

legumes

R-U
July-Aug

tundra and above treeline along windswept ridges, hilltops and slopes

barely enters U.S. lower 48 in Okanogan County, Washington and in Glacier NP, Montana

only sulphur in its range with a greenish topside; individuals that are off-white above are common

Plateau Mtn. Alberta
male

HW cell spot usually sharply pointed outwardly
North Slope Bor., AK
female
pale band usually goes to margin
strong green tint

Labrador Sulphur *Colias nastes*

legumes

U
June-Aug

boggy tundra

most treat as *Colias tyche*

similar to Labrador Sulphur but Labrador normally flies very close to the ground while Booth's flight is normally higher

unlike Labrador, male Booth's have a black FW border w/o white intrusions

solid black border
male

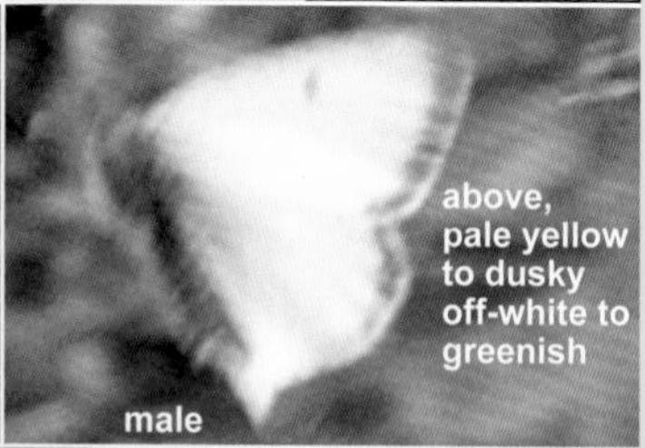
above, pale yellow to dusky off-white to greenish
male

most frequently w/ a satellite red spot
pale band stops before margin
female

Booth's Sulphur *Colias nastes* x *Colias hecla*

milkvetches and other legumes

LC-LA mid July-mid Aug

alpine and subalpine meadows

Hinsdale Co., CO
Sublette Co., WY
Sublette Co., WY

deep dusky orange above

The size and shape of the HW cell spot is quite variable as is the amount of HW overscaling

some populations have many white females

dusky orange FW disk
greenish HW
Park Co., WY

Mead's Sulphur *Colias meadii*

Northern Sweetvetch

LC July

hilly tundra

possibly conspecific with Mead's Sulphur

museum specimens
male
female

female
male

Coppermine Sulphur *Colias johanseni*

unknown

LC mid July-early Aug

recently described from west Hudson Bay and possibly conspecific wtih Hecla

reportedly smaller and duller than Hecla
museum specimens
male
female

female
male

Rankin Inlet Sulphur *Colias rankinensis*

milkvetches

LR-C
mostly July

wet tundra

males are orange above

topsides of most females are orange, some are off-white

female

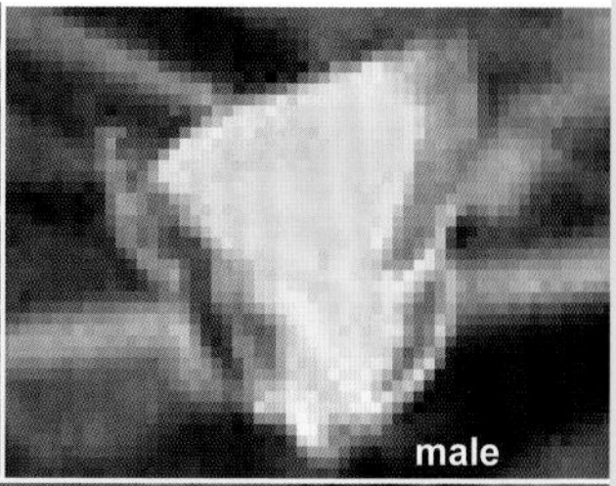
male

orange disk
HW cell spot usually sharply pointed outwardly

Hecla Sulphur *Colias hecla*

legumes

U
May-July

open taiga, shrub-tundra

variable

males are orange or golden-yellow above (male in rightmost inset is same individual as in main photo)

below, males FW cell-end spot has faint black edging

topside of females ranges from off-white to pale orange

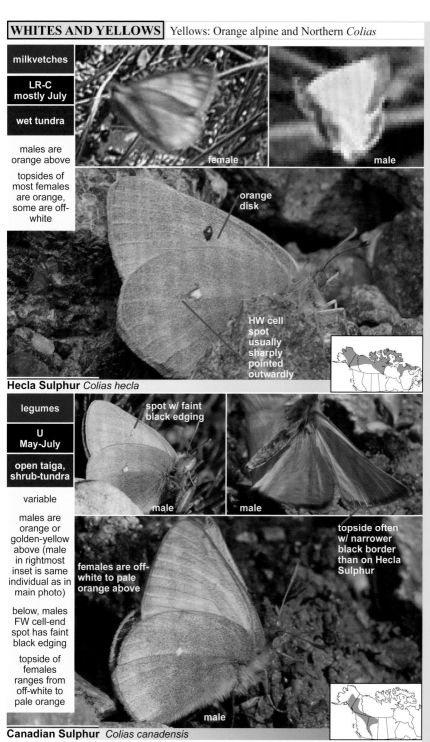

spot w/ faint black edging
male

male

topside often w/ narrower black border than on Hecla Sulphur
females are off-white to pale orange above
male

Canadian Sulphur *Colias canadensis*

prairieclovers and other legumes

three broods C-A all year

elsewhere mostly R-U summer immigrant

open areas such as open pine woods, thorn scrub, and farmland

larger than other *Colias*, bright yellow and black

females have a more sloping "forehead." Most are yellow (see top left), some are off-white (see top right)

female

male

caterpillar

"eye" near the back of the "dog's head"
black marginal spots weak or absent
male

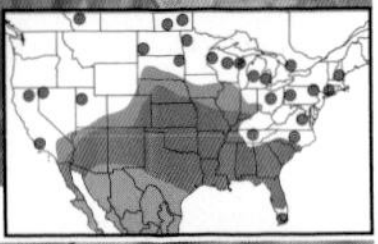

Southern Dogface *Colias* (*Zerene*) *cesonia*

California False Indigo

LU-LC Apr-May; late July-Sept

foothill canyons and meadows

males are bright yellow above with a beautiful violet sheen when fresh

females are off-white and usually lack black borders; they easily can be confused in flight with Cloudless Sulphurs

male

"eye" near the front of the "dog's head"
strong black spots
male

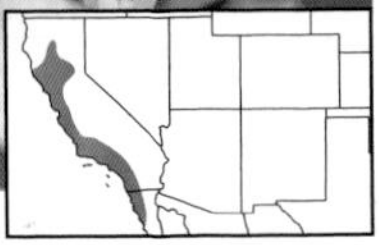

California Dogface *Colias* (*Zerene*) *eurydice*

sennas

an irregular stray to southeastern Arizona

more frequent in the LRGV

mostly thorn-scrub

one of our largest butterflies

both males and females are off-white above, but males have a yellow patch in the FW cell

powerful flight can approach 20 mph

very large
male
spot rounded
greenish below w/ prominent raised veins
diagonal line
this vein prominent

White Angled-Sulphur *Anteos clorinde*

sennas

R
an irregular visitor to the LRGV

mostly thorn-scrub

males are bright yellow above; females are pale yellowish-white and easily confused with White Angled-Sulphurs in flight

flight is powerful and fast

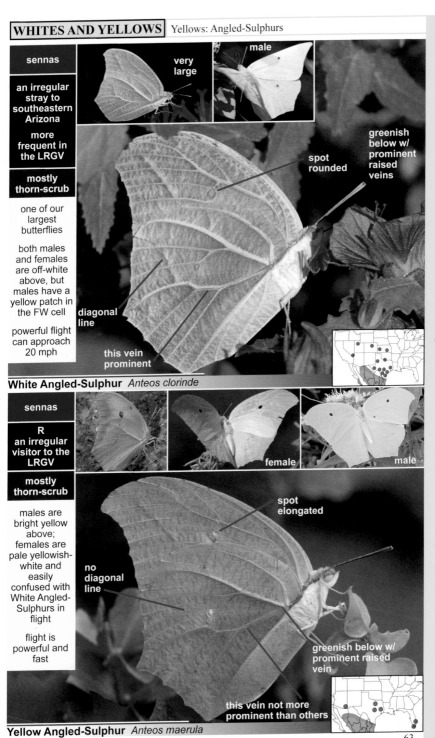

female
male
spot elongated
no diagonal line
greenish below w/ prominent raised vein
this vein not more prominent than others

Yellow Angled-Sulphur *Anteos maerula*

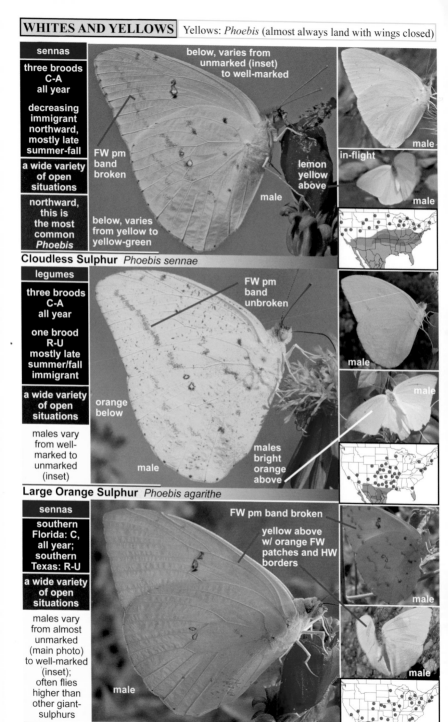

sennas

three broods
C-A
all year

decreasing immigrant northward, mostly late summer-fall

a wide variety of open situations

northward, this is the most common *Phoebis*

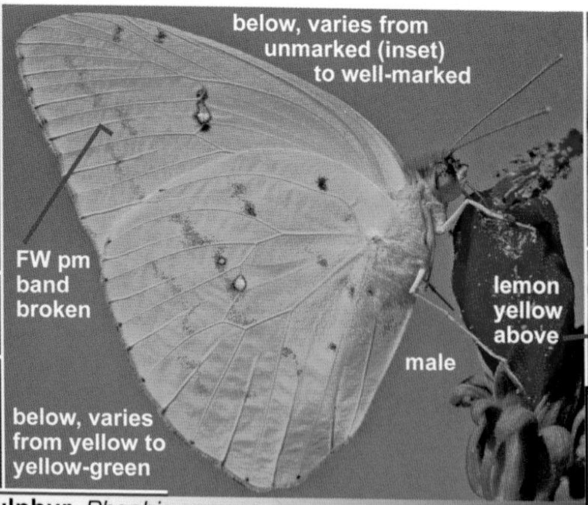
below, varies from unmarked (inset) to well-marked
FW pm band broken
lemon yellow above
male
below, varies from yellow to yellow-green

male

in-flight
male

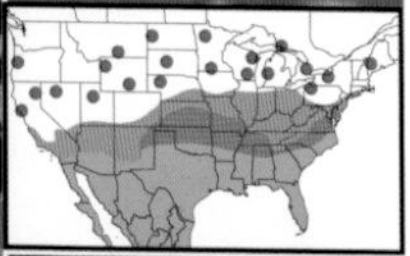

Cloudless Sulphur *Phoebis sennae*

legumes

three broods
C-A
all year

one brood
R-U
mostly late summer/fall immigrant

a wide variety of open situations

males vary from well-marked to unmarked (inset)

FW pm band unbroken
orange below
male
males bright orange above

male

male

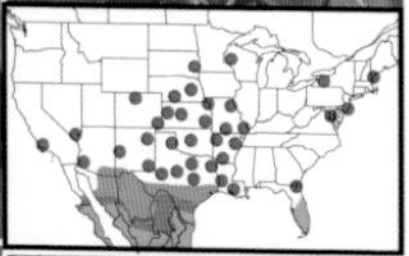

Large Orange Sulphur *Phoebis agarithe*

sennas

southern Florida: C, all year; southern Texas: R-U

a wide variety of open situations

males vary from almost unmarked (main photo) to well-marked (inset); often flies higher than other giant-sulphurs

FW pm band broken
yellow above w/ orange FW patches and HW borders
male

male

male

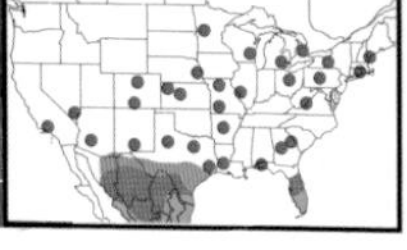

Orange-barred Sulphur *Phoebis philea*

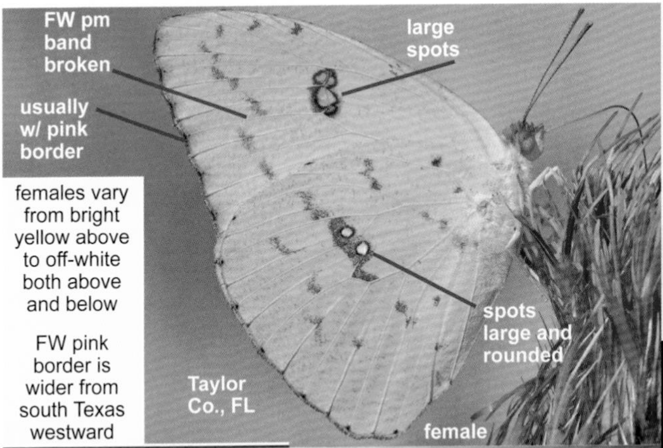
FW pm band broken
large spots
usually w/ pink border
spots large and rounded
Taylor Co., FL
female

females vary from bright yellow above to off-white both above and below

FW pink border is wider from south Texas westward

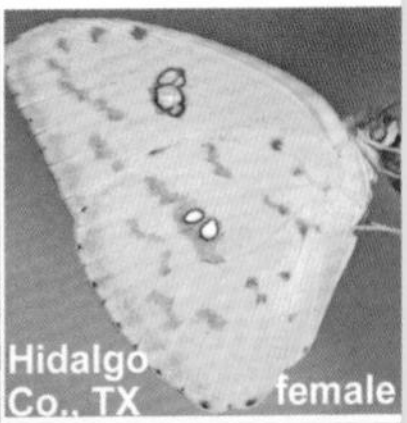
Hidalgo Co., TX
female

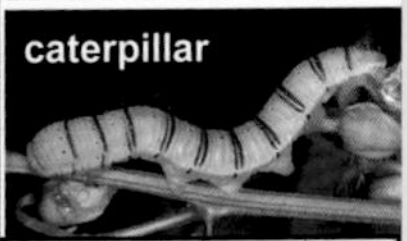
caterpillar

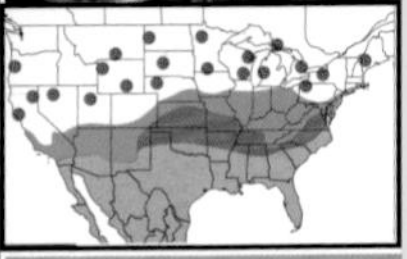

Cloudless Sulphur *Phoebis sennae*

FW pm band unbroken
female

most females in Florida are orange; in Texas and the Southwest most females are off-white (see top inset)

female

female

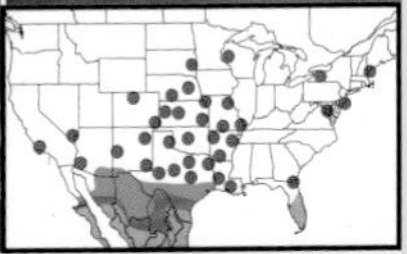

Large Orange Sulphur *Phoebis agarithe*

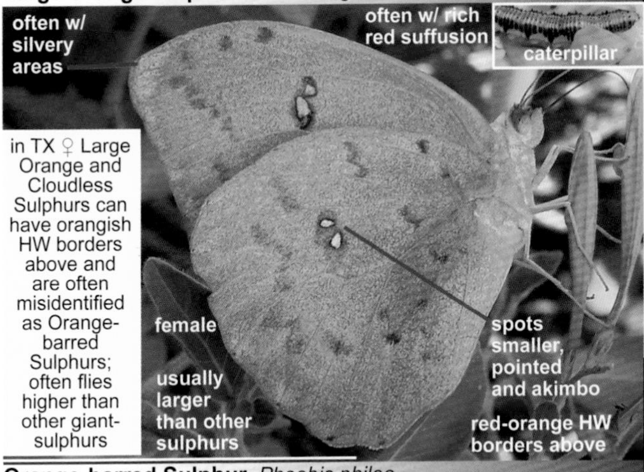
often w/ silvery areas
often w/ rich red suffusion
female
usually larger than other sulphurs
spots smaller, pointed and akimbo
red-orange HW borders above
caterpillar

in TX ♀ Large Orange and Cloudless Sulphurs can have orangish HW borders above and are often misidentified as Orange-barred Sulphurs; often flies higher than other giant-sulphurs

female
rarely off-white

female

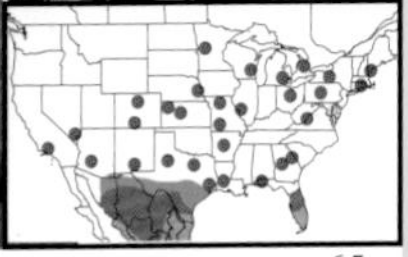

Orange-barred Sulphur *Phoebis philea*

mainly *Dalbergia*, but also sennas and other legumes

south Florida
LU
all year

LRGV
R
all year

outer one-third of wings usually with puckered look

males usually unmarked below

often confused with Cloudless Sulphurs on the one hand and w/ Lyside Sulphurs on the other!

male

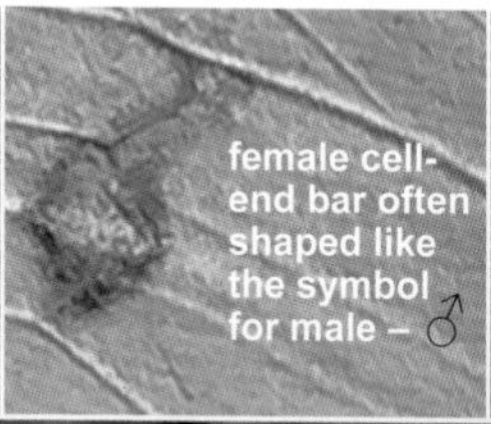
female cell-end bar often shaped like the symbol for male – ♂

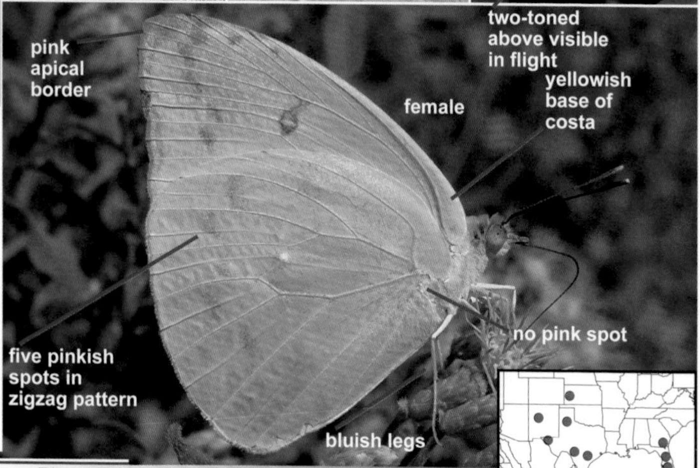
two-toned above visible in flight
pink apical border
yellowish base of costa
female
no pink spot
five pinkish spots in zigzag pattern
bluish legs

Statira Sulphur *Phoebis* (*Aphrissa*) *statira*

reportedly Horseflesh Mahogany

U
all year

native to Cuba and Bahamas

until recently, overlooked due to similarity to Cloudless and Statira Sulphurs; now seems to be resident

its reported foodplant is also non-native

see Cloudless Sulphur, previous two pages — males are similar

unmarked below
male
pink spot

female

male

pale yellow above
pm line not broken
pink spot
female
yellow legs

Pink-spot Sulphur *Phoebis* (*Aphrissa*) *neleis*

lignum vitaes

three broods C-A all year (major irruptions can occur)

one brood U-C immigrant mainly late summer/fall

Florida Keys R periodic colonist

tropical and subtropical thorn-scrub

size is extremely variable; frequently lands upside-down under leaves where its color camouflages it remarkably well

in Arizona, males usually w/ a "thumb" mark
yellow FW wing base
usually greenish below, but can be pale or quite yellow
in south Texas, rarely w/ a "thumb" mark
vein often prominent

Lyside Sulphur *Kricogonia lyside*

multiple families

male
FW pm line broken
strong basal line
bright orange above
see Large Orange Sulphur pg 62

not yet LRGV

Apricot Sulphur *Phoebis argante*

unknown

male
narrow wings
straight line

LRGV twice

Costa-spotted Mimic-White *Enantia albania*

legumes

large and tailed

se AZ LRGV

Tailed Sulphur *Phoebis neocypris*

male
yellow wing bases
female
double squiggle
pink spot

FL Keys

Orbed Sulphur *Phoebis orbis*

sennas, Partridge Pea and other legumes

Deep South C-A

decreasing abundance northward where it is a late-season immigrant

many open habitats, especially open disturbed areas

by far the most common and widespread small yellow

sun-loving; flight is usually rapid and low

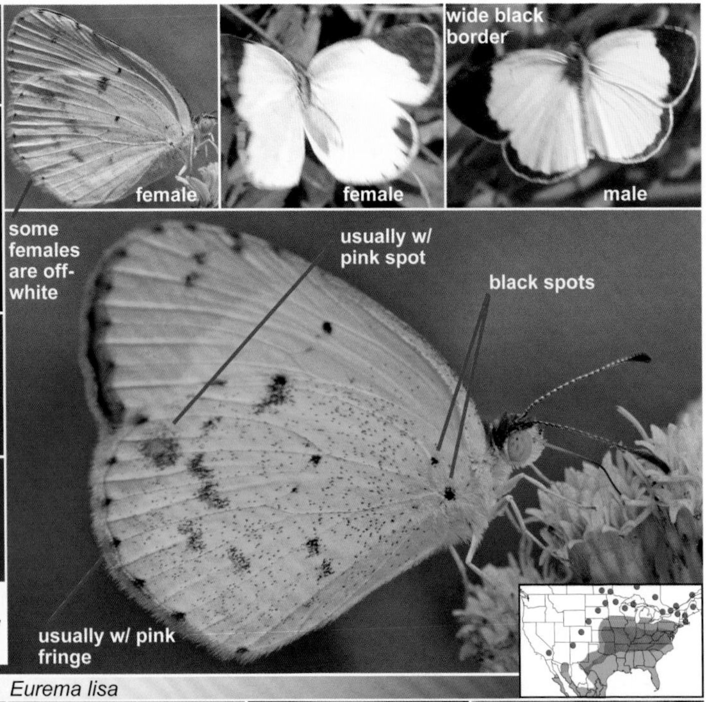
female
female
wide black border
male
some females are off-white
usually w/ pink spot
black spots
usually w/ pink fringe

Little Yellow *Eurema lisa*

Mimosa

south Texas, C all year

Miami-Dade Co., Florida R all year

central Texas and se AZ R immigrant

open tropical woods and edges

shade-loving (especially in Florida)

flight is usually languid and low

without white females

black border not as wide
female
male
no black spot
fringe not pink
male

Mimosa Yellow *Eurema nise*

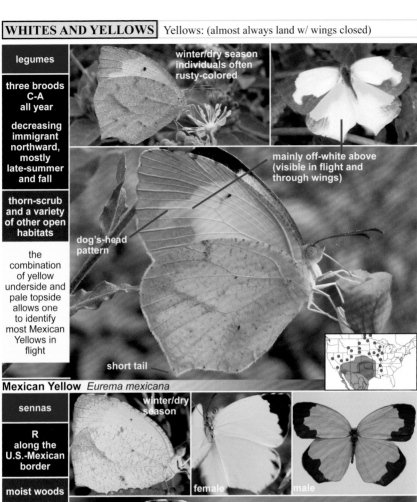

legumes

three broods
C-A
all year

decreasing immigrant northward, mostly late-summer and fall

thorn-scrub and a variety of other open habitats

the combination of yellow underside and pale topside allows one to identify most Mexican Yellows in flight

winter/dry season
individuals often
rusty-colored

mainly off-white above
(visible in flight and
through wings)
dog's-head
pattern
short tail

Mexican Yellow *Eurema mexicana*

sennas

R
along the U.S.-Mexican border

moist woods

larger than Little Yellow and Mimosa Yellow

bright yellow topside

winter/dry
season

female

male

bright
yellow
rusty
diagonal line
wide black
border
HW angled

Boisduval's Yellow *Eurema boisduvaliana*

sennas

Southeast
U-C

south Texas to southeastern Arizona
C-A

decreasing abundance northward where it is an immigrant

a wide variety of open areas

the name "sleepy" does not refer to this species flight but rather to it's "closed" FW "eye"

winter form

female

male

black
spot
diagonal
line (some-
times faint)

Sleepy Orange *Eurema nicippe*

legumes

LRGV
C-A
All year

elsewhere mainly a late summer immigrant; influx varies yearly

tropical woods and thorn-scrub

the seasonal forms are so disimilar that they were once thought to be two species

both forms can sometimes be found at the same time

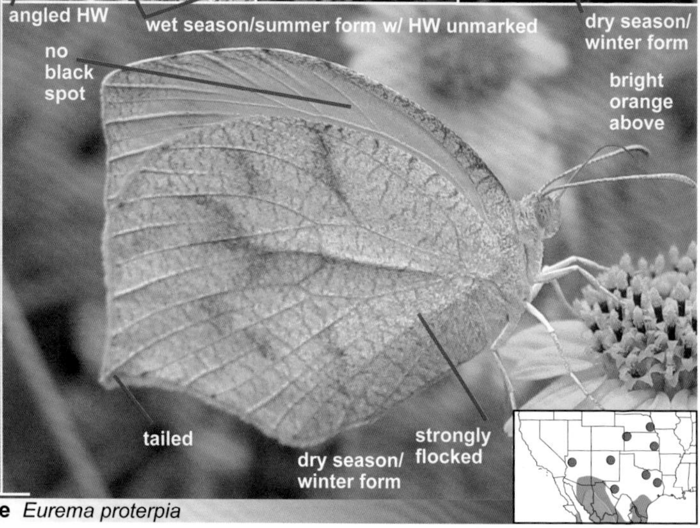
angled HW
wet season/summer form w/ HW unmarked
dry season/
winter form
no
black
spot
bright
orange
above
tailed
dry season/
winter form
strongly
flocked

Tailed Orange *Eurema proterpia*

quassia family

Miami-Dade County, Florida
LU
all year

southeastern Arizona
R immigrant
mostly mid Aug.-mid Sept

LRGV
RS

brushy woods and thorn-scrub

more golden and larger than Little Yellow

male
males are rarely almost unmarked

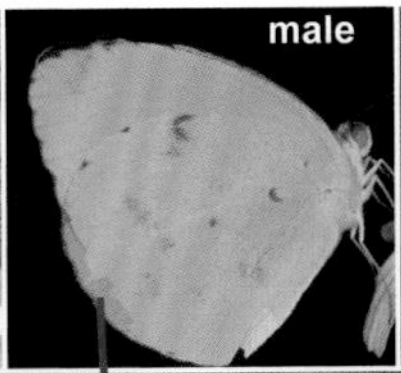
male

male

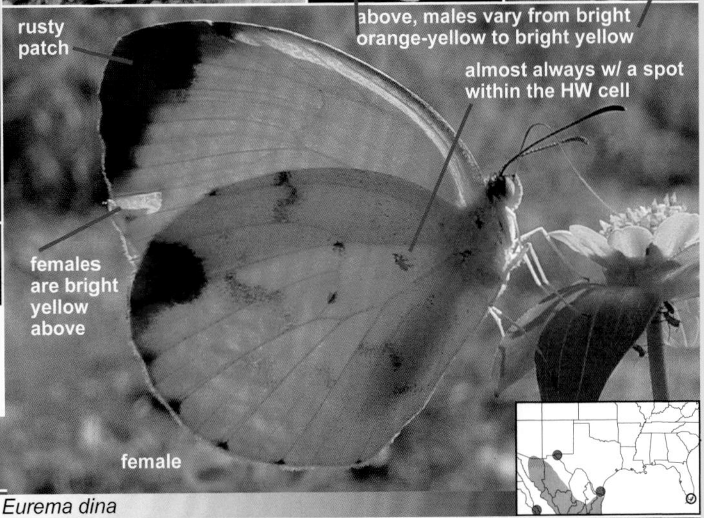
above, males vary from bright orange-yellow to bright yellow
rusty patch
almost always w/ a spot within the HW cell
females are bright yellow above
female

Dina Yellow *Eurema dina*

aster family

U-A
decreasing immigrant northward and westward

many open habitats, especially with low or mowed plants

small

appears smaller and duskier in flight than do Little or Mimosa Yellows

flies very close to ground

wet season/ summer form

dry season/ winter form

dusky yellow above
photo in flight

strong black spots
wet season/ summer form
green tints below

Dainty Sulphur *Nathalis iole*

legumes

Florida
C-A
most of year

decreasing immigrant northward

LRGV and se AZ
R

open areas, especially disturbed areas

small with weak flight

can be white or pale yellow above, or with FWs yellow and HWs white

males have a black bar along the FW inner margin that is often visible in flight

HW usually with dark overscaling

see Dainty Sulphur, page 71

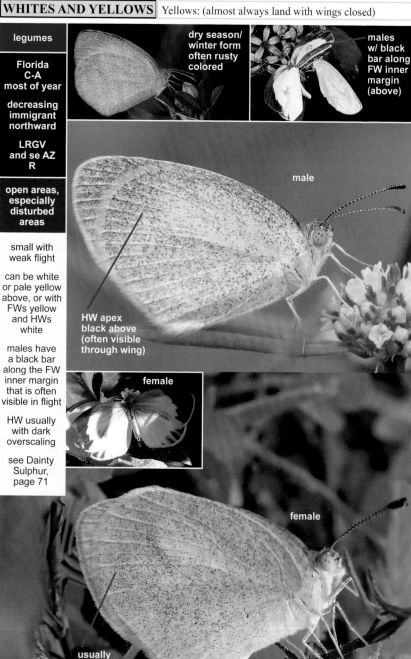

dry season/
winter form
often rusty
colored

males
w/ black
bar along
FW inner
margin
(above)

male
HW apex
black above
(often visible
through wing)

female

female
usually
heavily
overscaled
with gray

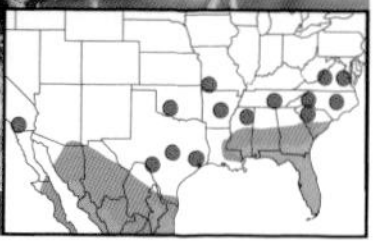

Barred Yellow *Eurema daira*

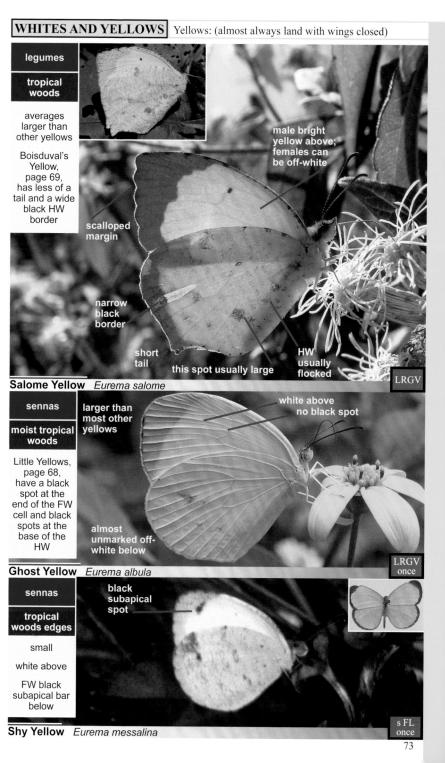

legumes

tropical woods

averages larger than other yellows

Boisduval's Yellow, page 69, has less of a tail and a wide black HW border

male bright yellow above; females can be off-white
scalloped margin
narrow black border
short tail
this spot usually large
HW usually flocked
LRGV

Salome Yellow *Eurema salome*

sennas

moist tropical woods

Little Yellows, page 68, have a black spot at the end of the FW cell and black spots at the base of the HW

larger than most other yellows
white above
no black spot
almost unmarked off-white below
LRGV once

Ghost Yellow *Eurema albula*

sennas

tropical woods edges

small

white above

FW black subapical bar below

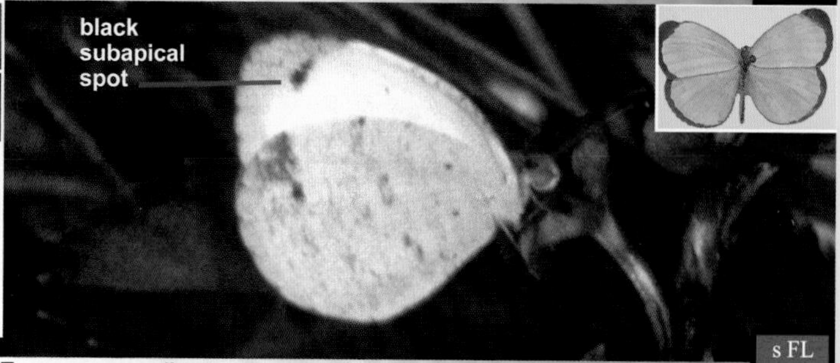
black subapical spot
s FL once

Shy Yellow *Eurema messalina*

Species in the well-named gossamerwing family (Lycaenidae) are usually small and delicate. Many species have iridescent blue or purple on their topsides. The caterpillars of many gossamerwing species associate with ants. The caterpillars possess special glands that secrete "honey-dew," a sweet substance that the ants love. The ants protect the caterpillars from predatory ants and other insect threats.

There are four recognizable subfamilies:

Coppers are primarily a northern group, with only a few species in the tropics.

On the other hand, hairstreaks (page 84) are most well developed in the tropics. About 1300 species inhabit the Neotropics alone! Many hairstreaks have a large spot at the outer angle of the HW below. This spot, and the adjacent long tail, often appear to be an eye and an antenna. Predators are sometimes fooled by this duplicity, especially when the hairstreak saws its two HWs together to attract attention to its back end.

Blues (page 122) are another predominantly northern group, with many more species in the temperate zone than in the tropics.

Harvesters (page 83) are the only butterflies in North America whose caterpillars are carnivorous — feeding on aphids. In the Old World, there are a number of carnivorous blues.

docks, especially Bitter Dock

U-LC
mid June-mid Aug

moist prairies and meadows, drainage ditches, pond and stream edges

large

squiggly orange marginal HW band above

Acadian Hairstreak, page 90, has tails, blue at HW outer angle and no black basal spots

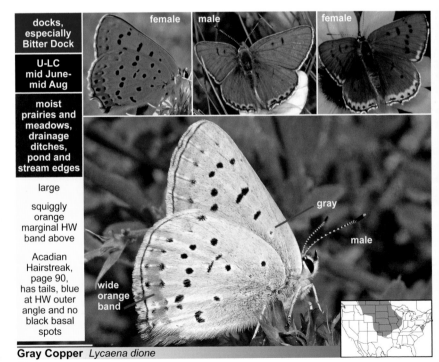

female
male
female
gray
male
wide orange band

Gray Copper *Lycaena dione*

docks and horkelias

C-A
June-Aug

sagebrush flats and mountain meadows

unlike close relatives, Gray and Great Coppers, Edith's Coppers can swarm in appropriate habitat

averages smaller than Gray or Great Coppers and is more heavily mottled

Sublette
Co., WY

female

female

Modoc
Co., CA
large brown spots, usually w/ darker outlines
male

Edith's Copper *Lycaena editha*

docks

LU-LC
late Apr-June in lowlands and south, June-July/Aug higher and north

lowland grasslands and chaparral generally below 6500 ft.

large

squiggly orange marginal HW band above

Gorgon Copper, page 77, has HW w/ red-orange submarginal spots

female

female

male

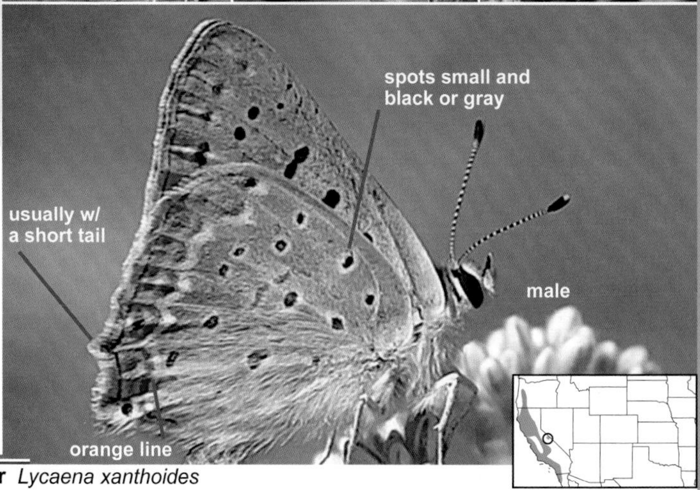
spots small and black or gray
usually w/ a short tail
male
orange line

Great Copper *Lycaena xanthoides*

docks, especially non-native sheep sorrels

C-A in the Northeast decreasing abundance in the MidWest and Appalachians Apr-Oct

West LR July-Aug

East: primarily disturbed dry open areas, but also some native grasslands

West: above or at treeline

called "small copper" in Europe

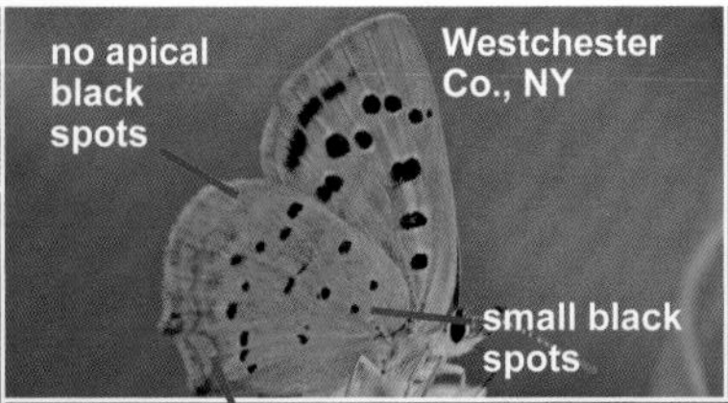
no apical black spots
Westchester Co., NY
small black spots

Glacier Co., MT
in West, FW usually greasy yellow-orange

narrow red-orange line inwardly paler
Westchester Co., NY
intense red-orange
usually w/ blue spots
small with whirling flight

American Copper *Lycaena phlaeas*

docks and sorrels

California Sierra Nevada C

elsewhere RU

June-Aug depending upon elevation

California Sierra: lush meadows and forest openings

elsewhere: rocky alpine meadows and ridgetops

apical black spots
Tuolomne Co., CA

Salt Lake Co., UT

female
no black spot

narrow red-orange line
bold black spots
red-orange on both FW and HW
male

Lustrous Copper *Lycaena cupreus*

docks, especially Water Dock and Curly Dock

LR-LU
May-Oct
mostly
June-Aug

transiently wet open areas, such as floodplains and pond edges

decreasing over a wide area

large with slow flight

females vary from yellow to orange; males w/ iridescent purple or dull gray-brown

wide
orange
border

black spot
female

male

black spot
female
wide orange
border
male
wide orange
border

Bronze Copper *Lycaena hyllus*

buckwheats, especially Naked, see page 132 for photo, and Longstem Buckwheats

U-C
Apr-Aug
about three weeks at any locality

mostly chaparral, foothills and canyons

males often perch in low areas

a California near-endemic

female

male
Siskiyou
Co., CA

no spots
Modoc
Co., CA
above, males
vary from orange
-brown to dull
iridescent purple
(see inset)
male

Gorgon Copper *Lycaena gorgon*

buckwheats

C-A but LR in southern California June-early Sept mostly June-July low and south, July-Aug high and north

sagebrush flats, dry rocky hillsides, dry mountain meadows

Blue and Ruddy Coppers are closely related

ground color below is white to blue-white

Boisduval's Blue, page 140, is usually grayer, w/ FW apical sm spots and HW black spots w/ white rings

most females are gray-brown with some blue at wing bases, but some populations have dull blue females

Blue Coppers are larger with a more powerful flight than blues with which they could be confused

Sublette Co., WY
male

Jackson Co., OR
male

Wasco Co., OR
male

HW varies from almost unmarked to strongly black spotted (especially along the eastern base of the Cascades from N. CA to extreme S. WA — see top right inset)
male
bright blue, usually w/ pronounced black veining

female
black spot
faded spots

female
some populations have dull blue females

female

Blue Copper *Lycaena heteronea*

docks

LC-A
mid May
-Aug,
depending
upon latitude
and altitude;
flies for
about one
month at any
particular
location

wet
meadows,
streamsides
and other
moist areas
in arid
country

some treat
the Arizona
populations,
'Ferris'
Ruddy
Copper, as
a separate
species

off-white
to cream
HW
Modoc
Co., CA
orange
FW
disk
male

Apache
Co., AZ
male

Apache
Co., AZ
male

a sensational butterfly!
Brilliant red-orange shot
with violet
Mono
Co., CA
male

most females
are orange-
tawny above
(main photo)
but some are
duller
(inset photo)

female

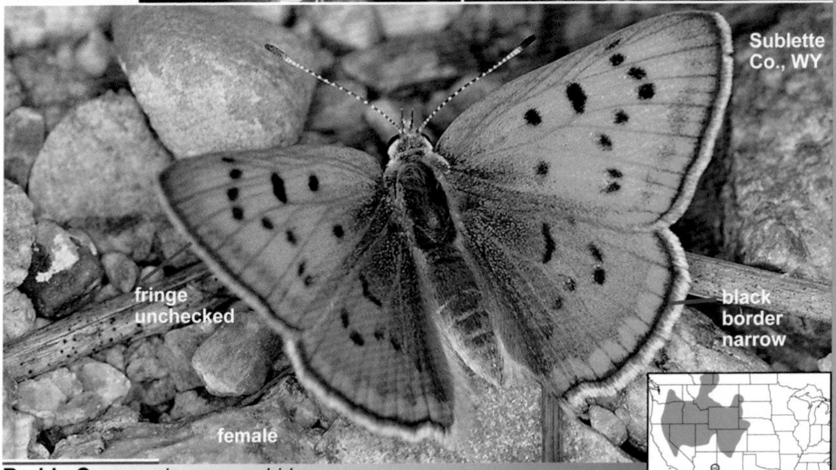
Sublette
Co., WY
fringe
unchecked
black
border
narrow
female

Ruddy Copper *Lycaena rubidus*

docks and knotweeds

C-A but LR in southern California and toward east edges of range; late May-Sept

moist grassy areas, including disturbed habitats

many high Rocky Mountain populations closely resemble Dorcas Coppers and the affinities of these populations is is uncertain

male
high Rockies male
male
narrow black borders
more orange
female
HW uniformly pale pink-purple
usually w/ much orange

Purplish Copper *Lycaena helloides*

cinquefoils, especially Shrubby Cinquefoil

LR-LU mid-June-early Aug in MidWest; late July-late Aug in Maine

wet meadows, marshes and bogs with cinquefoils

the Maine-New Brunswick subspecies is endangered; populations in salt marshes of Quebec/New Brunswick are treated as a separate species by some

wide dark border
female
wide black borders
male
less orange
below, very similar to Purplish Copper

Dorcas Copper *Lycaena dorcas*

knotweeds

C-A
late May-early Sept, depending upon latitude and altitude; about 3 weeks at any particular locality

sagebrush flats, mountain meadows

the strongly contrasting lilac and yellow on the HW makes most individuals an easy ID; but some can be confused w/ Purplish Coppers

Teton Co., WY
Modoc Co., CA
male
males vary from dull above to iridescent purple
two-tone HW
Calaveras Co., CA
female
black spots small and few, except in Warner Mtns of CA (see inset - Modoc Co.)

Lilac-bordered Copper *Lycaena nivalis*

cranberries

LR-LC
mostly June in New Jersey; mainly July Wisconsin; mainly July-Aug northward

cranberry bogs

usually emerges in close synchrony with the flowering of cranberry

very small, weak-flying; normally restricted to cranberry bogs, where other coppers rarely occur

male
pm spots absent or weak
male
female
dull gray-brown w/o orange on FW
HW gray-white or yellowish, not pale purple
female

Bog Copper *Lycaena epixanthe*

mainly blueberries, but also cranberries in some Washington State localities

mostly C but LU California late June-Aug

openings in coniferous woods

Behr's Hairstreak, page 87, is similar but has evenly dark fringes and a gray FW disk

female
male
male
strongly checked
males vary from bright iridescent purple to orange-brown
strongly checked
black chevrons point inward
soft gray with black curls

Mariposa Copper *Lycaena mariposa*

gooseberries

LU-C May-Sept about three weeks at any particular locality

most frequent in wooded foothills along streams; also in sagebrush and mountain meadows

males perch on shrubs or low tree branches

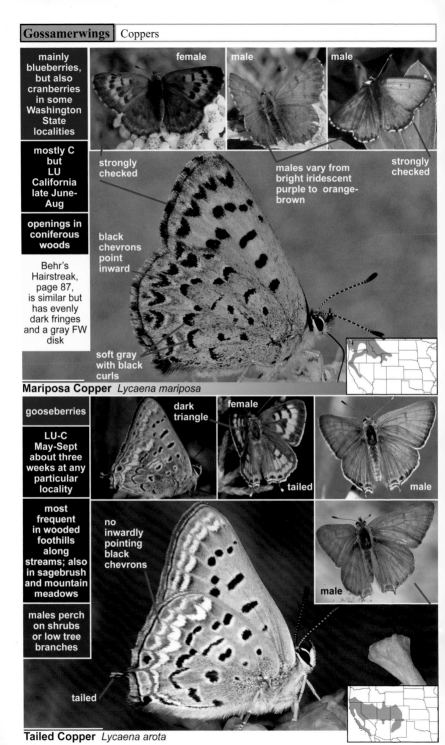

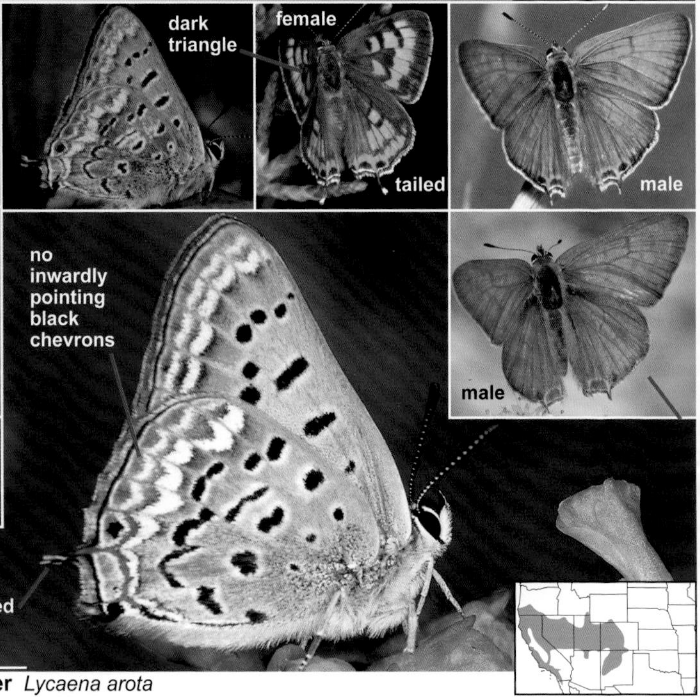
dark triangle
female
tailed
male
no inwardly pointing black chevrons
male
tailed

Tailed Copper *Lycaena arota*

Redberry Buckthorn

LR
mid May-mid July
restricted to San Diego Co., north to Fallbrook and east to Descanso, and to adjacent Baja California

chaparral and thorn-scrub

although not listed by the U.S. government as endangered, in reality this is one of the most endangered truly distinct species in the U.S.

males and females are similar, but females are slightly duller
golden yellow underside
tailed

Hermes Copper *Lycaena hermes*

aphids

LR-LU
Apr/May-Sept/Oct

most frequent in or near wet woods with alders, but also occurs in many other habitats, including suburbia

this is the only butterfly in North America whose caterpillars are carnivorous

small, w/ large black patch in the FW cell

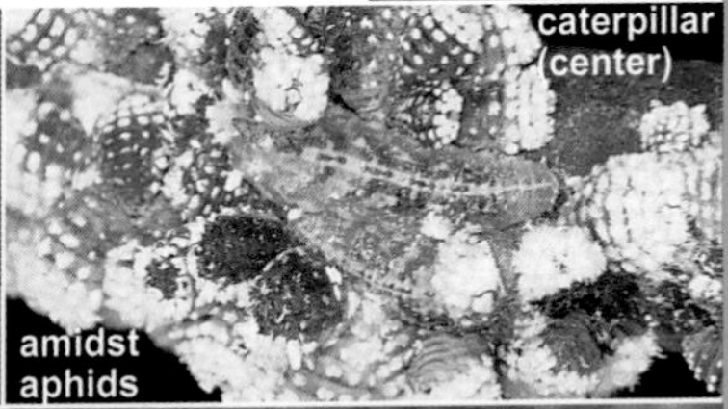
caterpillar (center)
amidst aphids

red-brown ground color
lacey white markings

Harvester *Feniseca tarquinius*

Gambel's Oak

U-LC mostly July-Aug, but also late May-Oct

hillsides with Gambel's oak

this species and Golden Hairstreak are the only two New World hairstreaks that have affinities w/ Old World hairstreaks rather than w/ other New World hairstreaks

large

mainly purple
above (often
rendered as
blue in photos)

foodplant

white basal line

Colorado Hairstreak *Hypaurotis crysalus*

Canyon Live Oak and, in Oregon, chinquapins

California and Oregon LC-LA

Arizona R

mostly late June-Aug, but as early as early June and as late as late Sept

mostly hillsides in chaparral, foothill canyons, but can occur in mountains

partially crepuscular

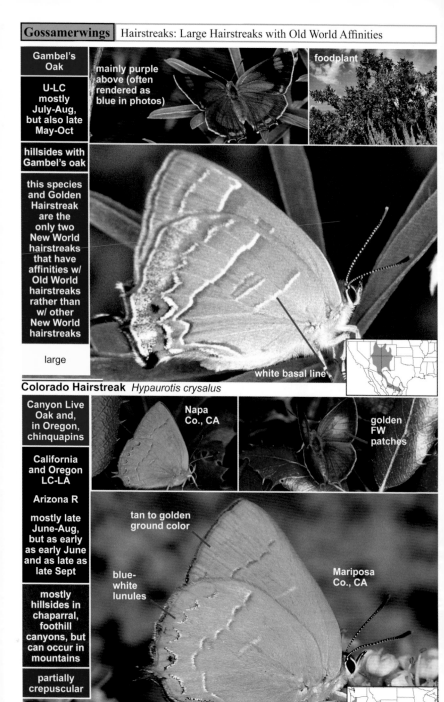

Napa
Co., CA

golden
FW
patches

tan to golden
ground color
blue-
white
lunules
Mariposa
Co., CA

Golden Hairstreak *Habrodais grunus*

native Coontie and other introduced cycads

LR-LA all year

anyplace w/ cycads, sometimes even in native habitats!

whirring flight is seemingly mothlike

once thought to be endangered, even extinct, this species' population levels can vary greatly from year to year

caterpillars are just as incredible as the adults!

Coontie

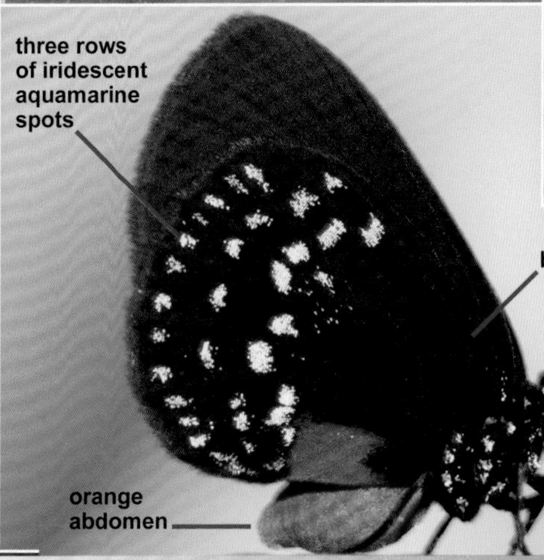
three rows of iridescent aquamarine spots
black
orange abdomen

Atala ***Eumaeus atala***

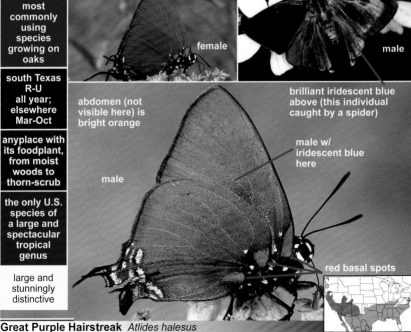

mistletoes, most commonly using species growing on oaks

south Texas R-U all year; elsewhere Mar-Oct

anyplace with its foodplant, from moist woods to thorn-scrub

the only U.S. species of a large and spectacular tropical genus

large and stunningly distinctive

female

male

brilliant iridescent blue above (this individual caught by a spider)
abdomen (not visible here) is bright orange
male w/ iridescent blue here
male
red basal spots

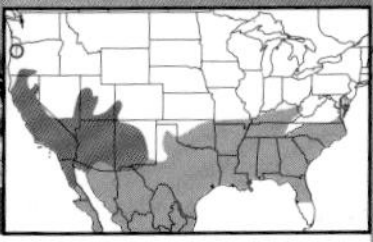

Great Purple Hairstreak *Atlides halesus*

oaks

southern portion of range
U-C
Feb-Oct

northern portion
LR
Apr-Sept

openings in and edges of oak woods

Oak Hairstreaks, page 94, have an orange spot that doesn't jut inward, lack the white dash and are smaller

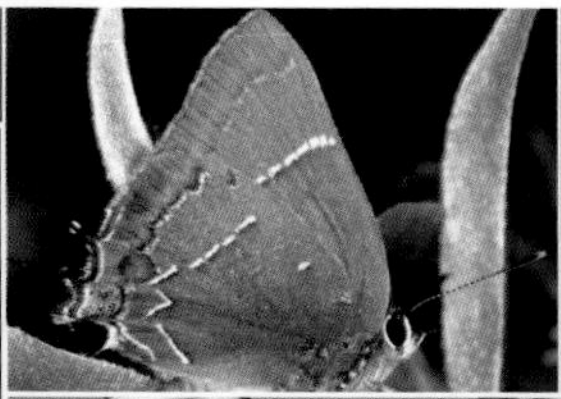

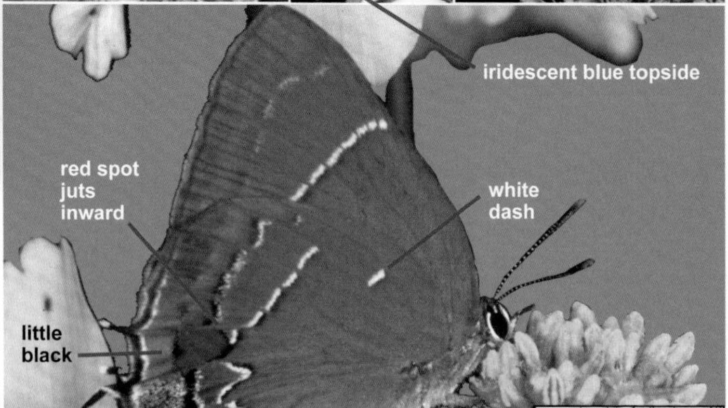
iridescent blue topside
red spot juts inward
white dash
little black

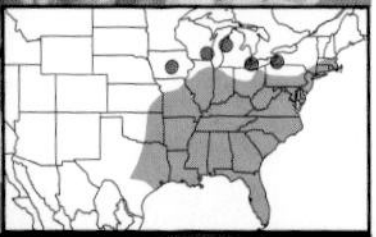

White M Hairstreak *Parrhasius m-album*

Western Soapberry

LU
May-June

openings in and edges of oak woods

probably occurs wherever its foodplant is found, although not yet recorded from south Texas

Gray Hairstreaks, page 110, and Oak Hairstreaks, page 94, lack the white cell-end bars

topside is dull gray-brown

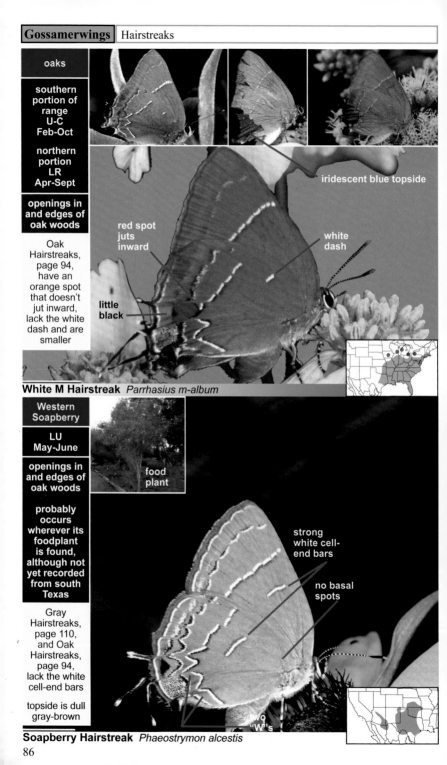

food plant

strong white cell-end bars
no basal spots
two "W"s

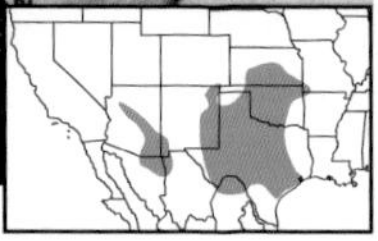

Soapberry Hairstreak *Phaeostrymon alcestis*

wild cherries and wild plums

east of Rockies U-C

west of Rockies LR-U

June-Aug

brushy areas, including overgrown fields and streamsides

well-named and gem-like — a real favorite!

topside is dull gray-brown

male

female

top-
side
(thru
wing
tear)
female

red-orange marginal spots
female
no tail
no blue spot

Coral Hairstreak *Satyrium titus*

Antelope Bitterbrush, Alderleaf Mountain Mahogany

C-A
May-Aug

dry, often rocky, areas, including sagebrush flats and foothill ridgetops

often swarms buckwheats along the east slope of the Sierras and Cascades

Mariposa Copper, pg 82, is similar but with checked fringes and orange FW disk

White Pine Co., CA
orange patches above

Tulare Co., CA

Teton Co., ID

bright orange above
Modoc Co., CA
strong black spots
gray overscaling
no tail

Behr's Hairstreak *Satyrium behrii*

oaks and hickories

U-C
Apr-July
about one month at each location

openings and edges of woods with oaks, including treed suburban areas

populations densities vary from year to year

below, varies from chalk gray (northwestern CO) to dark; topside is dull gray-brown

some w/ white on both sides
some in FL w/ much red and long tails

most w/ white only on outside of FW pm band
blue spot usually dark and doesn't jut inward of arc of orange spots (except in Colorado)
leading edge bars not aligned w/ cell-end bars

Banded Hairstreak *Satyrium calanus*

hickories

R-U
June-July

openings and edges of rich deciduous woods with hickories

topside is dull gray-brown

perhaps 10% of individuals cannot reliably be distinguished from Banded Hairstreak in the field

blue spot jut and leading edge bars are most important field marks

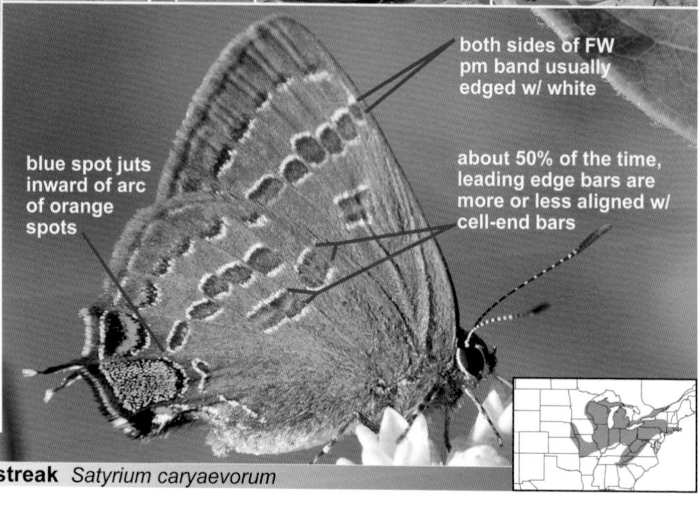
both sides of FW pm band usually edged w/ white
blue spot juts inward of arc of orange spots
about 50% of the time, leading edge bars are more or less aligned w/ cell-end bars

Hickory Hairstreak *Satyrium caryaevorum*

oaks, especially Bear Oak and other small oaks

LR-LC mid May-early Aug about one month at each location

openings and edges of oak woods and savannahs on sandy or barren soil

closely associated with small oaks and usually colonial

topside is dull gray-brown

Sussex
Co., NJ

Moore
Co., NC

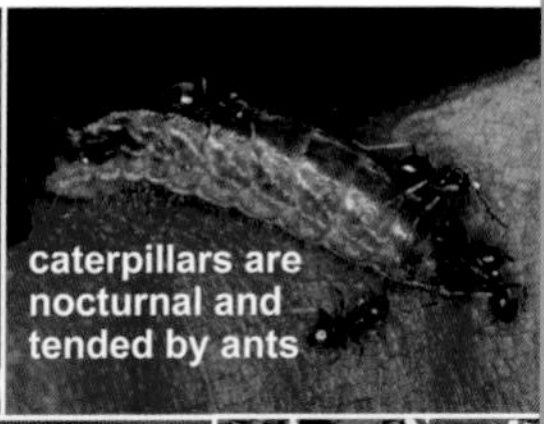
caterpillars are nocturnal and tended by ants

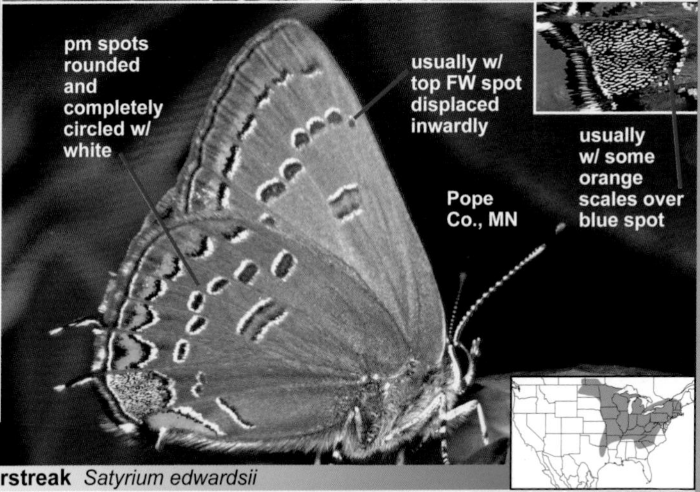
pm spots rounded and completely circled w/ white
usually w/ top FW spot displaced inwardly
usually w/ some orange scales over blue spot
Pope Co., MN

Edwards' Hairstreak *Satyrium edwardsii*

wild cherries, blueberries and others

R-U May-early Aug about one month at each location

not as colonial as most other *Satyrium* hairstreaks, one rarely encounters large numbers

above, brown w/ orange patches

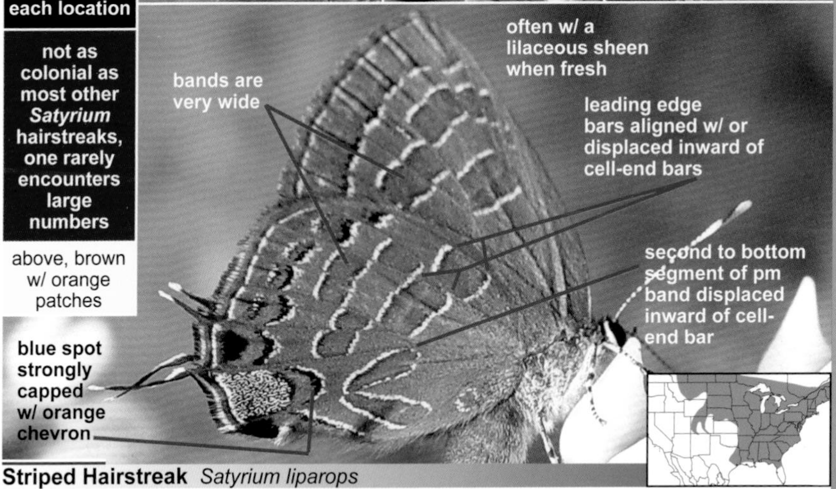
bands are very wide
often w/ a lilaceous sheen when fresh
leading edge bars aligned w/ or displaced inward of cell-end bars
second to bottom segment of pm band displaced inward of cell-end bar
blue spot strongly capped w/ orange chevron

Striped Hairstreak *Satyrium liparops*

Common Sweetleaf

LR
mid May-mid Aug
about three weeks at each location

mainly rich, moist woods

range closely mirrors the range of Common Sweetleaf

Banded Hairstreaks, page 88, lack orange cap

Striped Hairstreak, page 89, with different banding

topside is dull gray-brown

leading edge bars distal to cell-end bars
blue spot strongly capped w/ orange
second to bottom segment of pm band distal to cell-end bar

King's Hairstreak *Satyrium kingi*

willows

LU-LC
mainly June-July

wet thickets, streamsides w/ small willows

gray or gray-brown with pm bands of small black spots

Sylvan Hairstreaks lack orange caps

California Hairstreaks have wider HW cell-end bars

topside is dull gray-brown

small black spots
this spot far from sm band
ground color gray to gray-brown
cell-end bar narrow
blue spot strongly capped w/ orange

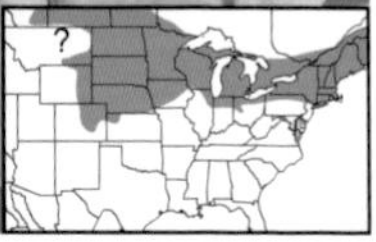

Acadian Hairstreak *Satyrium acadica*

willows

LU-LC
late May-
mid July

wet thickets,
streamsides
w/ small
willows

gray or gray-brown with pm bands of small black spots

Sylvan Hairstreaks lack orange caps

California Hairstreaks have wider HW cell-end bars

topside is dull gray-brown

Teton
Co., WY

Alameda
Co., CA

Elko
Co., NV

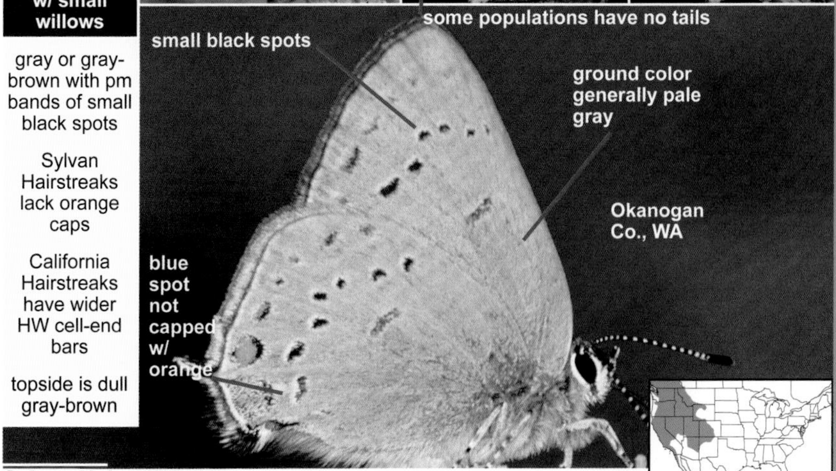
some populations have no tails
small black spots
ground color generally pale gray
Okanogan
Co., WA
blue spot not capped w/ orange

Sylvan Hairstreak *Satyrium sylvinus*

oaks and
mountain
mahoganies

LU-LC
mainly
June-July

chaparral,
sagebrush
flats, forest
openings

topside is gray-brown, usually with some orange-brown

Mono
Co., CA

Davis
Co., UT

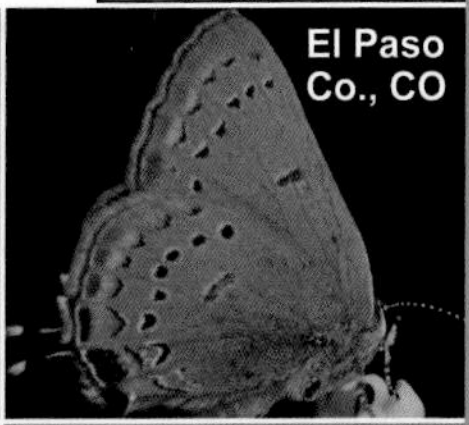
El Paso
Co., CO

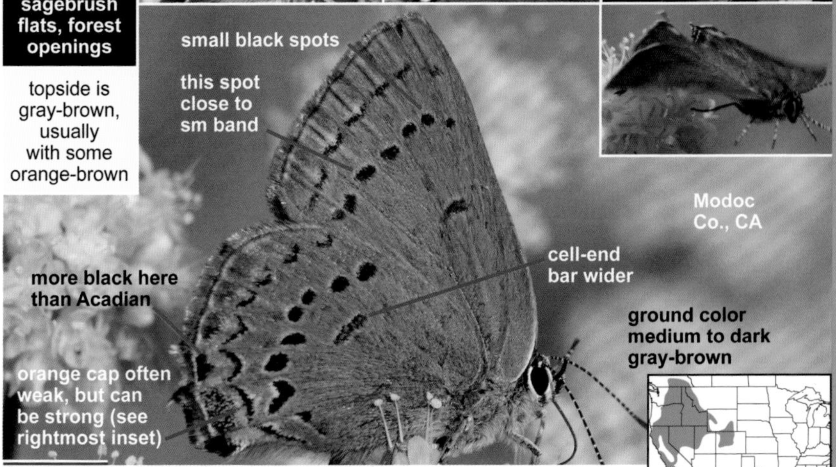
small black spots
this spot close to sm band
Modoc
Co., CA
cell-end bar wider
more black here than Acadian
ground color medium to dark gray-brown
orange cap often weak, but can be strong (see rightmost inset)

California Hairstreak *Satyrium californica*

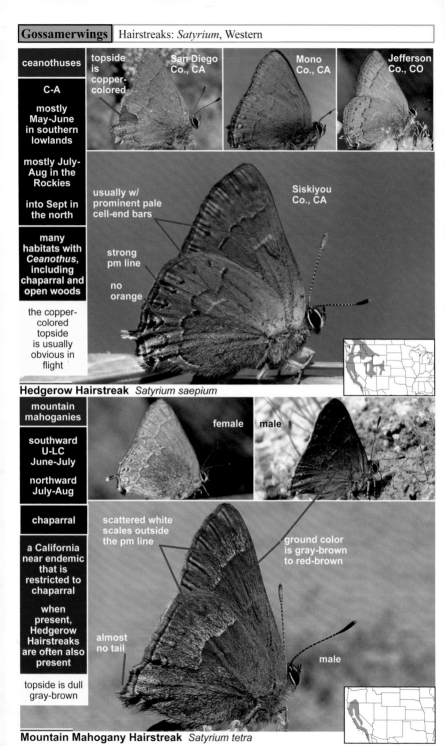

ceanothuses

C-A

mostly May-June in southern lowlands

mostly July-Aug in the Rockies

into Sept in the north

many habitats with *Ceanothus*, including chaparral and open woods

the copper-colored topside is usually obvious in flight

topside is copper-colored
San Diego Co., CA

Mono Co., CA

Jefferson Co., CO

usually w/ prominent pale cell-end bars
strong pm line
no orange
Siskiyou Co., CA

Hedgerow Hairstreak *Satyrium saepium*

mountain mahoganies

southward U-LC June-July

northward July-Aug

chaparral

a California near endemic that is restricted to chaparral

when present, Hedgerow Hairstreaks are often also present

topside is dull gray-brown

female

male

scattered white scales outside the pm line
ground color is gray-brown to red-brown
almost no tail
male

Mountain Mahogany Hairstreak *Satyrium tetra*

oaks

R-LU
June-July

chaparral and open woods w/ oaks

when found, often co-occurs with California Hairstreak

topside is dull brown; females w/ some orange

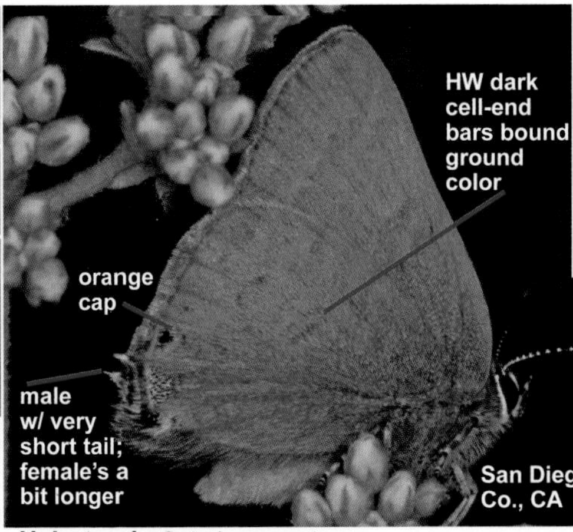
HW dark cell-end bars bound ground color
orange cap
male w/ very short tail; female's a bit longer
San Diego Co., CA

LA Co., CA

Gold-hunter's Hairstreak *Satyrium auretorum*

lupines

LU
late June-early Aug

mountain meadows

some treat ***S. f. semiluna*** (below) as a distinct species from nominate ***S. fuliginosa***, but they appear to interbreed

most w/ dark fringe
ground color is warm brown (mostly) to gray

Sooty Hairstreak *Satyrium fuliginosa fulginosa*

lupines

U-C
May-Sept; mostly July-Aug

high altitude sagebrush flats and mountain meadows

topside is dull gray-brown

see Boisduval's Blue, pg 140

most w/ white fringe
Teton Co., WY
ground color is gray to gray-brown
spots rather fuzzy and, circled w/ white

Park Co., WY

Deschutes Co., OR

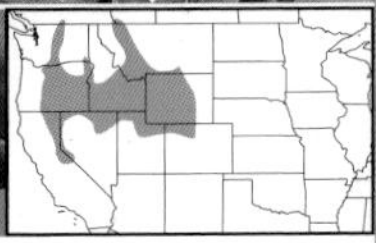

Sooty Hairstreak *Satyrium fuliginosa semiluna*

oaks

R-U
Apr-May at south end of range; June-July at north end of range

areas with oaks, including open pineland, brushland, and edges of deciduous woods

where their populations meet, there is a blend zone between 'Northern' and 'Southern'

Westchester
Co., NY

Goliad
Co., TX

topside is dull
gray-brown
Goliad
Co., TX
cell-end bars
faint or absent
usually (but
not always –
see inset) w/
a white dash
here
blue
spot w/
orange
cap
Northern
Southern

'Northern' Oak Hairstreak *Satyrium favonius ontario*

oaks

U-C
Apr-May

areas with oaks, including open pineland, scrub, and edges of deciduous woods

topside is dull gray-brown with orangish patches

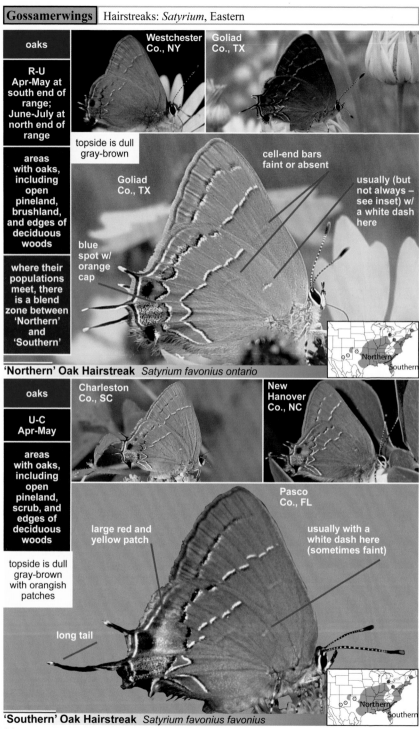

Charleston
Co., SC

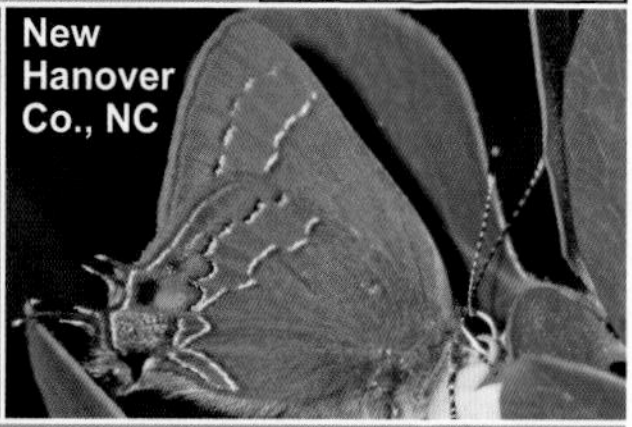
New
Hanover
Co., NC

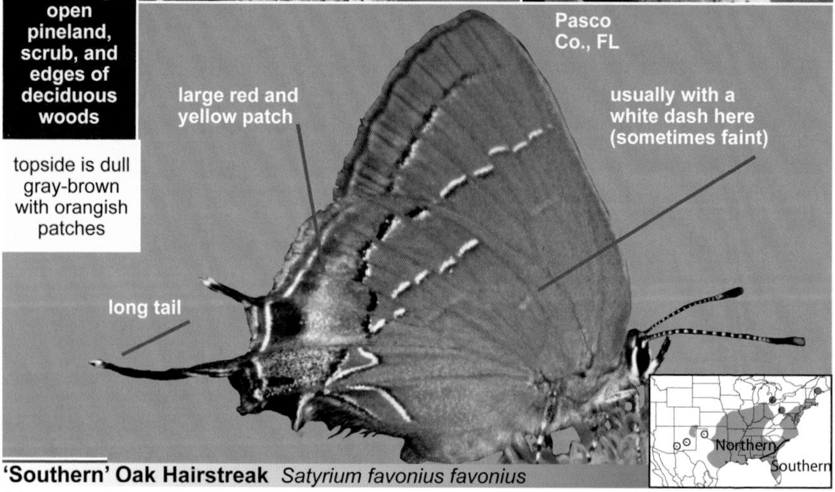
Pasco
Co., FL
large red and
yellow patch
usually with a
white dash here
(sometimes faint)
long tail
Northern
Southern

'Southern' Oak Hairstreak *Satyrium favonius favonius*

Gray Oak and Emory Oak

R-LC
May-June

open woods with oaks

Big Bend National Park and Guadalupe Mountains National Park are two good places to find this restricted range species

topside is dull gray-brown

absent or weak submarginal band
pm bands placed farther out on wings
HW fringe dark
blue spot w/o orange cap
strong W

Poling's Hairstreak *Satyrium polingi*

Sonoran Scrub Oak

R-LC
May-June

dry hilly areas with Sonoran Scrub Oak thickets

topside is dull gray-brown w/ orangish patches which can sometimes be seen in flight

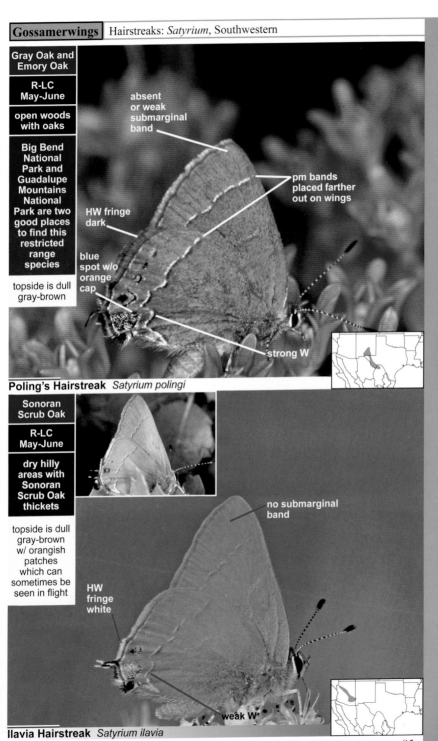

no submarginal band
HW fringe white
weak W

Ilavia Hairstreak *Satyrium ilavia*

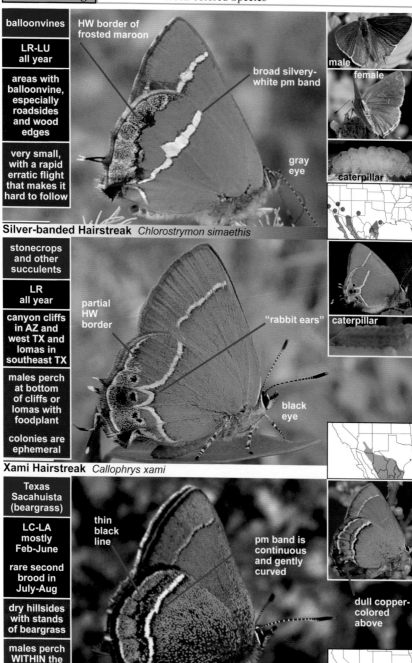

balloonvines

LR-LU
all year

areas with balloonvine, especially roadsides and wood edges

very small, with a rapid erratic flight that makes it hard to follow

HW border of
frosted maroon
broad silvery-
white pm band
gray
eye

male

female

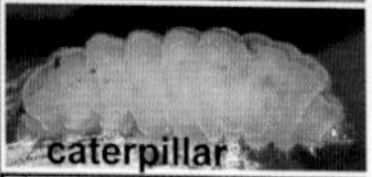
caterpillar

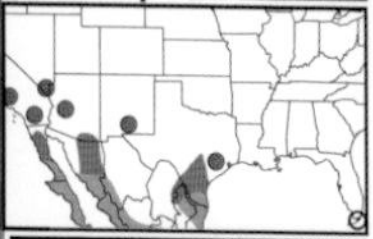

Silver-banded Hairstreak *Chlorostrymon simaethis*

stonecrops and other succulents

LR
all year

canyon cliffs in AZ and west TX and lomas in southeast TX

males perch at bottom of cliffs or lomas with foodplant

colonies are ephemeral

partial
HW
border
“rabbit ears”
black
eye

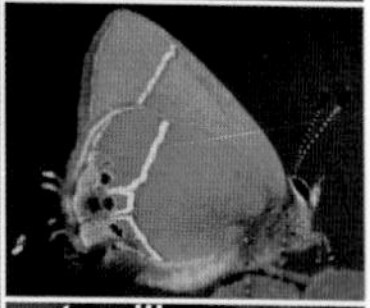

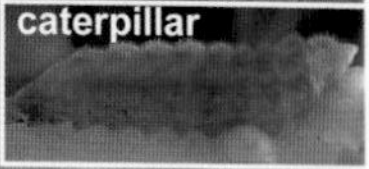
caterpillar

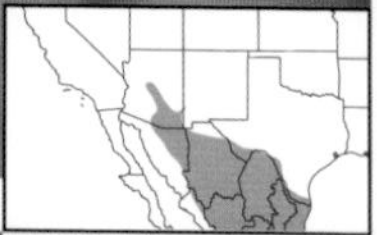

Xami Hairstreak *Callophrys xami*

Texas Sacahuista (beargrass)

LC-LA
mostly
Feb-June

rare second brood in July-Aug

dry hillsides with stands of beargrass

males perch WITHIN the beargrass

thin
black
line
pm band is
continuous
and gently
curved

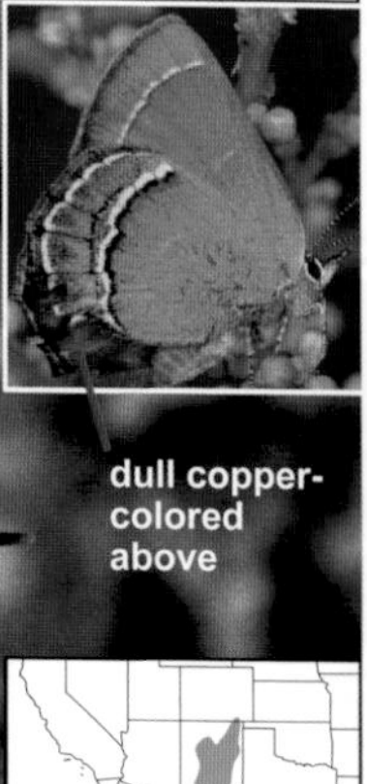

Sandia Hairstreak *Callophrys mcfarlandi*

Florida Fish-poison Tree, Button Mangrove
R all year, mainly May; occurrence is very erratic
tropical woods
wide partial HW border
no white on pm band
flies at tops of trees, mating near dusk

Amethyst Hairstreak
Chlorostrymon maesites
FL Keys

many families
wide partial HW border

Telea Hairstreak
Chlorostrymon telea
LRGV

unknown
black spot
face is all brown
w/ tails
black eye

Clench's Greenstreak
Cyanophrys miserabilis
LRGV

many families
little or no black
face w/ some green
black eye
w/ or w/o tails

Tropical Greenstreak
Cyanophrys herodotus
LRGV

many families
gray eye
no tail

Goodson's Greenstreak
Cyanophrys goodsoni
LRGV

unknown
marginal spots
not yet reported from U.S., but probably strays to LRGV, possibly Big Bend
black eye
brown spot

Brown-spotted Greenstreak
Cyanophrys longula
not yet LRGV

many plant families

mostly U, but C-A in southern California

mostly early spring but subspecies *apama* in Arizona, June-mid July

chaparral, open woods, sagebrush

this and Sheridan's Hairstreak are a difficult group with much variability

there is little consensus on the best taxonomy or identification, in part because there is little data available regarding the genetics of this group

some treat Bramble Hairstreak as two or three species

some place California coastal *viridis* (shown in main photo at right) with Bramble Hairstreak, some with Sheridan's Hairstreak

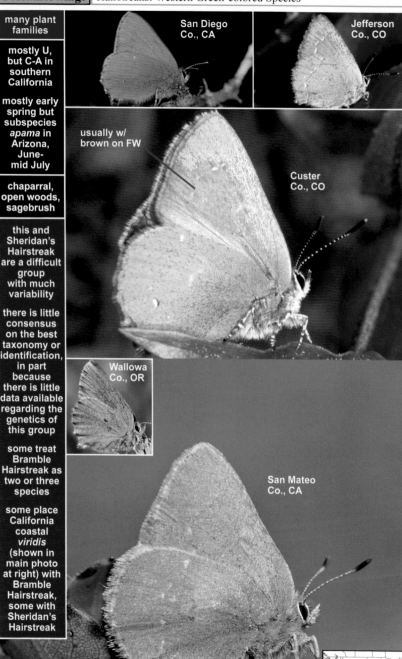

San Diego
Co., CA

Jefferson
Co., CO

usually w/
brown on FW
Custer
Co., CO

Wallowa
Co., OR

San Mateo
Co., CA

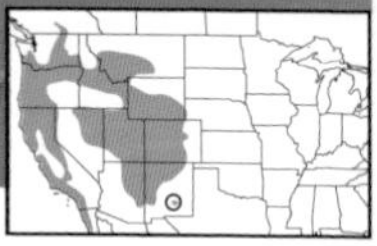

Bramble Hairstreak *Callophrys dumetorum*

buckwheats

LC in the Rockies, Mar-mid June

LR-LU in Pacific mid elevations Apr-May

LR-LU June-July for 'Alpine' form (shown in main photo of bottom panel) in California and Nevada

'Desert' Sheridan's in two brood area is LU, mid Mar-early May and late Aug-mid Sept

open mixed and conifer woods, sagebrush

'alpine' forms on high ridgetops

'desert' forms in canyons on lower slopes of desert mountains

a complicated group with much variation

most individuals in the Rockies are similar to the one shown in top panel

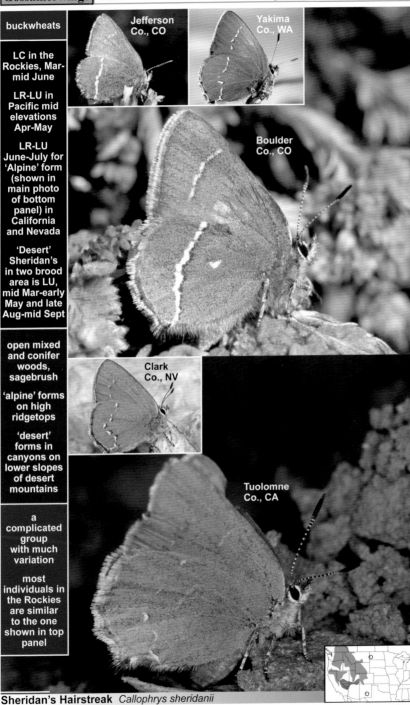

Jefferson Co., CO

Yakima Co., WA

Boulder Co., CO

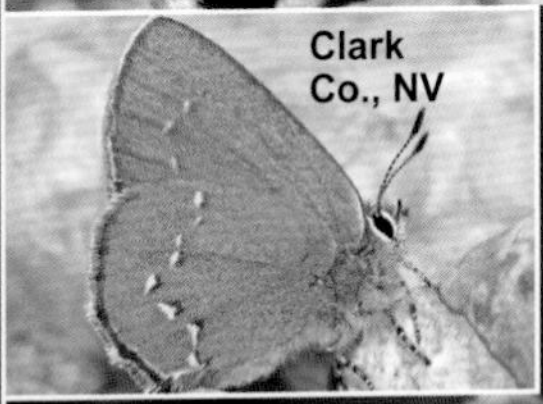
Clark Co., NV

Tuolomne Co., CA

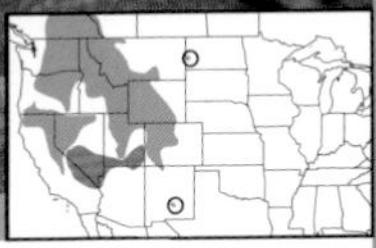

Sheridan's Hairstreak *Callophrys sheridanii*

'Olive' Juniper Hairstreak *Callophrys gryneus gryneus*

Eastern Redcedar

LC-LA but LR-LU in southeast and Midwest; early spring and mid summer

open woods and fields with the foodplant

this species is attracted to orange milkweed but, otherwise, it infrequently visits flowers; best found by shaking redcedars

Travis Co., TX
summer brood

Monmouth Co., NJ
spring brood

food plant

orangish topside
top pm spot aligned w/ spot below it
irregular pm line
Sussex Co., NJ
two spots curved in opposite directions

Hessel's Hairstreak *Callophrys hesseli*

Atlantic White Cedar

LR-LU late Apr-May, July-early Aug 2nd brood only partial in north

white cedar bogs

best found by searching flowers, such as those of blueberries or sand myrtle, along roads through or on the periphery of white cedar bogs

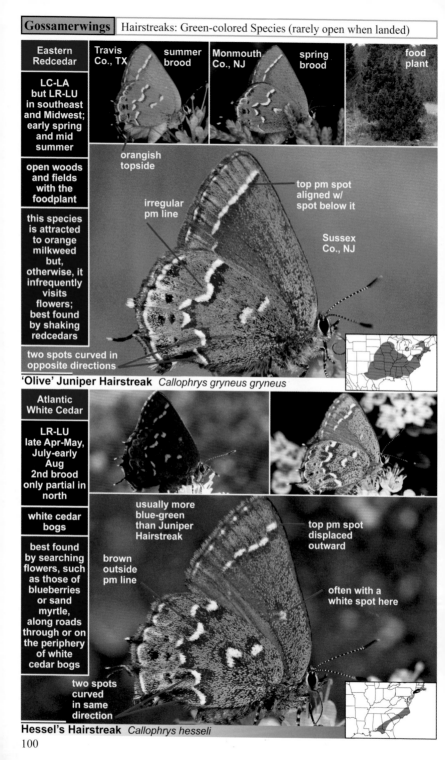

usually more blue-green than Juniper Hairstreak
top pm spot displaced outward
brown outside pm line
often with a white spot here
two spots curved in same direction

Southern Redcedar

LU
Mar-May,
Sept-Oct

open woods and fields with the foodplant

a few treat this as a full species; intermediates with 'Olive' occur where ranges meet

straight pm line
long tails
eyespot with less orange, more black

'Sweadner's' Juniper Hairstreak *Callophrys gryneus sweadneri*

junipers

U-C

southward spring and mid summer

northward early summer

open woods and fields with the foodplant

the commonest "green" hairstreak in much of the West

intermediates between 'Siva' and 'Olive' occur from eastern New Mexico to west Texas

Jefferson Co., CO

Santa Cruz Co., AZ

Cochise Co., AZ

some w/ purple gloss

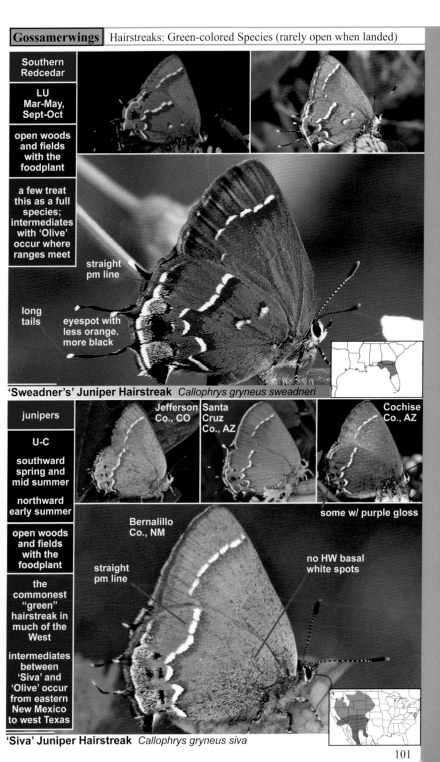

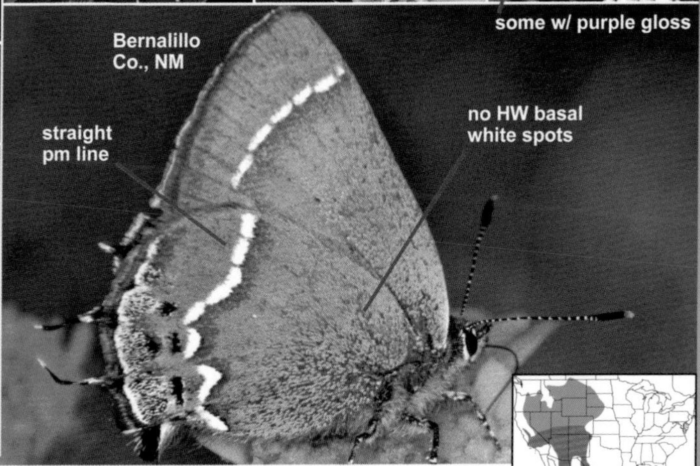
Bernalillo Co., NM
straight pm line
no HW basal white spots

'Siva' Juniper Hairstreak *Callophrys gryneus siva*

Incense Cedar and Western Redcedar

A mostly May-July

montane coniferous woods

some treat Juniper Hairstreak subspecies as full species

purple sheen when fresh
pm band varies from strong to weak

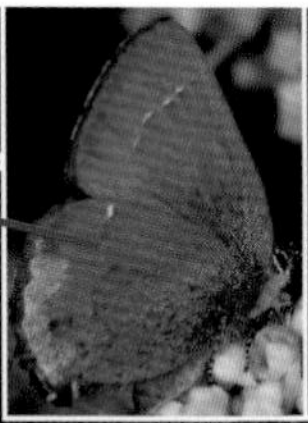

orangish topside

'Nelson's' Juniper Hairstreak *Callophrys gryneus nelsoni*

junipers

U-C spring and mid summer southward; early summer northward

hillsides w/ the foodplant

brown 'Siva's mainly in the northwestern portion of the range; see page 101 for green form

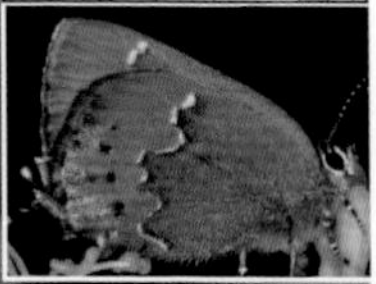

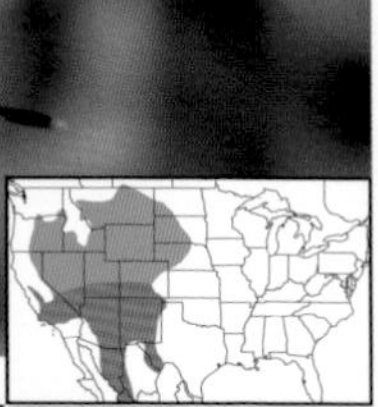

'Siva' Juniper Hairstreak *Callophrys gryneus siva*

Tecate Cypress for 'Thorne's' and junipers for 'Loki'

'Thorne's' LR-LU; 'Loki' LC Mar-Apr, Sept

canyons and hillsides w/ the foodplant

Thorne's on Otay Mountain

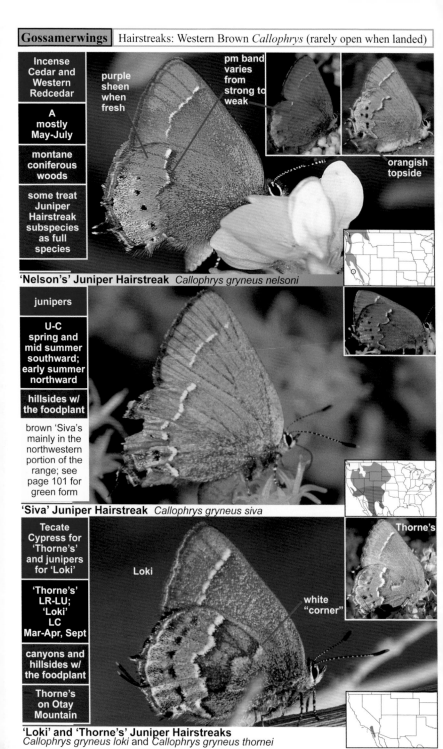

Loki
white "corner"

Thorne's

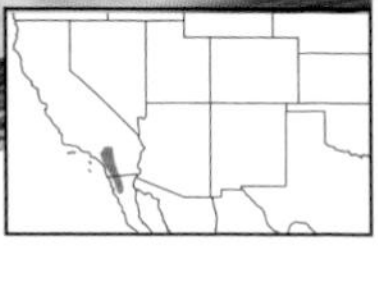

'Loki' and 'Thorne's' Juniper Hairstreaks
Callophrys gryneus loki and *Callophrys gryneus thornei*

dwarf mistletoes on conifers

U-C

two brood areas Mar-Sept

one brood areas May-July

openings in coniferous woods

topside is blue-gray to bright blue

Klamath
Co., OR

reddish-
brown
ground
color
Custer
Co., CO

bold white
pm line
white FW
cell-end bar
(sometimes
faint)
Pima
Co., AZ

Thicket Hairstreak *Callophrys spinetorum*

dwarf mistletoes on conifers

LR June-Aug

openings in coniferous woods

more often stumbled upon than found by an intentional search

similar to the much more common Thicket Hairstreak below

topside is orange-brown, unlike bluish topside of Thicket Hairstreak

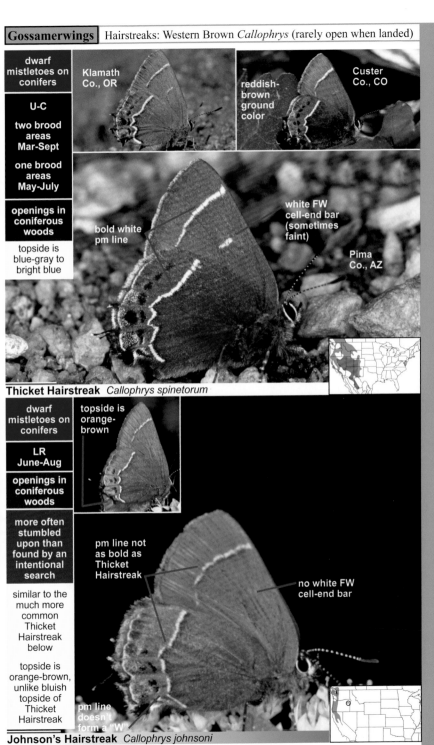

pm line not
as bold as
Thicket
Hairstreak
no white FW
cell-end bar
pm line
doesn't
form a "W"

Johnson's Hairstreak *Callophrys johnsoni*

Elfins

The delightful elfins are some of the first butterflies to fly in the spring, with most of the species flying in early spring (which can be in June or later in the high mountains or far north). Luckily for butterfliers, these diminutive gossamerwings are often stunningly garbed in iridescent scales of purple and aqua. Most of the species live in poor-soil habitats such as pine barrens and bogs and all of them have one brood each year. Some treat the elfins as forming a group distinct from the *Callophrys* hairstreaks.

Black Spruce

LR
mid May-
mid June

Black Spruce bogs

if you are willing to travel to remote Black Spruce bogs and feed ravenous mosquitoes and black flies, you'll have a chance of missing this mysterious butterfly yet again

smaller than either species of pine elfin

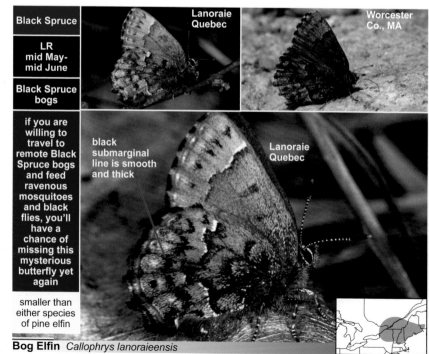

Lanoraie
Quebec

Worcester
Co., MA

black submarginal line is smooth and thick
Lanoraie
Quebec

Bog Elfin *Callophrys lanoraieensis*

pines, usually hard pines, but also soft pines, such as White Pine

LU-C
Mar-Apr at southern end of range; Apr-May north to about Virginia-Missouri; northward, late Apr-June

pine woods

dramatically patterned with pink, white, maroon and dark brown

usually with two bars in FW cell

Ocean Co., NJ
female
females w/ orange patches above
males dull brown above

Worcester Co., MA

Mineral Co., WV

pm line more disjointed
black submarginal line less jagged
Sussex Co., NJ
usually w/ two bars
pink bars on top of maroon bars

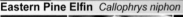

Eastern Pine Elfin *Callophrys niphon*

pines

West
C

East
LR

Apr-July, mostly Apr-May

pine woods

dramatically patterned with pink, white, maroon and dark brown

usually with only one bar in FW cell and jagged HW submarginal line

Tulare Co., CA

Jefferson Co., CO

Jackson Co., OR

pm line more connected
black submarginal line is very jagged and thin
Humboldt Co., CA
usually w/ only one bar
pink crescents on top of maroon spots

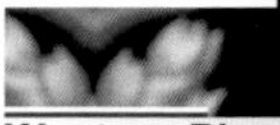

Western Pine Elfin *Callophrys eryphon*

east of Appalachians mostly American Holly

west of Appalachians mostly Eastern Redbud

Great Lakes area mostly blueberries

also non-native Alder Buckthorn

LR-LC early spring

brushy woods

Levy
Co., FL

Monmouth
Co., NJ

no frosting on FW; frosting on HW
pm line usually fairly straight
bold white
a few scattered gray hairs and scales
short tail
white

Henry's Elfin *Callophrys henrici*

Kinnikinnick (bearberry)

LR-LU early spring

sand and limestone barrens

best found by locating large stands of bearberry but, even then, absent from many areas of seemingly hospitable habitat

a small, dark elfin of barrens

Frosted Elfin is larger without frosting on the FW

food
plant

frosting on both FW and HW
prominent area w/ gray hairs and scales

Hoary Elfin *Callophrys polios*

in the East, mainly blueberries

in the West, a wide variety in many plant families

LC-LA
early spring

poor soil woods

hilltops

this is probably the most frequently encountered elfin

map shows eastern portion of range

Westchester Co., NY

Ocean Co., NJ

worn
Sevier Co., TN

Ocean Co., NJ
no frosting
rusty border
often w/ purple sheen

Brown Elfin *Callophrys augustinus*

Horseflyweed (wild indigo) and lupines

LR-LU
spring - early summer

cleared sandy or rocky areas such as burns, powerline cuts and roadsides

probably because its habitats are ephemeral and not being replaced, this species is declining over much of its range

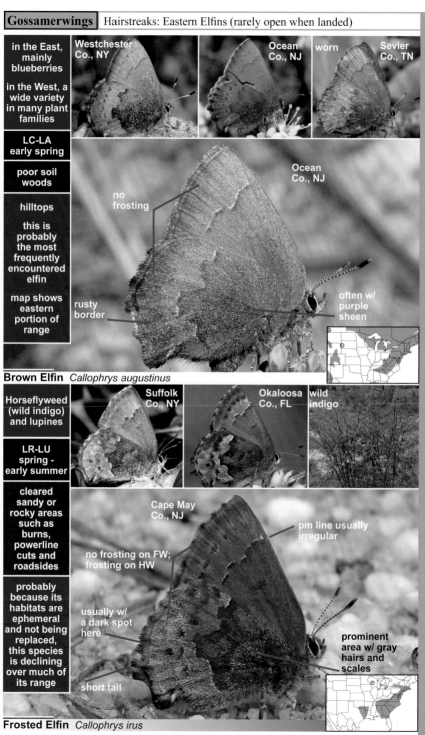

Suffolk Co., NY

Okaloosa Co., FL

wild indigo

Cape May Co., NJ
pm line usually irregular
no frosting on FW; frosting on HW
usually w/ a dark spot here
prominent area w/ gray hairs and scales
short tail

Frosted Elfin *Callophrys irus*

in the East, mainly blueberries

in the West, a wide variety in many plant families

LC-LA early spring

poor soil woods

hilltops

this is probably the most frequently encountered elfin

map shows western portion of range

often with a purple sheen when fresh

Kern
Co., CA

San Diego
Co., CA

Gila
Co., AZ

topside
in flight
no frosting
on wings
rusty
ground
color
San Luis Obispo
Co., CA

Brown Elfin *Callophrys augustinus*

Kinnikinnick (bearberry)

LR-LU early spring

barrens with its foodplant

as in much of the East, this butterfly is quite local and strangely absent from many areas with extensive stands of its foodplant

map shows western portion of range

the only dark elfin with frosting along the FW outer margin

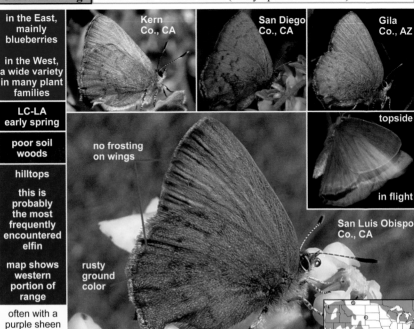

food
plant
frosting on
both FW
and HW

Hoary Elfin *Callophrys polios*

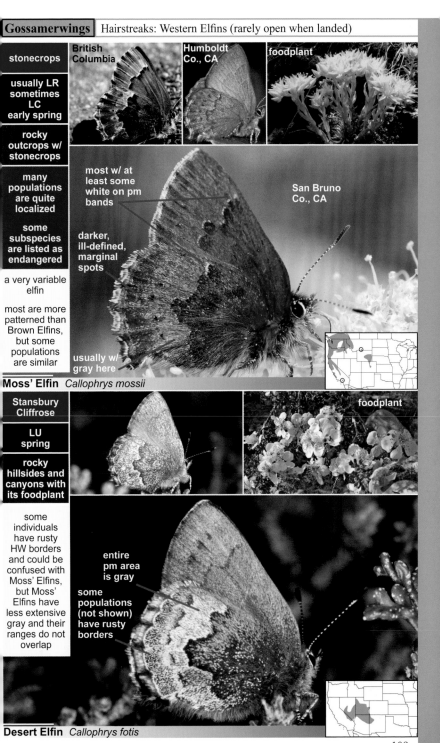

stonecrops

usually LR
sometimes
LC
early spring

rocky
outcrops w/
stonecrops

many
populations
are quite
localized

some
subspecies
are listed as
endangered

a very variable elfin

most are more patterned than Brown Elfins, but some populations are similar

Moss' Elfin *Callophrys mossii*

Stansbury
Cliffrose

LU
spring

rocky
hillsides and
canyons with
its foodplant

some individuals have rusty HW borders and could be confused with Moss' Elfins, but Moss' Elfins have less extensive gray and their ranges do not overlap

Desert Elfin *Callophrys fotis*

will use a large number of species in many plant families

southward C-A

far north LR-U

early spring through fall

all year in no-freeze areas

almost any open areas

hilltops

quite variable

a few are browner than shown

the inner side of the large orange spot is almost always flat, rarely is curved, as on the individual in lower main photo

red-orange HW pm line dashes are sometimes faint or lacking, see lower panel left inset

male w/ orange abdomen

ground color usually true gray
no strong spots inside pm line
orange spot is large, usually w/ flat inner edge

female w/ gray abdomen

black dashes
orange spot usually reaches pm line

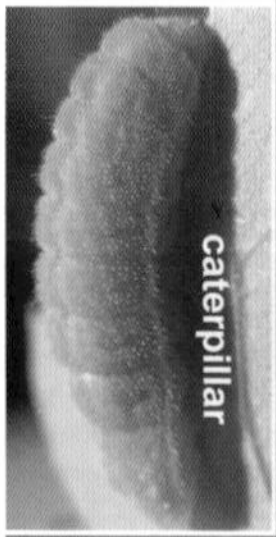
caterpillar

Gray Hairstreak *Strymon melinus*

Deerweed and Silver Bird's-foot Trefoil

U
Feb-Oct
most frequent in May

almost any open areas

Gray Hairstreaks also now occur on Santa Catalina Island

these are faded versions of Gray Hairstreaks, endemic to Santa Catalina Island
line displaced inward
orange spot small, crescent-shaped
Santa Catalina Island, south of Los Angeles

Avalon Scrub-Hairstreak *Strymon avalona*

bromeliads, Texas False Agave in TX

R
mainly late Mar-Apr, Sept

Big Bend NP population was recently described as *S. solitario*

males with some blue on topside

cell-end bar dark-centered
female
often w/o red basal spots in TX

Confusing Scrub-Hairstreak *Strymon megarus*

bromeliads

see Red-lined Scrub-Hairstreak, page 113

males with blue above

single row of dark gray spots
male
often w/ white distal to pm line

Bromeliad Scrub-Hairstreak *Strymon serapio*

LRGV once

bromeliads

males with some blue above

female
usually w/ red basal spots
cell-end bar white-centered

Red-spotted Scrub-Hairstreak *Strymon ziba*

not yet LRGV

Bay Cedar and Jamaican Nettletree

LU-LC all year

most frequent in May and Aug-Oct

shrubby shores and tropical hammock edges

the bright blue topside is visible when the butterfly saws its wings, or in flight

male

caterpillar

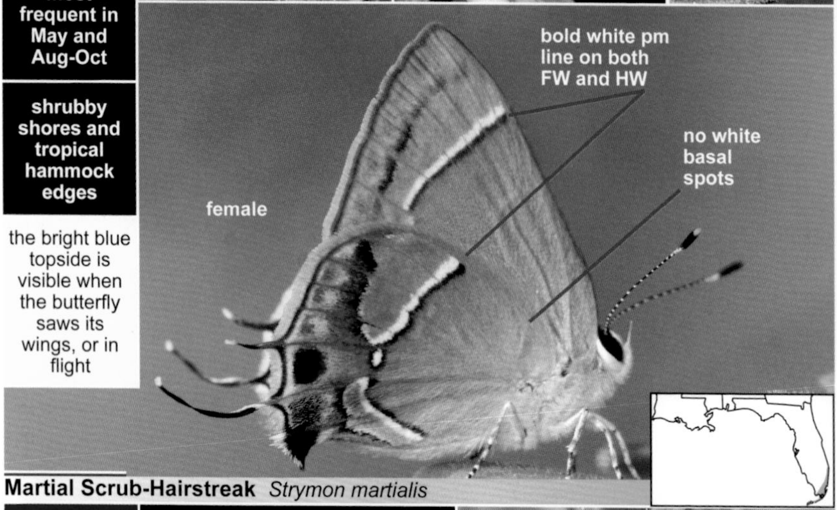
bold white pm line on both FW and HW
no white basal spots
female

Martial Scrub-Hairstreak *Strymon martialis*

Grannybush (pineland croton)

LR-LU all year

pine rockland

due to extensive habitat loss, and the unecessary use of anti-mosquito pesticides, this species, and almost all of the special butterflies of South Florida, are endangered

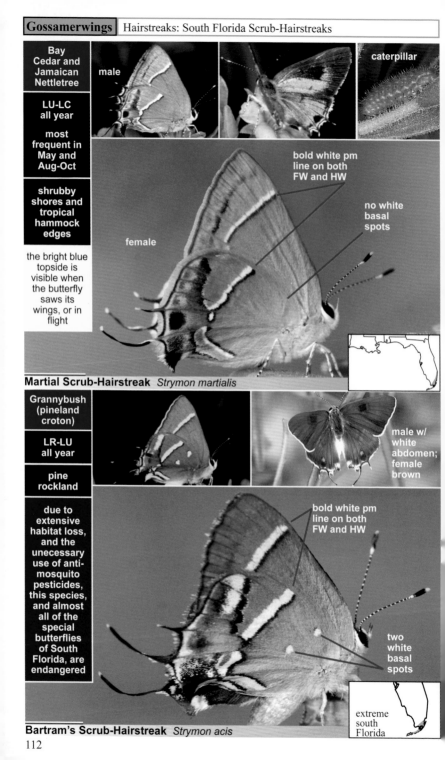

male w/ white abdomen; female brown

bold white pm line on both FW and HW
two white basal spots
extreme south Florida

Bartram's Scrub-Hairstreak *Strymon acis*

many plant families
wide band
extensive white
jagged basal line

White Scrub-Hairstreak *S. albata*

LRGV

many plant families
white cell-end bar
median stripe

Yojoa Scrub-Hairstreak *S. yojoa*

LRGV

Mouse's Eye (south-western myrtle-croton)
narrow band
smooth basal line
bold black spot

Lacey's Scrub-Hairstreak *S. alea*

balloon-vines
see Bromeliad Scrub-Hairstreak, page 111
wide red-orange band
orange spot doesn't reach pm line

Red-lined Scrub-Hairstreak *S. bebrycia*

verbena family
unchecked fringe
+ or - HW ray
gray eye
no tail

Lantana Scrub-Hairstreak
Strymon bazochii

LRGV

unknown
checked fringe
no tail
black eye

Tailless Scrub-Hairstreak
Strymon cestri

LRGV

mallow family

south Texas
C
all year

elsewhere
R-U
Mar-Aug

open woods, scrub and disturbed areas

Ceraunus Blues, page 124, lack tails and do not have a dark, defined HW pm band

male

female

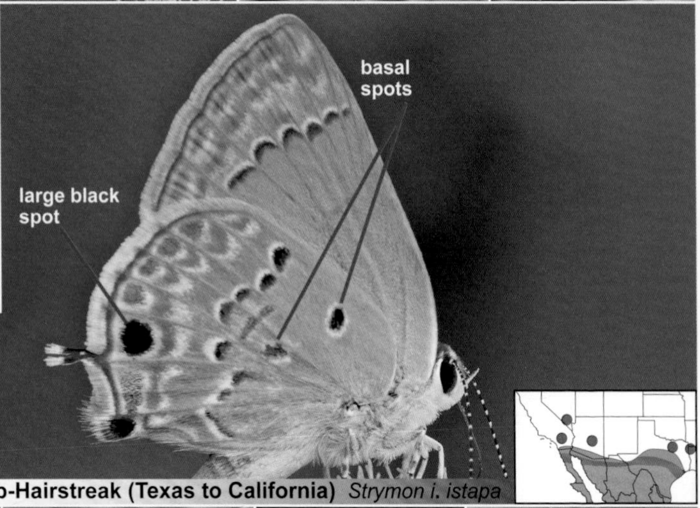
basal spots
large black spot

Mallow Scrub-Hairstreak (Texas to California) *Strymon i. istapa*

mallow family

U-C
all year

mainly disturbed areas

this subspecies is restricted to south Florida, other subspecies are found throughout the West Indies and from Texas to Argentina

Ceraunus Blues, page 124, lack tails and do not have a dark, defined HW pm band

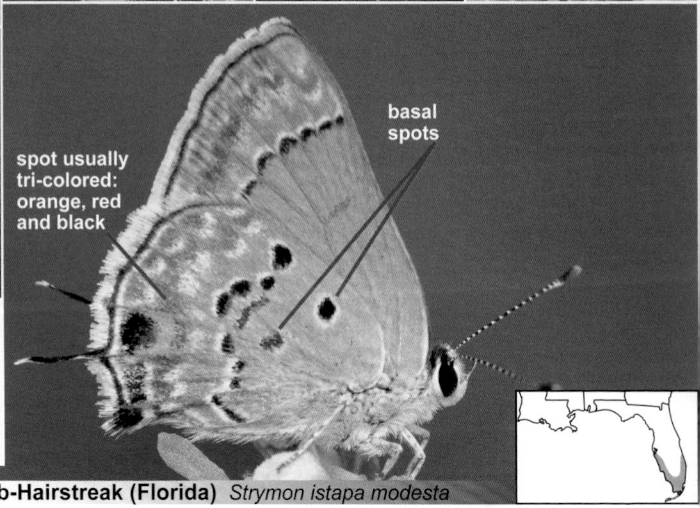
basal spots
spot usually tri-colored: orange, red and black

Mallow Scrub-Hairstreak (Florida) *Strymon istapa modesta*

mallow family

R-U
all year

mainly thorn-scrub

more common in the more arid northern and western parts of the LRGV where fewer butterfliers visit

most similar to Mallow Scrub-Hairstreak, but lacks HW basal spots and the red crescents are usually more prominent

worn
individual

pm bands
of red
crescents
no
basal
spots

Red-crescent Scrub-Hairstreak *Strymon rufofusca*

unknown

RS
from Cuba

similar to Mallow Scrub-Hairstreak, but note the more extensive orange, the white antennal patch and the differently shaped bottom part of the HW postmedian line

orange
lobe

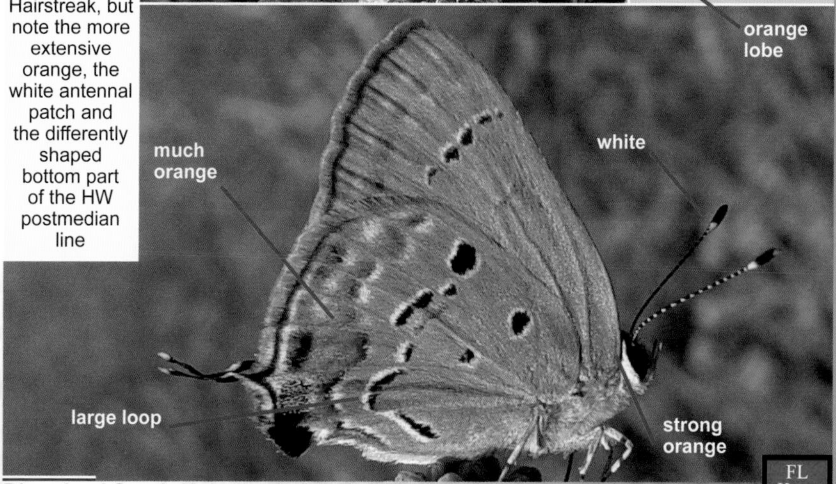
much
orange
white
large loop
strong
orange

Disguised Scrub-Hairstreak *Strymon limenia*

FL Keys

decaying plant matter, especially sumacs

southward C-A

northward mostly U

early spring through late fall

woods edges, brushy fields, suburban areas with ample vegetation

continues to expand its range northward, as it has over the past 25 years

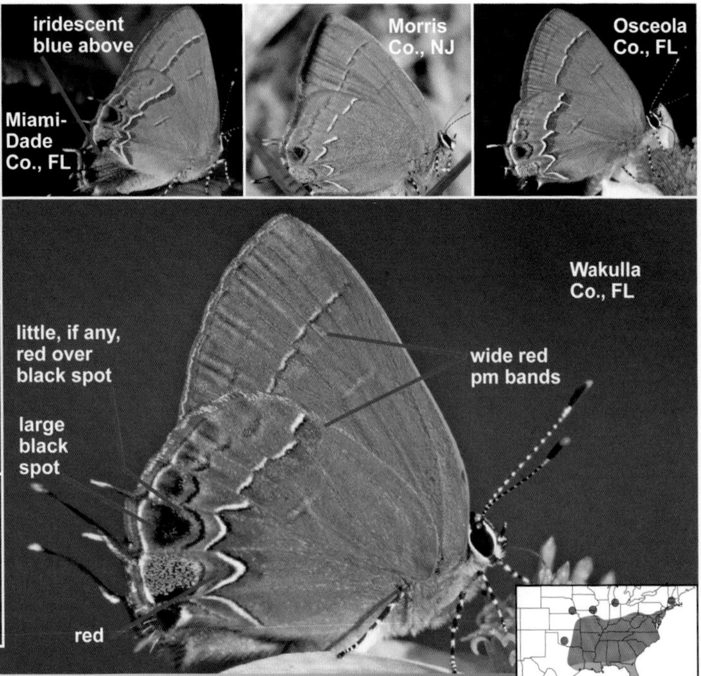
iridescent blue above
Miami-Dade Co., FL
Morris Co., NJ
Osceola Co., FL
Wakulla Co., FL
little, if any, red over black spot
wide red pm bands
large black spot
red

Red-banded Hairstreak *Calycopis cecrops*

decaying plant matter

C-A in south Texas all year; decreasing abundance northward, mostly late summer-fall

woods edges, thorn-scrub, brushy areas

intermediates between this species and Red-banded Hairstreaks are frequent south and west of Houston; one species or two? — a subjective decision

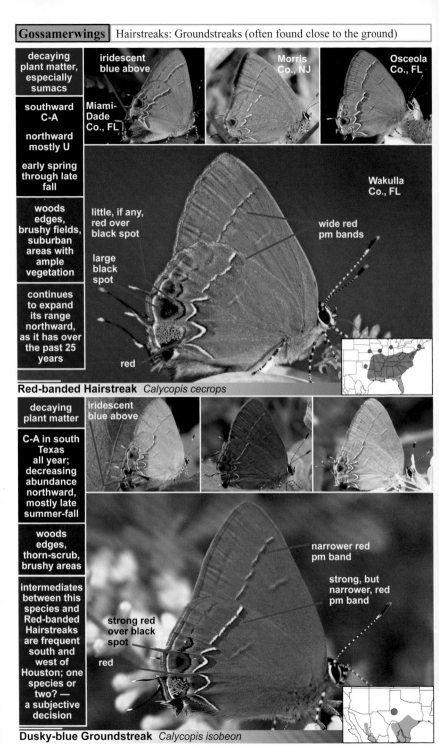

iridescent blue above
narrower red pm band
strong, but narrower, red pm band
strong red over black spot
red

Dusky-blue Groundstreak *Calycopis isobeon*

Brazilian Peppertree

south mainland Florida U-C

Florida Keys U

an Antillean species first established in Florida in 1974; using a non-native hostplant

strong white spot
copper colored above

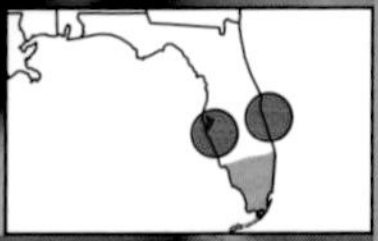

Fulvous Hairstreak *Electrostrymon angelia*

unknown

dark ground color, red on pm band

field ID of female Ruddy and Muted is unknown

males bright orange above; females duller
dark

Ruddy Hairstreak *Electrostrymon sangala*

LRGV

unknown

dark ground color, red on pm band

field ID of female Ruddy and Muted is unknown

both males and females are dull above
dark

Muted Hairstreak *Electrostrymon canus*

LRGV

unknown

similar to Ruddy but with iridescent (male) or pale (female) blue above

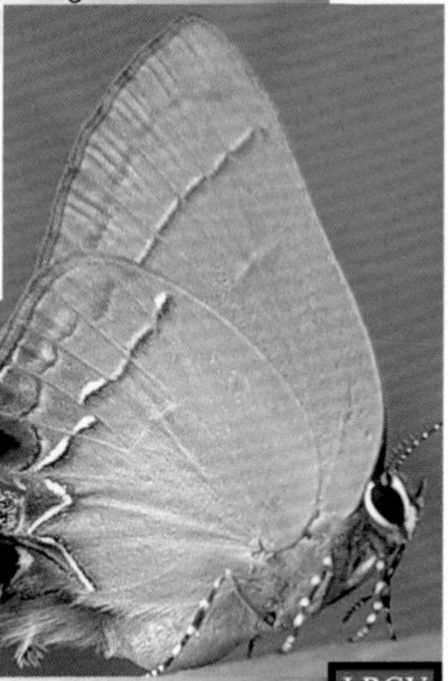
dark
iridescent blue above

Confused Groundstreak *Kisutam syllis*

LRGV once

unknown

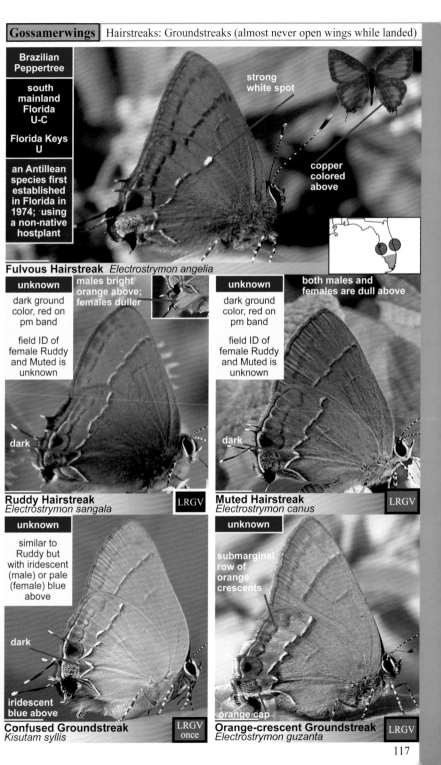

submarginal row of orange crescents
orange cap

Orange-crescent Groundstreak *Electrostrymon guzanta*

LRGV

American Beech and Beaked Hazelnut

LR-U three brood areas late Apr-early Sept; two brood areas mid May-mid Aug

rich woods

although rarely observed, when it is it is usually on dirt roads; it is possible that it is fairly common but spends most of its time in the tree canopy

mint
green
below
red-orange
submarginal
spots

Early Hairstreak *Erora laeta*

oaks

U Mar-Aug

oak canyons at moderate elevations

hilltops

dreamstreaks, a mainly tropical group, are green; the two in the U.S. are mint green and red-orange, definitely inducing sweet dreams

Arizona and Early Hairstreaks are best distinguished by range

red-orange
submarginal
spots
mint
green
below

Arizona Hairstreak *Erora quaderna*

mesquites

three and two broods C-A

R late season immigrant elsewhere

arid canyons and washes

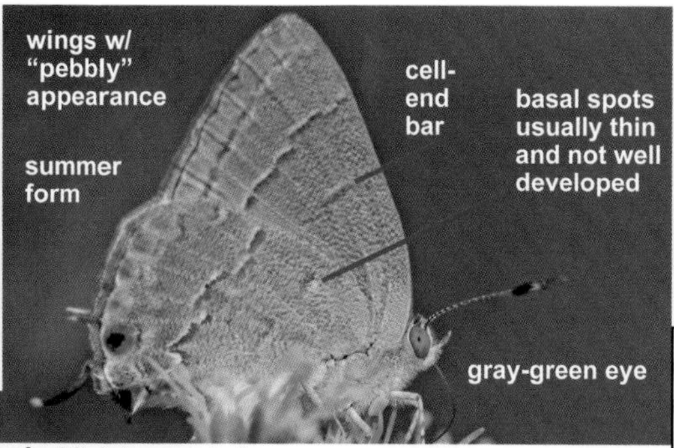
wings w/
"pebbly"
appearance
summer
form
cell-
end
bar
basal spots
usually thin
and not well
developed
gray-green eye

winter
form

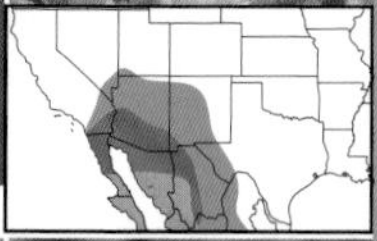

Leda Ministreak *Ministrymon leda*

Screwbean Mesquite and other legumes

U-C all year

tropical woods and thorn-scrub

summer
form
cell-
end
bar
pale
above
gray-green eye
basal spots
usually rounded
and well developed

winter
form

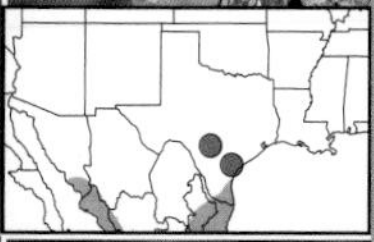

Clytie Ministreak *Ministrymon clytie*

White Leadtree and probably other tree legumes

LR-LU all year

scrub

no cell-
end bar
smooth wings
black eye
no basal
spots

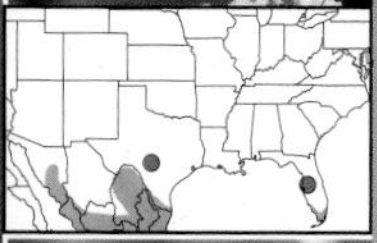

Gray Ministreak *Ministrymon azia*

Softleaf Mimosa and probably other tree legumes

scrub

described in 2013; confused w/ Gray Ministreak for 100 years

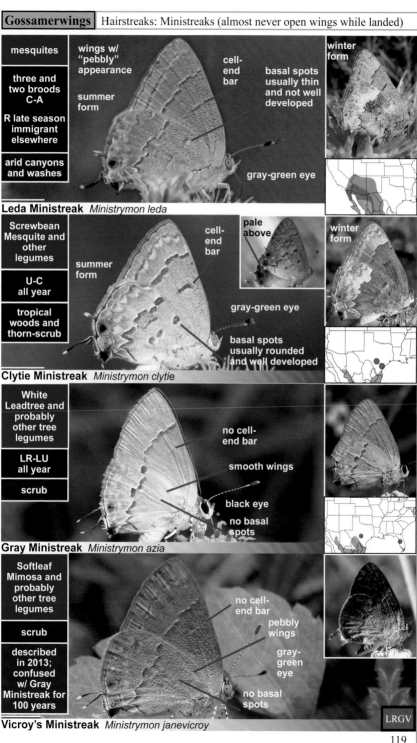

no cell-
end bar
pebbly
wings
gray-
green
eye
no basal
spots

LRGV

Vicroy's Ministreak *Ministrymon janevicroy*

nightshades, including Potatotree
powder-blue above
tan and off-white stripes

Creamy Stripe-streak se AZ
Arawacus jada

many plant families
gold border

Gold-bordered Hairstreak LRGV
Rekoa palegon

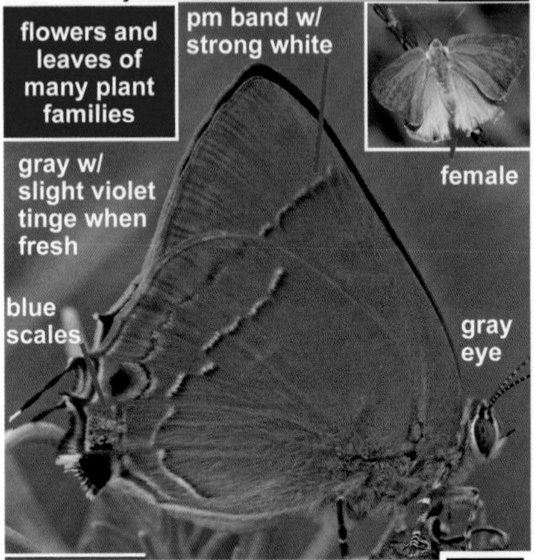
flowers and leaves of many plant families
pm band w/ strong white
gray w/ slight violet tinge when fresh
female
blue scales
gray eye

Marius Hairstreak LRGV
Rekoa marius

unknown
FW distal to pm band is often paler
pm band often wide & smudged
few, if any, blue scales
gray eye

Smudged Hairstreak LRGV once
Rekoa stagira

Barbados Cherry family
pm band w/ faint white
black eye

Strophius Hairstreak LRGV
Allosmaitia strophius

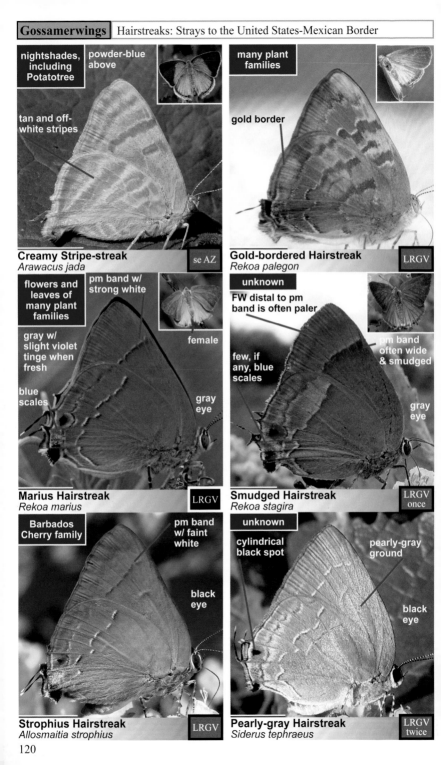

unknown
cylindrical black spot
pearly-gray ground
black eye

Pearly-gray Hairstreak LRGV twice
Siderus tephraeus

Annona globiflora
no pm spots
bold median spots
large blue area
large

Aquamarine Hairstreak LRGV
Oenomaus ortygnus

many plant families
iridescent-blue above
no cell-end bar
bold red spots

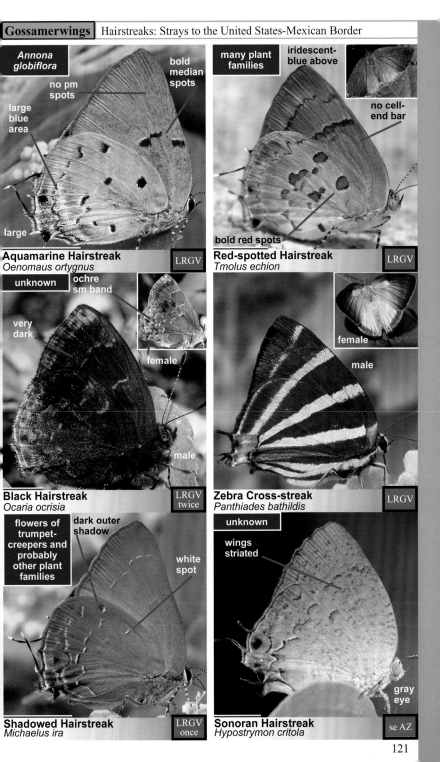

Red-spotted Hairstreak LRGV
Tmolus echion

unknown
ochre sm band
very dark
female
male

Black Hairstreak LRGV twice
Ocaria ocrisia

female
male

Zebra Cross-streak LRGV
Panthiades bathildis

flowers of trumpet-creepers and probably other plant families
dark outer shadow
white spot

Shadowed Hairstreak LRGV once
Michaelus ira

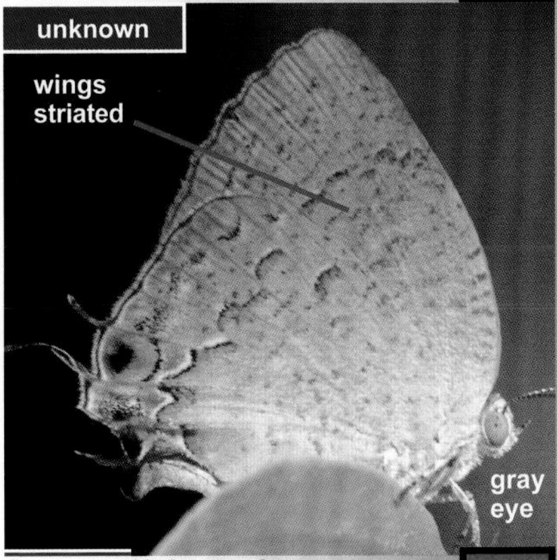
unknown
wings striated
gray eye

Sonoran Hairstreak se AZ
Hypostrymon critola

goosefoot family, esp saltbushes and goosefoots

three broods C-A

two broods R-U

Mexican border; all year decreasing flight period northward

open arid and disturbed areas

frequently basks w/ wings open

the smallest North American butterfly

copper colored above w/ blue-gray wing bases

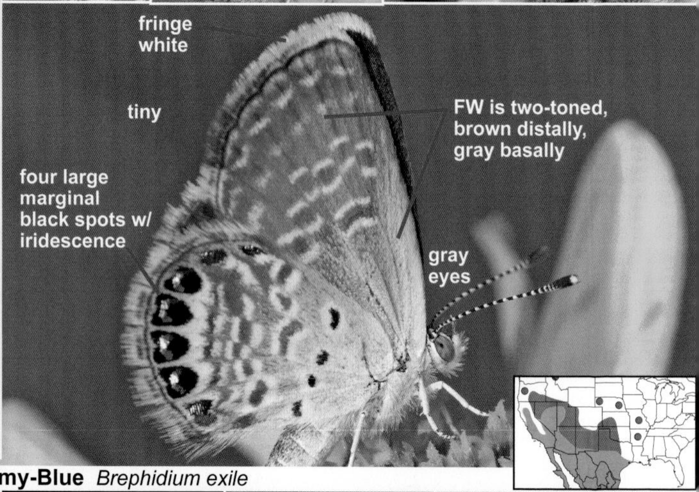
fringe white
tiny
FW is two-toned, brown distally, gray basally
four large marginal black spots w/ iridescence
gray eyes

Western Pygmy-Blue *Brephidium exile*

Salicornia

LU

southern Florida all year

elsewhere Mar-Oct

coastal salt flats and tidal marshes with *Salicornia*

Eastern Pygmy-Blues rarely open their wings while landed

caterpillars are tended by ants

flight is usually very low to the ground

food plant

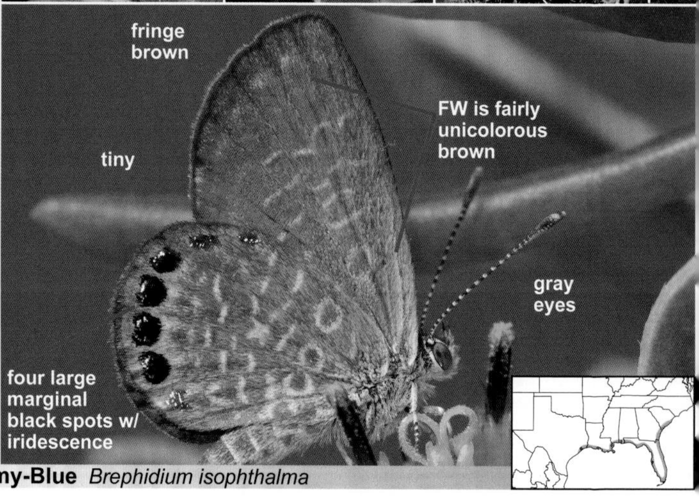
fringe brown
FW is fairly unicolorous brown
tiny
gray eyes
four large marginal black spots w/ iridescence

Eastern Pygmy-Blue *Brephidium isophthalma*

legumes and other plant families

along Mexican border C-A all year

emigrating northward, w/ decreasing abundance, as the warm season progresses

open areas

usually have more extensive brown striping and thus appear to be darker than Cassius Blues

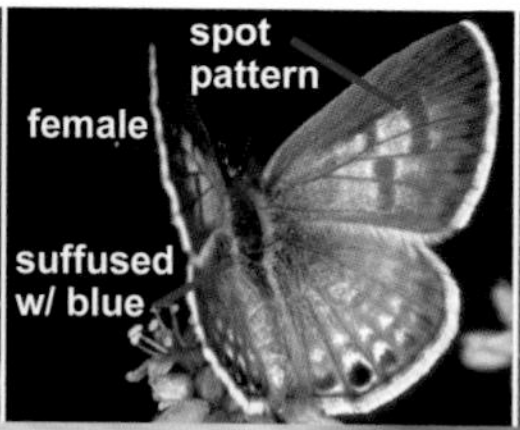
spot pattern
female
suffused w/ blue

darker blue at wing bases
male

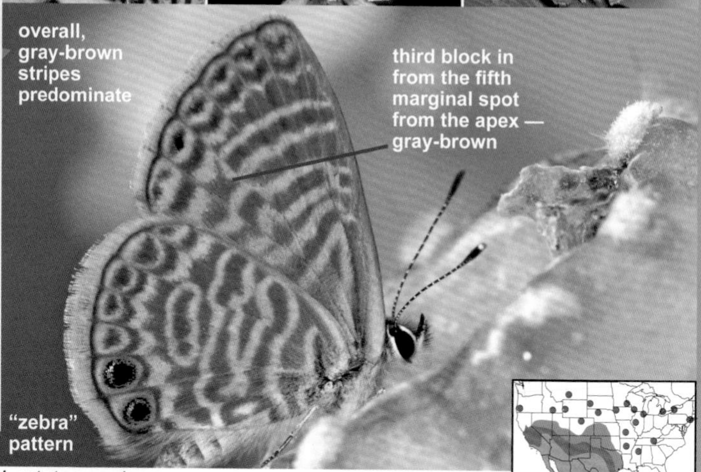
overall, gray-brown stripes predominate
third block in from the fifth marginal spot from the apex — gray-brown
"zebra" pattern

Marine Blue *Leptotes marina*

legumes and other plant families

south Florida C-A all year

south Texas U all year

decreasing abundance and flight times farther north

subtropical and tropical open woods

usually found low to the ground, Cassius Blues will seek nectar high in trees

Miami-Dade Co., FL

spot pattern
quite white
female

male

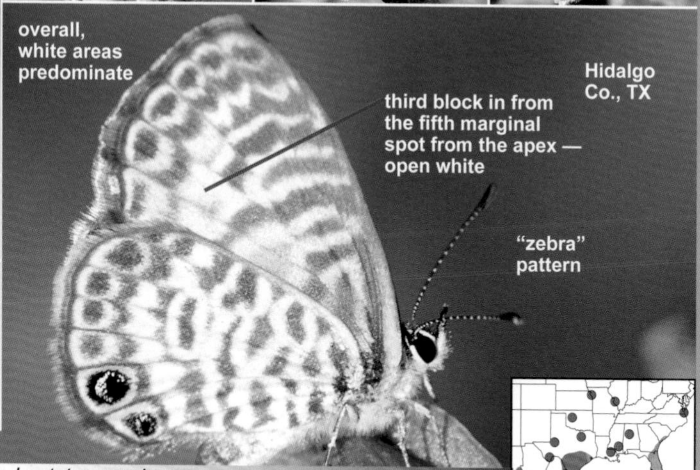
overall, white areas predominate
Hidalgo Co., TX
third block in from the fifth marginal spot from the apex — open white
"zebra" pattern

Cassius Blue *Leptotes cassius*

legumes

U-C

southern FL-south TX all year

northward Apr-Nov

a wide variety of open, especially disturbed, situations

HW outer margin varies, with two strong black spots in Texas, one or two strong spots in seAZ and only one strong spot in Florida (see inset) and California

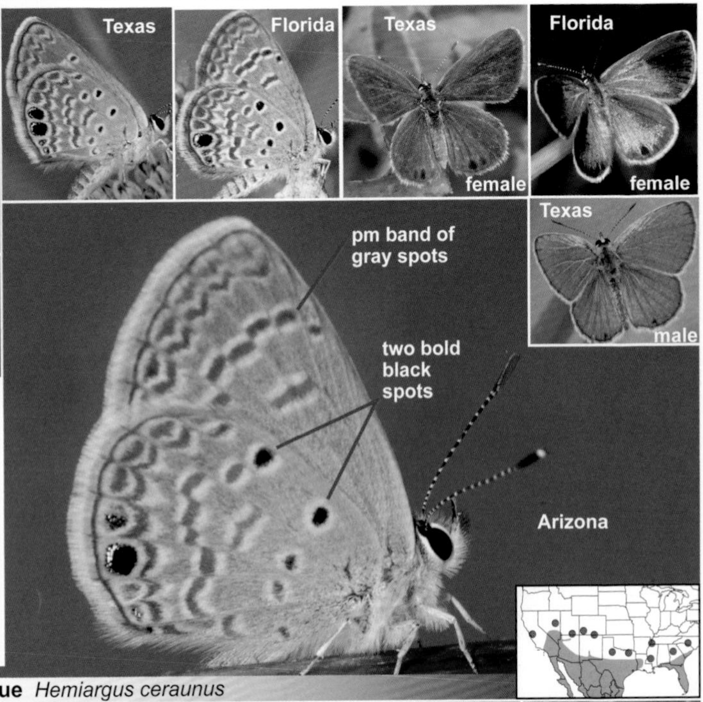
Texas
Florida
Texas
female
Florida
female
Texas
male
pm band of gray spots
two bold black spots
Arizona

Ceraunus Blue *Hemiargus ceraunus*

legumes

along Mexican border C-A all year

decreasing abundance northward

a wide variety of open, especially disturbed, situations

Silvery and Boisduval's Blues also have bold black FW spots, but they are larger and lack the HW outer angle black spot

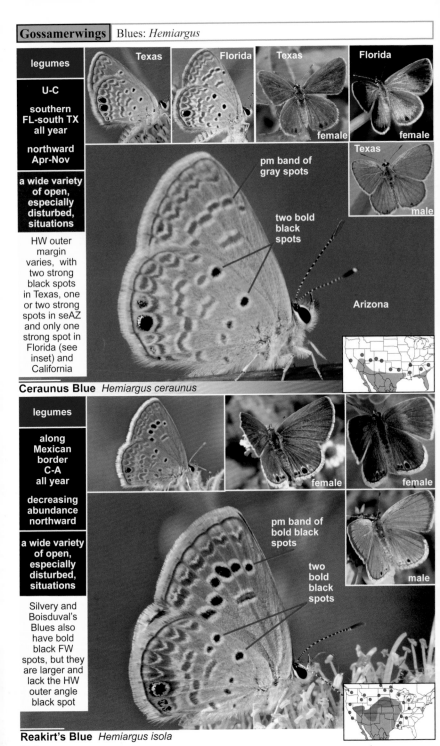

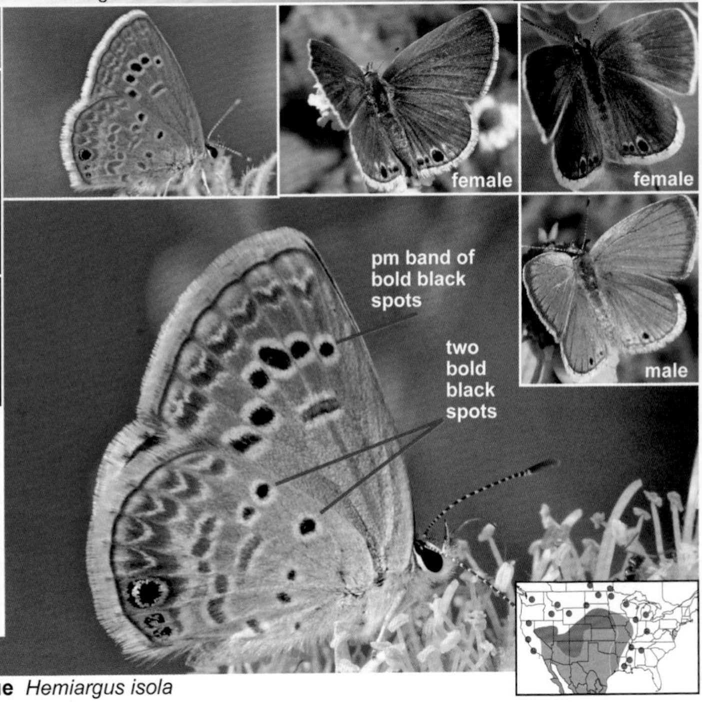
female
female
male
pm band of bold black spots
two bold black spots

Reakirt's Blue *Hemiargus isola*

balloonvines, monkeypods and nickers

U-C on the Marquesas

apparently extirpated from mainland Florida and the Keys

hardwood hammocks

habitat loss, anti-mosquito spraying and human ineptitude have pushed these butterflies to the brink of extinction

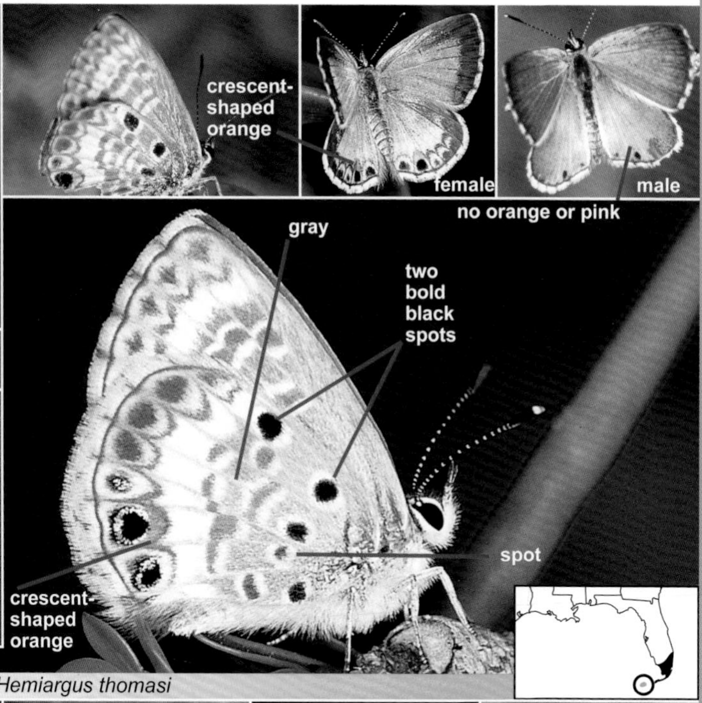
crescent-shaped orange
female
male
no orange or pink
gray
two bold black spots
spot
crescent-shaped orange

Miami Blue *Hemiargus thomasi*

nickers and acacias

This Cuban species became established on Big Pine Key in 1997, but none have been seen since 2007

pine rockland

some Antillean species occasionally become established in south Florida and then die out

bullet-shaped pink
male
female
bullet-shaped orange
white
two bold black spots
bullet-shaped orange
no spot

Nickerbean Blue *Hemiargus ammon*

Acanthus family

periodic colonist in LRGV, especially at the National Butterfly Center; RS elsewhere

thorn-scrub, gardens

African species in this genus also do wing waves

tiny

when landed, wings are closed and often waved in unison from side to side

black spots at base of FW
gray eye
no eyespots
white "bill" pointing out from cell-end bar

Cyna Blue *Zizula cyna*

liveforevers

LU-LC Feb-Apr into May in the mountains

canyons and cliffs w/ the foodplant

bright blue with bold red-orange FW spots both above and below, the only impediment to identification is finding them

try Plum Canyon in Anza-Borrego State Park, California

female

food plant

bright blue w/ bright orange FW spots
male

Sonoran Blue *Philotes sonorensis*

legumes

East: C-A
West: LR-LU
flies throughout warm weather

open areas, especially disturbed

at home in weedy situations, this is one of the few butterflies found in truly urban areas

Spring Azure, page 128, lacks tails and orange HW spot and flight is usually higher and stronger

female

female

usually w/
slightly rounded
outer margin
tail
orange spot

male
usually w/
orange spot
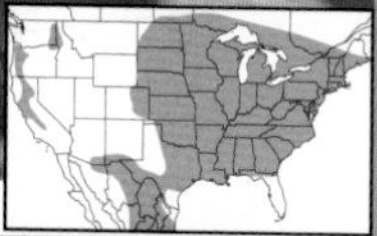

Eastern Tailed-Blue *Everes comyntas*

legumes

U-C
mostly Mar/Apr - Aug

many, including mountain meadows and chaparral

it is currently not known how to separate, with certainty, most Eastern and Western Tailed-Blues in the field

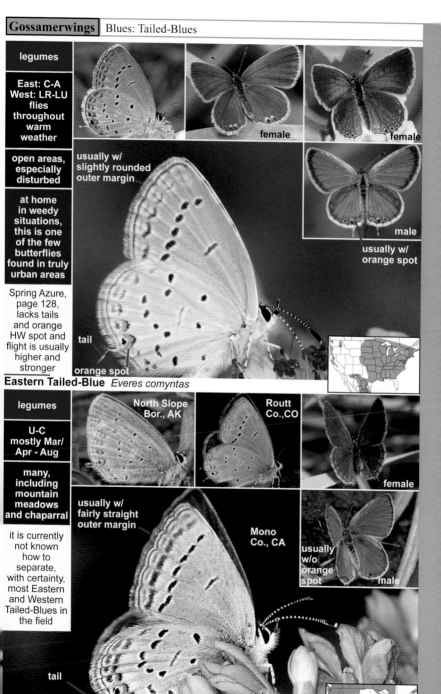

North Slope
Bor., AK
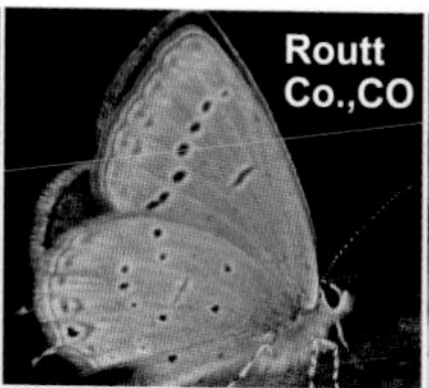
Routt
Co.,CO

female
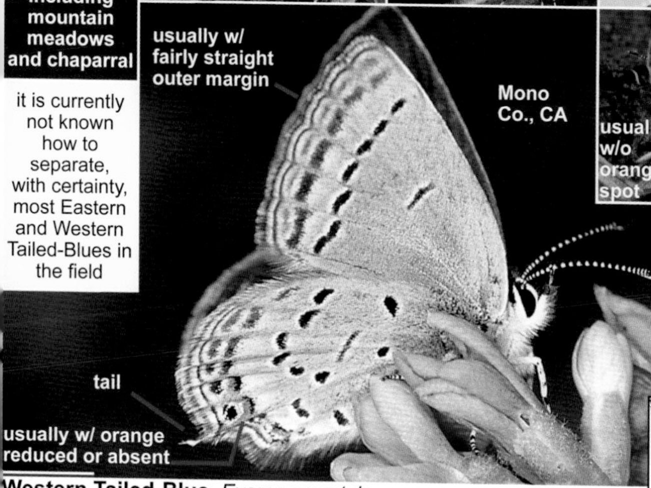
usually w/
fairly straight
outer margin
Mono
Co., CA
tail
usually w/ orange
reduced or absent

usually
w/o
orange
spot
male
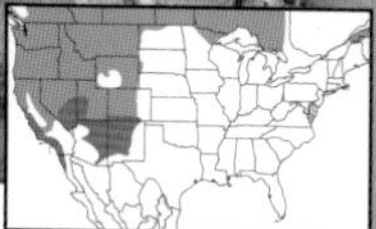

Western Tailed-Blue *Everes amyntula*

many plant families

C-U in spring
mostly R-U in summer/fall

woods, barrens, suburbia

mudpuddles

this complex has populations, using different foodplants with different flight times

some treat each population as a distinct species, but unpublished DNA data groups all spring populations as one species and summer and fall populations as another

males are bright blue above

in the East, the undersides of many spring individuals resemble one of the two individuals shown in top panel

in the West, and in summer/fall in the East, the undersides of most individuals resemble the individuals shown in bottom panel

female

male

no orange
no iridescence
generally flies
higher than
other blues
no tail

Westchester
Co., NY

Deschutes
Co., OR

Jefferson
Co., CO
female

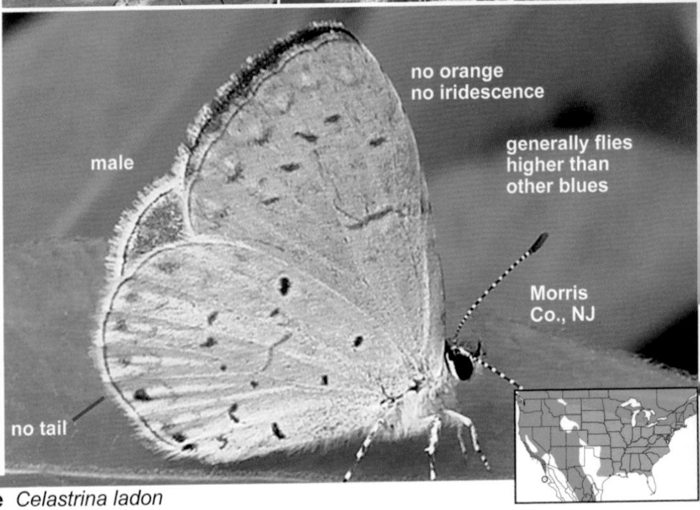
no orange
no iridescence
generally flies
higher than
other blues
male
Morris
Co., NJ
no tail

Spring Azure *Celastrina ladon*

Black Baneberry

C-U mid May - early June

rich woods

indistinguishable from Spring Azures (and possibly conspecific), Appalachian Azures are recognized by their relationship with Black Baneberry and their flight period, after most of the spring brood of azures and before most of the summer brood of azures

foodplant

female

male

Appalachian Azure *Celastrina neglectamajor*

Bride's Feathers

LR-LU Apr-early May

rich woods

frequently mudpuddles

because females, and the undersides of both males and females, are indistinguishable from Spring Azures, you'll have to see the upperside of a male in flight to be sure you're seeing a Dusky Azure

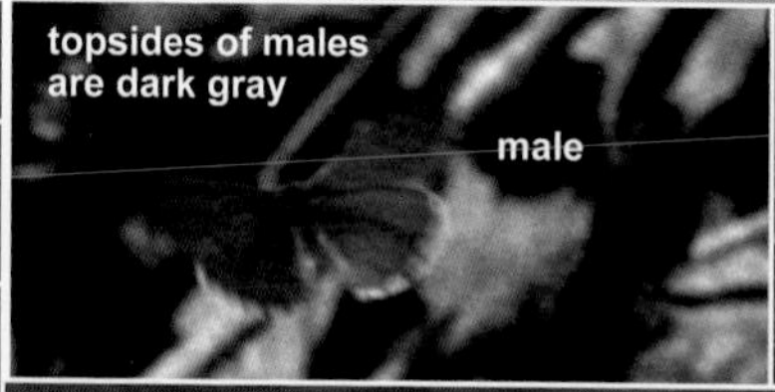
topsides of males are dark gray
male

foodplant

Dusky Azure *Celastrina nigra*

Sulphur-flower Buckwheat

LU California Sierras July-Aug

rocky alpine areas

even more than the azures, populations of buckwheat blues are often very local, with different hostplants and flight times

identifying associated buckwheats can be useful for ID of the butterfly

other blues w/ orange sm bands have iridescence

map shows range of all Square-spotted Blues, not subspecies

hostplant

thick black marginal line
fringe checked
sm band of fused orange spots
Tuolomne Co., CA

Square-spotted Blue *Euphilotes battoides battoides*

Eastern Mojave Buckwheat

C southwestern California Apr-June

arid slopes with the foodplant

although ID of unknown colony of buckwheat blues is often not possible in the field, in general Square-spotteds have a thicker black FW margin than Dotteds and orange sm band tends to be composed of fused spots

female

male

map shows range of all Square-spotted Blues, not subspecies

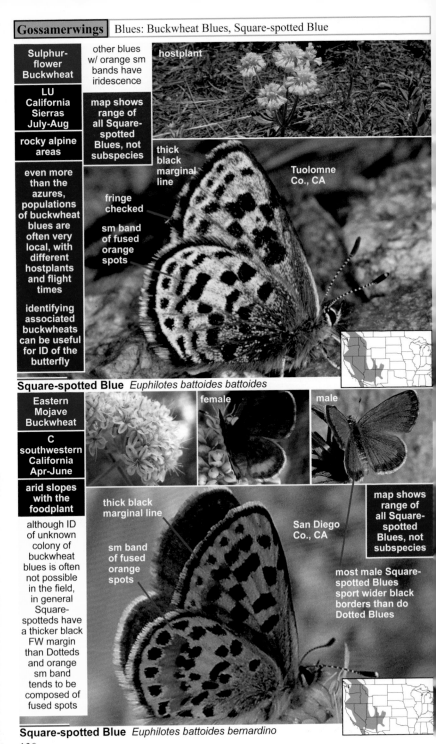

thick black marginal line
sm band of fused orange spots
San Diego Co., CA
most male Square-spotted Blues sport wider black borders than do Dotted Blues

Square-spotted Blue *Euphilotes battoides bernardino*

Sulphur-flower Buckwheat

U-LC British Columbia to California/ Nevada Apr-July

mountain slopes, canyons

some treat Square-spotted Blues as comprising as many as five species, including phenotypically indistinguishable *baueri*, *ellisi* and *intermedia* (not shown)

map shows range of all Square-spotted Blues, not subspecies

Jackson Co., OR

Alpine Co., CA

female

thick black marginal line
Klamath Co., OR
fringe checked
sm band of fused orange spots

Square-spotted Blue *Euphilotes battoides glaucon*

James' Buckwheat

LU southern Colorado, New Mexico, Arizona mid July-early Sept

arid slopes and canyons

map shows range of all Square-spotted Blues, not subspecies

host plant

female

male

fringe checked
Apache Co., AZ
sm band of fused orange spots

Square-spotted Blue *Euphilotes battoides centralis*

Naked Buckwheat

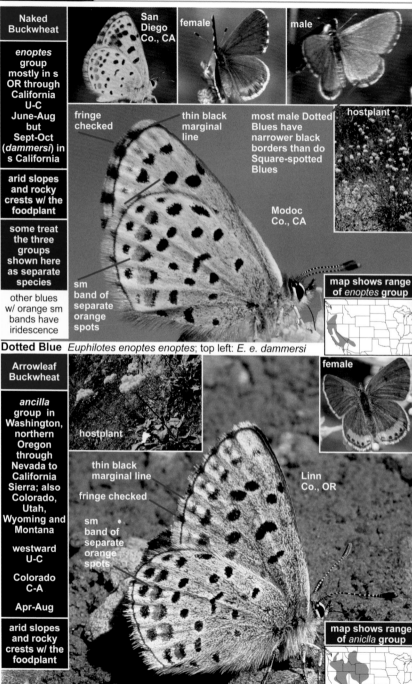

enoptes group mostly in s OR through California

U-C

June-Aug but Sept-Oct (*dammersi*) in s California

arid slopes and rocky crests w/ the foodplant

some treat the three groups shown here as separate species

other blues w/ orange sm bands have iridescence

San Diego Co., CA

female

male

fringe checked
thin black marginal line
most male Dotted Blues have narrower black borders than do Square-spotted Blues
Modoc Co., CA
sm band of separate orange spots

hostplant

map shows range of *enoptes* group

Dotted Blue *Euphilotes enoptes enoptes*; top left: *E. e. dammersi*

Arrowleaf Buckwheat

ancilla group in Washington, northern Oregon through Nevada to California Sierra; also Colorado, Utah, Wyoming and Montana

westward U-C

Colorado C-A

Apr-Aug

arid slopes and rocky crests w/ the foodplant

hostplant

female

thin black marginal line
Linn Co., OR
fringe checked
sm band of separate orange spots

map shows range of *anicla* group

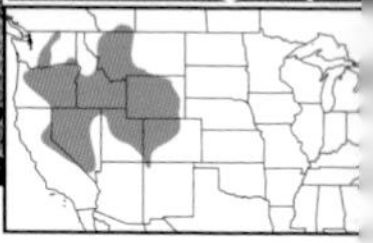

Dotted Blue *Euphilotes enoptes columbiae* (*ancilla* group)

Sulphur-flower Buckwheat

ancilla group in Washington, northern Oregon through Nevada to California Sierra; also Colorado, Utah, Wyoming and Montana

westward U-C

Colorado C-A

Apr-Aug

arid slopes and rocky crests with the foodplant

female

male
most males w/ narrower borders than Square-spotted Blues

fringe checked
thin black marginal line
Jefferson Co., CO
sm band of separate orange spots

map shows range of *anicla* group

Dotted Blue *Euphilotes enoptes ancilla* (*ancilla* group)

Yellow-turbans Buckwheat

U southern California Apr-May

arid slopes and rocky crests with the foodplant

map shows range of *E. e. mojave* group

spring flight in limited southern California range

Los Angeles Co., CA
fringe checked
thin black marginal line
sm band of separate orange spots

Dotted Blue *Euphilotes enoptes mojave* (*mojave* group)

Bastardsage (Wright's buckwheat) and Spreading Buckwheat

LU
Aug-mid Sept

open arid areas, such as short-grass prairie (eastern Colorado) and desert flats

some treat *rita* and *pallescens* as separate species

Weld
Co., CO

female

male

thick
black
line
fringe
unchecked
or lightly
checked
Pima
Co., AZ

Rita Blue *Euphilotes rita rita*

Money Buckwheat, Yucca Buckwheat and others

LU
July-Sept

open arid areas, such as desert flats

almost all populations are similar to the individual shown in the main photo; subspecies *calneva*, from Plumas and Lassen Cos., California and Washoe Co., Nevada, lacks the orange sm band and is shown in inset

sm
black
spots
Lassen
Co., CA

Churchill
Co., NV
female

thick
black
line
Mineral
Co., NV
fringe
unchecked
or lightly
checked

Rita Blue *Euphilotes rita pallescens*

Redroot Buckwheat

LR-U July-Aug

dry meadows and flats in foothills and mountains

closely associated with its foodplant, which it also prefers as a nectar source

the only buckwheat blue with a prominent orange FW sm band, however, some Square-spotted Blues, page 130, do have some orange on the FW

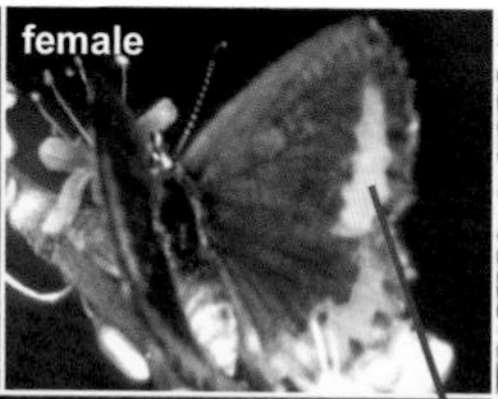
female

male

FW w/ extensive orange sm band
veins often w/ orange
strong orange band

host plant

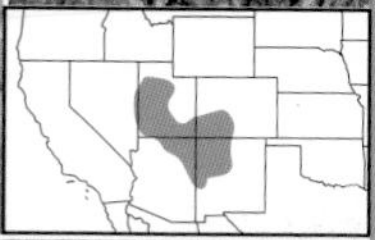

Spalding's Blue *Euphilotes spaldingi*

mainly Roundleaf Oxytheca and Kidneyleaf Buckwheat; Spurry Buckwheat in Oregon; California Spineflower in Santa Barbara Co.

LR and often unpredictable; mainly Apr-June, Mar-Apr near Mexican border; mid June-mid July in Oregon

mainly desert slopes but chaparral-oak in Santa Barbara and pine forest in Oregon

Roundleaf Oxytheca

Klamath Co., OR

no sm black spots
bold black spots
Santa Barbara Co., AZ
fringe checked
very small
no sm black spots
no orange

some treat *P. s. leona*, in Oregon, as a separate species

Small Blue *Philotiella speciosa*

legumes mainly vetches in the East, more varied in the West

Northeast C-A

elsewhere mostly LU-C

mostly spring but into July at high elevations and latitudes

many open habitats, especially moist meadows and grassy areas

caterpillars are tended by ants

northeastern population continues to expand southward, reaching Maine in 1967, Massachusetts in 1992 and northwestern New Jersey in 2011

meanwhile, the range of Appalachian Silvery Blues continues to constrict

as is true for many blues, in the West each isolated colony tends to be a little different

HW spots bold or muted

Los Angeles Co., CA
female
Humboldt Co., CA
female
Jefferson Co., CO
male
Boone Co., WV
unchecked fringes
male
Boone Co., WV
Lawrence Co., SD
San Diego Co., CA
North Slope Bor., AK
bold black spots
fairly even gray or gray-brown ground color
Oxford Co., ME
no marginal or submarginal spots

Silvery Blue *Glaucopsyche lygdamus*

lupines

LR-U

lowland and southern California late Mar-May

at higher elevations and farther north May-June/July

many open habitats

especially males, usually keep their wings closed when landed

caterpillars are tended by ants

FW with bold black pm spots and a cell end bar, as in Silvery Blue, but also with a black bar within the FW cell

HW with a distinctive submarginal band of white "arrowheads" and a horizontal white bar at the base of the wing

Jefferson Co., CO
male

LA Co., CA
male

checked fringes
Los Angeles Co., CA
female

Okanogan Co., WA

Denver Co., CO

Tulare Co., CA

bold black spots
white spike
Los Angeles Co., CA
white "arrowheads"

Arrowhead Blue *Glaucopsyche piasus*

many legumes, but especially lupines, Alfalfa and rattleweeds

C
two broods May-Sept except one brood, July-Aug, at high elevations

widespread, from disturbed habitats to prairies, sagebrush, and rocky ridgetops

some treat the Sierra crest population (top right) as a separate species

Custer Co., SD
female

Montezuma Co., CO
female

w/o orange on FW
female

Mono Co., CA
female

Custer Co., SD
male

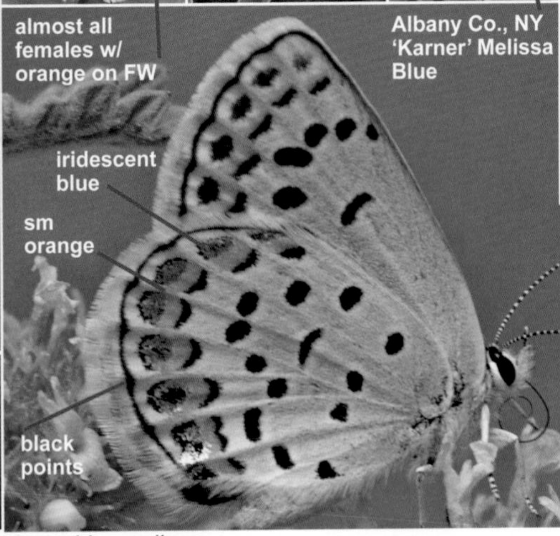
almost all females w/ orange on FW
Albany Co., NY 'Karner' Melissa Blue
iridescent blue
sm orange
black points
Modoc Co., CA

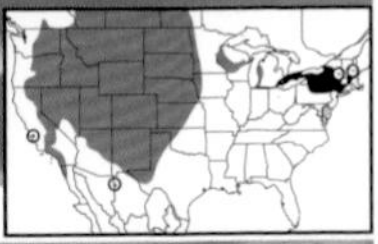

Melissa Blue *Lycaeides melissa*

legumes

LC
May-Sept

disturbed habitats

A Eurasian species first reported in North America in 2005, in Mirabel, Quebec

apparently spreading and probably already in New York

in time, likely to occupy much of North America

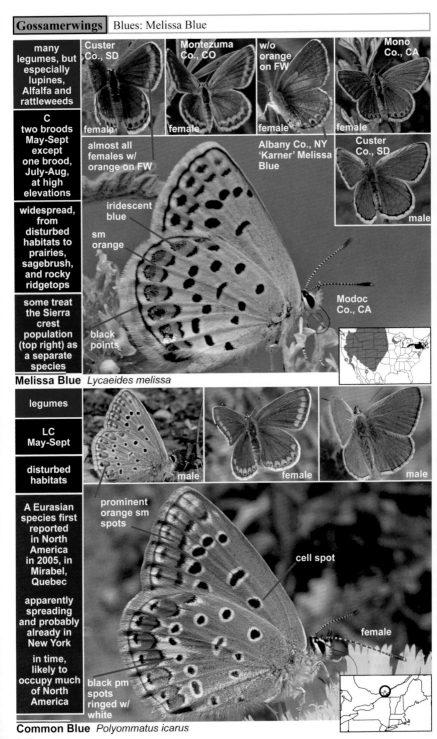

male

female

male

prominent orange sm spots
cell spot
female
black pm spots ringed w/ white

Common Blue *Polyommatus icarus*

East: Dwarf Bilberry

West: many legumes especially lupines and *Lotus*

R East
LU-C West
mid June-Aug

openings in moist coniferous woods, arid open areas at high elevation

although generally paler below, w/ less orange, many individuals are not distinguishable from Melissa Blue

Teton
Co., WY
female

Marinette
Co., WI
female

Flathead
Co., MT
male

females in most populations have reduced orange on the FW
iridescence
Teton
Co., WY
orange
sm
black
points

Northern Blue *Lycaeides idas*

many legumes, especially lupines and *Lotus*

LU-C
mainly July-Aug

openings in moist coniferous & mixed woods; arid open areas at high elevation

some treat 'Anna's' as a separate species

most individuals in most populations have relatively faint markings below with little orange

Modoc
Co., CA

Tuolomne
Co., CA
female

Tuolomne
Co., CA
male

Jackson
Co., OR
faint
orange
sm
Linn
Co., OR

'Anna's' Northern Blue *Lycaeides idas anna*

many different lupines, but most populations use only one species

C-A

mostly May-July

in southern lowlands mid Mar

at high elevations into Sept

open areas w/ lupines

caterpillars are tended by ants

forms isolated colonies

there are more than 25 described subspecies of Boisduval's Blue

bold black spots on FW combined with white spots on HW

see Silvery Blue, page 136

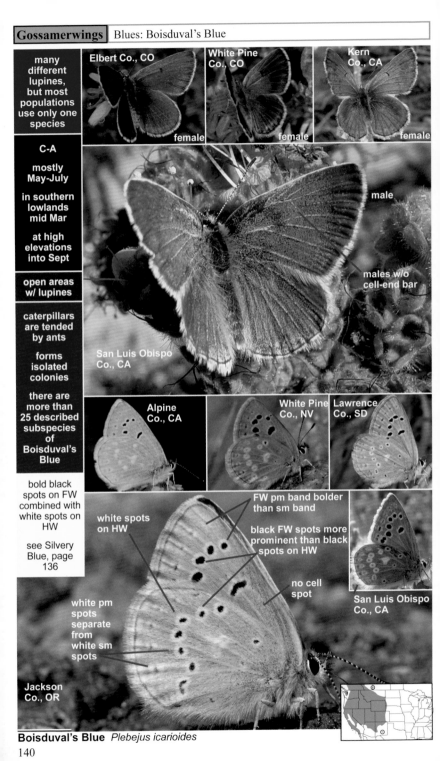

Elbert Co., CO
female

White Pine Co., CO
female

Kern Co., CA
female

male
males w/o cell-end bar
San Luis Obispo Co., CA

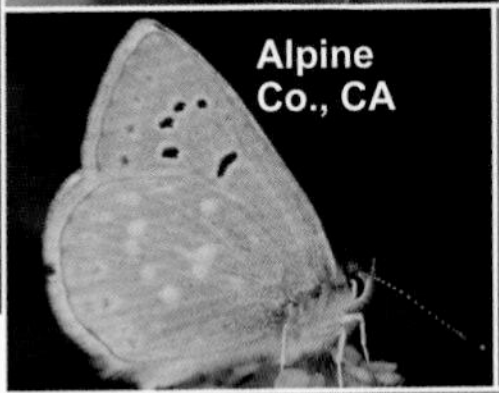
Alpine Co., CA

White Pine Co., NV

Lawrence Co., SD

FW pm band bolder than sm band
white spots on HW
black FW spots more prominent than black spots on HW
no cell spot
white pm spots separate from white sm spots
Jackson Co., OR

San Luis Obispo Co., CA

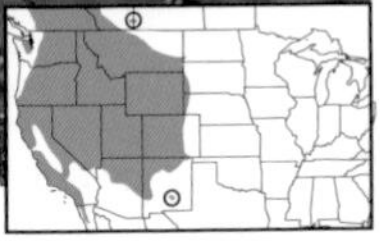

Boisduval's Blue *Plebejus icarioides*

clovers

LC-A

mostly June-July

in southern lowlands flies in May

at high elevations into Sept

also in eastern half of Alaska and most of Canada

mostly moist mountain meadows

also above treeline and to sea level on coast

although historically recorded from much of Maine, none have been seen there recently

undersides of females are usually tan, males, off-white

some females (see rightmost inset in bottom panel) have white rings around HW black spots and resemble Boisduval's Blues; but unlike Boisduval's Blues, FW pm and sm bands are usually of similar intensity

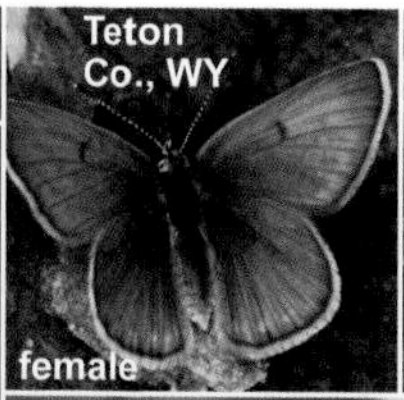
Teton Co., WY
female

Tulare Co., CA
female

Clallum Co., WA
female

Fairbanks Bor., AK
female

males w/ cell-end bar
Sublette Co., WY
male

Tuolomne Co., CA
male

Tuolomne Co., CA
male

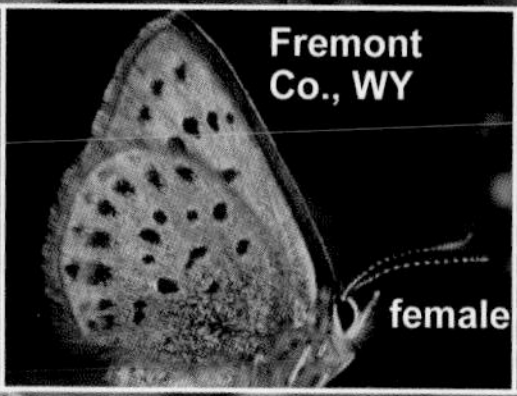
Fremont Co., WY
female

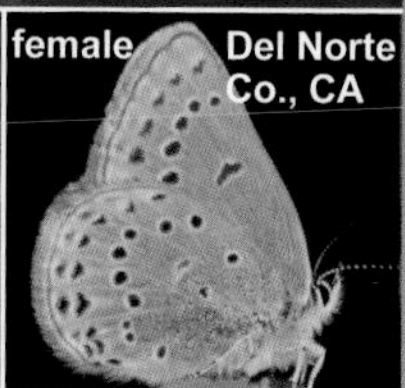
female
Del Norte Co., CA

usually w/ some obvious orange here
black FW spots not more prominent than black spots on HW
Jefferson Co., SD
male

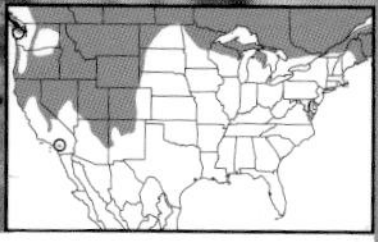

Greenish Blue *Plebejus saepiolus*

legumes and buckwheats

C except R-U east of Rockies mostly Mar-Sept, June-July at high elevations

many open habitats

some have recently treated most populations, previously thought to be Acmons, as Lupine Blues; while not impossible, there is little published data to support this hypothesis

female
female
male
Gila Co., AZ
male
LA Co., CA
fringe unchecked
iridescent blue spots
band often pinkish, especially in southern California

Acmon Blue *Plebejus acmon*

buckwheats

U-LC May-July

chaparral, sagebrush, rocky alpine

it is not currently known how to distinguish female Lupine Blues from female Acmon Blues

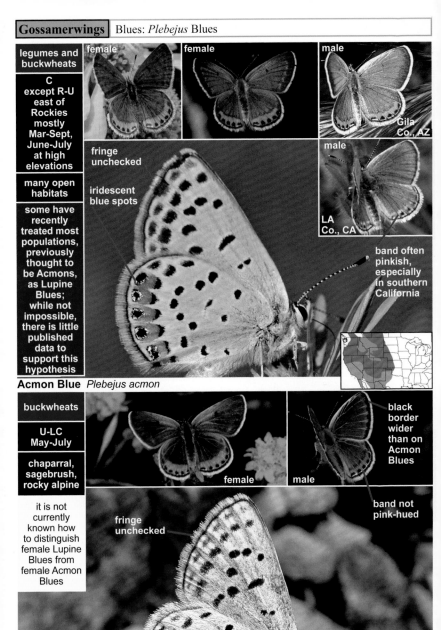

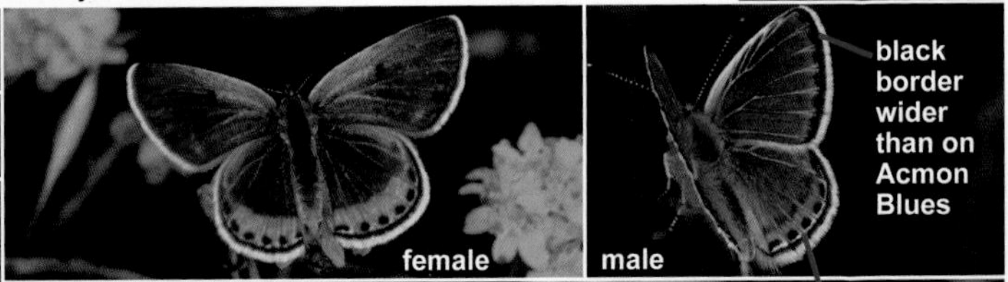
female
male
black border wider than on Acmon Blues
band not pink-hued

fringe unchecked
iridescent blue spots

Lupine Blue *Plebejus lupini*

saltbushes

LR-LU

late Apr-May, late June-early July, Aug - early Sept

second and third broods dependent upon rain

dry washes

one of the most range-restricted species in North America

spring
female

summer
female
black spots large

male
males w/ indistinct dull brown border

orange caps on iridescent spots are usually thinner
no spot here

San Emigdio Blue *Plebejus emigdionis*

Bastardsage (Wright's buckwheat)

LR
May-mid Aug

mid to high elevation openings in coniferous woods

as with most very local colonial species, this blue can be fairly common at its colony sites

one of the most range-restricted species in North America

foodplant

strong orange veining
black spots small

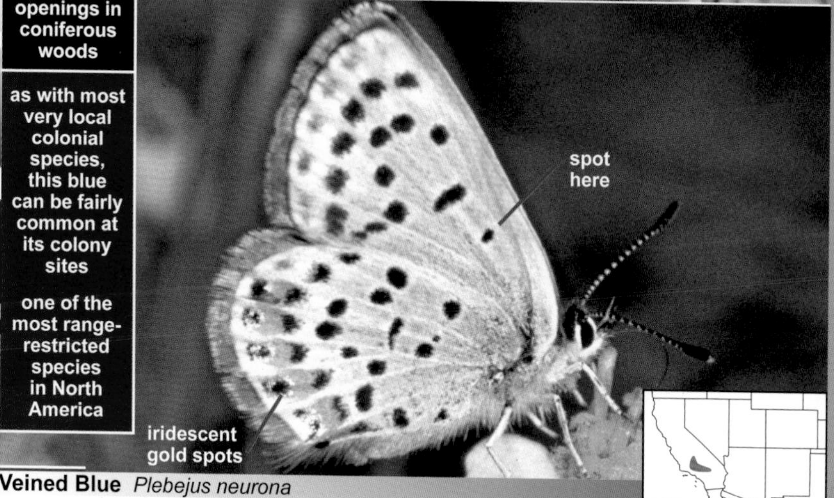
spot here
iridescent gold spots

Veined Blue *Plebejus neurona*

many, including primrose family

U-C
June-Aug-early Sept

rocky areas above treeline and high mountain meadows

Heather Blues, at high elevations in the Sierra Nevada, are probably best placed as Arctic Blues

Boisduval's Blue, pg 140, has HW white pm spots separated from white sm spots

Clallum
Co., WA

female

male

Clear Creek
Co., CO
sm band
usually weak
white pm
spots abut
white sm
spots
cell
spot
black spot
absent or
very small
Heather
Blue

Arctic Blue *Agriades glandon*

shooting-stars

mainly C-A but LR northward

lush subalpine mountain meadows

although treated as a subspecies of Arctic Blue on the NABA list, Sierra Blues will probably prove to be best treated as a separate species

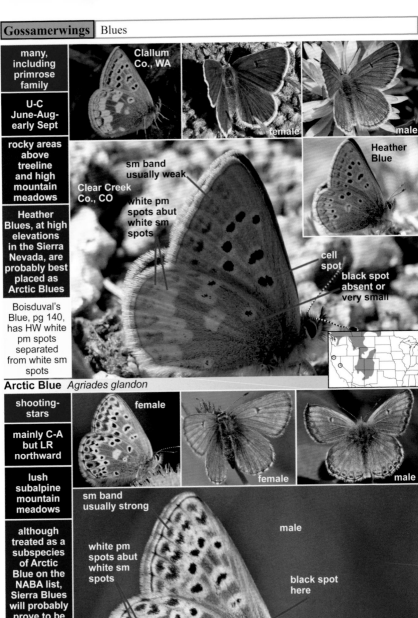

female

female

male

sm band
usually strong
male
white pm
spots abut
white sm
spots
black spot
here

'Sierra' Arctic Blue *Agriades glandon podarce*

milkvetches, clovers, and other legumes

LC
June-Aug

rocky areas above treeline, high mountain meadows, and sagebrush

HW below has an orange submarginal band with iridescent dark spots

postmedian band is orange or gray, not black

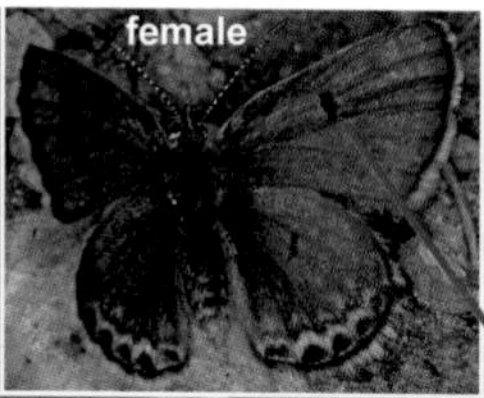
female

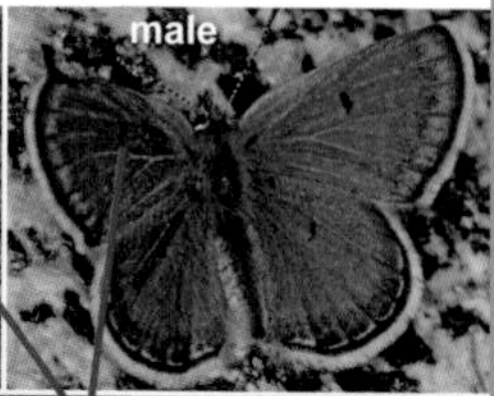
male

pm spots brown or gray, not black
strong cell-end bars

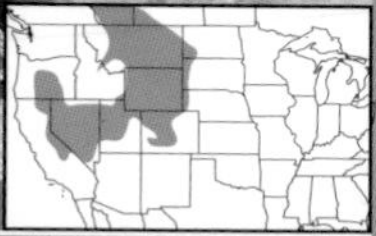

Shasta Blue *Plebejus shasta*

cranberries and blueberries

LU
July-Aug

arctic bogs

in its range, could be confused with Greenish Blue, page 141 or Arctic Blues, previous page

below, there is one prominent orange spot on the HW and no black spot in the FW cell

female

male

no black spot here
prominent orange spot

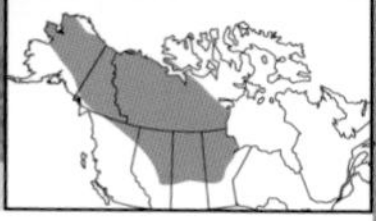

Cranberry Blue *Vacciniina optilete*

Monkeypod

R-U
all year

wherever its foodplant is planted

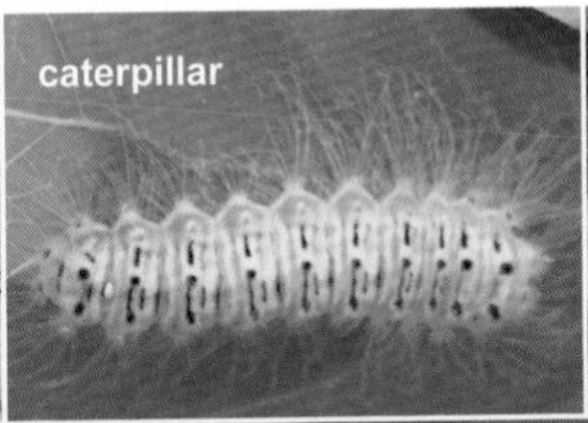
caterpillar

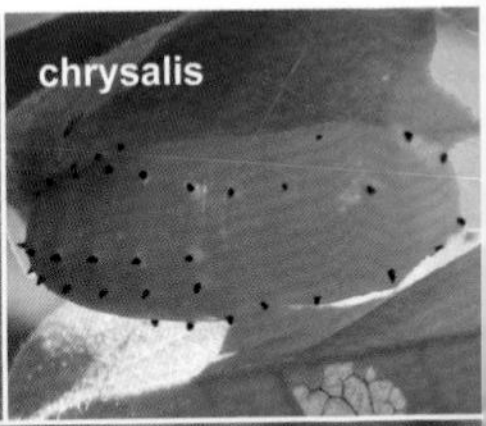
chrysalis

everyone enjoys these flying smiley faces!

nectars in early morning and late afternoon

often lands upside down under a leaf

hard to miss! black with bright red spots and bright yellow FW apexes

Red-bordered Pixie *Melanis pixe*

male

female

female
orange border

Spiny Hackberry

U
all year

thorn-scrub, gardens

the only greenmark (genus *Caria*) in the United States, this shows its affinity by the metallic green FW cell-end bars

curved wing
deep ultramarine blue
male

Red-bordered Metalmark *Caria ino*

legumes

usually LR-LU, rarely LA

all year

mostly in the eastern portion of the LRGV

thorn scrub, gardens

males are brilliant iridescent blue above

females are gray with black lines above

below, checkered white and brown/black

female
narrow
band

brilliant
iridescent
blue
male

Blue Metalmark *Lasaia sula*

LRGV

acacias

dark
patch
male

wide
band
female

Black-patched Bluemark *Lasaia agesilas*

not yet LRGV

spurge family

if you see one, you'll want to party too!

iridescent
silver streaks
and spots
fringed leggings
(for night-clubbing)
brick red
areas

Carousing Jewelmark
Anteros carausius

not yet LRGV

unknown

black
and
yellow
tiny
square
spot

Square-spotted Yellowmark
Baeotis zonata

se AZ once

Yellow Thistle

R-LC
Apr-Oct

open pine woods, wet prairies

bright orange with iridescent silvery lines

known range doesn't overlap with other scintillants

strong black spot

bright orange ground
thorax usually w/ orange
fringe unchecked gray

Little Metalmark *Calephelis virginiensis*

weak, or no, black spot

Sussex Co., NJ

second brood
Pulaski Co., AR

Roundleaf Ragwort

LR

one-brood areas mid June-July

two-brood areas late June and Aug

edges of woodland openings on limestone soils

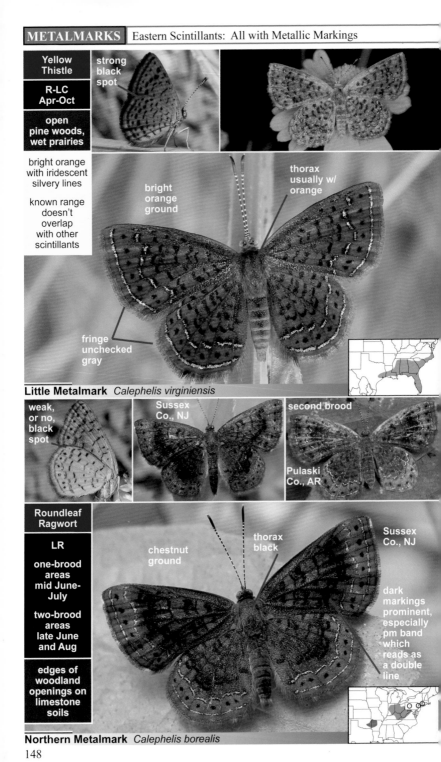

chestnut ground
thorax black
Sussex Co., NJ
dark markings prominent, especially pm band which reads as a double line

Northern Metalmark *Calephelis borealis*

Swamp Thistle

LR

one-brood areas July-mid Aug

two-brood areas June and Aug-early Sept

wet meadows

gone from quite a bit of its former range, this beautiful little species needs your help

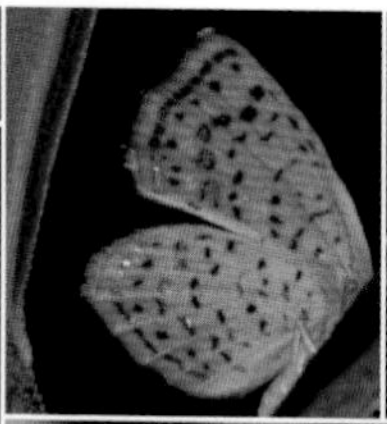

male

pm band reads as single line
female

Swamp Metalmark *Calephelis mutica*

Sweetbush

C Feb-Oct

desert canyons and washes

Fatal Metalmark, page 151, is not so reddish (individual in the top right inset is worn) and has median bands that are darkened

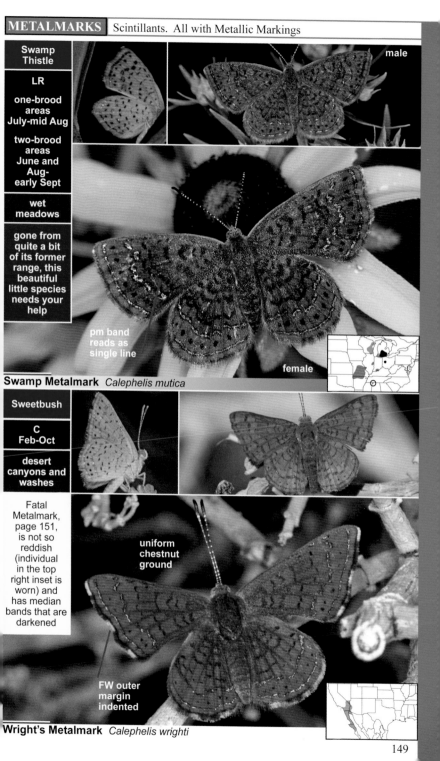

uniform chestnut ground
FW outer margin indented

Wright's Metalmark *Calephelis wrighti*

beggarticks

U-C all year

riparian areas in arid regions

often active in the afternoon

Fatal Metalmark, next page, the only other scintillant metalmark in its range, has darkened median bands

female

median band not usually darkened
male
fringes w/ strong white checks

Arizona Metalmark *Calephelis arizonensis*

Havana Snakeroot

LR-LU

riparian areas in arid regions

some Fatals can be similar, but below, Fatals have the third from the top black spot of the FW pm band set close to the pm metallic band (as do SOME Rawson's), don't have the top spot of the pm metallic band offset inward, and above have a paler, wider pm band

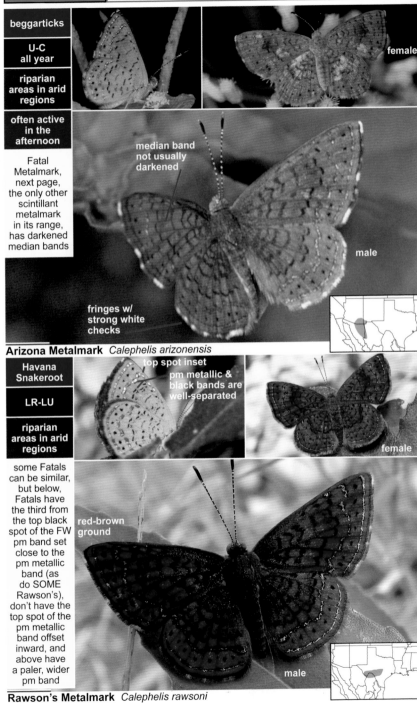

top spot inset
pm metallic & black bands are well-separated

female

red-brown ground
male

Rawson's Metalmark *Calephelis rawsoni*

baccharis and clematis

C
all year

thorn-scrub, riparian areas, chaparral

scintillants are often difficult to identify and, expecially with worn individuals, it is often best to just call them scintillants

top spot
not inset

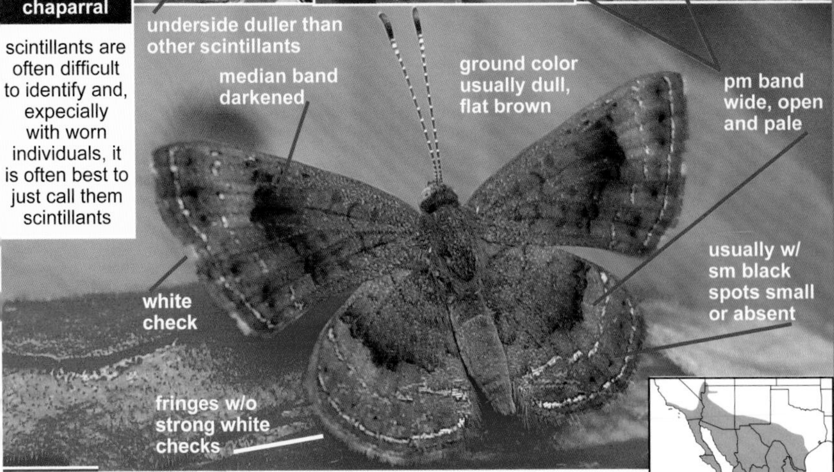
underside duller than
other scintillants
median band
darkened
ground color
usually dull,
flat brown
pm band
wide, open
and pale
usually w/
sm black
spots small
or absent
white
check
fringes w/o
strong white
checks

Fatal Metalmark *Calephelis nemesis*

Jack in the Bush (butterfly mistflower) and probably other mistflowers

U-C
all year

thorn-scrub, and tropical woods

FW pm band bulges outward (is rounded)

median bands are double-looped

usually more richly colored than Fatal Metalmarks

male

pm band
bulges
outward
no
white
check
female

Rounded Metalmark *Calephelis perditalis*

probably oaks

C
Mar-Apr, July-Aug

sycamore-lined canyons in mid-elevation oak woods

both at flowers and mudpuddling, often seems oblivious to human presence

fringes are weakly checked; usually with a wide black area below the FW apex (see female)

male

female

dark
patch
female
marginal spots tiny or absent

marginal
spots
usually
tiny or
absent
dark
patch
wingtip
slightly
falcate
male
orange

Zela Metalmark *Emesis zela*

oaks

U
June-Sept

mid-elevation oak woods

some individuals, intermediate between Ares and Zela, defy identification

whether these are hybrids or normal variants is unknown

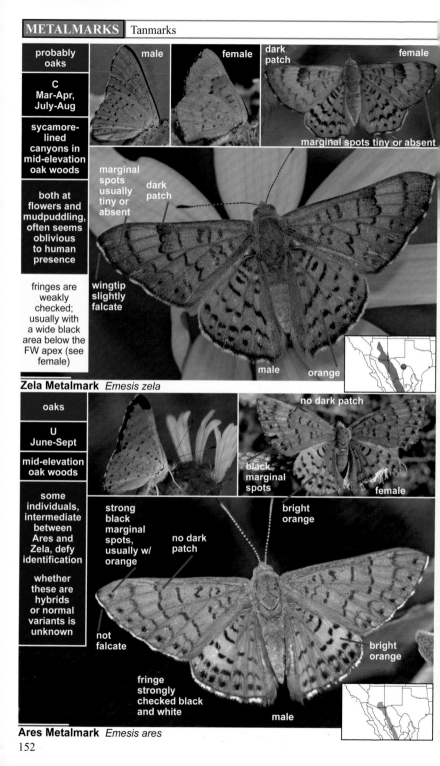

no dark patch
black
marginal
spots
female

bright
orange
strong
black
marginal
spots,
usually w/
orange
no dark
patch
not
falcate
bright
orange
fringe
strongly
checked black
and white
male

Ares Metalmark *Emesis ares*

clematis

a very rare stray to the LRGV

this species is C-A in Mexico, where it is widespread

female
large pale FW patch

gray pm band
gray bands on FW and HW
male

Falcate Metalmark *Emesis tenedia*

LRGV

nickers

the bumpy, humpy FW costal margin is quite dramatic

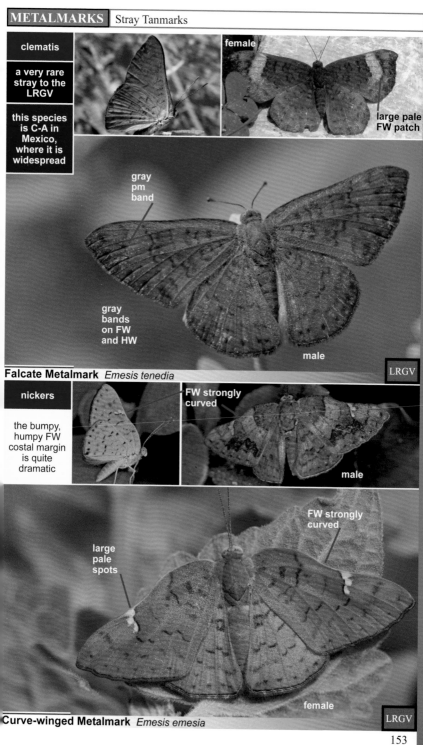

FW strongly curved
male

FW strongly curved
large pale spots
female

Curve-winged Metalmark *Emesis emesia*

LRGV

buckwheats and ratanys

LR-LC mostly LU number and timing of broods varies; some populations w/ spring and fall broods, others with spring or fall brood; some Mexican border populations may have three broods

dry habitats with its foodplants, including dunes, sagebrush, slopes and grasslands

the relationships among the different flight-time populations is uncertain, and some treat a number of the populations as distinct species

HW below varies from brown to silver to black, but always with large white spots

above, amount of black varies

large white spots
San Diego Co., CA, March

San Diego Co., CA, Sept

black and orange w/ white spots
San Diego Co., CA, March
black border

Santa Cruz Co., AZ, Aug

Santa Cruz Co., AZ, Aug

black and orange w/ white spots
large white spots
Dona Ana Co., NM, May

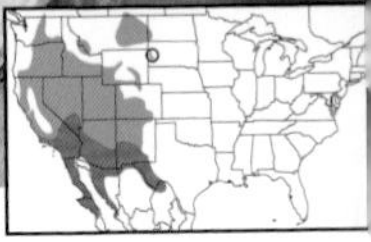

Mormon Metalmark *Apodemia mormo*

mesquites

se Arizona C-A

s California and w Texas U

Apr-Oct

dry habitats, especially low desert, with mesquites

almost all Palmer's Metalmarks are smaller than almost all Mormon Metalmarks

ground color averages increasingly darker from west to east

pale
wingbase

San Diego
Co., CA, Sept
orange
border

black/gray and
orange w/ white
spots
white sm spots
Pima Co.,
AZ, Aug
orange
border

Palmer's Metalmark *Apodemia palmeri*

Fendler's Ceanothus, except Havard's Plum for 'Chisos' Nais Metalmark

C-A June-Aug

'Chisos' U-C Apr-June

open pine woods

'Chisos' Nais, in w TX, may best be considered a separate species from Nais Metalmark; both appearance and foodplant differ

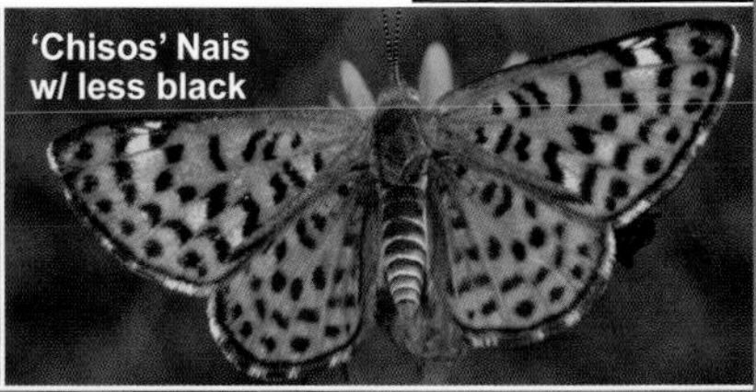
'Chisos' Nais
w/ less black

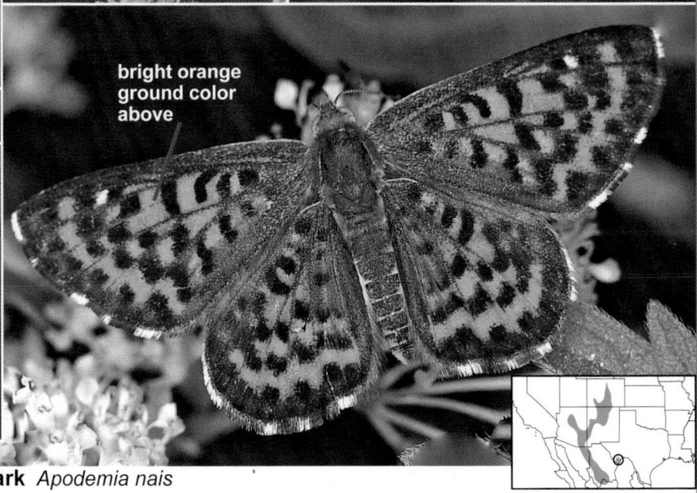
bright orange
ground color
above

Nais Metalmark *Apodemia nais*

unknown

black when fresh, fades to dark brown

large white spots both above and below

FW margin strongly concave

female similar but with some reddish brown on the HW

concave
margin
mainly
brown
below
black w/
large white
spots
concave
margin
male
LRGV
once

Narrow-winged Metalmark *Apodemia multiplaga*

unknown

R
all year almost all records are from Cameron County

thorn-scrub

Resaca de la Palma State Park is a good place to find this rare species

below, similar to Palmer's Metalmark, page 155, but browner

female

dark
patch
orange
margin
male
LRGV

Walker's Metalmark *Apodemia walkeri*

unknown

see Palmer's Metalmark, page 155

Murphy's Metalmark, found in Baja California could stray to s Cal.; has HW sm white spots above and a prominent HW pm white band below

sm white spots
tiny or absent
orange HW base

se AZ
w TX

Hepburn's Metalmark *Apodemia hepburni*

clematis

resembles crescent, page 215 or checkerspot, page 194, but lacks HW submarginal pale crescent spots

The two subapical white spots often have a thin white streak between them

two
subapical
white spots

se AZ
twice

Crescent Metalmark *Apodemia phyciodoides*

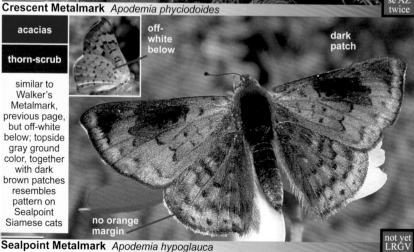

acacias

thorn-scrub

similar to Walker's Metalmark, previous page, but off-white below; topside gray ground color, together with dark brown patches resembles pattern on Sealpoint Siamese cats

off-
white
below
dark
patch
no orange
margin

not yet
LRGV

Sealpoint Metalmark *Apodemia hypoglauca*

passion-flowers

s FL and s TX
C all year

farther north
U-C

open woods, woodland edges and gardens

forms communal roosts at night

may become established northward during warm weather, then killed off by freezes

graceful with an often hovering flight

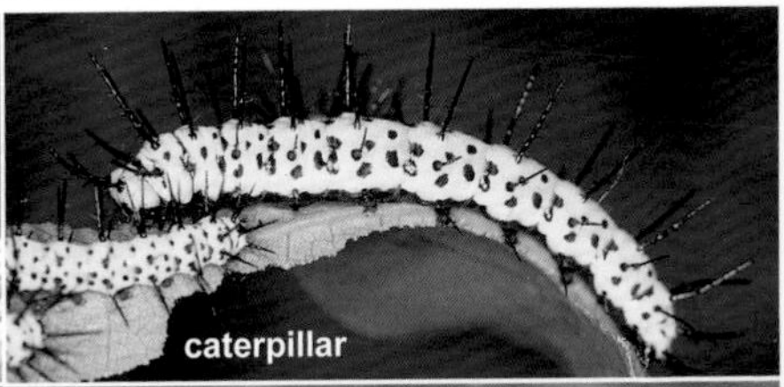
caterpillar

dramatically striped
black-and-yellow

Zebra Heliconian *Heliconius charithonia*

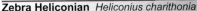

passionflowers

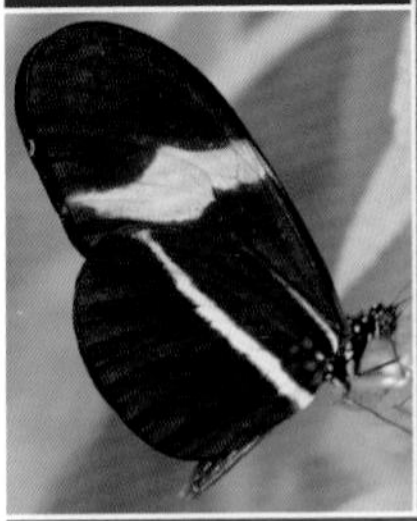

black with red band
on elongated FW
LRGV

Erato Heliconian *Heliconius erato*

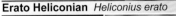

passionflowers

black-and-orange
striped "tiger" pattern
pointed
spot
black body w/
yellow spots
LRGV

Isabella's Heliconian *Eueides isabella*

passion-flowers

s FL and s TX
C
all year

farther north
U-C

open woods, scrub and gardens

males are bright satiny orange, females duller

Florida males usually w/ some black in the FW cell, Texas males usually w/o black

flies quickly on stiff wings w/ shallow wingbeats

male
bright satiny orange
Hidalgo Co., TX
male
orange brown w/ elongated FWs
Miami-Dade Co., FL
Hidalgo Co., TX
female

Julia Heliconian *Dryas iulia*

passionflowers

female
male
FW w/ two parallel black bands

LRGV

Banded Orange Heliconian *Dryadula phaetusa*

passionflowers

bold silvered spots
black bar within cell
falcate FW

LRGV once

Juno Heliconian *Dione juno*

passion-flowers

three brood areas C-A; decreasing immigrant northward; most common in late summer/fall

open woods, scrub, disturbed habitats, gardens

a common, widespread, large butterfly that is dazzlingly beautiful — how lucky can we get!

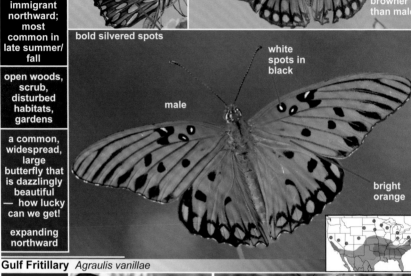

expanding northward

white spots in black

female
browner than male

bold silvered spots
white spots in black
male
bright orange

Gulf Fritillary *Agraulis vanillae*

passion-flowers

LRGV R but regular stray

elsewhere, a very rare stray

slightly larger than Gulf Fritillaries and darker, more chestnut colored

no white spots
bold silvered spots

two-toned FW
no spots

Mexican Silverspot *Dione moneta*

passion-flowers, violets, et al.

three brood areas C-A throughout warm weather; decreasing immigrant northward in summer and fall

open areas, including old fields, grassland, and scrub

has boom years and bust years

variable size, and wingshape (squared or elongated)

HW variegated

black median band

Variegated Fritillary *Euptoieta claudia*

Damiana, passion-flowers, violets, et al.

LRGV U-C

se AZ occasional temporary colonist

thorn-scrub, gardens, disturbed areas

resident in the Bahamas, this species could also stray to the Florida Keys

almost always brighter orange-brown than Variegated Fritillary

HW reticulated, more evenly colored than Variegated

Damiana

no black median band

Mexican Fritillary *Euptoieta hegesia*

Prairie Violet and other violets

LR-U
June-Sept

mostly tall-grass prairie; also short-grass prairie, wet meadows

the greater fritillaries contain two species clusters; one, including Regal Fritillary, has amber/brown eyes, the other has gray-blue eyes

this regal animal, formerly widespread, disappeared from the East in the 1970s and 80s; the cause is unknown, but probably includes changing land use patterns and less extensive open space; currently occurs in the East only at Fort Indiantown Gap Military Reservation in PA and Radford Army Ammunition Plant, VA

large

female

male

female
HW black w/ median white spotband

habitat

HW dark w/ large silvered spots
dark brown eye

Regal Fritillary *Speyeria idalia*

violets

LR-LU
June-Sept

openings in rich Appalachian/Ozark mountain woods, especially in valleys

males tend to emerge before females

one of North America's more striking examples of sexual dimorphism

populations in the Ohio River Valley, and in tidewater Virginia, have disappeared

male, top panel, is very large, with bright orange outer one-third of wings, black-brown inner two-thirds, there is really no other eastern butterfly to confuse with this spectacular fritillary

Red-spotted Purple is smaller than females Dianas

Pipevine Swallowtail has tails and more brilliant blue

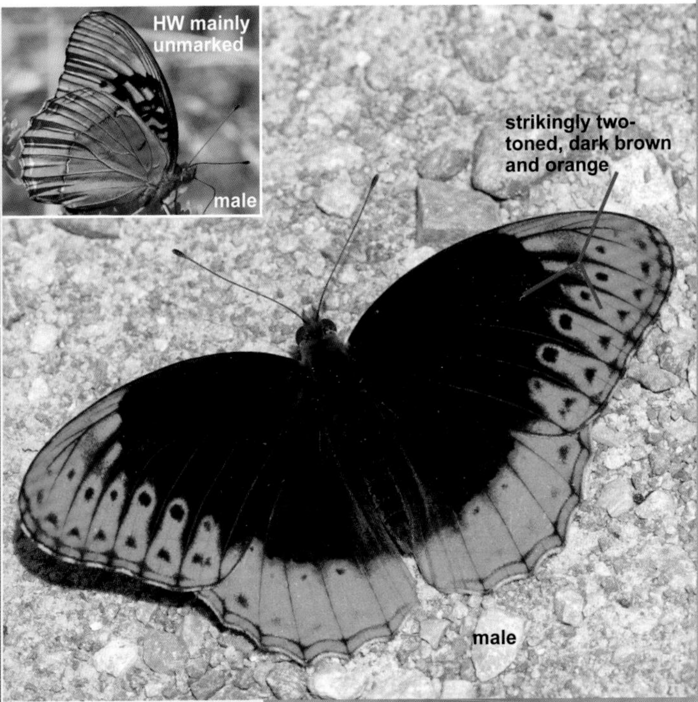
HW mainly unmarked
male
strikingly two-toned, dark brown and orange
male

female
female
black spots in blue lozenges

Diana Fritillary *Speyeria diana*

violets

C
widespread
mid May/
June-Sept

open areas including meadows, grasslands, roadsides, old fields, open woods and suburbia

see page 166 for Great Spangled Fritillary in the West

females persist later into the fall

As do most fritillaries, females lay eggs on dry vegetation, caterpillars then find violets the following spring

large

above, orange-brown with black bars

females are usually darker and larger than are males

female

female

no
basal
spot
amber
eye
male

female

male

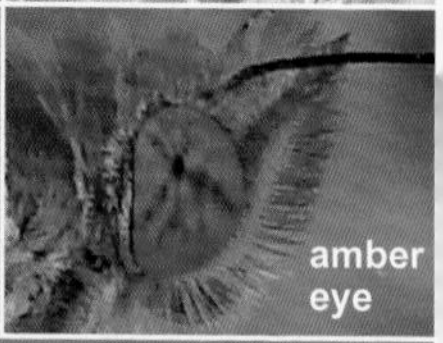
amber
eye

male
wide cream band; basal ground color stops at pm silver spots

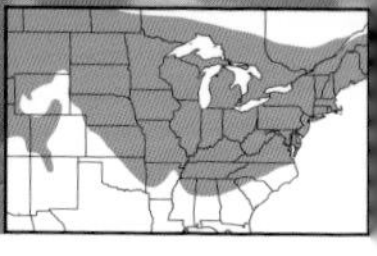

Great Spangled Fritillary *Speyeria cybele*

violets

southward
R-U

northward
U-C

mid/late June-Aug/ early Sept

cool openings in northern woods, meadows, moist prairie

see page 171 for Aphrodite Fritillary in the West

usually smaller and less robust than are Great Spangled Fritillaries

above, orange-brown with black bars

females are usually darker and larger than are males

especially in the Midwest, some individuals, especially females, have the HW dark ground color completely obscuring the cream sm band

Atlantis Fritillaries have blue-gray eyes

female

Essex Co., VT
male

Hamilton Co., TN
basal spot
amber eye
male

Door Co., WI
female

male
Columbia Co., NY

amber eye

narrow cream band; basal ground color extends beyond pm silver spots
Hamilton Co., TN
amber eye
male

Aphrodite Fritillary *Speyeria aphrodite*

violets

Oregon to Montana LC

southward R-U

June-Sept mostly July-Aug

open woods, meadows, prairies

see page 164 for eastern populations

some treat western populations as distinct from eastern populations, although they reportedly intergrade in Montana and Alberta

sexes are strongly dimorphic above

most populations have reduced spotting below

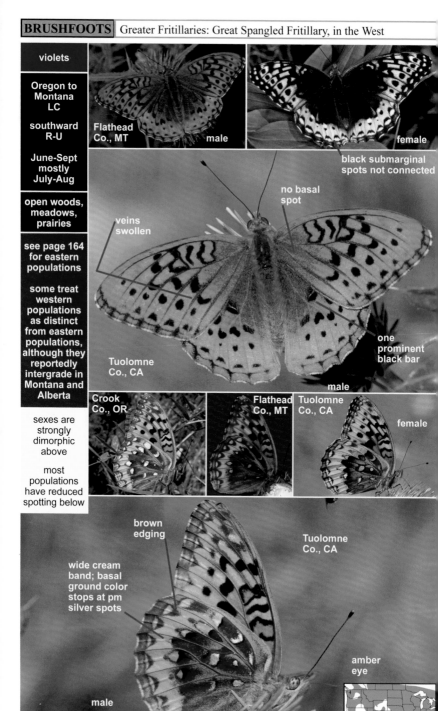

Flathead Co., MT
male

female
black submarginal spots not connected

no basal spot
veins swollen
one prominent black bar
Tuolomne Co., CA
male

Crook Co., OR

Flathead Co., MT

Tuolomne Co., CA
female

brown edging
Tuolomne Co., CA
wide cream band; basal ground color stops at pm silver spots
amber eye
male

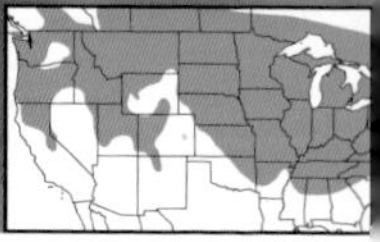

Great Spangled Fritillary *Speyeria cybele leto*

violets

LR-LU
mid July-mid Oct
mostly Aug-Sept

wet meadows, and seeps in dry regions

a population with beautiful blue females, formerly occurring in the Santa Catalina Mountains of Arizona, is now extirpated; similar populations still survive in northern Mexico

sexes strongly dimorphic above

populations in California and Nevada have yellowish ground color on the HW below; more eastern populations are darker brown

female
Mono Co., CA
black submarginal spots connected
Greenlee Co., AZ
no basal spot
veins not swollen
two prominent black bars
male

Mono Co., CA
female

male
Greenlee Co., AZ

Mono Co., CA
black edging
male
amber eye

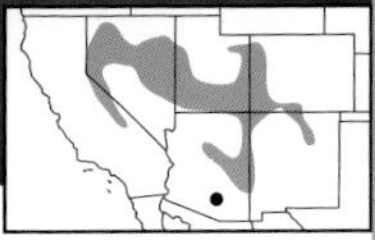

Nokomis Fritillary *Speyeria nokomis*

violets

C
mid June-mid Sept

moist meadows and openings in or adjacent to mixed woods

see pages 169 and 170 for western populations

some treat western populations as distinct from eastern populations, largely based upon the fact that two populations of "Atlantis" Fritillaries exist in the Black Hills of South Dakota; but the truth is that no one really knows

smaller than Great Spangled Fritillary

in the East, most often confused with Aphrodite Fritillary, page 165, but Atlantis Fritillaries have blue-gray eyes while Aphrodite Fritillaries have amber eyes

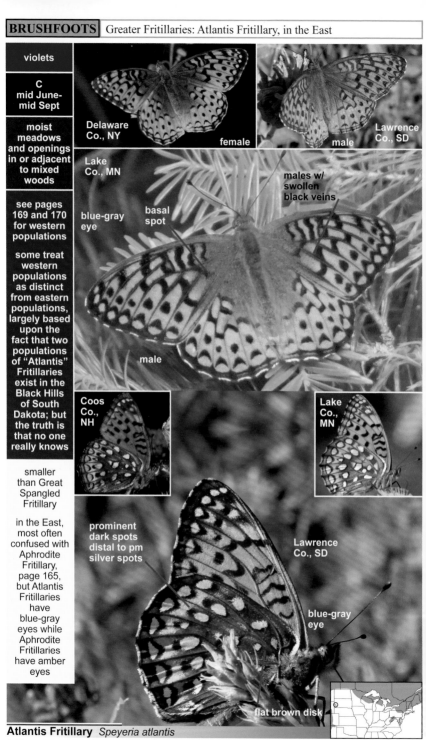

Delaware Co., NY
female

male
Lawrence Co., SD

Lake Co., MN
males w/ swollen black veins
basal spot
blue-gray eye
male

Coos Co., NH

Lake Co., MN

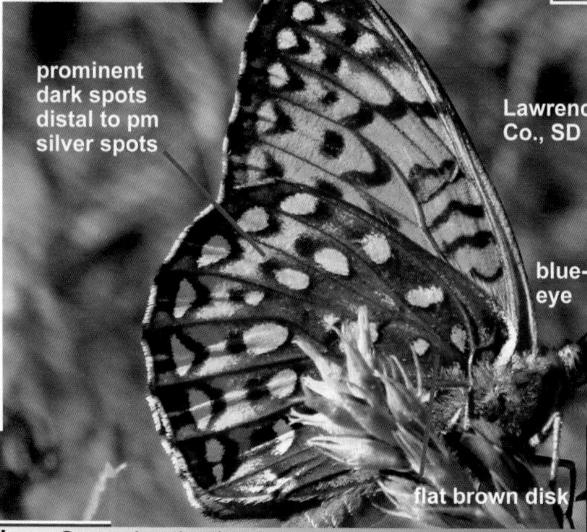
prominent dark spots distal to pm silver spots
Lawrence Co., SD
blue-gray eye
flat brown disk

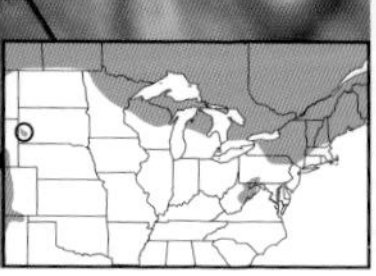

Atlantis Fritillary *Speyeria atlantis*

violets

C-A
June-Sept,
mostly July

moist meadows and openings in or adjacent to mixed woods

mid-sized to small

best distinguished from Aphrodite Fritillary, page 171, by blue-gray eyes

similar to Great Basin Fritillary, pages 178-179, and Zerene Fritillary, pages 173-174, both of which usually have more mottled HW disks

above, Zerene Fritillary males, page 174, has bold, inky black FW markings

Flathead Co., MT
female

Lawrence Co., SD
male

Routt Co., CO

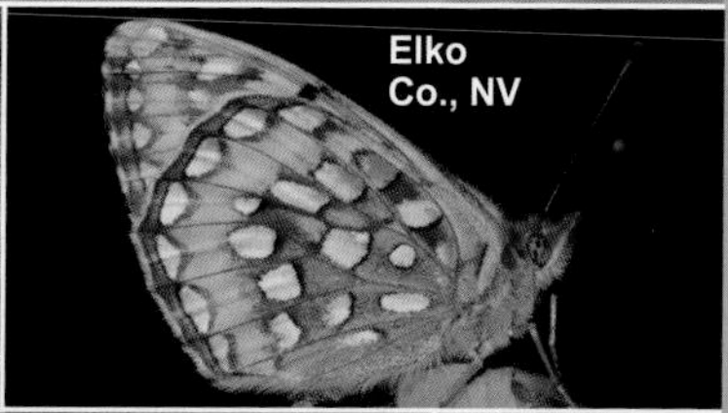
Elko Co., NV

Flathead Co., MT
reddish-brown disk

blue-gray eye

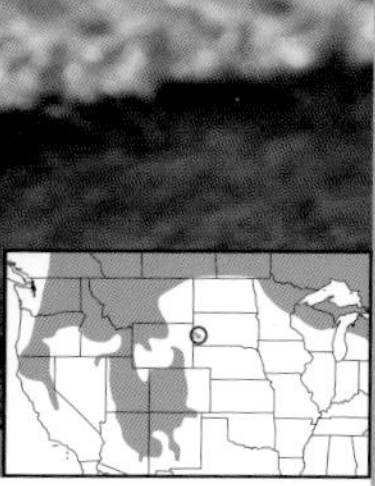

Atlantis Fritillary *Speyeria atlantis hesperis* (complex)

males are bright orange above; females duller, usually w/ a pale area on the FW costal margin near the subapex

Teton Co., WY
female

Jefferson Co., CO
male
males w/ swollen black veins

most western populations have a reddish-brown HW disk below

HW spots are usually silvered but some populations, including California and Oregon, are unsilvered

Teton Co., ID

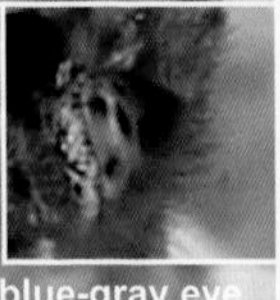
blue-gray eye

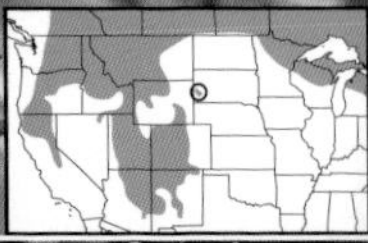

Atlantis Fritillary *Speyeria atlantis hesperis* (complex)

LC
June-Aug

the brightly colored "Atlantis" in the Southwest (including named subspecies, *schellbachi*, *nausicaa*, *dorothea* and *capitanensis* — with *dorothea* being the oldest name) have a yellower eye color than other Atlantis Fritillaries; when better studied, they may prove to be a separate species

Otero Co., NM

Bernallilo Co., NM

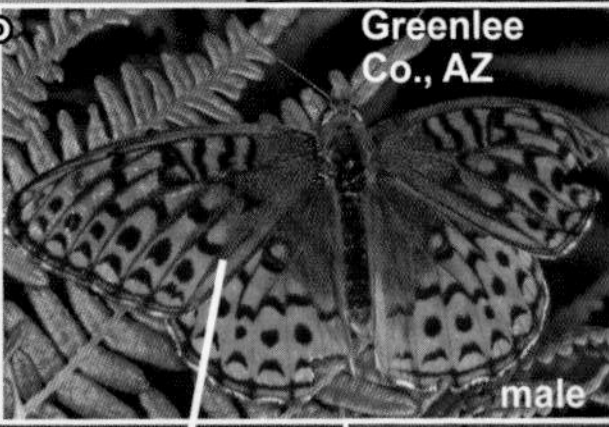
Greenlee Co., AZ
male
males w/ swollen black veins

Greenlee Co., AZ

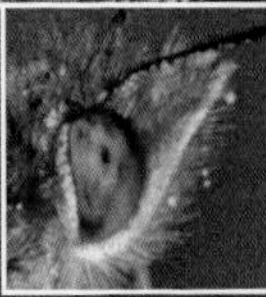
amber eye

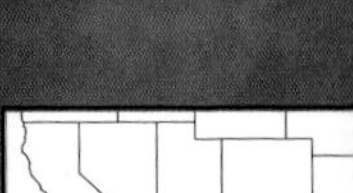

'Southwestern' Atlantis Fritillary *Speyeria atlantis dorothea*

violets

C
June-Aug

cool openings in northern and mountain woods, meadows, moist prairie

see page 165 for Aphrodite Fritillary in the East

males are bright orange above; females duller, usually with a pale area on the FW costal margin near the subapex

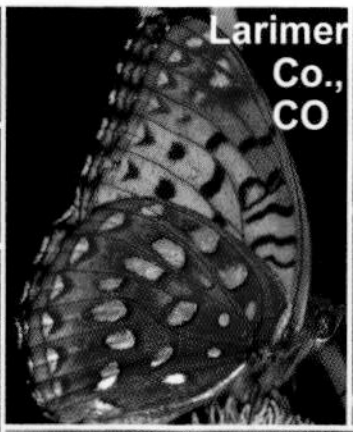
Larimer Co., CO

Custer Co., SD
female

male
w/o swollen black veins
Jefferson Co., CO

Jefferson Co., CO

amber eye

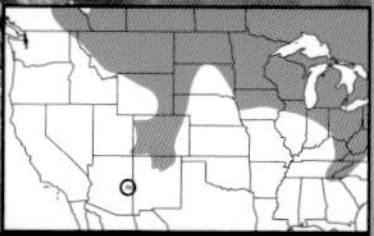

Aphrodite Fritillary *Speyeria aphrodite*

violets

U
in the White Mountains of Arizona
July-Aug

mountain meadows

males do not have swollen black veins on the FW, and eyes are more amber, otherwise very difficult to separate from co-occurring Atlantis Fritillaries

Apache Co., AZ
male
males w/o swollen black veins

Greenlee Co., AZ
amber eye

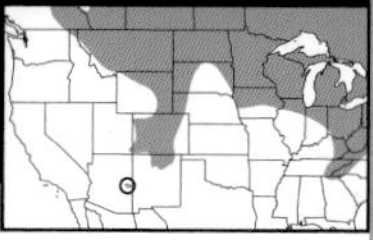

'White Mountains' Aphrodite Fritillary *Speyeria aphrodite byblis*

violets

U-C
mid June-mid Sept, mostly July-Aug

openings and edges of moist coniferous or aspen woods

some populations hilltop

the most widespread greater fritillary in the Northwest

relatively small

bold, wide black FW spots

males w/ swollen black FW veins

below, HW spots usually unsilvered (except on Vancouver Island, BC)

below, HW pm spots come close to touching, making them form a more coherent band than on other fritillaries

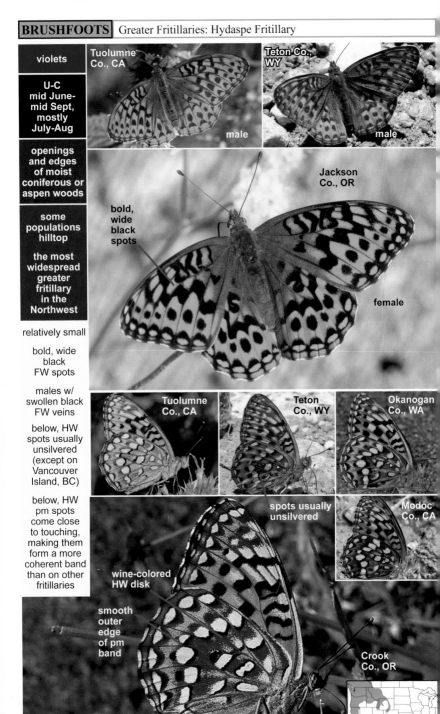

Tuolumne Co., CA
male

Teton Co., WY
male

Jackson Co., OR
bold, wide black spots
female

Tuolumne Co., CA

Teton Co., WY
spots usually unsilvered

Okanogan Co., WA

Modoc Co., CA

wine-colored HW disk
smooth outer edge of pm band
Crook Co., OR

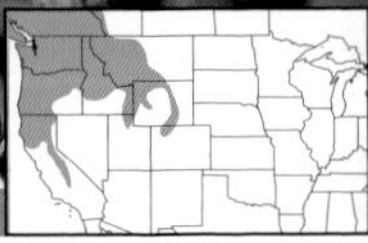

Hydaspe Fritillary *Speyeria hydaspe*

violets

C-A
May-Sept
mostly
July-Aug

openings in woods, grasslands, coastal dunes

'Carol's' Zerene, in the Spring Mtns of Nevada, is treated as a full species by some

mid-sized

extremely variable

above, with wide black FW spots

above, males with swollen black veins

below, HW spots usually silvered, but unsilvered in parts of California

below, red-purple from west slope of California Sierras to southern Oregon; distinguish from Hydaspe by less coherent HW pm band

brown-disked elsewhere on Pacific Coast

pale-disked east of the Sierra Nevada crest

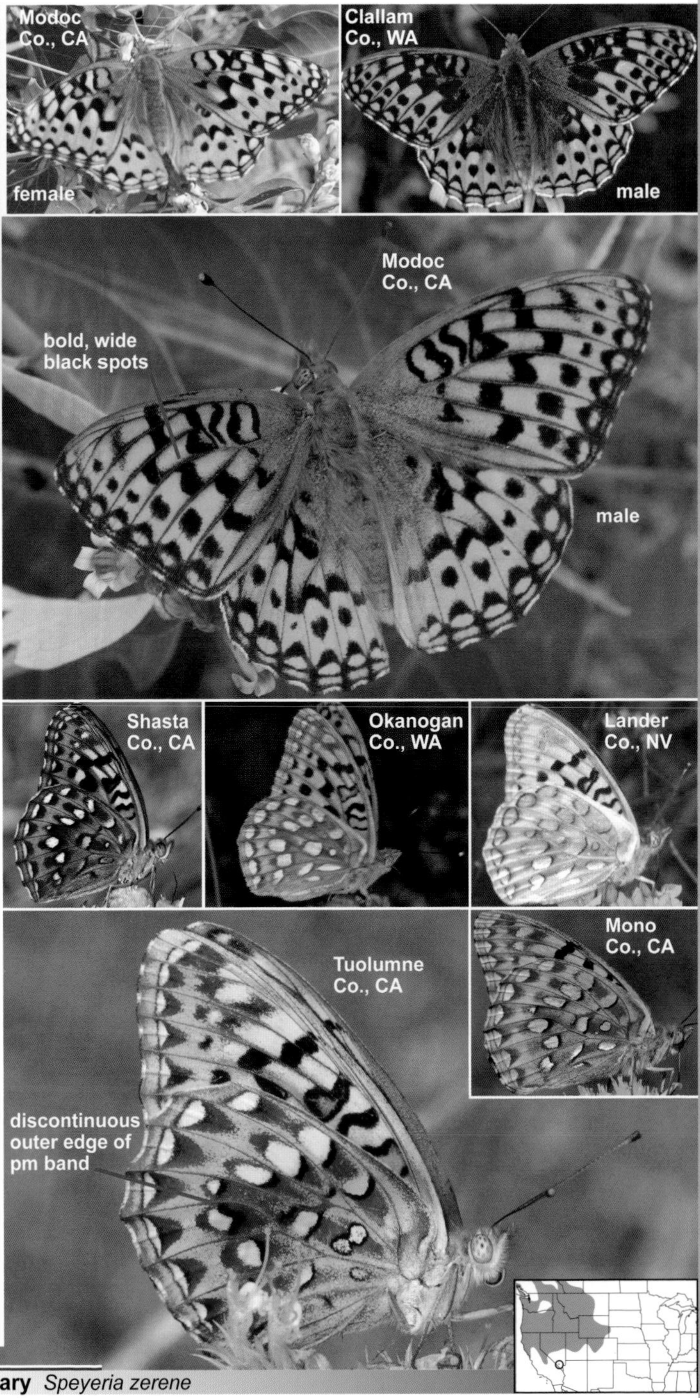
Modoc Co., CA
female
Clallam Co., WA
male
Modoc Co., CA
bold, wide black spots
male
Shasta Co., CA
Okanogan Co., WA
Lander Co., NV
Mono Co., CA
Tuolumne Co., CA
discontinuous outer edge of pm band

Zerene Fritillary *Speyeria zerene*

violets

C-A
May-Sept
mostly
July-Aug

openings in woods, grasslands, coastal dunes

mid-sized

above, with bold, wide black FW spots

above, males with swollen black FW veins

below, HW spots usually silvered

east of Great Basin, HW disk below usually unevenly tan and blotchy, with much individual variation

Coronis Fritillary, next page, averages larger with narrower, less intense black markings above

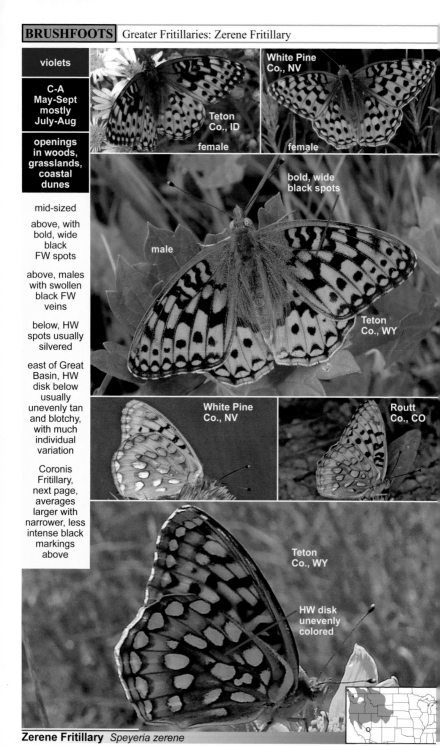

Teton
Co., ID
female

White Pine
Co., NV
female

bold, wide
black spots
male
Teton
Co., WY

White Pine
Co., NV

Routt
Co., CO

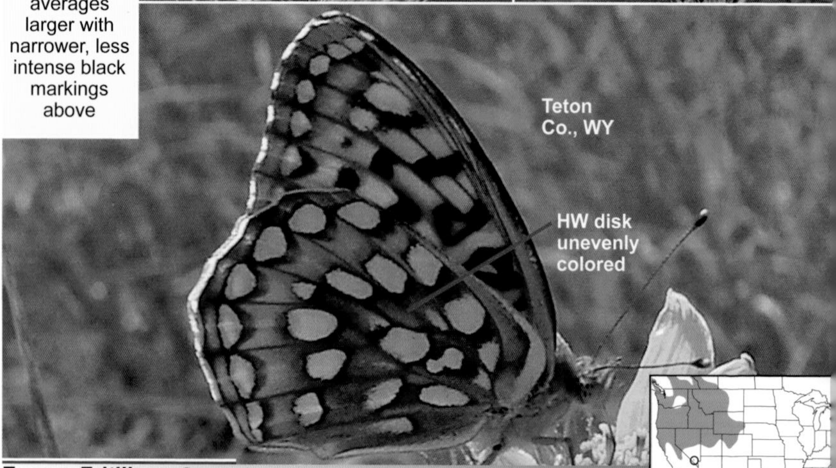
Teton
Co., WY
HW disk
unevenly
colored

Zerene Fritillary *Speyeria zerene*

violets

R-A depending upon location May-Sept mostly July-Aug

moist openings in woods, sagebrush, and chaparral

large to mid-sized

above, most females have FW apical marginal spots paler than on other fritillaries (except for much smaller Mormons)

above, FW black spots not usually as bold as on Zerene Fritillaries

below, HW spots silvered and large

below, similar to Zerene Fritillary over much of range but averages larger and HW disk is more evenly colored

in southern California, very similar to Callippe Fritillary, pages 176-177, but slightly larger and brighter orange

four different subspecies are shown at right

San Bernardino Co., CA
male

White Pine Co., NV
female

pale apical marginal spots
Crook Co., OR
female

Monterrey Co., CA

Lander Co., NV

Fremont Co., CO

Modoc Co., CA
FW base often w/ pink-orange

Coronis Fritillary *Speyeria coronis*

violets

C-A mainly July-Aug; mostly May-June in coastal California south of San Francisco

open woods, sagebrush, chaparral, grassy areas

often begins flying earlier in the season than other greater fritillaries

hilltops

mid-sized

below, most populations wtih triangular HW marginal spots with inward edging that is usually thin and/or not very dark

tan to brown populations in California, s. Oregon (see top panel)

intermediate to green in Oregon, Washington

green-tinged populations east of the Sierra Nevada and Cascades (see bottom panel)

some populations are silvered, some unsilvered

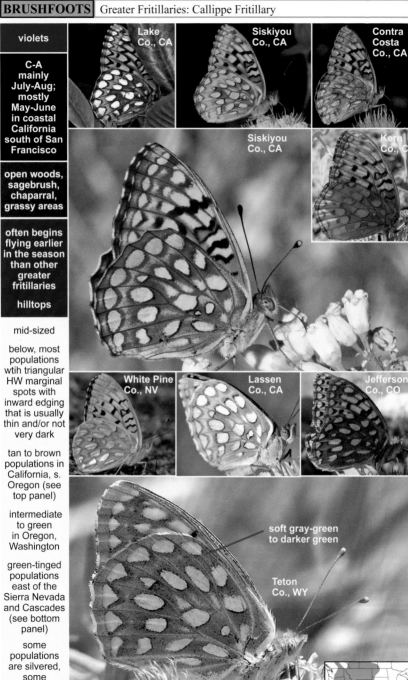

Lake Co., CA
Siskiyou Co., CA
Contra Costa Co., CA
Siskiyou Co., CA
Kern Co., CA
White Pine Co., NV
Lassen Co., CA
Jefferson Co., CO
soft gray-green to darker green
Teton Co., WY

Callippe Fritillary *Speyeria callippe*

violets

silvered spots (if present) show through HW, creating pale spots when topside is seen

see Coronis Fritillary, page 175

female
Siskiyou Co., CA

male
Lake Co., CA

male
Lake Co., OR
silvered spots show through to topside

Callippe Fritillary *Speyeria callippe*

violets

U-C
late May-early Sept

grasslands, open woods in foothills

less variable than other greater fritillaries

large

green reflections below (dependent upon light)

green reflections below (dependent upon light)
marginal spots rounded inwardly

Edwards' Fritillary *Speyeria edwardsii*

violets

U-C
June-Sept

mostly
July-Aug

mountain and/or northern meadows, usually dry, in mixed or conifer woods

mid-sized to small

in California Sierra Nevada, similar Mormon Fritillary males, pages 180-181, lack FW thick black veins on topside

extremely variable

some populations resemble Mormons, others Zerene, Atlantis, Callippe or Coronis!

usually w/ mottled brown HW disk, a few populations with a greenish tint (see individuals from White Pine Co., inset)

silvering can vary within a population

wing bases usually darkened, often w/ green tint
Tuolumne Co., CA
female

Jackson Co., OR
male

Tuolumne Co., CA
male

Tuolumne Co., CA

Jackson Co., OR

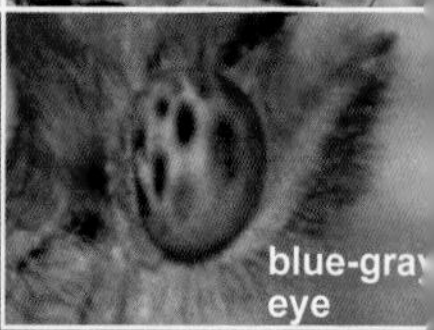

spots can be silvered or unsilvered
west of Rockies, this spot usually elongate
Calaveras Co., CA

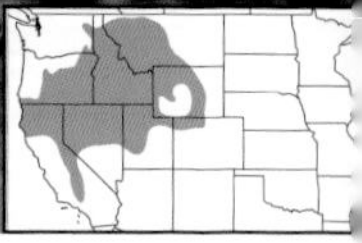

Great Basin Fritillary *Speyeria egleis*

U-C
June-Sept; mostly July-Aug

mountain and/or northern meadows in mixed or conifer woods

mid-sized to small

populations near eastern edge of range w/ darker brown disk

some populations in center of range w/ green tints below

Teton Co., WY
female

Teton Co., WY
male
thick black veins

Routt Co., CO
disk mottled

Salt Lake Co., UT

Great Basin Fritillary *Speyeria egleis*

LR-LU
June-July/ early Aug

open areas in redwood forest (San Mateo and Santa Cruz Counties)

mountain meadows (Monterey and San Luis Obispo Cos.)

this pink-flushed ghostly charmer has one subspecies down and two to go — it's continued survival is tenuous

small

white streak (in north)
female

thick black veins
male

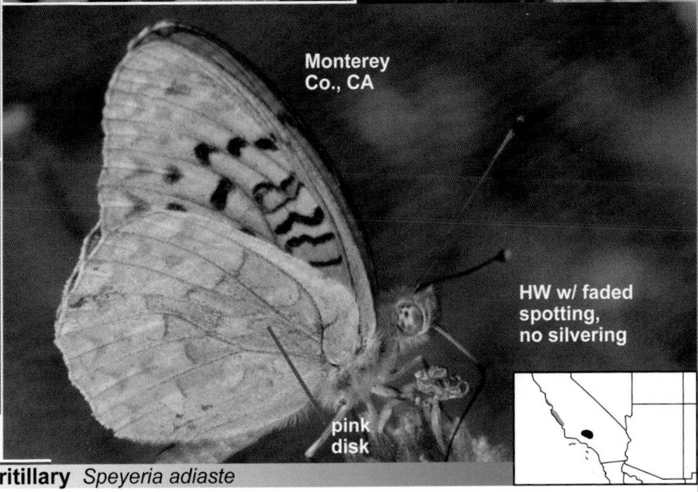
Monterey Co., CA
HW w/ faded spotting, no silvering
pink disk

Unsilvered Fritillary *Speyeria adiaste*

violets

C-A
June-Sept; mostly July-Aug

high mountain meadows, usually moist

the smallest greater fritillary

below, HW disk is pale, varying from yellow to tan w/ green tints to brown in Black Hills of South Dakota

most populations are yellow-tinted below

below, HW spots vary from silvered to unsilvered but pale, to almost matching the ground color

silvering can vary within a population

In California Sierra, eye color is amber (see main photo at right), not blue-gray, distinguishing Mormons, which fly in moist areas, from Great Basin Fritillaries, which fly in drier areas. It is possible California "Mormons" are a separate species.

Teton
Co., WY

Carbon
Co., WY

Hinsdale
Co., CO

outside CA
Sierra, eye
is blue-gray
Park
Co., WY

Apache
Co., AZ

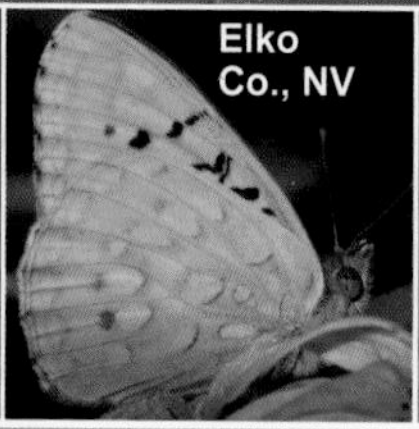
Elko
Co., NV

Lawrence
Co., SD

in CA Sierra,
eye is amber
Mono
Co., CA

Mormon Fritillary *Speyeria mormonia*

violets

C-A
June-Sept;
mostly
July-Aug

high mountain meadows, usually moist

the smallest greater fritillary

FWs are short and rounded

above, females usually have a black border containing pale spots that are more prominent than on other greater fritillaries

above males are bright orange, w/o thick black scaling on FW veins

above, the six black FW pm spots are usually more uniform and thus read more as a group than on other greater fritillaries, where the bottom three spots tend to be larger and indented

Tuolomne Co., CA
female

Apache Co., AZ
female

FW round and short
Sublette Co., WY
marginal pale spots
female

Hinsdale Co., CO
male

Lawrence Co., SD
male

FW round and short
Tuolomne Co., CA
FW veins not thick
male

Mormon Fritillary *Speyeria mormonia*

violets

East
LC-C
Apr-Sept

West
LR-LU
May-Sept;
June-July
where one
brood

moist meadows and grassy fields in East; moist mountain meadows and willow thickets in the West

expanding range in some areas while disappearing from others

Burnet
Co., WI

lower spot
much larger
and inset
bar open
sm black
spots not
chevrons
male

female

outer margin
comes to a
shallow point
Sussex
Co., NJ

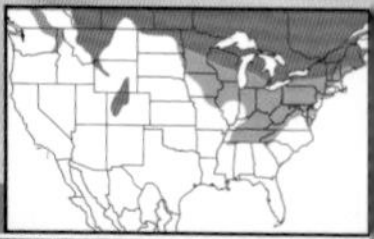

Meadow Fritillary *Boloria bellona*

violets

C-A
May-Aug
mostly
June-July

moist meadows, especially in woods openings

the FW chevrons are weakly expressed from Montana and British Columbia north

lesser fritillaries are smaller than greater fritillaries, but larger than crescents

Mariposa
Co., CA

two spots not
dissimilar
sm black
outward
chevrons

outer margin
comes gently
rounded
Siskiyou
Co., CA

Pacific Fritillary *Boloria epithore*

shrub willows

LR-LU
May-July, but less than a month at any one spot

also found throughout most of Canada and Alaska

willow thickets and northern bogs

this species is named for the Norse goddess of love and marriage

NW Arctic
Bor., AK

bar
closed
black
bars
point
out
wing bases
very dark

white patch
large and
prominent

Frigga Fritillary *Boloria frigga*

Snow Willow and other prostrate willows

LR

San Juan Mountains of Colorado mid July-early Aug

Wind River Mountains of Wyoming early-mid Aug

wet areas above treeline

the population in Colorado is listed by the United States as endangered

North Slope
Bor., AK

Hinsdale
Co., CO
male
rounded wings

Hinsdale
Co., CO
female

black chevrons
are flat or point
outward
Hinsdale
Co., CO

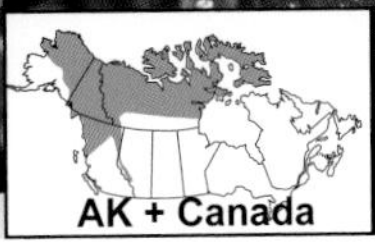
AK + Canada

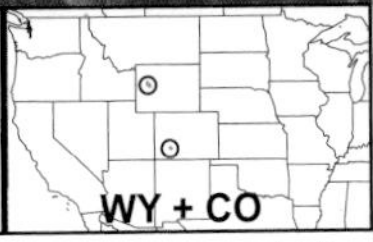
WY + CO

Dingy Fritillary *Boloria improba*

violets

most of the East and Alberta-Montana
LC

West and southern edge of range in East
LR-LU

May-Sept

wet meadows, wet prairies, bogs

more tolerant of drier conditions in the north

Middlesex Co., NJ

Flathead Co., MT
black chevrons point inward

marginal and pm white spots
Coos Co., NH
pm spots black-centered

Silver-bordered Fritillary *Boloria selene*

many, including willows and bistorts

LR-LU
June-early Aug

also found throughout most of Canada and Alaska

bogs and wet alpine areas

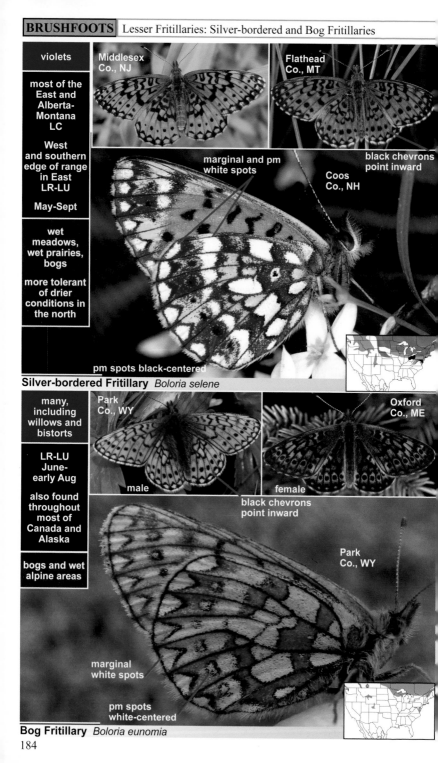

Park Co., WY
male

Oxford Co., ME
female
black chevrons point inward

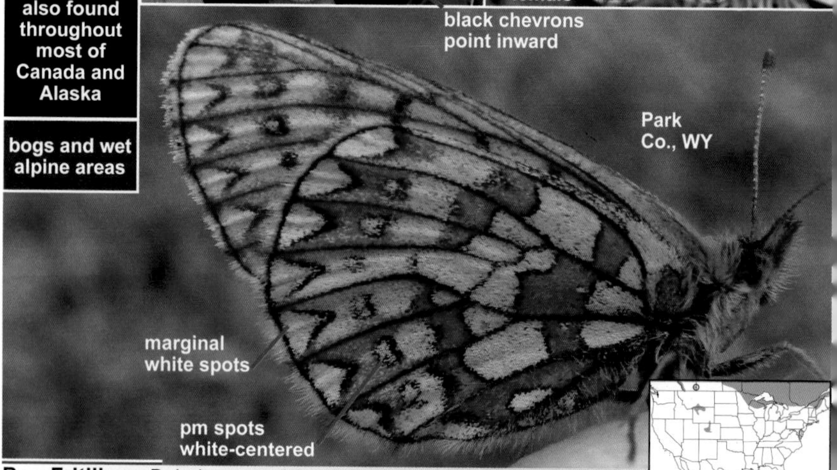
Park Co., WY
marginal white spots
pm spots white-centered

Bog Fritillary *Boloria eunomia*

violets

LR-LU
June-
early Aug

moist openings in montane conifer woods and wet areas above treeline

Pacific Fritillary, page 182, also has outwardly pointing chevrons, but they are discontinuous and below, Pacific and Relict are very different

male

female
black chevrons point outward

creamy median band
chestnut sm line
no marginal white spots
pm spots pale-centered

Relict Fritillary *Boloria kriemhild*

Eightpetal Mountain-Avens

LR
July-
early Aug

in the United States, reported only from Glacier National Park

rocky ridges and slopes above treeline

because of its rarity, it's iffy flight times and the inaccessible nature of its habitat, very few people have seen this butterfly

food plant

museum specimens
large (for a lesser fritillary)
dully colored with no strong markings
faded black triangles w/ flat bottoms

Alberta Fritillary *Boloria alberta*

willows and violets

East
LU

West
C-A

July-Aug/Sept

open meadows and bogs in conifer woods

some treat Purplish Fritillary populations as subspecies of Arctic Fritillaries

widespread throughout Canada and Alaska, a relict population exists at and above treeline in the White Mtns of New Hampshire

quite variable

only Purplish, Arctic and Alberta Fritillaries have flat-bottomed HW submarginal black triangles

Alberta Fritillaries are very dull and below, the black triangles are faded

female
Sublette Co., WY

male
Yukon Koyukuk Bor., AK

Coos Co., NH
male
black triangles w/ flat bottoms

near Blairmore Alberta

Sublette Co., WY

pale horizontal bars
Coos Co., NH
black triangles w/ flat bottoms
white spots

Purplish Fritillary *Boloria montinus*

heaths, including blueberries and bearberries

LU-LC
Apr-July
mostly May-June during snowmelt

generally flies earlier than Friggas at the same location

also found throughout most of Canada and Alaska

willow thickets and moist tundra

North Slope Bor., AK

black, inwardly pointing chevrons or triangles

prominent white pm band
white "poles" or spots
contrasting dark area
white x
Douglas Co., WI

Freija Fritillary *Boloria freija*

probably willows

LU
late June-mid July

wet tundra

some treat Purplish and Arctic Fritillaries as one species

HW median line usually sharply angled (see inset)

separation from Purplish Fritillaries is problematical, with habitat and flight period the best current clues

female

white spots

Arctic Fritillary *Boloria chariclea*

knotweeds

in the lower U.S. found only high in the Wind River Mountains of Wyoming, where it is LR early-mid Aug

LC Alaska and Canada late June-July Aug/Sept

moist meadows above treeline

some treat North American populations as *B. alaskensis*

female

dark wing bases well-defined
male
HW to a shallow point

thin and continuous reddish pm band
not white
white
HW comes to a shallow point

Mountain Fritillary *Boloria napaea*

Bog Blueberry, mountain-avens, and probably others

C
June-July

many populations fly every year, but some fly mainly in even-numbered years and some mainly in odd-numbered years

tundra

female

male

pale "telephone poles"
prominent, wide and continuous reddish pm band
big "eye" in "duck head"
female
white "telephone poles"

Polaris Fritillary *Boloria polaris*

Entireleaf Mountain-Avens

LR-LC mid June-mid July

dry rocky hilltops and rock slides

known from very few locations, but probably more widespread

similar to Freija Fritillary, page 187, but darker, with a duller, more blurry topside, often w/ a blue sheen when fresh and underside is usually darker

food plant

usually w/ large marginal white spots

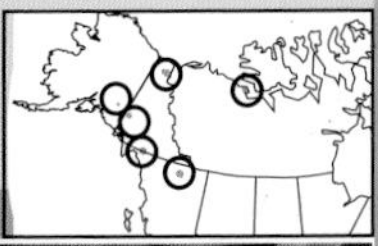

Cryptic Fritillary *Boloria natazhati*

Yellowdot Saxifrage

in lower U.S. in Okanogan Co., WA and n Glacier NP, MT; LR late July-early Aug

LC Alaska and Canada mid June-mid Aug

above treeline on scree slopes and rocky ridges

the largest lesser fritillary

like a large, dull Silver-bordered Fritillary w/o strong marginal black triangles

black margin

foodplant

well defined white median band
white pm band

Astarte Fritillary *Boloria astarte*

Parish's Goldeneye

C mostly Mar-Apr partial broods in June and Sept-Nov, depending upon rain

high desert canyons and washes

hilltops

most species in the genus *Chlosyne* have white spots on the top of their head

foodplant

white dots in black sm band
orange marginal spots

California Patch *Chlosyne californica*

aster family, especially sunflowers

three brood areas: C most of the year; a decreasing immigrant northward, mainly in late summer and fall

brush fields, thorn-scrub, and other open habitats

extremely variable

from west Texas eastward, most individuals resemble the main photo on pg 191 top

Hidalgo Co., TX
cream-yellow band

La Paz Co., AZ

caterpillar

Hidalgo Co., TX
usually w/ white pm dots
rarely w/ orange marginal spots

Bordered Patch *Chlosyne lacinia*

aster family, especially sunflowers

three brood areas
C
most of the year

a decreasing immigrant northward, mainly in late summer and fall

brush fields, thorn-scrub, and other open habitats

like other members of the genus *Chlosyne*, Bordered Patches lay eggs in large clusters, under leaves

one of the most variable butterflies in the world

orange bands vary from extensive to absent

from New Mexico westward, most individuals have reduced orange and vary from the individual shown on right to the individual shown on page 190 in the top right inset of the lower panel

Hidalgo Co., TX
Hidalgo Co., TX
chrysalis
cream-yellow band
Hidalgo Co., TX
usually w/ white pm dots
Dona Ana Co., NM
Starr Co., TX
cream-yellow band
Cochise Co., AZ
usually w/ white pm dots

Bordered Patch *Chlosyne lacinia*

acanthus family

LR-LU mostly June-Nov population numbers fluctuate

tropical woods and thorn-scrub

large and attractive

black with a large red-orange patch

some Bordered Patches can be very similar above but have only one, or no, white spots in the outer portion of the FW cell

yellow patch w/ black spots
large yellow sm spots

caterpillar

two white spots
large, fairly unicolorous red-orange patch

Crimson Patch *Chlosyne janais*

acanthus family

yellow patch w/o black spots on its outer half

w/o large yellow sm spots

one, or no, cell spots
patch usually two-toned

Rosita Patch, *Chlosyne rosita*

probably acanthus family

red spot at outer angle

red

yellow
red spots

LRGV se AZ

Red-spotted Patch *Chlosyne marina*

Early Shaggytuft

R-LU mostly Mar-Nov

thorn-scrub, especially in limestone areas, but also along rocky or clay embankments

often present at Palo Alto Battlefiield National Historical Park in Cameron Co., Texas

see Theona Checkerspot, page 196 and Arachne Checkerspot, page 195

inverted orange "Y"
pale spot
black-and-white
male
antennas black, not checked
female
spot reduced

Definite Patch *Chlosyne definita*

acanthus family

LR mostly Mar-Nov

thorn-scrub

of the butterflies that are resident in the lower United States, this is one of the least seen

inverted orange "Y"
white bounded by black
antennas checked
middle spot tiny
white rings

Banded Patch *Chlosyne endeis*

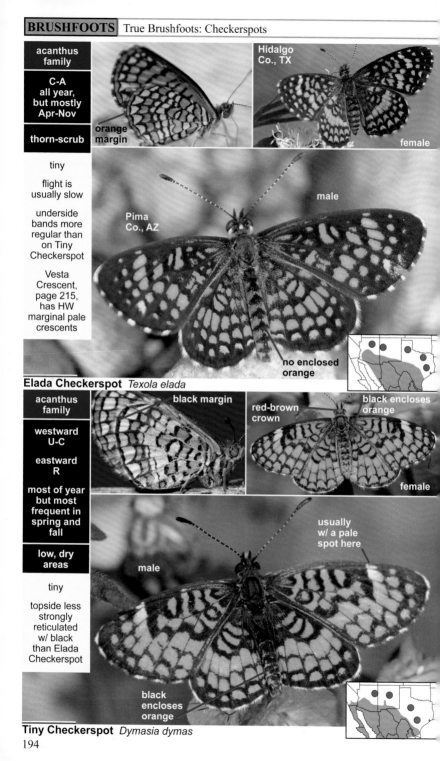

acanthus family

C-A
all year, but mostly Apr-Nov

thorn-scrub

tiny

flight is usually slow

underside bands more regular than on Tiny Checkerspot

Vesta Crescent, page 215, has HW marginal pale crescents

orange
margin

Hidalgo
Co., TX
female

male
Pima
Co., AZ
no enclosed
orange

Elada Checkerspot *Texola elada*

acanthus family

westward
U-C

eastward
R

most of year but most frequent in spring and fall

low, dry areas

tiny

topside less strongly reticulated w/ black than Elada Checkerspot

black margin

red-brown
crown
black encloses
orange
female

usually
w/ a pale
spot here
male
black
encloses
orange

Tiny Checkerspot *Dymasia dymas*

eardtongues

R-LC
Apr-Oct

at high altitudes, only one brood, June-Aug,

grasslands and mountain meadows

hilltops

underside pattern is similar to Tiny Checkerspot, but Arachne Checkerspots are much larger

male

black
dots in
white
band
female
blue-gray
eyes
red-orange rings
on abdomen

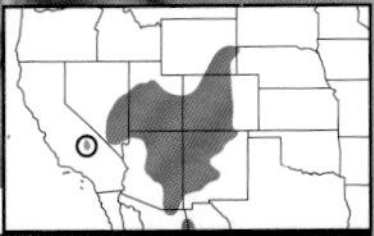

rachne Checkerspot *Poladryas arachne*

eardtongues

LR-LU
Apr-Sept

open woods on limestone

hilltops

only *Euphydryas* Checkerspots, pgs 204-207, also have red-orange abdominal rings, but *Euphydryas* have brown eyes

Arachne Checkerspots have narrower orange bands below and more extensive black above

black
dots in
white
band

blue-gray
eyes
reduced
black
markings
red-orange rings on abdomen

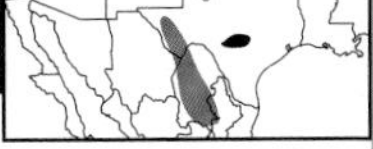

otted Checkerspot *Poladryas minuta*

mostly barometer bushes in Texas, mainly Indian paintbrushes in Arizona

U-C mostly Mar-Nov

thorn-scrub

hilltops

extremely variable, even within one population

above, most males are similar to the one shown at right

flight is usually low to the ground

below, orange and white bands are more regular than on related checkerspots

FW below, with a black cell-end bar (sometimes faint)

female
Hidalgo Co., TX

male
Hidalgo Co., TX
wide black border

Cochise Co., AZ

Big Bend NP, TX

Hidalgo Co., TX
bold orange and white bands

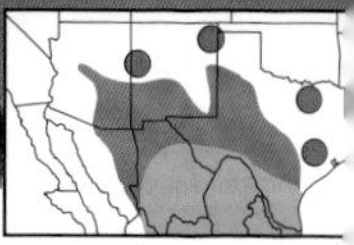

Theona Checkerspot *Chlosyne theona*

mostly barometer bushes in Texas, mostly Indian paintbrushes in Arizona

U-C
mostly Mar-Nov

thorn-scrub

hilltops

extremely variable, even within one population

most females are similar to the one shown at right

low-flying

Hidalgo
Co., TX
female

Cochise
Co., AZ
female

Zapata
Co., TX
female

Theona Checkerspot *Chlosyne theona*

barometer bushes

R
Apr-Oct

mid elevation scrub and open brush

treated by some as a subspecies of Theona Checkerspot

below, there is no FW cell-end bar

above, there are no post-median black bands

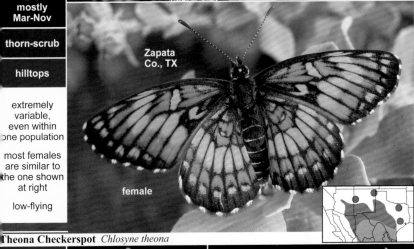

male

female
no black
pm band
or spots
wide black
border w/o
pale spots

Chinati Checkerspot *Chlosyne chinatiensis*

Indian paintbrushes

LR-LU
Mar-July
mostly
Apr-June

abundance fluctuates

hillsides with its foodplant in a variety of habitats

hilltops

most populations west of the Sierra Nevada have black individuals; east of the Sierra Nevada mostly with orange

Leanira, Fulvia and Black Checkerspots all have nifty, and similar, black and white patterns on their HW undersides

rarely, individuals will lack the underside black bands

Leanira is most easily distinguished from the other two species by the yellow-brown antennal clubs

San Bernardino Co., CA

end of antennal club is yellow/brown
orange palps
Siskiyou Co., CA
abdomen black

San Bernardino Co., CA

food plant

end of antennal club is yellow/brown
orange palps
black band w/ white spots

Leanira Checkerspot *Chlosyne leanira*

Indian paintbrushes

LR-U

three broods mostly Apr, June, Aug-Sept

two broods mostly May-July, Aug-Sept

hillsides with its foodplant, usually on limestone

hilltops

palps are black above, white below

thin black cell-end bar
black band w/ white spots
white palps

male

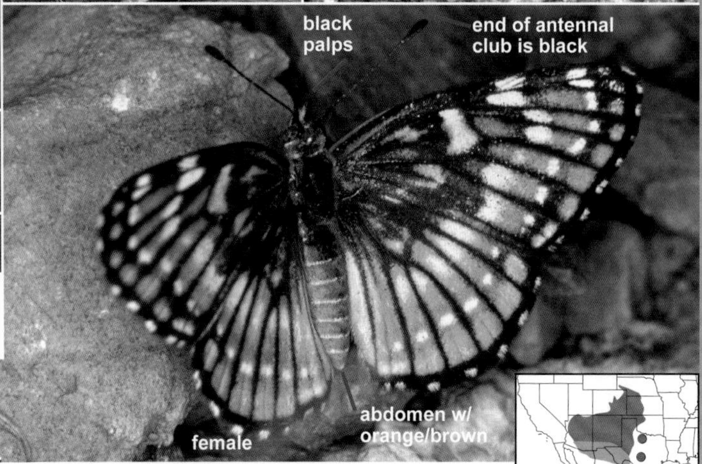
black palps
end of antennal club is black
abdomen w/ orange/brown
female

Fulvia Checkerspot *Chlosyne fulvia*

Indian paintbrushes

R-C Apr-Nov; abundance fluctuates

mountain canyons with streams at mid elevations

hilltops

very similar to Fulvia Checkerspot, but blacker above and yellower on the HW below

Bordered Patch, pgs 190-191, lacks white abdominal rings

black band w/ white spots
no black cell-end bar
abdomen black

Black Checkerspot *Chlosyne cyneas*

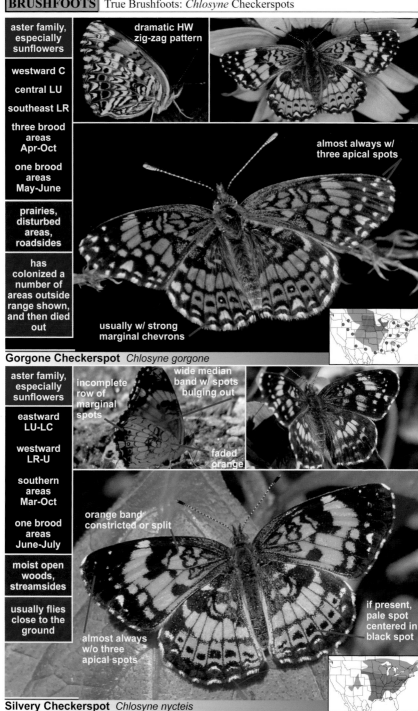

aster family, especially sunflowers

westward C

central LU

southeast LR

three brood areas Apr-Oct

one brood areas May-June

prairies, disturbed areas, roadsides

has colonized a number of areas outside range shown, and then died out

dramatic HW
zig-zag pattern

almost always w/
three apical spots
usually w/ strong
marginal chevrons

Gorgone Checkerspot *Chlosyne gorgone*

aster family, especially sunflowers

eastward LU-LC

westward LR-U

southern areas Mar-Oct

one brood areas June-July

moist open woods, streamsides

usually flies close to the ground

incomplete
row of
marginal
spots
wide median
band w/ spots
bulging out
faded
orange

orange band
constricted or split
almost always
w/o three
apical spots
if present,
pale spot
centered in
black spot

Silvery Checkerspot *Chlosyne nycteis*

Parasol Whitetop

LR-LU

southward June

northward June-July

wet meadows and marshes w/ the foodplant

males are frequent mudpuddlers

Gorgone and Silvery Checkerspot, whose ranges partially overlap this species, don't have bright orange on the HW below

West-
chester
Co., NY

Pope
Co., MN
bright
orange

Pope
Co., MN

caterpillar

complete row of
marginal spots
orange band
across cell
Westchester
Co., NY
if present, pale spot is
at top of black spot

Harris' Checkerspot *Chlosyne harrisii*

fleabanes

R-U July-Aug

rockslides and scree slopes at and above treeline

some treat the populations in the California Sierra Nevada as a separate species

ID by habitat

see Northern Checkerspot, page 203, and Sagebrush Checkerspot, page 202

Rockslide Checkerspot *Chlosyne whitneyi*

aster family, especially sandasters

U
Mar-June

chaparral, dunes, washes

closest populations of Sagebrush Checkerspots are bright orange with little black (see Sagebrush Checkerspot inset)

it is possible that Gabb's, Sagebrush and Northern Checkerspots are one species

median
band is
white

Gabb's Checkerspot *Chlosyne gabbii*

rabbitbrushes in most of range, Mojave Woodyaster and Orcutt's Aster in se California and Arizona

mostly C, but LR northeastward

southward Mar-May

northward May-July

open dry regions

generally flies earlier in the season than Northern Checkerspots in the same area

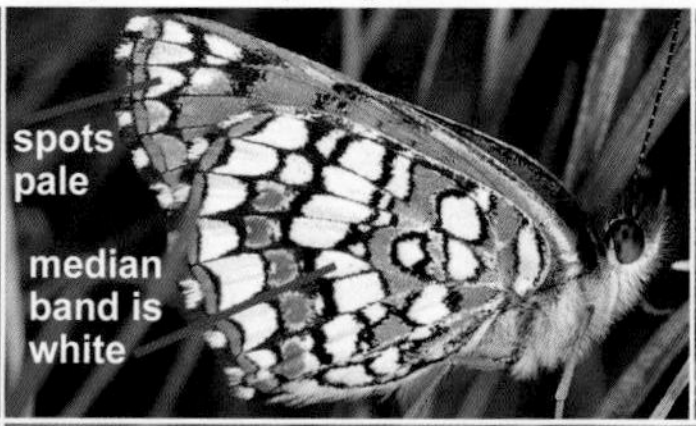
spots
pale
median
band is
white

San Bernardino
Co., CA

in Oregon,
topside is
darker
Teton
Co., WY

Sagebrush Checkerspot *Chlosyne acastus*

asters and rabbitbrushes

C
Apr-Aug

many including sagebrush, woods openings

varies, especially females, from mainly orange to mainly black

the four species shown on these two pages, along w/ Rockslide Checkerspot, page 201, are closely related; range is often the best clue to identity

median band
is creamy
wings don't appear
as two-toned

Northern Checkerspot *Chlosyne palla*

asters

southward
C

northward
R-LU

June-Aug

montane conifer woods openings

northern Cascades populations are very similar to Northern Checkerspots, but range doesn't overlap

spots
yellow
median band
off-white

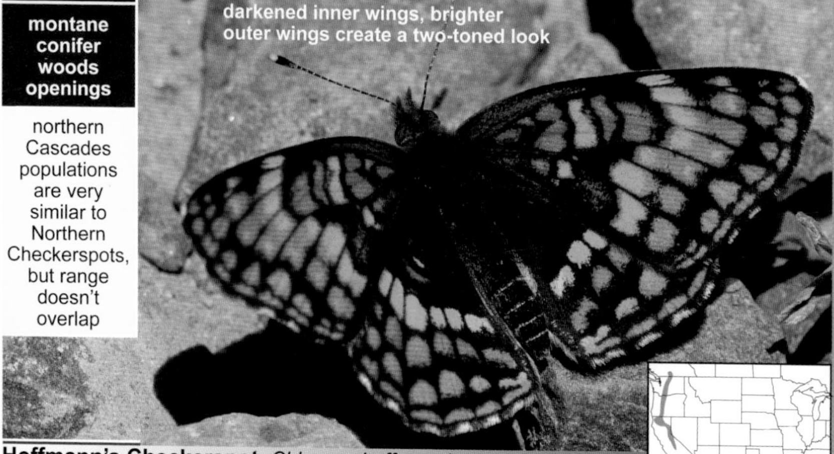
darkened inner wings, brighter
outer wings create a two-toned look

Hoffmann's Checkerspot *Chlosyne hoffmanni*

figwort family, including beardtongues, Indian paintbrushes, over most of range

snowberries in the northwest

C-A

southward Apr-May

northward mainly June-July

many open habitats, including desert canyon, mtn meadows and above treeline

map shows range of, *E. c. chalcedona* + *E. c. colon*

Euphydryas checkerspots have brown eyes, other checkerspots have blue-gray eyes

individuals w/ white abdominal spots are almost always this species, not Edith's Checkerspot

it is not known how to separate many Variable/ Edith's Checkerspots in the field

see more photos, pages 206-207

San Diego
Co., CA

San Luis
Obispo
Co., CA

San Diego
Co., CA
abdomen w/ or w/o white dots

San Mateo
Co., CA

Tuolomne
Co., CA

Tuolomne
Co., CA
w/o
red here

Variable Checkerspot *Euphydryas chalcedona*

figwort family, including Indian paintbrushes, beardtongues, and blue-eyed marys

LR-U
Mar-Apr low and south, July-Aug high and north

poor soil areas, including rocky areas above treeline, desert hills, bluffs

E. e. quino, shown at right, is federally endangered

lacks white abdominal spots

in general, Pacific states Edith's are redder than nearby Variables, but see Tuolomne Co., CA, Variable Checkerspot, previous page

only Edith's have red inner edging to the black pm line, but many Edith's populations lack the red

in general, flies earlier in the season than nearby Variable Checkerspots

see page 207 for more photos

Tuolomne Co., CA
Alberta, Canada
San Diego Co., CA
abdomen w/o white dots
Park Co., WY
San Diego Co., CA
Teton Co., WY
Linn Co., OR
Linn Co., OR
w or w/o red here

Edith's Checkerspot *Euphydryas editha*

figwort family, including beardtongues, Indian paintbrushes

C-A

low and southward Apr-May

high and northward mostly June-Aug

many open habitats, including desert canyon, mtn meadows and above treeline

map shows range of, *E. c. chalcedona* + *E. c. colon*

Apache
Co., AZ

Siskiyou
Co., CA

Apache
Co., AZ

Variable Checkerspot *Euphydryas chalcedona*

snowberries and other figwort family

open wooded canyons, slopes, snowberry thickets

C
Apr-Aug

in lowlands mainly June

in mountains mainly July-Aug

map shows range of, *E. c. chalcedona* + *E. c. colon*

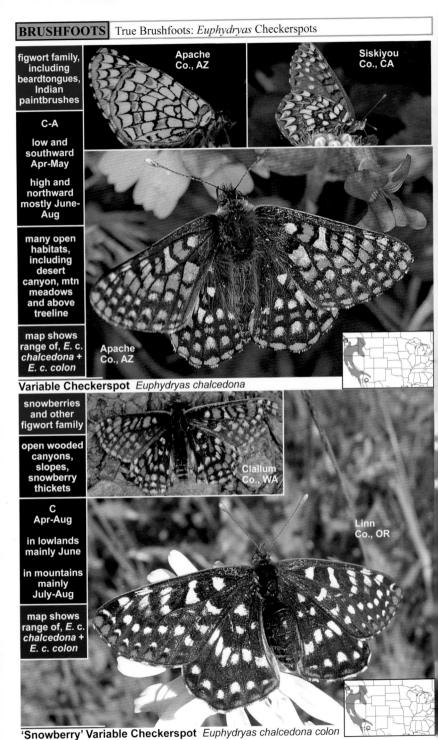

Clallum
Co., WA
Linn
Co., OR

'Snowberry' Variable Checkerspot *Euphydryas chalcedona colon*

Salt Lake
Co., UT

Jefferson
Co., CO
male

female
white spots, when
present, are diagnostic
Jefferson
Co., CO

ble Checkerspot *Euphydryas chalcedona anicia*

White Pine
Co., NV

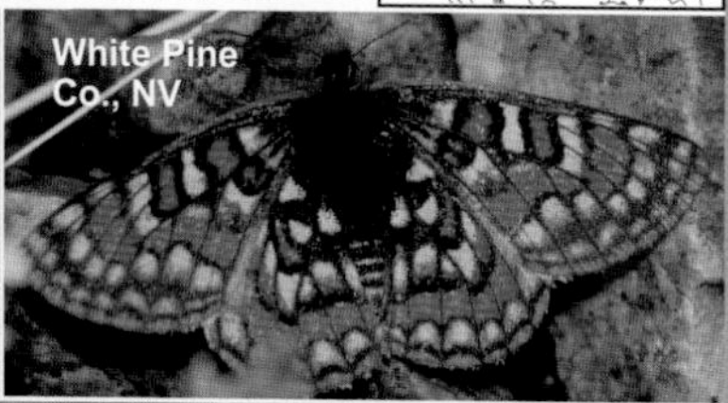
White Pine
Co., NV

red, when present,
is diagnostic
Tulare
Co., CA

kerspot *Euphydryas editha*

figwort family, especially White Turtlehead; and plantains, especially Narrowleaf Plantain

LU-LA mainly June-July, May-June southward

formerly restricted to wet meadows w/ turtlehead, now also occurs in dry fields w/ plantain

finally, a *Euphydryas* checkerspot that is easy to identify!

named for the orange-and-black colors of Lord Baltimore

prepare to be dazzled!

on the wing may appear to be small and mainly black

seen well, there is nothing similar in its range

caterpillar

rows of pale spots on black ground
bright orange marginal spots

rows of white spots on black ground
bright orange marginal spots

Baltimore Checkerspot *Euphydryas phaeton*

Twinberry Honeysuckle

LR
late June-July

wet mountain meadows

along with Relict Fritillary and Hayden's Ringlet, a northern Rockies specialty

caterpillars in web

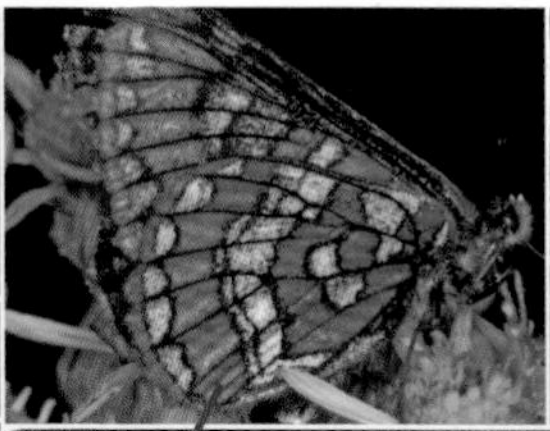

Twinberry
Honeysuckle

wide red-orange
submarginal band
black w/
white spots

Gillett's Checkerspot *Euphydryas gillettii*

hairy fournwort, water-willows, and other Acanthus family species

historically a RS to southeastern AZ, recently this species has become a regular, but R-U, late summer immigrant

mid elevation canyon washes and stream edges

small

black with bold bright orange bands

black w/ bold
orange bands

Elf *Microtia elva*

asters

C-A throughout warm weather

fields, meadows, roadsides, disturbed habitats

one of our most common and widespread butterflies

Pearl, Northern and Tawny Crescents can be very difficult to distinguish

considering that Pearl and Northern are probably best considered as one species, while Tawny is local and rare, you'll almost always be right if you call them Pearl Crescents

small, bright orange and black

flight is low to the ground

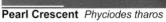

females w/ pm band paler
female

female

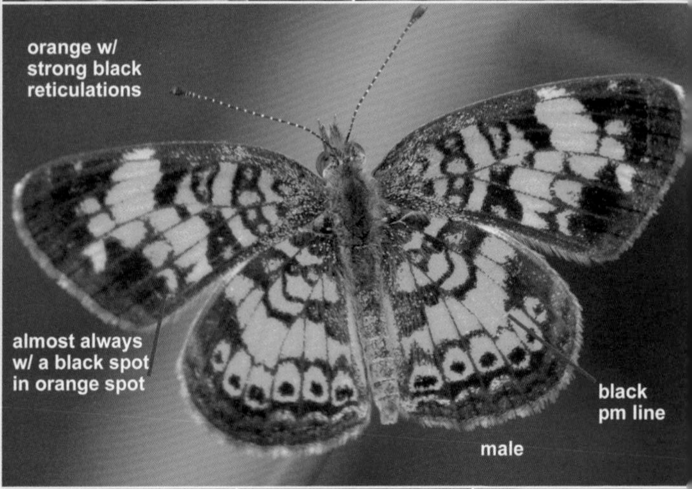
orange w/ strong black reticulations
almost always w/ a black spot in orange spot
black pm line
male

dark area
HW varies from highly reticulated (see insets) to pale w/ a dark crescent

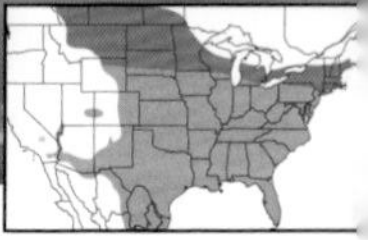

Pearl Crescent *Phyciodes tharos*

asters

C-A
mostly
June-July

openings in woods, fields, meadows, roadsides, disturbed habitats

of the orange crescents, only the three species on these pages, and Phaon Crescent, page 216, have a black spot in the orange spot along the FW innner margin

dark
area

females w/ pm
band paler
female

male
black
spot
no black
pm line

Northern Crescent *Phyciodes selenis*

asters

LR-U
mostly
June-July

woods openings and edges

northeastern populations disappeared in the 1970s, for unknown reasons

the crescents mapped in Colorado and Utah may not be this species

males especially with extensive black above

apex and
margin
are tan
black bar
usually straight
pale,
weakly
marked
HW

females w/ pm
band paler
female

wide black bar
black
spot
male
?

Tawny Crescent *Phyciodes batesii*

aster family

C-A throughout warm weather

many types of open areas from sea level to above treeline

in much of the West, the most frequently encountered crescent

usually appears as quite black above, other Western crescents appear to be primarily orange

underside varies from weakly patterned to highly patterned

antennal club color, often mentioned as a way to distinguish various crescent species, appears to be variable within each species

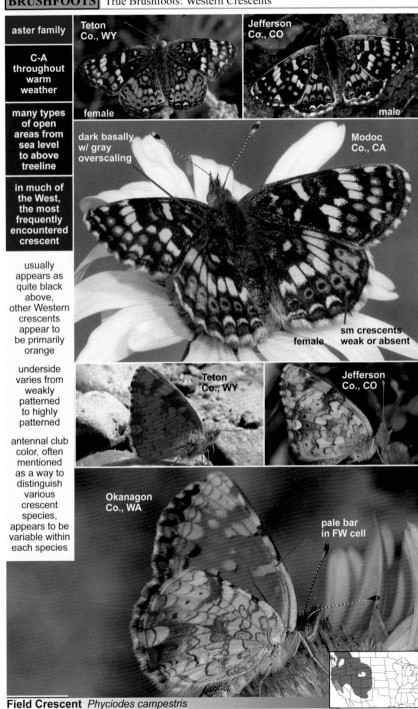

Teton Co., WY
female

Jefferson Co., CO
male

dark basally w/ gray overscaling
Modoc Co., CA
female
sm crescents weak or absent

Teton Co., WY

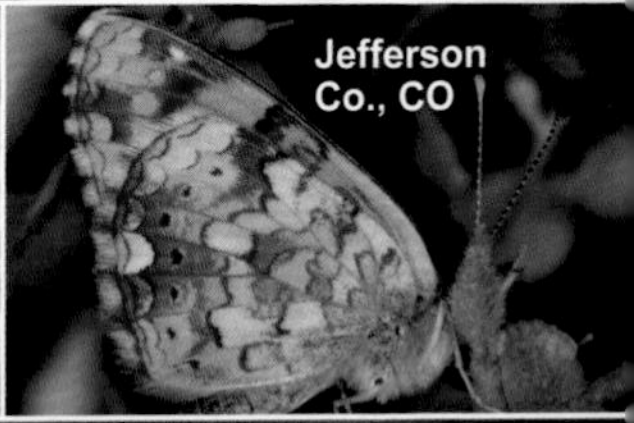
Jefferson Co., CO

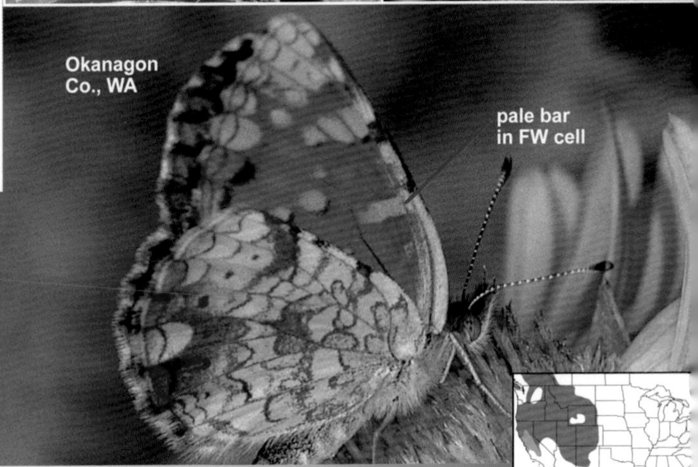
Okanagon Co., WA
pale bar in FW cell

Field Crescent *Phyciodes campestris*

aster family

U in the California mountains, one brood high, mainly July-early Aug

especially in the mid to high California Sierra Nevada, but also elsewhere, some populations have much orange

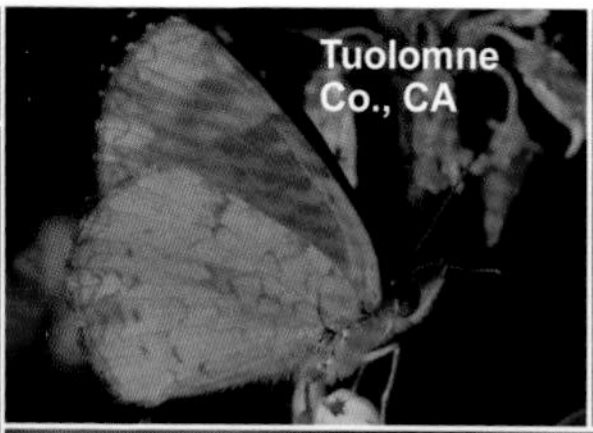
Tuolomne
Co., CA

Del Norte
Co., CA
male

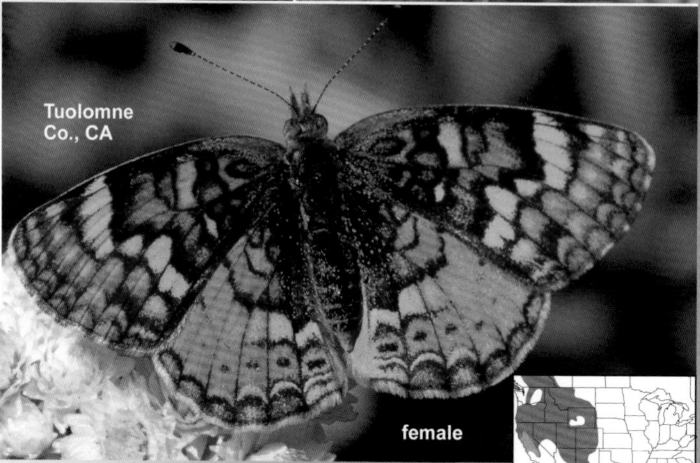
Tuolomne
Co., CA
female

Field Crescent *Phyciodes campestris*

thistles

LR-LU mostly Mar-June, July-Aug at high elevations

mountain streamsides

below similar to Mylitta, w/o FW black bar

in California Sierra Nevada, similar to co-occurring Field Crescent

if you're very lucky, and see an association with thistles, this will be a good clue to identification

Mono
Co., CA
male

Jackson
Co., OR
female

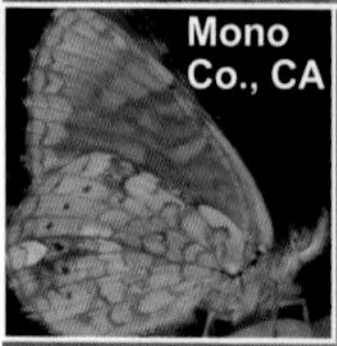
Mono
Co., CA

sm crescents
complete
Mono
Co., CA
female

California Crescent *Phyciodes orseis*

thistles

U-C
Mar-Oct

many types of open areas from sea level to above treeline

males often patrol paths and gullies

a Mexican subspecies is found in Nuevo Leon and could stray to south Texas

unlike the Pearl Crescent group, there is no black spot within the FW inner margin orange spot

males especially are brighter orange overall than other crescents in the range

from about southern Colorado south, Mylitta Crescents tend to have wide black FW inner margin spots

Jefferson
Co., OR

Lake
Co., CA
female

Jefferson
Co., OR
no black
in orange
spot
black
spot
narrow
male

Greenlee
Co., AZ

Dona Ana
Co., NM
female

Cochise
Co., AZ
male

Mylitta Crescent *Phyciodes mylitta*

thistles

LU-C
mid Apr-Aug

dry woods openings, arroyos in dry regions, prairie gullies

black spot in middle of FW inner margin is usually wide, Mylitta Crescents in range of Pale Crescents have a narrow spot; this is more definitive on underside, but unfortunately, can rarely be seen in the field

White Pine
Co., NV

White Pine
Co., NV

Jefferson
Co., CO
black
spot
wide

Pale Crescent *Phyciodes pallida*

Gregg's Tubetongue

C
through warm weather

thorn-scrub, gardens, wood edges

above, the orange ground color is strongly patterned with black

Elada Checkerspot, page 194, is smaller and lacks HW marginal pale crescents

below, the FW has black outlining pale areas

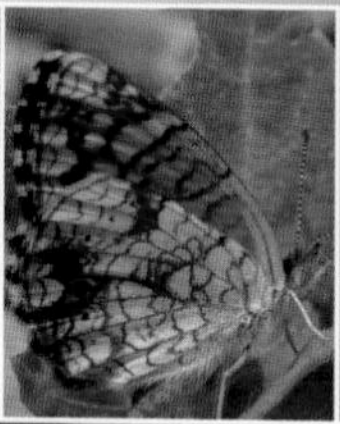
black
outline

female

male
w/o black
spot in
orange spot

Vesta Crescent *Phyciodes vesta*

fogfruits

Florida and south Texas C-A

elsewhere U

flying throughout warm weather

moist open areas w/ the foodplant, including gardens

over most of its range, the cream-colored median band is distinctive

may become established northward

wide
black
bar

orange

female

spot weak
or absent
cream-
colored
band
wide
orange
spots
black spot
in orange
male

Phaon Crescent *Phyciodes phaon*

acanthus family, including Sixangle Foldwing and Shrimpplant

LU all year

woods edges

a south Florida specialty whose population numbers vary greatly from year to year

pale sm band
borderd by
crescents

male

female
three large
orange spots
narrow,
even
black
line

Cuban Crescent *Phyciodes (Anthanassa) frisia*

Field Bindweed and aster family

LU-LC

southward Mar-Oct

northward May-Aug

moist areas in desert and dry grassland

even paler below than Phaons

the FW subapex is pale (see middle inset) where Phaon Crescents have a dark smudge (see left Phaon inset)

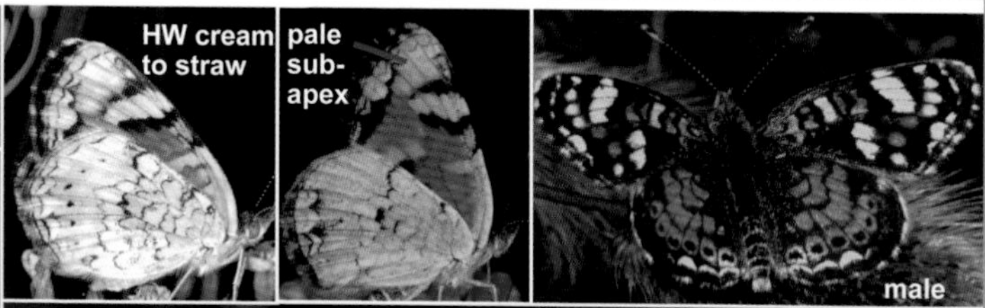
HW cream to straw
pale sub-apex
male

some sm spots pale
female
narrow orange spots
no black in orange spot
spot usually pale

Painted Crescent *Phyciodes picta*

unknown

perhaps overlooked due to their similarity to Painted and Phaon Crescents

underside is darker than on Painted Crescent

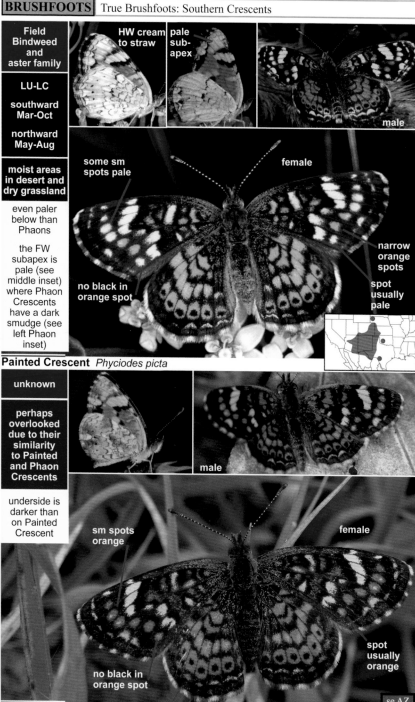

male

sm spots orange
female
spot usually orange
no black in orange spot

Mexican Crescent *Phyciodes pallescens*

se AZ
LRGV

acanthus family

where resident (three broods) C all year

decreasing immigrant northward, mainly June-Oct

trails and streams through woods or thorn-scrub, gardens

males love to patrol paths

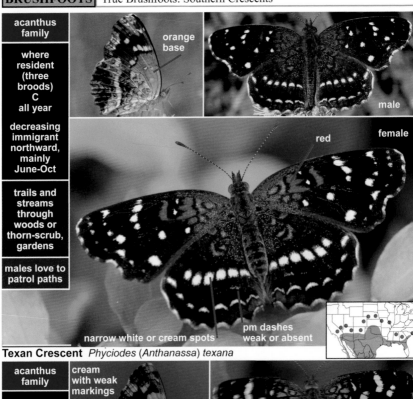

orange
base

male

female
red
narrow white or cream spots
pm dashes
weak or absent

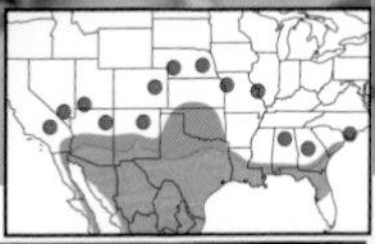

Texan Crescent *Phyciodes (Anthanassa) texana*

acanthus family

LRGV R-U sometimes resident for prolonged periods, sometimes absent

elsewhere RS

thorn-scrub and tropical woods edges

similar to Texan Crescents but with less red and with a wide cream HW median band

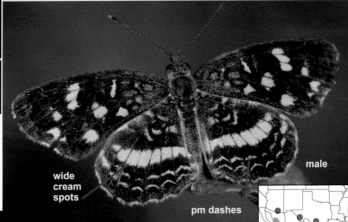

cream
with weak
markings

female

male
wide
cream
spots
pm dashes

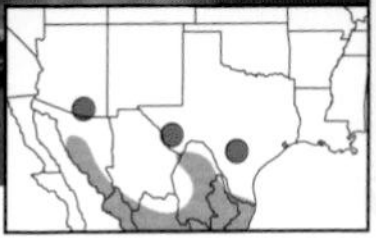

Pale-banded Crescent *Phyciodes (Anthanassa) tulcis*

unknown

males are chestnut and black and don't resemble any LRGV resident species

females are similar to Pale-banded Crescents, but the prominent white median band on the HW is white, not cream and there is no prominent pale spot along the FW inner margin near the wing base

gray w/ white patch

no pale spot
red
wide white spots
female
pm dashes

male

Chestnut Crescent *Phyciodes (Anthanassa) argentea*

LRGV

unknown

mottled HW

wide cream spots
pm dashes weak or absent

Black Crescent *Phyciodes (Anthanassa) ptolyca*

LRGV twice

water-willows

narrow white or cream spots
pm dashes

Ardent Crescent *Phyciodes (Anthanassa) ardys*

not yet LRGV

black form
(mainly summer)
horizontal
black bar

red form (most frequent in fall/spring)
margin
often violet

rarely
w/o dot

hackberries, nettles, elm family, and others

U-C
Mar/Apr-Oct

woods and adjacent open areas, suburbia

fall adults winter in tree holes and other shelters, then fly and mate in early spring, producing a brood that flies during summer

migrates south in fall, north in spring, overwintering north to about New York City

larger; flight more powerful w/ slower wingbeats than Eastern Comma

zigzagging flight often returns it to original perch

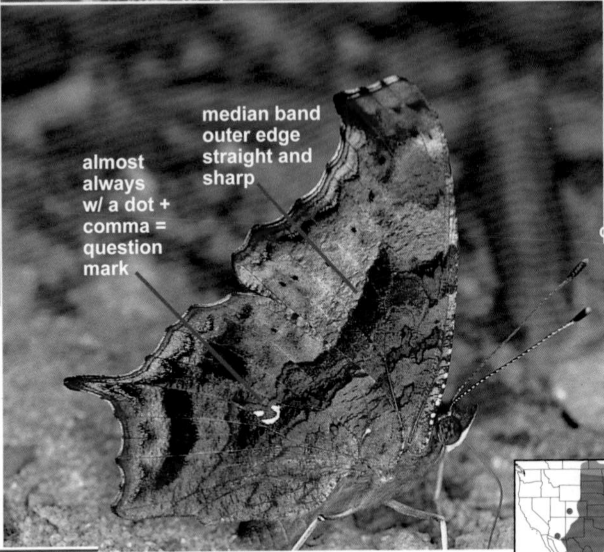
median band
outer edge
straight and
sharp
almost
always
w/ a dot +
comma =
question
mark

caterpillar

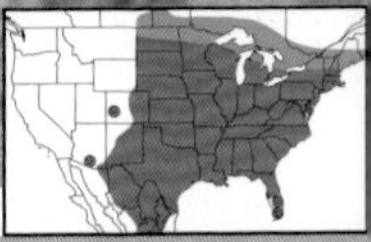

Question Mark *Polygonia interrogationis*

probably currants and gooseberries

very recently has been recorded as a rare stray to the Davis Mountains — may become resident

pine-oak woodlands

spots
faint or
absent

Spotless Comma *Polygonia haroldii*

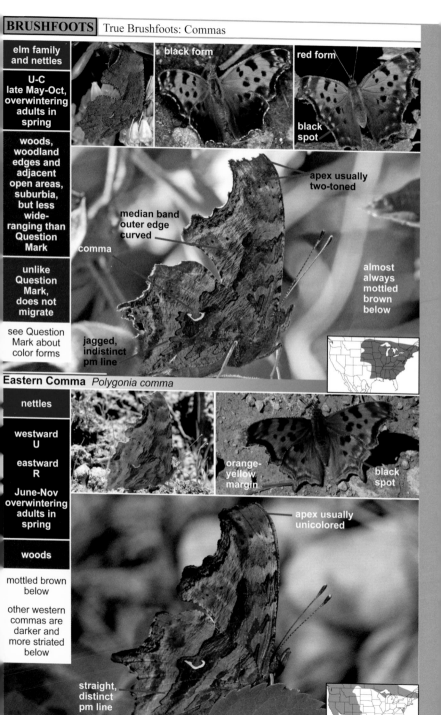

elm family and nettles

U-C
late May-Oct, overwintering adults in spring

woods, woodland edges and adjacent open areas, suburbia, but less wide-ranging than Question Mark

unlike Question Mark, does not migrate

see Question Mark about color forms

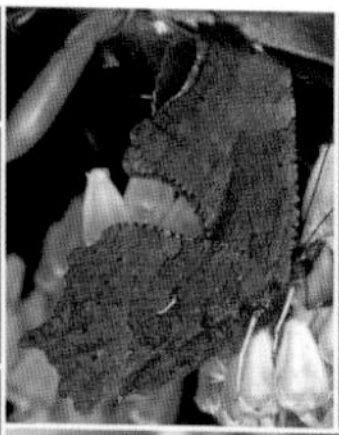

black form

red form
black spot

apex usually two-toned
median band outer edge curved
comma
almost always mottled brown below
jagged, indistinct pm line

Eastern Comma *Polygonia comma*

nettles

westward U

eastward R

June-Nov overwintering adults in spring

woods

mottled brown below

other western commas are darker and more striated below

orange-yellow margin
black spot

apex usually unicolored
straight, distinct pm line

Satyr Comma *Polygonia satyrus*

currants and gooseberries

C
June-Sept, overwintering adults in spring

woods openings and edges from sea level to treeline in the West; more restricted to Canadian zone forest in the East

some treat eastern and western populations as separate species

in the East, strongly two-toned
Coos Co., NH

no black spot
no, or faint, black spot
Mono Co., CA

Jefferson Co., CO
both FW and HW pale outwardly
heavily striated gray

Hoary Comma *Polygonia gracilis*

willows and birches

LR-U
July-Oct, overwintering adults in spring

moist openings in northern or mountain conifer woods or mixed woods

most individuals with obvious extensive green, but some individuals and populations are more subtly adorned with smaller green spots

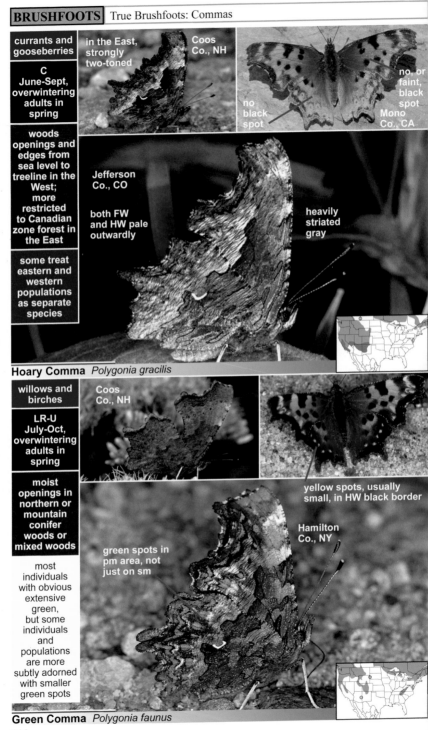

Coos Co., NH

yellow spots, usually small, in HW black border

Hamilton Co., NY
green spots in pm area, not just on sm

Green Comma *Polygonia faunus*

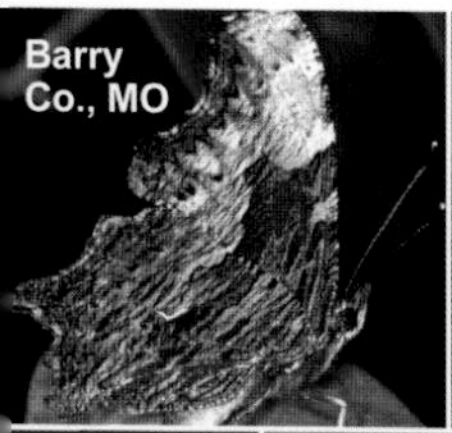
Barry Co., MO

Essex Co., VT

no black spot
usually w/ small yellow spots in HW black border

currants and gooseberries

R-U
June-Oct, overwintering adults in spring

deciduous woods

heavily striated, like Hoary Comma, but HW is not two-toned

Hunterdon Co., NJ
FW pale outwardly, HW not
long bar

Gray Comma *Polygonia progne*

currants and gooseberries

R-U
June-Sept, overwintering adults in spring

moist woods

some treat Oreas Commas as a subspecies of Gray Commas

similar to Gray Commas but ranges don't overlap

San Mateo Co., CA

usually w/ black spot
dark margin

often "blushing"
San Mateo Co., CA
about one-half the time w/ a very faint white spot here (as seen on this individual)

Oreas Comma *Polygonia oreas*

mainly willows, but also other trees and shrubs

U-C, but R in Florida, Texas, s California; June-Oct, overwintering adults in spring

mainly woods, but adaptable situations, including suburbia

some move south or downslope in the fall

comes to tree sap, rarely to flowers

dark w/
cream
border

deep mahogany brown
blue
spots
cream
border

Mourning Cloak *Nymphalis antiopa*

nettles

R-C June-Oct, overwintering adults in spring

moist open fields and meadows near woods

a few Small Tortoise-shells, a European butterfly, have been seen in the Northeast; these may be strays or accidental or deliberate imports

smaller than other tortoiseshells

dark w/ broad paler
pm band
Small Tortoiseshell,
Nymphalis urticae
paler
pm band
bright
orange
sm band

Milbert's Tortoiseshell *Nymphalis milberti*

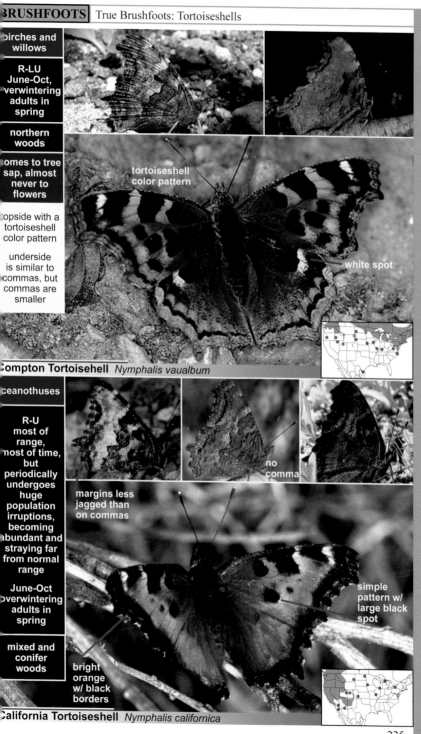

birches and willows

R-LU
June-Oct, overwintering adults in spring

northern woods

comes to tree sap, almost never to flowers

topside with a tortoiseshell color pattern

underside is similar to commas, but commas are smaller

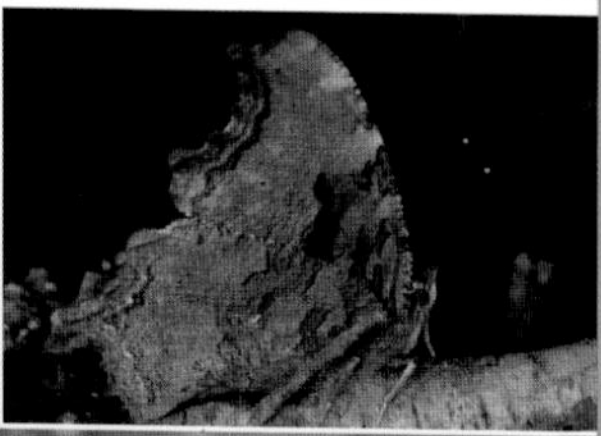

tortoiseshell color pattern
white spot

Compton Tortoisehell *Nymphalis vaualbum*

ceanothuses

R-U
most of range, most of time, but periodically undergoes huge population irruptions, becoming abundant and straying far from normal range

June-Oct
overwintering adults in spring

mixed and conifer woods

no comma

margins less jagged than on commas
simple pattern w/ large black spot
bright orange w/ black borders

California Tortoiseshell *Nymphalis californica*

thistles and many others in many families

R-A, depending upon year and location

any open areas

doesn't survive winter freezes; repopulates north each year from Mexico, often with dramatic flights

the planet's most cosmopolitan butterfly

four small eye-spots
HW w/ cobweb pattern
pale

often w/ pink suffusion

black band usually thick and "closed"
apex not strongly squared

Painted Lady *Vanessa cardui*

pearly everlastings and other aster family

mainly U-C but R in Northwest Mar-Nov

any open areas

remember "American Ladies have big eyes"

averages smaller with a less powerful flight than Painted Lady

caterpillar

cobweb pattern

two large eyespots
black bar broken
black band usually missing (or thin)
apex strongly squared
usually (but not always — see top right inset) w/ white dot

American Lady *Vanessa virginiensis*

mallow family

R-U
Mar-Nov

a wide variety open habitats, including disturbed areas and gardens

the most range-restricted lady in the continental United States (but see pg 400 for Kamahameha Lady in Hawaii), this species still manages to cover a lot of ground

pink
black
bar
crosses
cell

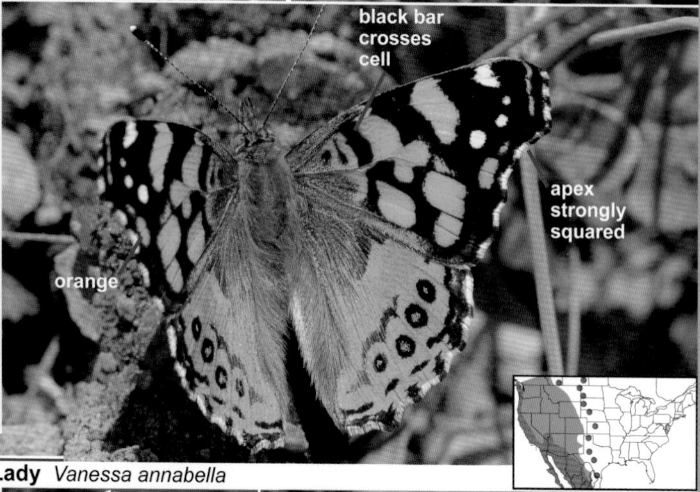
black bar
crosses
cell
apex
strongly
squared
orange

West Coast Lady *Vanessa annabella*

nettles

U-C
Mar-Nov in Southwest, mainly May-Oct elsewhere

any open areas, including urban areas

similarly to Painted Ladies, Red Admirals don't survive freezing winters and often have spectacular movements northward

often flies by one with a whirlygig flight

red,
white,
and blue!

bright
orange to
red-orange
band

Red Admiral *Vanessa atalanta*

figwort family, but also others

most of range C-A

decreasing immigrant northward

through warm weather

open areas, including fields, prairie, gardens, disturbed areas and beaches

a favorite! moves north in spring, south in fall, especially on east coast

orange bars
cream band
orange bars
cream
large eyespots
wide orange sm band

Common Buckeye *Junonia coenia*

Black Mangrove

LU all year; also reported from south Texas, but I have seen no credible records

Black Mangrove swamps and nearby areas

population relationships of the buckeyes is complex and the best taxonomic treatment is uncertain

averages larger than other buckeyes

orange band
orange
large eyespots
wide orange sm band

Mangrove Buckeye *Junonia evarete*

figwort family, including twintips and false-foxgloves

U-C
all year

dry
open areas

in south Texas, intermediates vary in appearance from typical Common to very dark; there appears to be much hybridization and the taxonomy of buckeyes is very uncertain

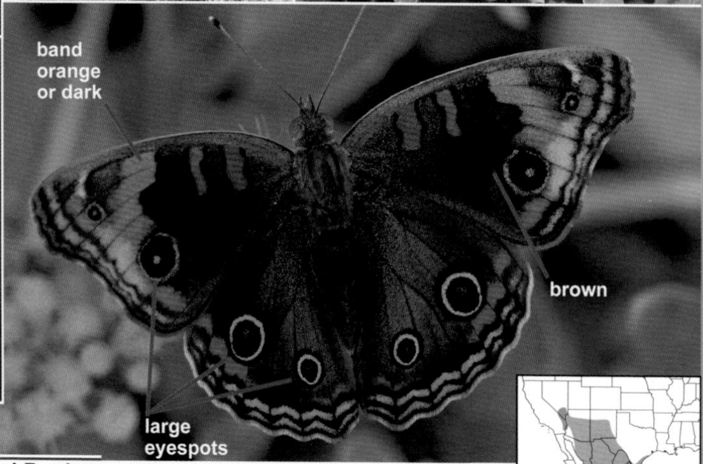
band orange or dark
brown
large eyespots

'Dark' Tropical Buckeye *Junonia genoveva nigrosuffusa*

porterweeds and probably others in the verbena family

LR
all year

open areas

abundance varies year to year

at the very least, appears to hybridize with Common Buckeyes

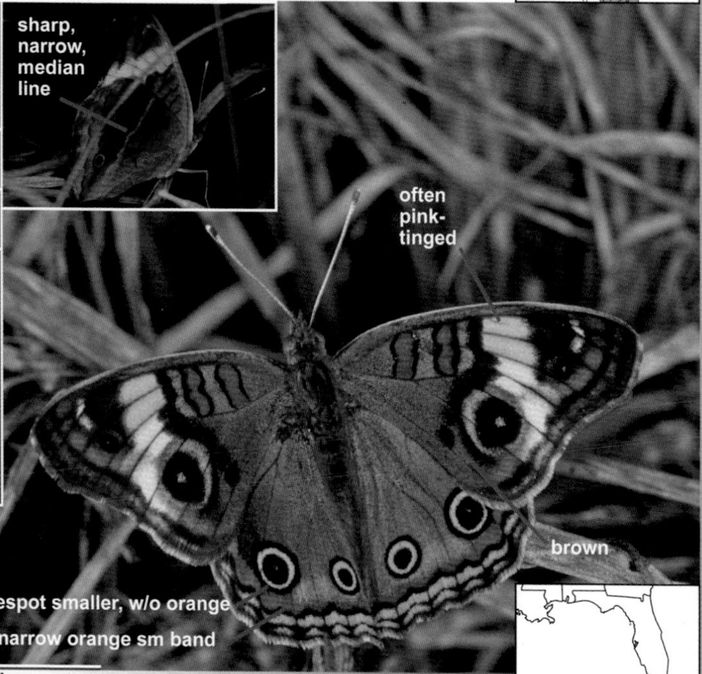
sharp, narrow, median line
often pink-tinged
brown
eyespot smaller, w/o orange
narrow orange sm band

Tropical Buckeye *Junonia genoveva*

mostly water-hyssops and fogfruits, but also others in the verbena, figwort and acanthus families

south Florida and LRGV
C-A
all year

northward
R-U
mostly in fall

open areas, gardens

often with less orange in Texas, compared to Florida

flight is usually low, with rapid wingbeats

silvery white
eyespots

White Peacock *Anartia jatrophae*

acanthus family

RS to LRGV
some years becomes temporarily established

disturbed open areas, gardens, thorn-scrub

median bands white or cream
red spots

Banded Peacock *Anartia fatima*

acanthus family

reported a few times in the early 1970s from the Lower Keys

large white patch
small tail

Cuban Peacock *Anartia chrysopelea*

FL Keys

acanthus family

south Florida LU

south Texas U all year

tropical woods, gardens

a flying emerald

the only large green butterfly in the United States

flight is graceful

Malachite *Siproeta stelenes*

nettle family

LRGV once?

Orange Mapwing *Hypanartia lethe*

LRGV once, Houston once, NM once

acanthus family

Lorquin's Admiral, pg 231, is much smaller, w/o tails

possibly zoo escapees

Rusty-tipped Page *Siproeta epaphus*

an African species that has become established in the Carribean and is capable of wandering widely

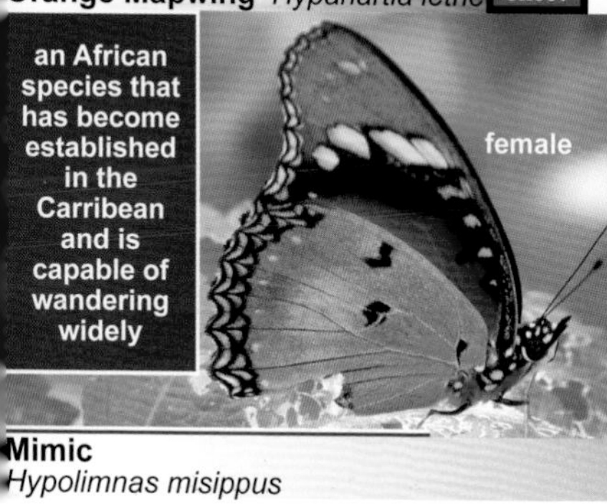

multiple families

Mimic
Hypolimnas misippus

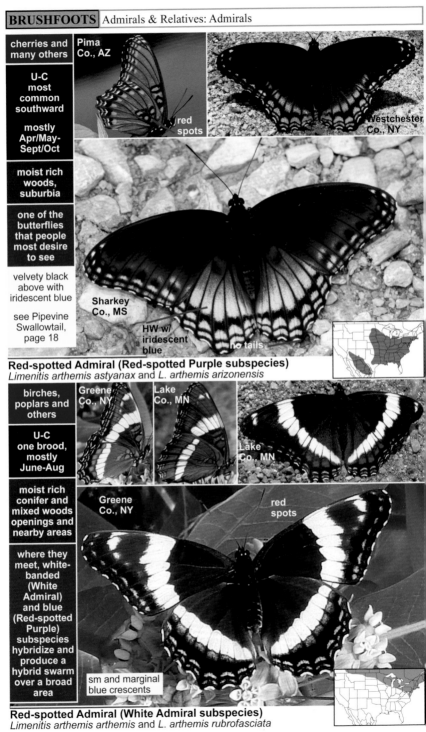

cherries and many others

U-C
most common southward

mostly Apr/May-Sept/Oct

moist rich woods, suburbia

one of the butterflies that people most desire to see

velvety black above with iridescent blue

see Pipevine Swallowtail, page 18

Pima
Co., AZ
red
spots

Westchester
Co., NY

Sharkey
Co., MS
HW w/
iridescent
blue
no tails

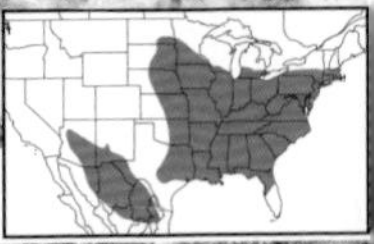

Red-spotted Admiral (Red-spotted Purple subspecies)
Limenitis arthemis astyanax and *L. arthemis arizonensis*

birches, poplars and others

U-C
one brood, mostly June-Aug

moist rich conifer and mixed woods openings and nearby areas

where they meet, white-banded (White Admiral) and blue (Red-spotted Purple) subspecies hybridize and produce a hybrid swarm over a broad area

Greene
Co., NY

Lake
Co., MN

Lake
Co., MN

Greene
Co., NY
red
spots
sm and marginal
blue crescents

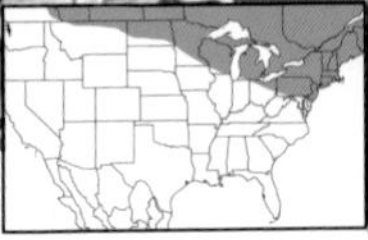

Red-spotted Admiral (White Admiral subspecies)
Limenitis arthemis arthemis and *L. arthemis rubrofasciata*

willows, poplars and others

C-A

two brood areas Apr-Sept

one brood areas June-Aug

moist rich woods openings and nearby areas

see California Sister, page 234, which has a round FW orange patch that doesn't reach the border

Modoc
Co., CA

Okanogan
Co., WA

wing base white w/
brown markings
white spot in cell
FW border
orange-brown
Tuolomne
Co., CA

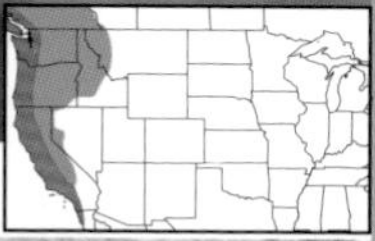

Lorquin's Admiral
Limenitis lorquini

willows, aspens and others

U-C
June-Aug

moist mountain woods, riparian areas in dry country

sometimes hybridizes with Lorquin's Admirals where they meet

there is also a population in the Sierra del Carmen of northern Coahuila, Mexico

Lawrence
Co., SD

wing base white w/
black markings
usually w/ white
spot in cell
Teton
Co., WY
sm pale spots, but
no marginal spots

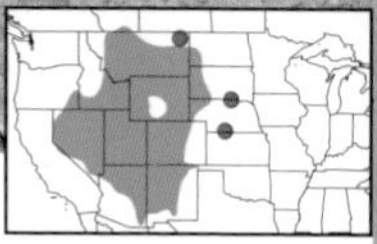

Weidemeyer's Admiral
Limenitis weidemeyerii

willows

U-C
South
Apr-Oct;
North
mostly
June-Sept

open wetlands and nearby areas

northward, Viceroys mimic Monarchs; southward they mimic Queens and are darker

smaller than Monarchs, Viceroys fly with shallow wingbeats; Monarchs fly with wings in a V

Chesa-
peake
Co.,
VA
Citrus
Co.,
FL
Okechobee
Co., FL
caterpillar
Sussex
Co., NJ
black
pm line

Viceroy *Limenitis archippus*

oaks

C
Apr-Oct

oak covered hillsides and canyons

usually fly high in and over oaks, when not puddling at damp sand or rocks

the California (*californica*) and southwestern (*eualia*) populations may be different species — and some treat them that way

californica
lilac band
weak and
erose
orange
here
wing base
lilac and
orange
eualia
lilac band
strong and
straight
no
orange
here
wing base
lilac and
orange
white
spots
large
orange
patch

California Sister *Adelpha bredowii*

indigoberries
a close relative – Twisted Sister – also has a band

white band crosses cell
LRGV

Band-celled Sister *Adelpha fessonia*

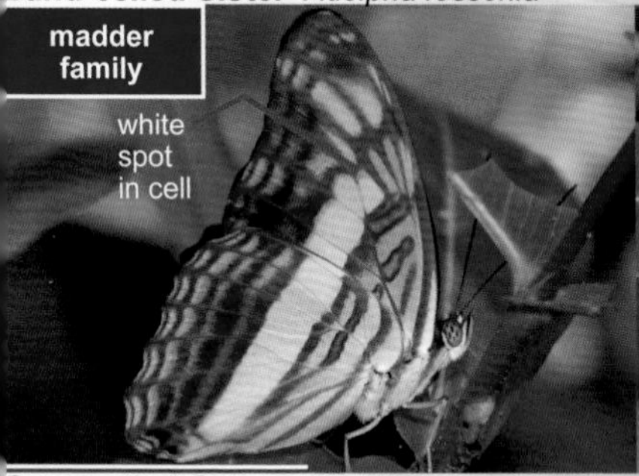
madder family
white spot in cell

white spot in cell
LRGV

Spot-celled Sister *Adelpha basiloides*

unknown
orange "eye"
three diamonds

no white in cell
orange "eye"
not yet LRGV

Eyed Sister *Adelpha paroeca*

Combretum
no orange "eye"
three diamonds

no white in cell
no orange "eye"
not yet LRGV

Bates' Sister *Adelpha paraena*

Vasey's Wild Lime

U-C all year

woods

not attracted to flowers

prefer shaded areas

can appear to be iridescent blue or purple, depending upon the angle of light

males lack FW median white spots that females have

often glide on flat wings with some flaps

underside resembles tree bark

male

horizontal blue/purple and black stripes
female

Mexican Bluewing *Myscelia ethusa*

noseburns

RS temporary colonist in Arizona

thorn-scrub, woods

not attracted to flowers

NW Mexican females are similar to males; females of other Mexican populations (see inset), which might stray to LRGV are very similar to female Mexican Bluewings

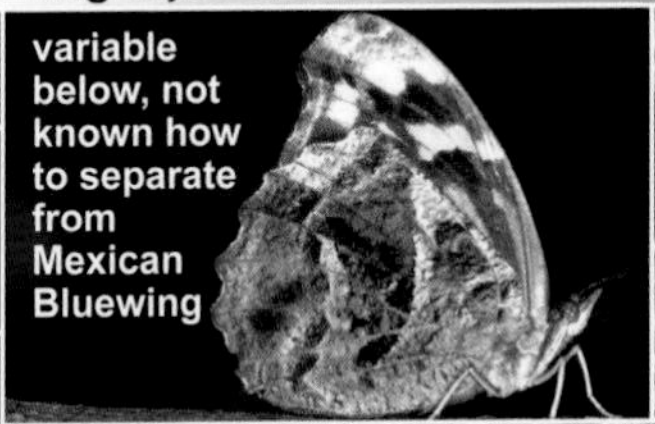
variable below, not known how to separate from Mexican Bluewing

female

male
FW w/ extensive black

Blackened Bluewing *Myscelia cyananthe*

oysterwoods

Florida LR all year; LRGV: RS

tropical woods

often lands head down on tree trunks

not attracted to flowers

Lignum Vitae Key may be your best bet to see this species

there are about 40 species of purplewings, all in the New World

falcate
pm chain of smal spots

falcate
strong blue iridescence

Florida Purplewing *Eunica tatila*

Gumbo Limbo in Florida; probably also other *Bursera* in Mexico

Florida LR all year

elsewhere RS

tropical woods

not attracted to flowers

Castellow Hammock Park, in Miami-Dade Co., is one of the more reliable spots to find this butterfly

rounded
two sets of pm spots

usually w/ little or no blue iridescence
rounded

Dingy Purplewing *Eunica monima*

noseburns

south Texas
U-C,
sometimes A
all year

northward
R
mostly
Aug-Oct

thorn-scrub, open woods

wanders surprisingly far afield, given its small size and weak flight

flight is slow and graceful, often hovering

white and gray
apricot HW borders

Common Mestra *Mestra amymone*

noseburns and others in the spurge family

LRGV
R

some years forms temporary colonies north to San Antonio

not attracted to flowers

this large satiny black butterfly w/ a red/pink squiggly HW submarginal band is difficult to misidentify – a Hostess cupcake with red icing!

Red Rim *Biblis hyperia*

soapberry family vines

although not resident in the LRGV, this spectacular species has been seen there in most recent years

woods

the iridescent blue and bright yellow striped males proudly carry the butterfly banner

yellow FW stripe

cream band
falcate
female

vertical blue and yellow stripes are striking
male

Common Banner *Epiphile adrasta*

LRGV

soapberry family

falcate

yellow tongue
falcate
evenly orange

Orange Banner *Temenis laothoe*

LRGV once

soapberry family

small

strong median line

smooth

Little Banner *Nica flavilla*

not yet LRGV

pumpwoods
a few reports; first seen in LRGV in 2011
huge
powerful flight
strong "stem"
red-orange antennas

LRGV Keys

Orion Cecropian *Historis odius*

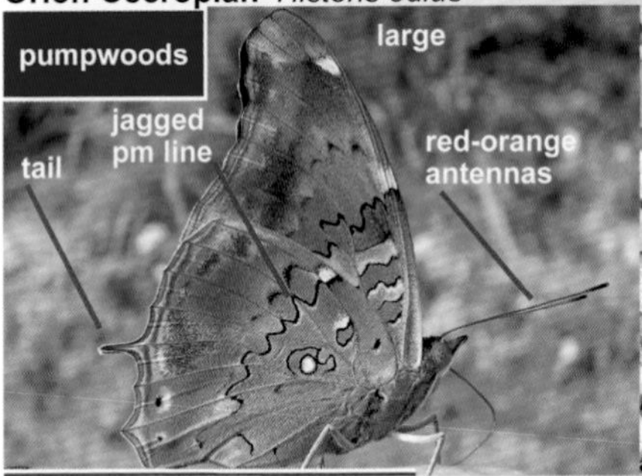
pumpwoods
large
jagged pm line
tail
red-orange antennas

Tailed Cecropian *Historis acheronta*

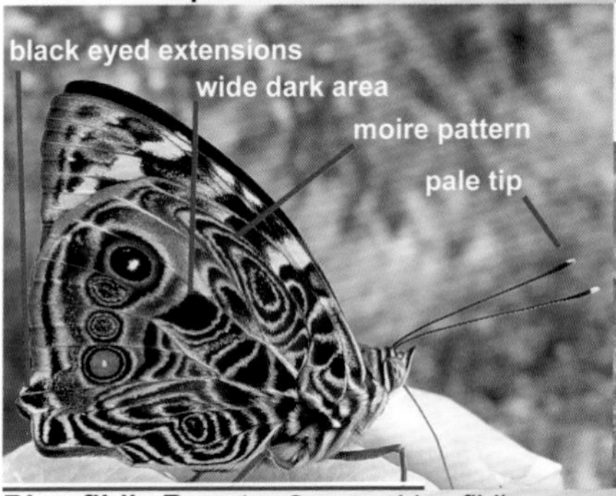
black eyed extensions
wide dark area
moire pattern
pale tip

female
pale tip
male

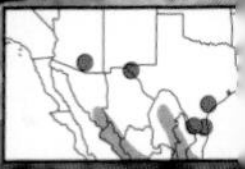

Blomfild's Beauty *Smyrna blomfildia*

not black
narrow dark area
moire pattern
black tip

black tip
male
LRGV once

Karwinski's Beauty *Smyrna karwinskii*

male
green-
gold

female
one white
band

Blue-eyed Sailor *Dynamine dyonis*

noseburns
brown
band
reaches
leading
edge
no orange
bar
cream

male
blue
FW w/
four
black
spots

two white
bands
female
LRGV

Four-spotted Sailor *Dynamine postverta*

soapberry
family
HW is self
descriptive

FW band
aqua or straw,
depending
upon
individual
and/or light

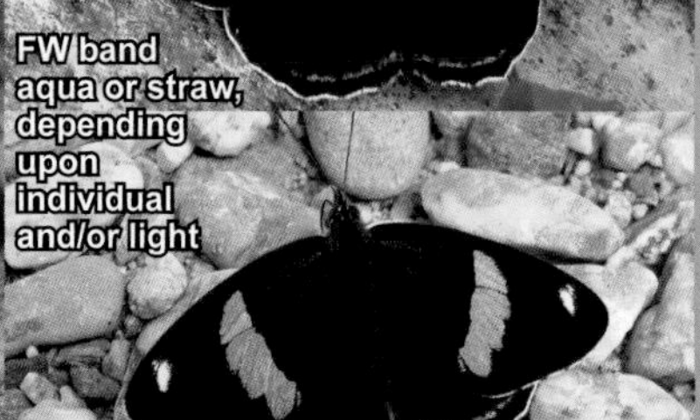
not yet
LRGV

Anna's Eighty-eight *Diaethria anna*

R
all year
woods
no white spot in black
brown
brown
brown
dull red bar
outlined
LRGV

Gray Cracker *Hamadryas februa*

brown
no brown
black w/ white center; two blue rings
outlined
no red bar
not yet LRGV

Brownish Cracker *Hamadryas iphthime*

R
all year
woods
strong white spot
tan
brown center; two blue rings
spot frosted
filled
red bar
black antenna
LRGV

Guatemalan Cracker *Hamadryas guatemalena*

weak, or no, white spot
tan
black w/ white center; one blue ring
spot not frosted
filled
red bar
LRGV twice

Variable Cracker *Hamadryas feronia*

no white
spot in
black

brown
some red

Pale Cracker *Hamadryas amphichloe*

FL Keys

white spot
in black

pm line less
intense than
on Gray
Cracker
brown
much
white
(on
male)
no red bar

Glaucous Cracker *Hamadryas glauconome*

se AZ
LRGV

large black patch
(on male)
black spots w/
blue centers
museum
specimen

black w/ blue center; two blue rings
little or no white

Black-patched Cracker *Hamadryas atlantis*

se AZ
once

red-orange

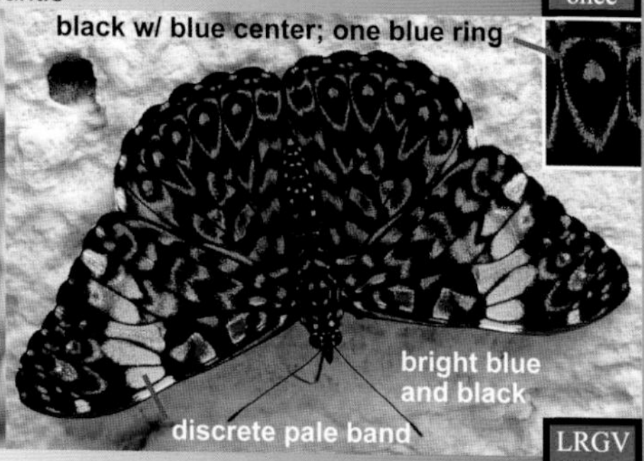
black w/ blue center; one blue ring
bright blue
and black
discrete pale band

Red Cracker *Hamadryas amphinome*

LRGV
once

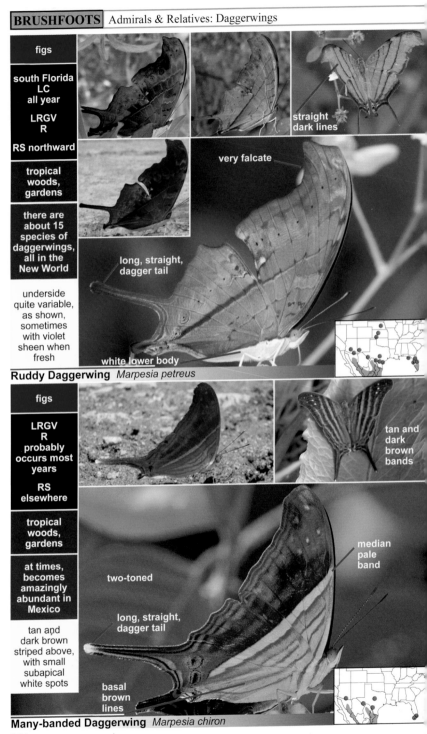

figs

south Florida
LC
all year

LRGV
R

RS northward

tropical woods, gardens

there are about 15 species of daggerwings, all in the New World

underside quite variable, as shown, sometimes with violet sheen when fresh

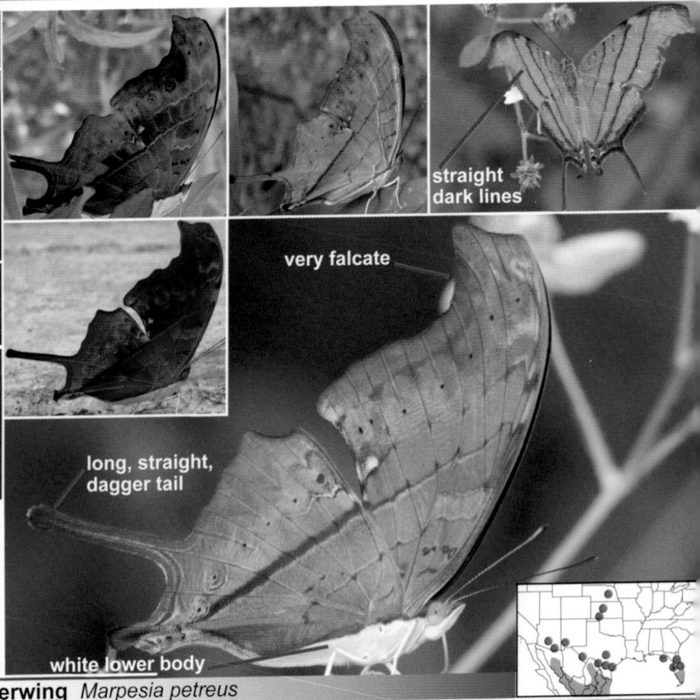
straight dark lines
very falcate
long, straight, dagger tail
white lower body

Ruddy Daggerwing *Marpesia petreus*

figs

LRGV
R
probably occurs most years

RS
elsewhere

tropical woods, gardens

at times, becomes amazingly abundant in Mexico

tan and dark brown striped above, with small subapical white spots

tan and dark brown bands
median pale band
two-toned
long, straight, dagger tail
basal brown lines

Many-banded Daggerwing *Marpesia chiron*

figs

RS
here are only a few reliable reports, one quite recent

smaller than Ruddy Daggerwing with a sharply angled median black line above and with a less falcate FW and less irregular wing margins below

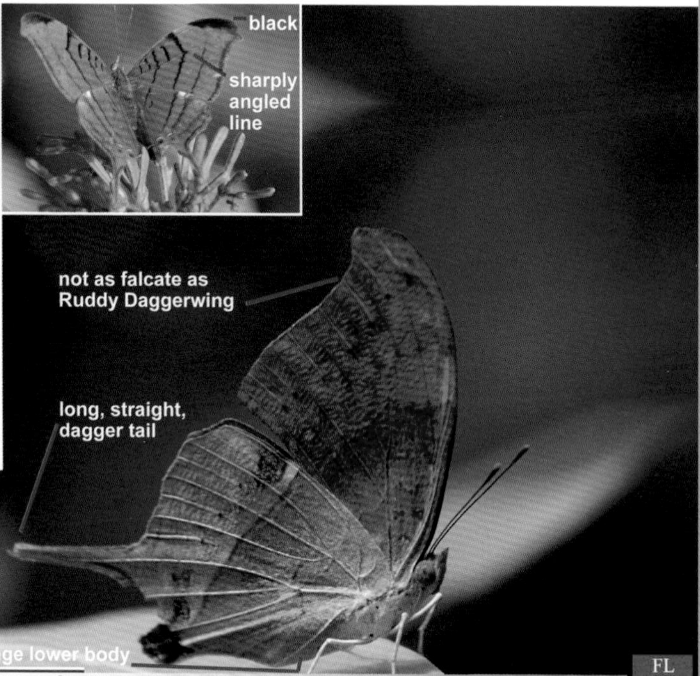
black
sharply angled line
not as falcate as Ruddy Daggerwing
long, straight, dagger tail
orange lower body

Antillean Daggerwing *Marpesia eleuchea*

FL Keys

figs

reported once from west Texas and once from south Texas

the validity of these reports is uncertain and, to the best of my knowledge, this species hasn't been reported from the Mexican states of Tamaulipas or Nuevo Leon

if you are fortunate enough to see one, you will be well served

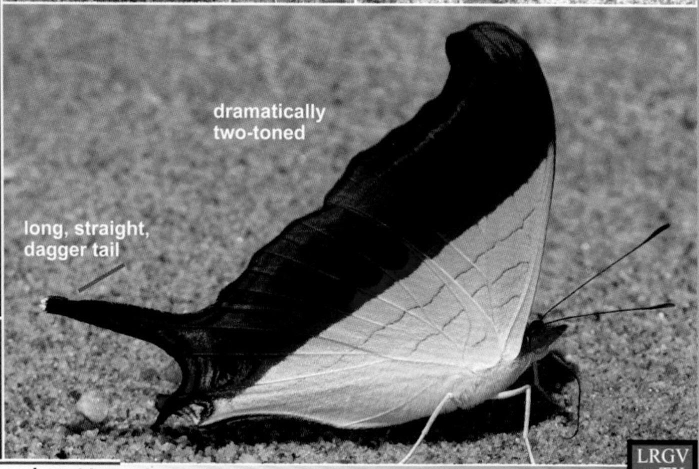
dramatically two-toned
long, straight, dagger tail

Waiter Daggerwing *Marpesia coresia*

LRGV w TX

crotons

U-LC
Mar-Oct

open woods, scrub

overwinters as an adult

larger than anglewings

fall brood individuals (see inset male) usually have more pointed wings than summer brood individuals (see main photo)

often sallies out from tree perches

female

male

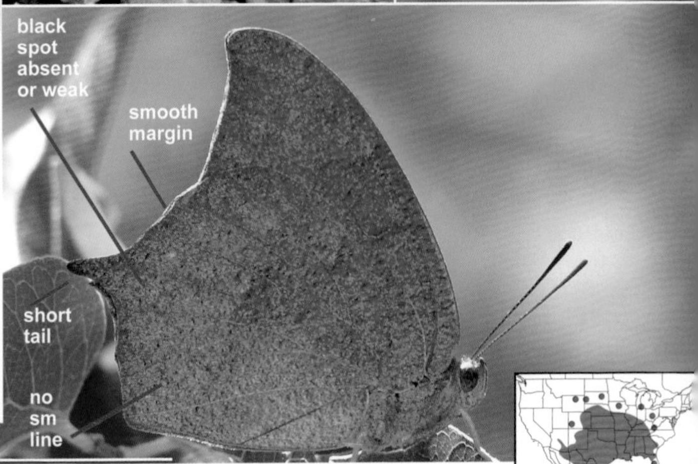
black spot absent or weak
smooth margin
short tail
no sm line

Goatweed Leafwing *Anaea andria*

Grannybush (a croton)

LR
Mar-Oct

pine rockland

formerly in much of south Florida, now a few at Everglades National Park, this may soon be the first full species of U.S. butterfly to become extinct — consider joining the North American Butterfly Association to save the rest

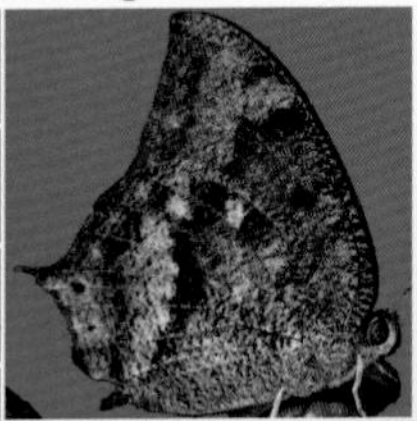

food plant

black spot
sm line

Florida Leafwing *Anaea floridalis*

crotons

C
all year

woods, thorn-scrub

adults live for many months

extremely variable underside

seasonal variation in wingshape: summer individuals usually with more rounded FWs than winter individuals

female

male

wavy margin at veins
sm line

Tropical Leafwing *Anaea aidea*

crotons

smooth margin
sm line

female

black band
male

not yet LRGV

Pointed Leafwing, *Anaea eurypyle*

crotons

sharply concave
wavy margin

no black band

LRGV

Angled Leafwing *Anaea glycerium*

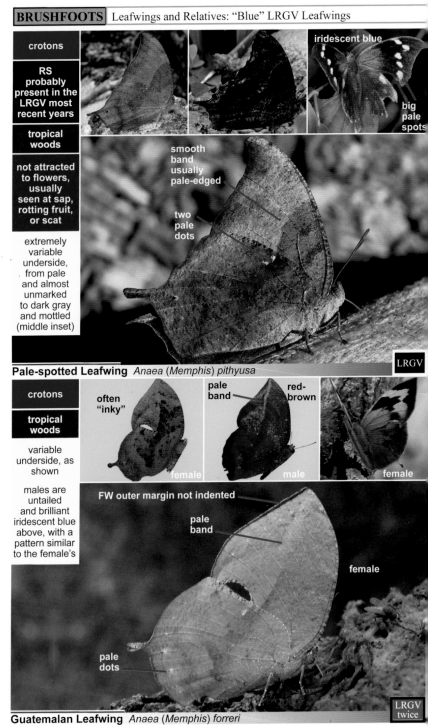

crotons

RS probably present in the LRGV most recent years

tropical woods

not attracted to flowers, usually seen at sap, rotting fruit, or scat

extremely variable underside, from pale and almost unmarked to dark gray and mottled (middle inset)

iridescent blue
big pale spots

smooth band usually pale-edged
two pale dots

LRGV

Pale-spotted Leafwing *Anaea (Memphis) pithyusa*

crotons

tropical woods

variable underside, as shown

males are untailed and brilliant iridescent blue above, with a pattern similar to the female's

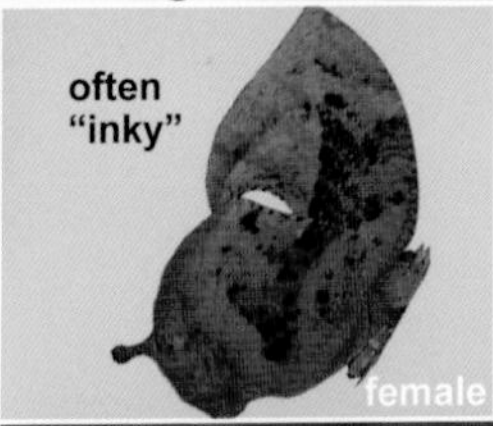
often "inky"
female
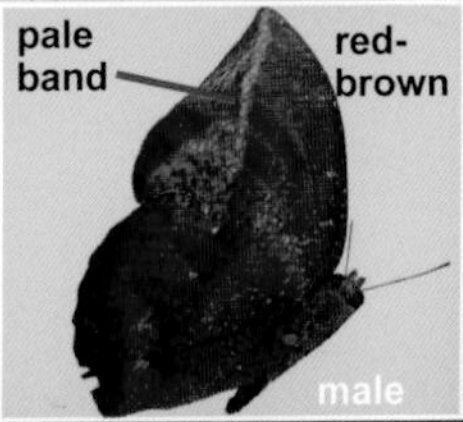
pale band
red-brown
male

female

FW outer margin not indented
pale band
female
pale dots

LRGV twice

Guatemalan Leafwing *Anaea (Memphis) forreri*

plants in a number of plant families

tropical woods

very large

iridescent blue bands above

see Orion Cecropian, page 240

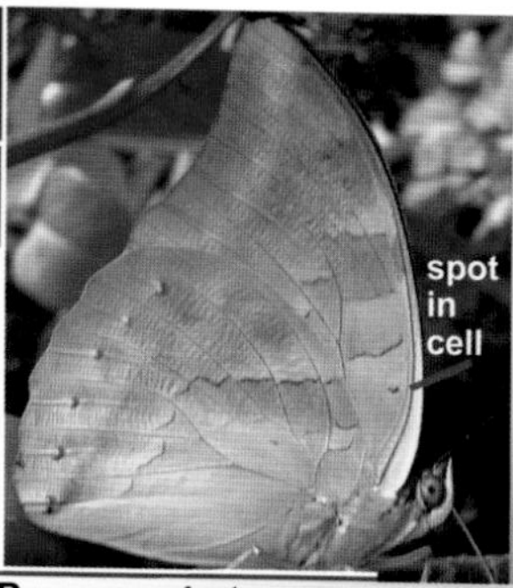
spot
in
cell

metallic eye

LRGV once

One-spotted Prepona *Archaeoprepona demophon*

Coco Plum

tropical woods

escaped from Butterfly World (a Broward County zoo) circa 2013. Now locally established

spots like
feathers
near the
nock of
an
arrow

south FL

Feathered Prepona *Prepona laertes*

plants in a number of plant families

huge and iridescent blue

not yet LRGV

Common Morpho *Morpho helenor*

multiple plant families

amazingly graceful

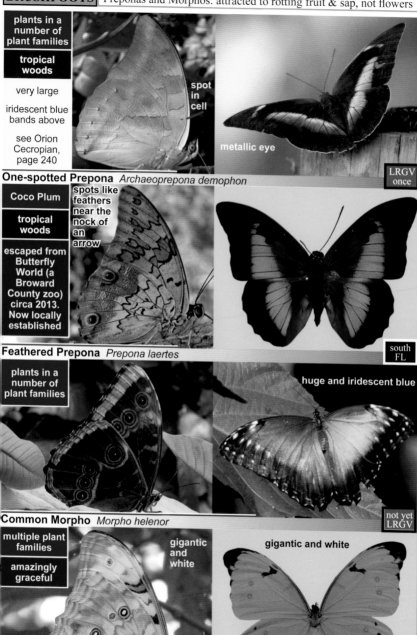

gigantic
and
white

gigantic and white

se AZ once

White Morpho *Morpho polyphemus*

hackberries

LU-A

LRGV all year

elsewhere mostly Mar-Oct

Dakotas June-July

anyplace with a hackberry tree, mainly woods

frequently seen on tree trunks

along with Tawny Emperor, the butterfly most likely to land on people, in search of the salts in perspiration

there is much geographical variation and some populations have at times been considered as separate species

rapid, nervous flight often brings it high into the trees

females with more rounded wings than males

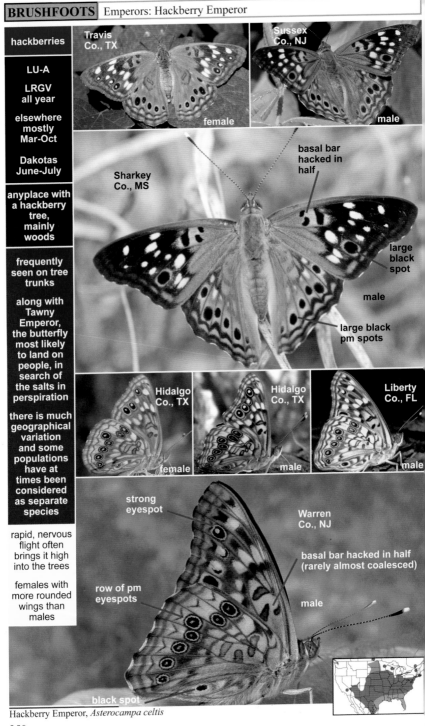

Travis Co., TX
female

Sussex Co., NJ
male

Sharkey Co., MS
basal bar hacked in half
large black spot
male
large black pm spots

Hidalgo Co., TX
female

Hidalgo Co., TX
male

Liberty Co., FL
male

strong eyespot
Warren Co., NJ
basal bar hacked in half (rarely almost coalesced)
row of pm eyespots
male
black spot

Hackberry Emperor, *Asterocampa celtis*

hackberries

most of range
U-C
May-Oct

LRGV
A
all year

western edge of range
R-U

anyplace w/ a hackberry tree, mainly woods

frequently seen on tree trunks

in some populations, females are much larger than males

there is much geographical variation and some populations have at times been considered as separate species

Tawny Emperors lack strong black FW eyespots

usually more orange above than Hackberry Emperors

Hidalgo Co., TX
female

Scott Co., MN
male

Sharkey Co., MS
basal bar crosses cell
no large black spot
large black pm spots
male

male
Sussex Co., NJ

Hidalgo Co., TX
female

thronging butterfly "brew"

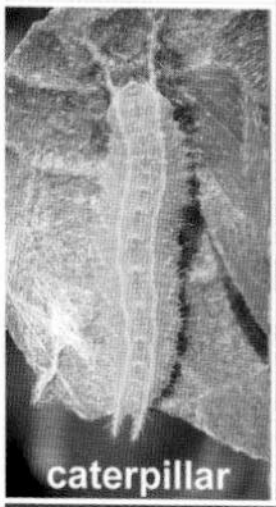
caterpillar

no strong eyespot
Hidalgo Co., TX
basal bar crosses cell
row of pm eyespots
male
no black spot

Tawny Emperor, *Asterocampa clyton*

hackberries, especially Spiny Hackberry

Arizona
C
Mar-Nov

south Texas
U
all year

dry woods, thorn-scrub, washes, canyons

most often seen on the ground on rocks, gravel or damp sand

two eyespots
bar crosses cell

male

wide brown bar crosses cell
female
two prominent eyespots
large black pm spots

Empress Leilia *Asterocampa leilia*

hackberries

also a possible stray to the LRGV

hilltops

probably best treated as a full species, distinct from Dusky Emperor, which is West Indian

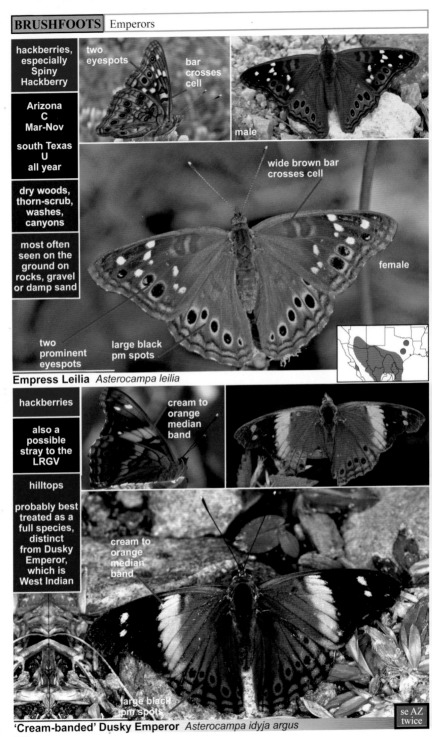

cream to orange median band

cream to orange median band
large black pm spots
se AZ twice

'Cream-banded' Dusky Emperor *Asterocampa idyja argus*

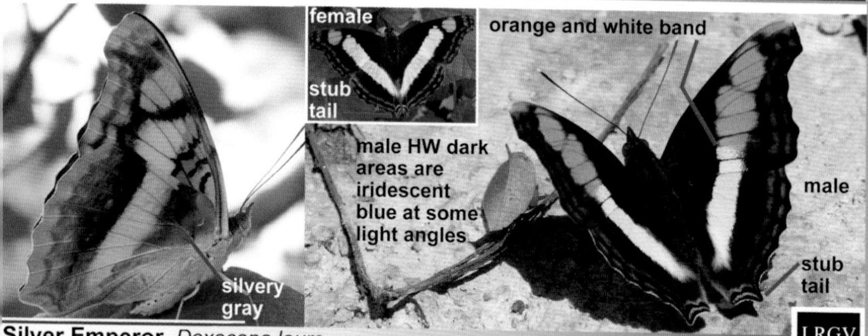
female
stub
tail
orange and white band
male HW dark
areas are
iridescent
blue at some
light angles
male
silvery
gray
stub
tail
LRGV

Silver Emperor *Doxocopa laure*

female
female
no
stub
tail
iridescent
blue-purple
male
LRGV

Pavon Emperor *Doxocopa pavon*

three brood areas C-A, all year

two brood areas, U-C, May-Sept

one brood areas R as immigrant

woods and gardens with hackberries

in big years in south Texas, millions of these butterflies can darken the sky

variable underside

ID certain if it sings Inka Dinka Doo

very long
palps (snout)
very long
palps (snout)
squared
apex

American Snout *Libytheana carinenta*

sedges

U-A, but LR-U at southern edge of range late June-early Aug

sedge-marshes, wet meadows

browns are larger than Little Wood-Satyrs, page 258

some populations in upper Midwest are quite dark, as shown in left inset

two spots w/
same intensity

pm line jagged
four eyespots in a "peapod"
smooth margin
pm line jagged
inwardly directed "tooth"

Eyed Brown *Satyrodes eurydice*

sedges

R-C, three brood area Apr-Oct; two brood May-Aug; one brood June-Aug

wet woods, swamps

this species and Eyed Brown may hybridize — there are individuals that seem intermediate between the two; there have been no studies of gene flow between these populations

top spot
less intense

each spot surrounded by white — a bull's-eye
pm line smooth
basal line straight
smooth margin
pm line smooth

Appalachian Brown *Satyrodes appalachia*

grasses

two brood areas
U-LC
May-Sept

one brood areas
LC-A
June-Aug

wet rocky deciduous woods

angled margin
clubs w/ black

Northern Pearly-eye *Enodia anthedon*

Giant Cane

LC
Apr-Nov

wooded bottomlands with cane

pearly-eyes are larger than browns, with angled HW margins

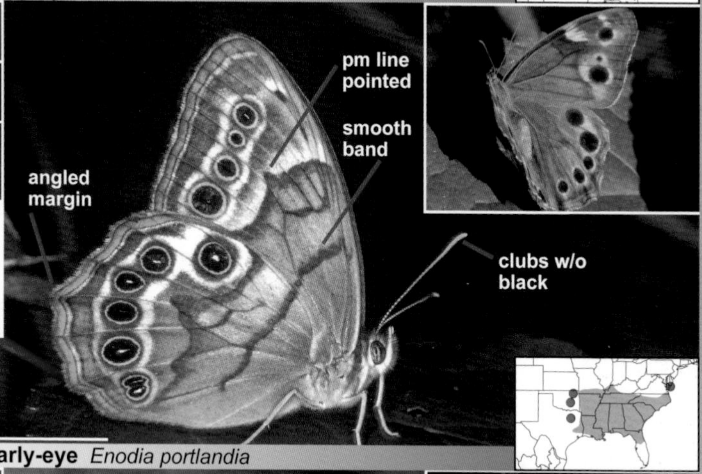
pm line pointed
smooth band
angled margin
clubs w/o black

Southern Pearly-eye *Enodia portlandia*

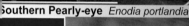

Giant Cane

LR-U
Apr-Sept

wooded bottomlands with cane

the least frequently encountered pearly-eye

pm line bulges
spiked band
angled margin
clubs w/ black

Creole Pearly-eye *Enodia creola*

grasses

C-A
May-Sept,
mostly
June-Aug

a variety of grasslands, including meadows, prairie, moist grassy areas in dry areas, and coastal marshes

larger than other wood-nymphs

the black line on the map divides most yellow FW populations from dark FW populations

Charleston Co., SC
White Pine Co., NV
Pennington Co., SD
bottom spot larger or equal in size to top spot, except that some in southeast lack bottom spot (see top left inset)
yellow or dark
Teton Co., ID
Mercer Co., NJ
Sussex Co., NJ
pm line not indented here

Common Wood-Nymph *Cercyonis pegala*

grasses

U-C
May-Sept,
mostly
July-Aug

grassy woods, especially with pinyon pine-juniper; moist grassy areas in dry areas

can be difficult to distinguish from Common Wood-Nymph

usually found in drier habitats than Common Wood-Nymph

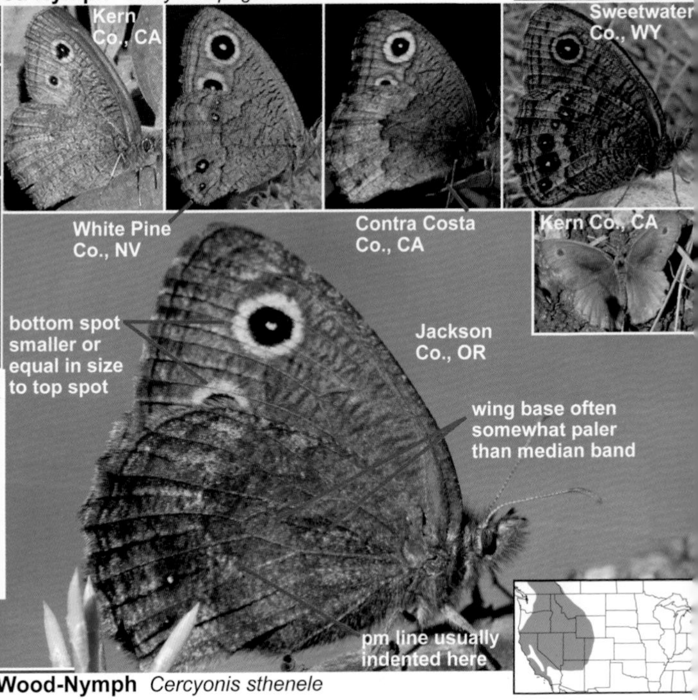
Kern Co., CA
Sweetwater Co., WY
White Pine Co., NV
Contra Costa Co., CA
Kern Co., CA
bottom spot smaller or equal in size to top spot
Jackson Co., OR
wing base often somewhat paler than median band
pm line usually indented here

Great Basin Wood-Nymph *Cercyonis sthenele*

grasses

Utah-Colorado south
U-LC
July-Sept

Wyoming north
R
July-Aug

grassy woods, sagebrush, canyons

Red Satyr, page 258, s smaller with only one FW eyespot, a straight HW pm line, and a black, not gray, eye

red-orange disk

ead's Wood-Nymph *Cercyonis meadii*

grasses

C-A
June-Sept

grassland, sagebrush, open woods

Okanogan Co., WA

Greenlee Co., AZ

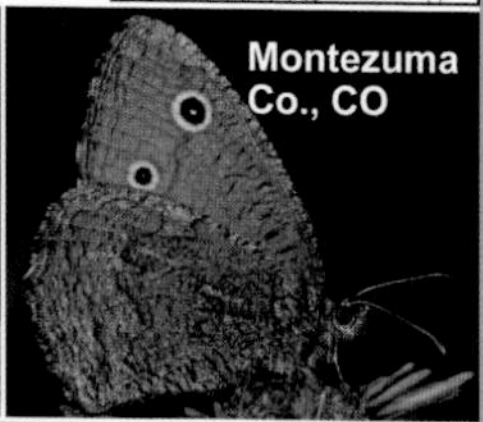
Montezuma Co., CO

a more frequent lower visitor than are other wood-nymphs

smaller than other wood-nymphs

Mono Co., CA
bottom spot smaller than top spot (or absent, as here) and displaced outwardly
pm band weak or absent
Modoc Co., CA
HW pm band with "twin peaks"

mall Wood-Nymph *Cercyonis oetus*

grasses

C-A
Apr-Sept
mostly
May-June

woods/grass edge; open grassy woods, brushy fields and meadows near woods

its size, larger than ringlets and smaller than wood-nymphs and browns, along with its characteristic bouncing flight, make it easy to ID on the wing

Morris
Co., NJ
eyespots

Alachua
Co., FL

large
eyespot
black eye

Little Wood-Satyr *Megisto cymela*

grasses

C-A
May-Sept

dry open woods and canyons

replaces Little Wood-Satyr in the arid Southwest

Canyonland Satyr, next page, has the FW below somewhat red flushed but lacks FW eyespot and has HW gemming

red-orange
disk

one large
eyespot
red-
orange
disk
black eye

Red Satyr *Megisto rubricata*

grasses

Florida and Deep South C-A all year

northward R-U Apr-Oct

LRGV U-C all year

grassy woods

some treat the populations from south Texas south as a separate species, *H. hermes*

usually flies within a foot of the ground, lower than Little Wood-Satyr

Hidalgo Co., TX
female
no eyespots
male
no large eyespot
slight bow in
straight
entire FW darkened basally
gray eye
Miami-Dade Co., FL

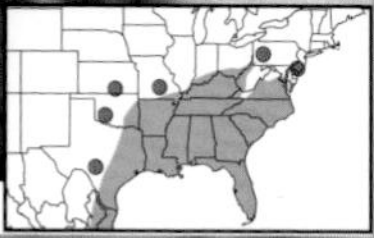

Carolina Satyr *Hermeuptychia sosybius*

presumably grasses

R-U probably all year

grassy woods

recently described and not yet evaluated by the NABA Names Committee

almost identical to the common and variable Carolina Satyr

topside of male is darkened only in the FW cell

slight bow out
straight

'Cryptic' Carolina Satyr *Hermeuptychia sosybius* form *intricata*

grasses

R-LC
Mar-Oct

grassy moist woods

Hidalgo
Co., TX

Hidalgo
Co., TX

Comal
Co., TX

most easily separated from Canyonland Satyr, page 261, by range

Colbert
Co., AL
gray patch
w/ "gems"
median
line bulges
inward

Gemmed Satyr *Cyllopsis gemma*

grasses

C-A
Apr-Nov

oak woods

until not too long ago, many treated the spring/summer and late summer/fall broods of this species as two separate species

pm line
reaches
lead
median line
is relatively
straight
gray
patch w/
"gems"

Nabokov's Satyr *Cyllopsis pyracmon*

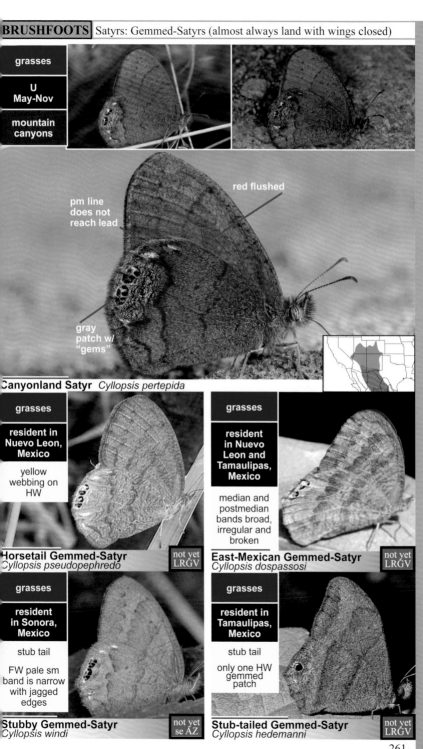

grasses

U
May-Nov

mountain canyons

red flushed
pm line does not reach lead
gray patch w/ "gems"

Canyonland Satyr *Cyllopsis pertepida*

grasses

resident in Nuevo Leon, Mexico

yellow webbing on HW

Horsetail Gemmed-Satyr *Cyllopsis pseudopephredo*

not yet LRGV

grasses

resident in Nuevo Leon and Tamaulipas, Mexico

median and postmedian bands broad, irregular and broken

East-Mexican Gemmed-Satyr *Cyllopsis dospassosi*

not yet LRGV

grasses

resident in Sonora, Mexico

stub tail

FW pale sm band is narrow with jagged edges

Stubby Gemmed-Satyr *Cyllopsis windi*

not yet se AZ

grasses

resident in Tamaulipas, Mexico

stub tail

only one HW gemmed patch

Stub-tailed Gemmed-Satyr *Cyllopsis hedemanni*

not yet LRGV

sedges and grasses

LC; Florida all year; two brood areas Mar-Oct; New Jersey June-July

wet grassy pine woods; pine-barren bogs in NJ

some treat the NJ and NC (and other) populations, as a separate species, Lakehurst Satyr, *N. helicta*; data supporting this treatment is weak

Ocean
Co., NJ

Osceola
Co., FL

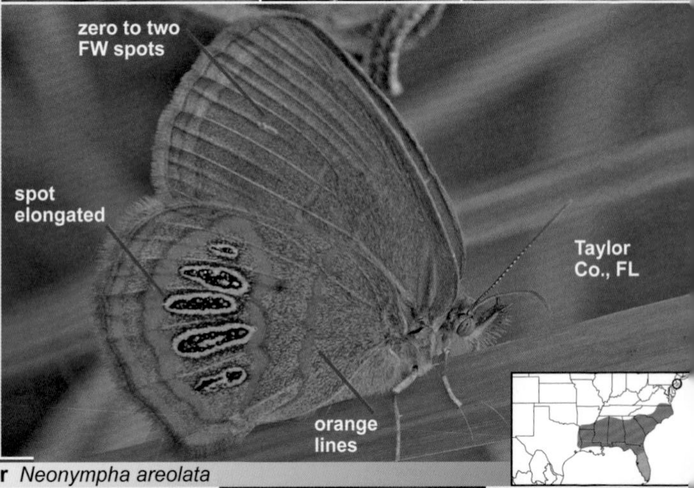
zero to two
FW spots
spot
elongated
Taylor
Co., FL
orange
lines

Georgia Satyr *Neonympha areolata*

sedges

LR southward two broods, May-June & July-Aug; northward one brood July

fens in the North; dense semi-shaded bogs in the South

federally endangered

the proximal cause of the New Jersey extinction was people who killed these butterflies as a hobby

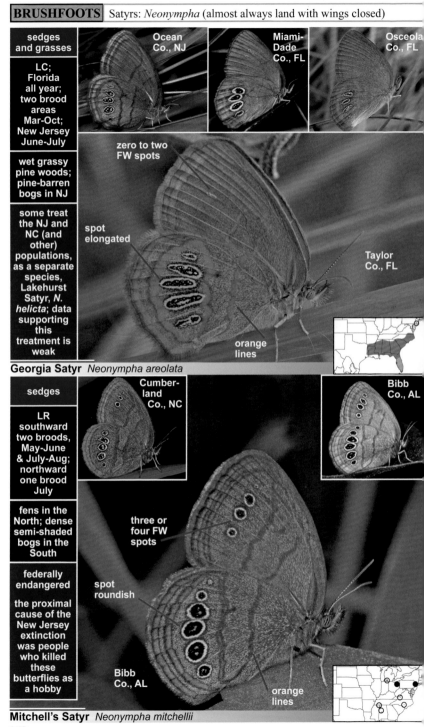

Bibb
Co., AL

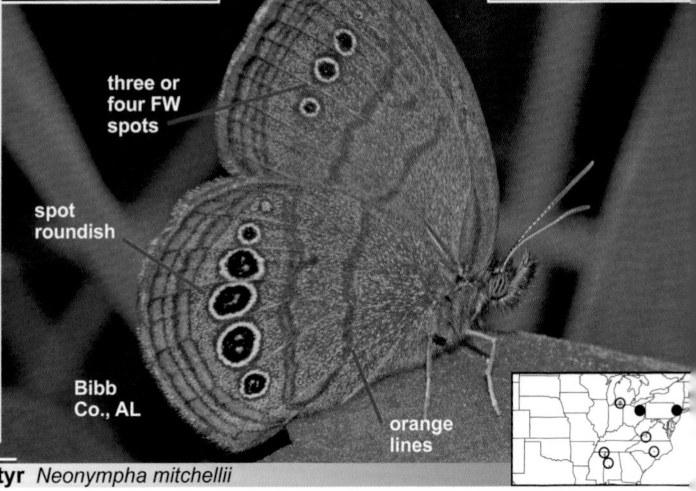
three or
four FW
spots
spot
roundish
Bibb
Co., AL
orange
lines

Mitchell's Satyr *Neonympha mitchellii*

Bullgrass and probably other grasses

C-A
Aug-Oct

mountain canyons in mixed or conifer woods

unmistakable! large and dark

white dots
broad pink-red/blue border

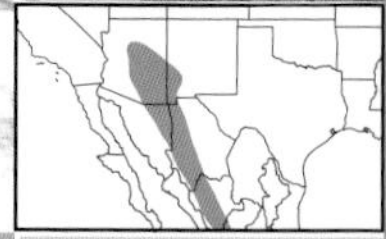

Red-bordered Satyr *Gyrocheilus patrobas*

unknown

first seen in the United States in 2011

very large

see Florida Purplewing, page 237

prominent curved pm band of eyespots

white spots

LRGV once

White-spotted Satyr *Manataria hercyna*

grasses

LU-LC
June-Aug

in U.S., limited to the Huachuca and Chiracahua Mountains

probably best treated as a subspecies of the central Mexican *xicaque*

a good-sized satyr with a pale HW pm band and a large and prominent FW apical eyespot

pale median band
mauve sheen when fresh

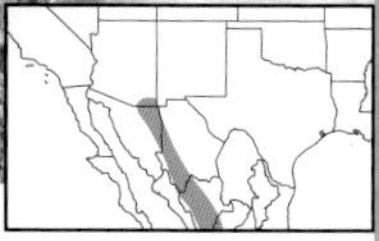

Pine Satyr *Paramacera allyni*

grasses

C-A
Apr-Sept,
mostly
June-July
in one brood
areas

open grassy
areas

having mutated to having two broods in the 1960s, the northeastern population has been moving steadily south, from southern Canada, now to West Virginia; it will reach Georgia along the Appalchians in about 40 years, unless global warming stops them!

small with bouncy flight and (mostly) bright tawny above

HW below is very variable, but with similar gestalt; quoting myself from BTB: West "As the U.S. Supreme Court has said about pornography, it is difficult to define, but you'll recognize it when you see it"

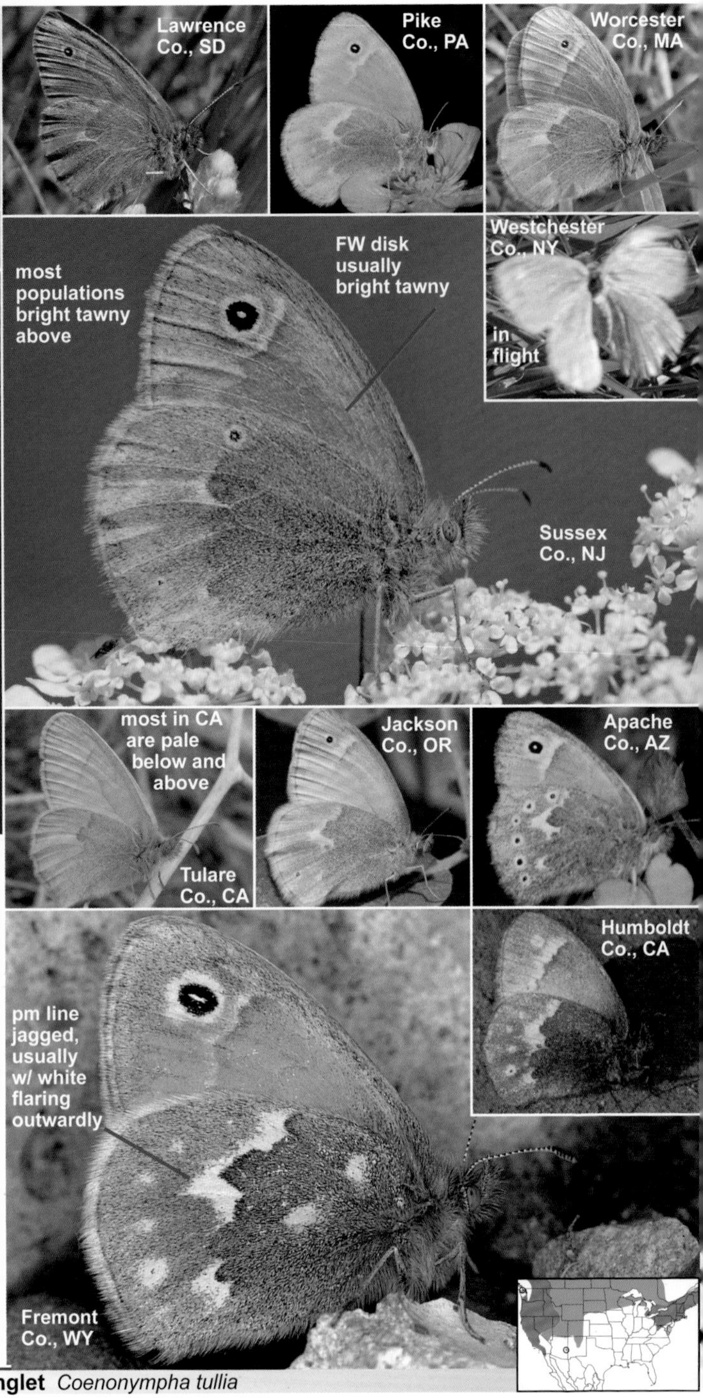
Lawrence Co., SD
Pike Co., PA
Worcester Co., MA
most populations bright tawny above
FW disk usually bright tawny
Westchester Co., NY
in flight
Sussex Co., NJ
most in CA are pale below and above
Tulare Co., CA
Jackson Co., OR
Apache Co., AZ
Humboldt Co., CA
pm line jagged, usually w/ white flaring outwardly
Fremont Co., WY

Common Ringlet *Coenonympha tullia*

grasses

U-C
late June-mid Aug

alpine and subalpine meadows

a U.S. Rocky Mountain endemic with a very restricted range

topside is soft gray/black

flight is slow

bright orange rings quickly fade to yellow (see right inset)

evenly dark brown ground color
marginal spots ringed w/ orange

Hayden's Ringlet *Coenonympha haydenii*

grasses

LR-LC
June-Sept

sagebrush, shortgrass prairie, open grassy woods

usually found when one disturbs an individual landed on the ground which then flies a short distance and lands; its camouflage attire blends with the earth, rocks and dry grass

"claws"

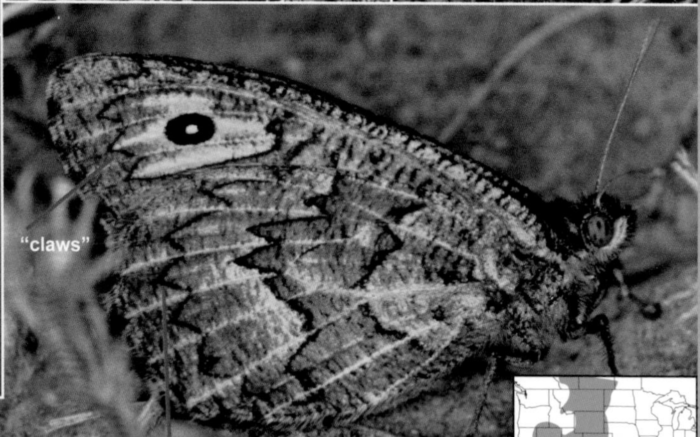
"claws"
very jagged pm line

Ridings' Satyr *Neominois ridingsii*

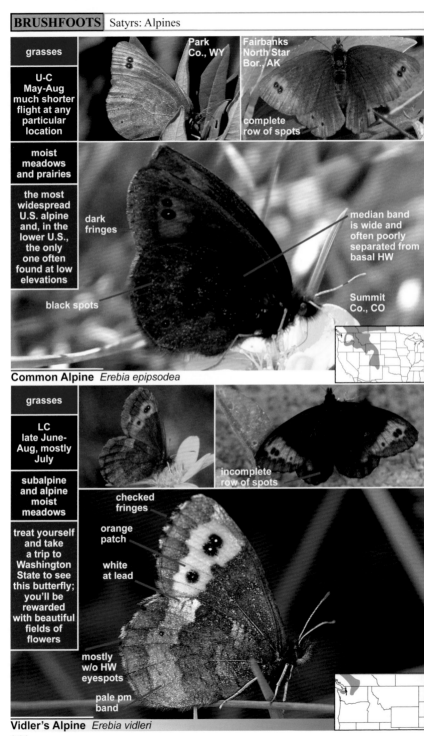

grasses

U-C
May-Aug
much shorter flight at any particular location

moist meadows and prairies

the most widespread U.S. alpine and, in the lower U.S., the only one often found at low elevations

Park
Co., WY

Fairbanks
North Star
Bor., AK
complete
row of spots

dark
fringes
median band
is wide and
often poorly
separated from
basal HW
black spots
Summit
Co., CO

Common Alpine *Erebia epipsodea*

grasses

LC
late June-Aug, mostly July

subalpine and alpine moist meadows

treat yourself and take a trip to Washington State to see this butterfly; you'll be rewarded with beautiful fields of flowers

incomplete
row of spots

checked
fringes
orange
patch
white
at lead
mostly
w/o HW
eyespots
pale pm
band

Vidler's Alpine *Erebia vidleri*

unknown probably grasses or sedges

LC
mid June-mid July

wet tundra

until recently, Taiga Alpine (this page, bottom) populations were treated as part of Disa Alpine

female

lower two eyespots as large as upper two, but displaced outwardly
pale, checked fringe
broad gray border
pale spot often prominent
male

Disa Alpine *Erebia disa*

unknown probably grasses or sedges

Canada + Alaska
LC

Minnesota
LR

late May-June

bogs and bog edges in Black Spruce and tamarack woods

widespread in Canada, this species is found in the Lower United States only in extreme northeastern Minnesota

eyespots w/o pupils
pale spot

Taiga Alpine *Erebia mancinus*

grasses and sedges

LU-LC July-Aug

alpine meadows

the combination of gray HW and reddish FW can often be seen in flight

when fresh, the topside often has a beautiful greenish sheen

Park
Co., WY

rusty patch juts
inward

extensive
rusty on FW
Hinsdale
Co., CO
soft gray
HW

Colorado Alpine *Erebia callias*

grasses

R-U July-early Aug

alpine scree and rockslides

some treat populations with a red patch on the FW underside as a separate species

upperside is all dark

northern Canadian and Alaskan populations have a reddish patch on the FW, see insets

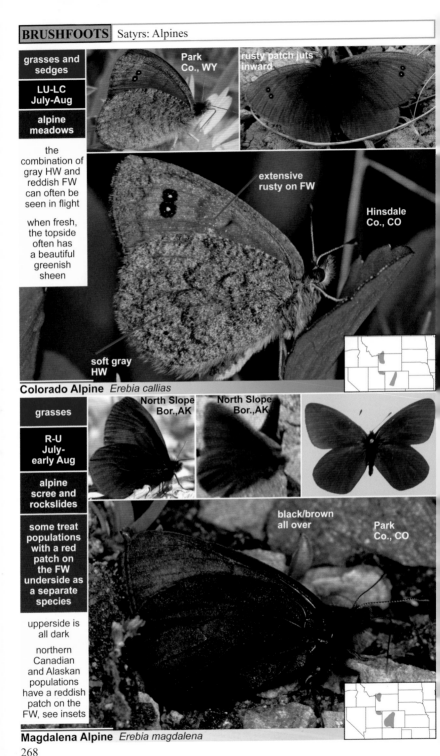

North Slope
Bor.,AK

North Slope
Bor.,AK

black/brown
all over
Park
Co., CO

Magdalena Alpine *Erebia magdalena*

bluegrasses

R-LU
Apr-
early June

bog edges, boggy open pine forest

flies in high grasses and sedges

this species holds a special place in my heart since I accidentally drove my car into a bog, leading to my finding the butterfly; the car, however, needed to be towed

rusty
disk
checked
costa
frosted
outer HW

Red-disked Alpine *Erebia discoidalis*

unknown

LC
mid June-
July

scree slopes, gravelly ridges

closely related to Four-dotted and Reddish Alpines, page 271

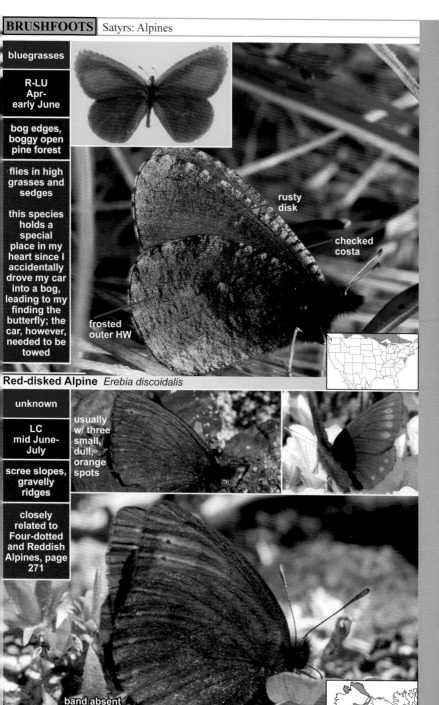

usually
w/ three
small,
dull,
orange
spots

band absent
(or faint)

Eskimo Alpine *Erebia occulta*

unknown

LU
mostly
July-Aug

alpine and subalpine meadows

also in Alaska, the Yukon and northern British Columbia

some treat *theano* as a subspecies of the Eurasian *Erebia pawloskii*

Hinsdale Co., CO

orange rectangles

no black spots
orange rectangles
Sublette Co., WY
cream spotband

Theano Alpine *Erebia theano*

sedges

C
June-July

boggy and wet areas in tundra

if present FW lower to eyespots are small and displaced outwardly

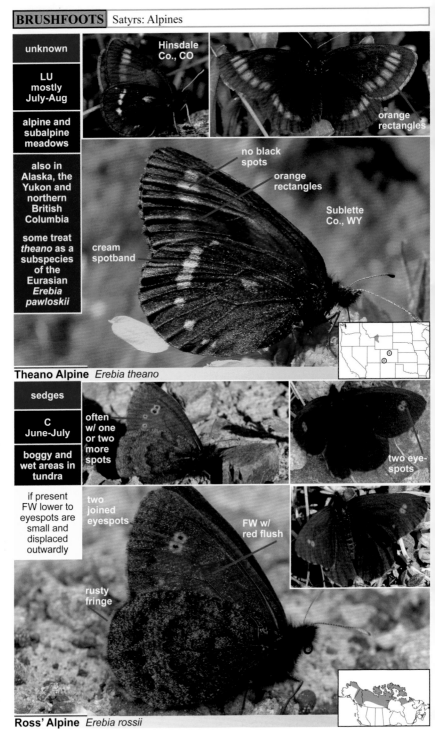

often w/ one or two more spots

two joined eyespots
FW w/ red flush
rusty fringe

Ross' Alpine *Erebia rossii*

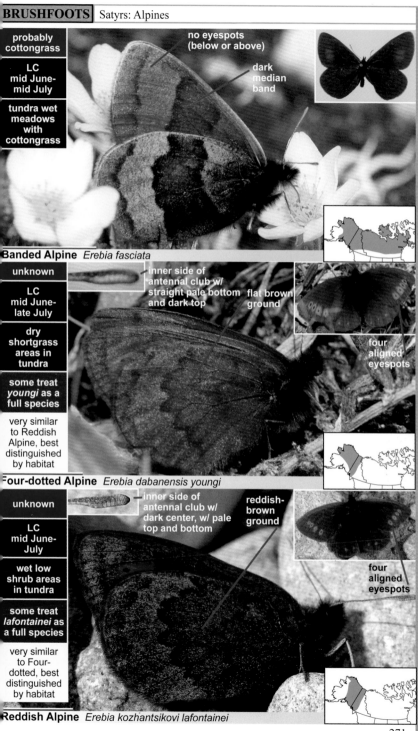

probably cottongrass

LC
mid June-mid July

tundra wet meadows with cottongrass

no eyespots
(below or above)
dark
median
band

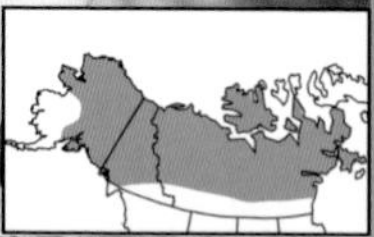

Banded Alpine *Erebia fasciata*

unknown

LC
mid June-late July

dry shortgrass areas in tundra

some treat *youngi* as a full species

very similar to Reddish Alpine, best distinguished by habitat

inner side of
antennal club w/
straight pale bottom
and dark top
flat brown
ground
four
aligned
eyespots

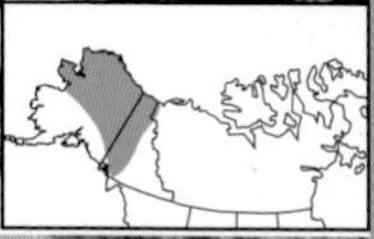

Four-dotted Alpine *Erebia dabanensis youngi*

unknown

LC
mid June-July

wet low shrub areas in tundra

some treat *lafontainei* as a full species

very similar to Four-dotted, best distinguished by habitat

inner side of
antennal club w/
dark center, w/ pale
top and bottom
reddish-
brown
ground
four
aligned
eyespots

Reddish Alpine *Erebia kozhantsikovi lafontainei*

grasses

East
LC-A
Apr-June,
mostly May

West
June-Sept
mostly July

open grassy areas in mountains and conifer woods; open sandy jack pine and flat rock areas in the eastern part of range

quite variable

most with bright tawny topsides

some in high Sierra Nevada are pale

Jefferson Co., CO

Alpine Co., CA

bright tawny above

Alpine Co., CA

most w/ orange
most populations w/ double loop
Clear Creek Co.,, CO

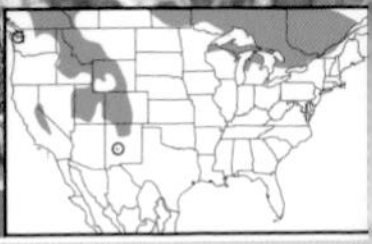

Chryxus Arctic *Oeneis chryxus*

unknown

LU
late June-
mid July

wet tundra

hilltops

Chryxus Arctic (this page), is very similar but range overlaps only in extreme northwestern Canada

Sentinel normally with FW eyespots oval, Chryxus normally FW eyespots round

eyespot
richly colored

Sentinel Arctic *Oeneis alpina*

sedges

U.S.: LR-LU; Canada: LC; late June-mid Aug

wet alpine or arctic meadows

some treat North American populations as subspecies of *Oeneis bore*

other arctics, pages 272-273, can have white veins, but have FW eyespots and are found in different habitats

Sublette Co., WY

Hinsdale Co., CO

no eyespots
most w/ pm band
North Slope Bor., AK
white veins through median band

North Slope Bor., AK

White-veined Arctic *Oeneis taygete*

grasses

LR-LC Apr-July, mostly May-June

arid, open grasslands

flight is usually fast and low

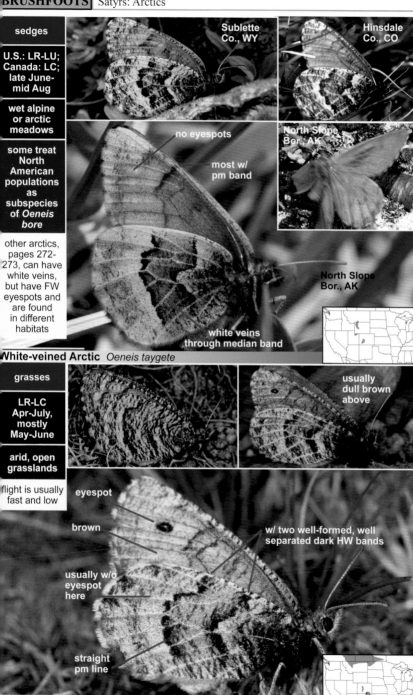

usually dull brown above

eyespot
brown
w/ two well-formed, well separated dark HW bands
usually w/o eyespot here
straight pm line

Alberta Arctic *Oeneis alberta*

grasses

LU-LC
May-July
more common in even-numbered years

clearings in moist mountain conifer woods

large

Chryxus Arctic, page 272, is much smaller

best distinguished from Macoun's Arctic, this page, by range

Del Norte
Co., CA

Deschutes
Co., OR

Okanogan
Co., WA
leading edge
is whitened

Great Arctic *Oeneis nevadensis*

grasses and sedges

LU-LC
May-July
more common in odd-numbered years in the western part of its range; in even-numbered years in the eastern part of its range

openings in jack pine woods

large

best distinguished from Great Arctic, this page, by range

Cook
Co., MN

much frosting at apex
leading edge
is whitened
eastern
Manitoba
AK + Canada
lower U.S.

Macoun's Arctic *Oeneis macounii*

cotton-grasses and other sedges

LR-LU

East
mid May-early July

West
late June-mid Aug

East: edges of Black Spruce bogs

West: openings in Lodgepole Pine woods

often perches on tree trunks or logs

Oxford
Co., ME

orange
patch

cottongrass

orange-ringed eyespot
Sublette
Co., WY
HW mostly unicolorous

Jutta Arctic *Oeneis jutta*

sedges

U-LC
late June-early Aug

high elevation rock fields, rocky mountaintops and gravelly ridges in tundra

light or dark colored individuals will choose appropriately colored rocks to blend into

variable below, from fairly pale and mottled to almost black

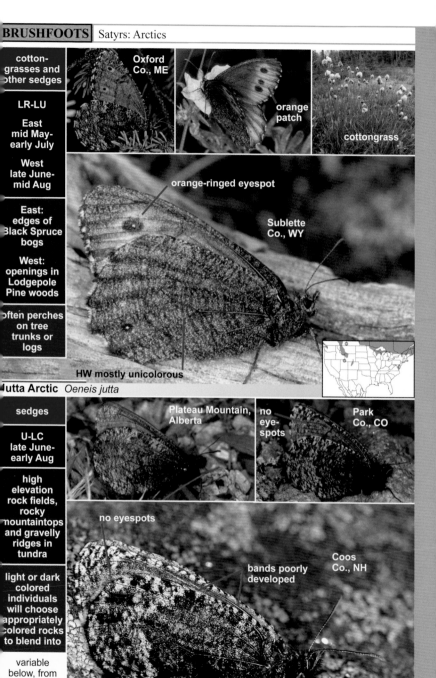

Plateau Mountain,
Alberta

no
eye-
spots
Park
Co., CO

no eyespots
bands poorly
developed
Coos
Co., NH

Melissa Arctic *Oeneis melissa*

grasses

LC
mid May-mid July

arid, open grasslands

flight is usually slow and high

usually w/o two well-formed, well separated dark HW bands
usually w/ eyespot here
highly striated

tawny above

Uhler's Arctic *Oeneis uhleri*

sedges and grasses

LR-LU
mid June-early Aug

dry rocky, grassy alpine or arctic tundra

Mt Katahdin, Maine individuals (see inset) have small FW eyespots, both above and below

w/ or w/o small eyespot
partly translucent
FW disk w/o strong markings
Park Co., CO
bands strongly developed
dark median band

Piscataquis Co., ME

Polixenes Arctic *Oeneis polixenes*

cotton-grasses

LU
late May-June

spruce bogs

often lands on trees

larger than Polixenes Arctic, flying earlier in year

more gray outwardly

dark median band
gray

Early Arctic *Oeneis rosovi*

broad, dark apex
curved out
no vein
transparent wings

Thick-tipped Greta *Greta morgane*

LRGV once

broad, dark apex
angled in vein
transparent wings

Broad-tipped Clearwing *Pteronymia cotytto*

LRGV once

translucent wings
female

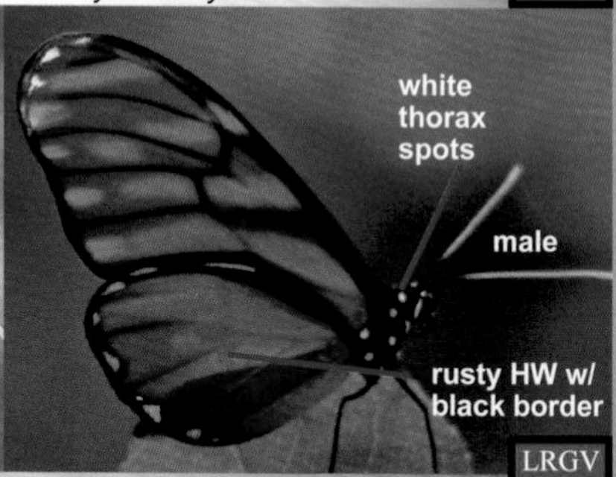
white thorax spots
male
rusty HW w/ black border

LRGV once

Klug's Clearwing *Dircenna kluggii*

striped thorax
dot closure
black band

LRGV once

Heliconoid Ticlear *Melinaea lilis*

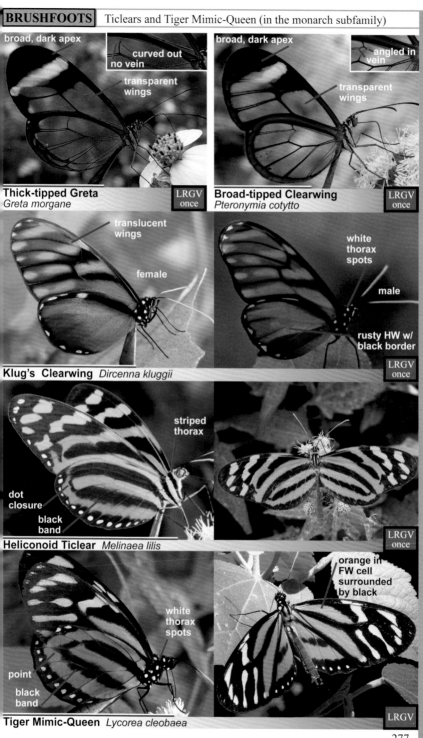

white thorax spots
point
black band

orange in FW cell surrounded by black

LRGV

Tiger Mimic-Queen *Lycorea cleobaea*

milkweeds

mainly C R-U in the Northwest; mostly Mar/Apr-Oct-Nov

any open areas with milkweeds

the one butterfly that almost everyone knows

millions of Monarchs from the Rockies eastward migrate south in the fall and overwinter in the Mexican mountains (see top middle inset); their overwintering sites are threatened by logging

western Monarchs overwinter along the California coast and are declining

native to North and South America, Monarchs are now established in Europe and Asia

larger than Viceroys, Monarchs fly with wings in a V; Viceroys fly with shallow wingbeats

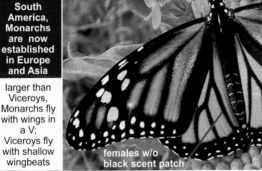

on Common Milkweed
male

overwintering site in Mexico

caterpillar

large and orange, w/ a powerful, sailing flight
black band crosses apex
males w/ black scent patch
male

female

Swamp Milkweed

chrysalis

on Butterfly Milkweed
female
females w/o black scent patch

Monarch *Danaus plexippus*

milkweeds and milkweed family vines

U-A
common south Florida and along the Mexican border where it flies all year; decreasing, but widespread, immigrant northward

any open areas with milkweeds

in boom years, tens of millions of Queens move south into Mexico in the fall; where they go, no one knows

orange-brown

female

caterpillar

in West, often w/ variable amount of white along veins
strong white spots
no black band crossing FW apex
male

Queen *Danaus gilippus*

milkweeds and milkweed family vines

R-U

most common in south Florida and south Texas, where it flies all year

decreasing immigrant northward

any open areas with milkweeds

males the same as females, except for presence of black scent patches on HWs

pm "water-marks"
dark

Okechobee Co., FL
faint spots in Florida
female

caterpillar

Hidalgo Co., TX
male
w/o white spots in Texas

Soldier *Danaus eresimus*

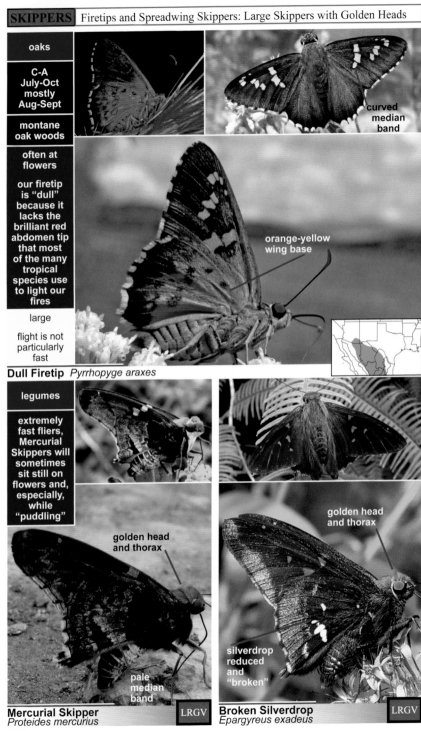

oaks

C-A
July-Oct
mostly
Aug-Sept

montane
oak woods

often at
flowers

our firetip is "dull" because it lacks the brilliant red abdomen tip that most of the many tropical species use to light our fires

large

flight is not particularly fast

curved
median
band

orange-yellow
wing base

Dull Firetip *Pyrrhopyge araxes*

legumes

extremely fast fliers, Mercurial Skippers will sometimes sit still on flowers and, especially, while "puddling"

golden head
and thorax
pale
median
band

Mercurial Skipper
Proteides mercurius

LRGV

golden head
and thorax
silverdrop
reduced
and
"broken"

Broken Silverdrop
Epargyreus exadeus

LRGV

caterpillar

gold band

large
white
spot

legumes

C-A
July-Oct
mostly
Apr-Sept;
all year in
south Florida

open woods,
fields,
suburban
gardens

common,
widespread
and a favorite
garden
butterfly

perhaps our
most easily
recognizable
widespread
skipper

silver spot
obvious, even
in flight

Silver-spotted Skipper *Epargyreus clarus*

foodplant

pale median band

Florida
Hammock
Milkpea

was LR
all year

tropical
hammocks

last seen
in 2004 on
Stock Island,
this butterfly
may be
extirpated
from the
United
States,
a victim of
the over-
development
of the Florida
Keys

like a Silver-
spotted
Skipper w/o its
spot & a more
deliberate
flight

Zestos Skipper *Epargyreus zestos*

Red Mangrove

LC
all year

mangrove swamps and nearby areas, including gardens

the Florida + Bahamas + Cuba populations may prove to be a distinct species

Hammock Skipper, page 285, has large white FW spots

usually lands with its wings flat, often under leaves

iridescent cobalt blue when fresh
iridescent turquoise blue pm band

Mangrove Skipper *Phocides pigmalion*

guavas, and other plants in the myrtle family

R-U
all year

open woods and gardens

a skipper that even skipper-phobes can't skip!

usually lands with its wings flat, often under leaves

orange face

caterpillar

FW beams
blue thorax stripes
red spots
iridescent ultramarine blue

Guava Skipper *Phocides polybius*

unknown

the one LRGV record, from the 1850s, is suspect, however this species occurs in nearby northern Mexico

no thorax stripes
FW beams
green-blue stripes

Teal Beamer *Phocides urania*

LRGV once

soapberry family

seen Apr 13, 2003 at Bentson-Rio Grande Valley State Park (see inset photo at right)

Hammock Skipper, page 285, has large white FW spots, no “beams” or thorax stripes

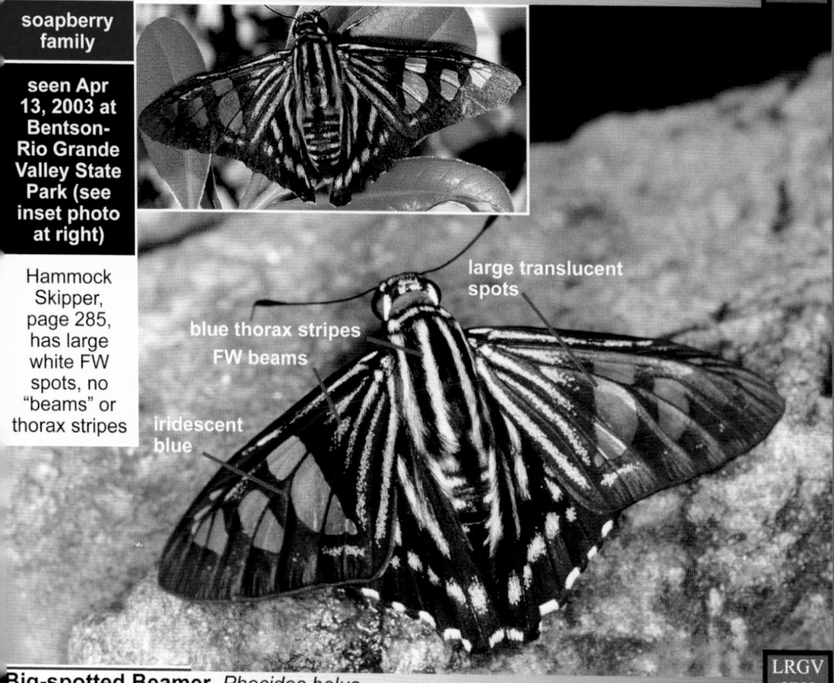
large translucent spots
blue thorax stripes
FW beams
iridescent blue

Big-spotted Beamer *Phocides belus*

LRGV once

oaks

C
Mar-June

montane oak woods

hilltops, often landing on trees or shrubs

also an avid mudpuddler

note the short tails and the unusual cream-colored HW postmedian area

short
tail

gray ground color
short
tail
cream patch

Short-tailed Skipper *Zestusa dorus*

variable shape and intensity of HW white median band
Hidalgo
Co., TX
usually
frosted

Jalisco,
Mexico
Bauhinia
gold spot
tawny
head
LRGV
se AZ

Gold-spotted Aguna *Aguna asander*

gold
spot
bold white
median band
blue-green
head and
thorax
green
on
abdomen
LRGV

Emerald Aguna *Aguna claxon*

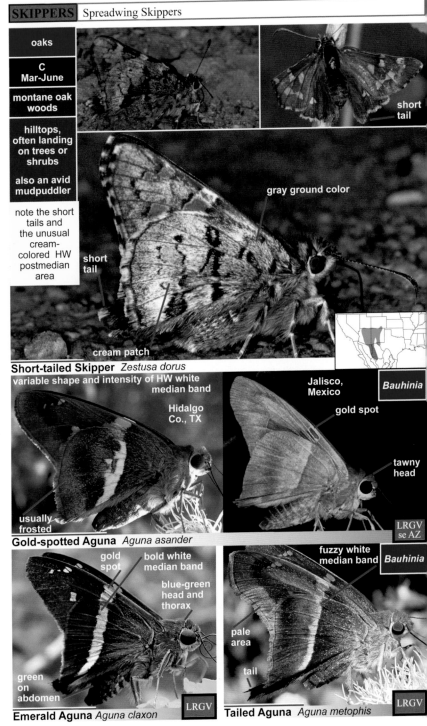

fuzzy white
median band
Bauhinia
pale
area
tail
LRGV

Tailed Aguna *Aguna metophis*

legumes

in Florida, especially Florida Poisonfish Tree and Pongame Oiltree

Florida Keys
U
all year

elsewhere
RS
although some years multiple individuals occur far north of normal range

hammocks in south Florida, more general in northern Mexico

spot not square
Hidalgo Co., TX

Monroe Co., FL

blue iridescence not intense

Hammock Skipper *Polygonus leo*

legumes

the few museum specimens labeled as from Florida, are possibly mislabeled

above, intensely iridescent blue is clue to ID

below, the HW top median band spot is squarish, not elongated as in Hammock Skipper and the basal spot is usually less intense than it usually is on Hammock Skipper

spot square

w/ intense blue iridescence

LRGV
twice

Manuel's Skipper *Polygonus manueli*

legume family vines

LRGV
C
all year

northward
R-U
immigrant

open woods, thorn-scrub, gardens

rarely open their wings when landed

the tail is so long that it often kinks in flight

inverted black triangle
very long tail
bold white stripe

White-striped Longtail *Chioides catillus*

legume family vines

R-U
LRGV
all year

thorn-scrub, gardens

rarely open their wings when landed

similar to White-striped Longtails but without a white stripe

unlike RS White-crescent Longtail, Zilpas white patches are oriented horizontally along the HW trailing edge

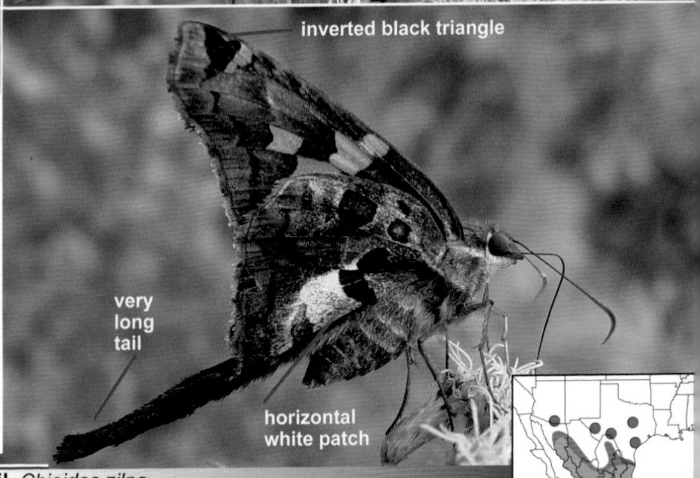
inverted black triangle
very long tail
horizontal white patch

Zilpa Longtail *Chioides zilpa*

see pgs 288-289

four or five spots
circle spot
holds wings flat
long tail
LRGV se AZ

Mexican Longtail *Polythrix mexicanus*

female w/ long tail
three spots
bar
legume family
holds wings flat
male w/ short tail
LRGV se AZ

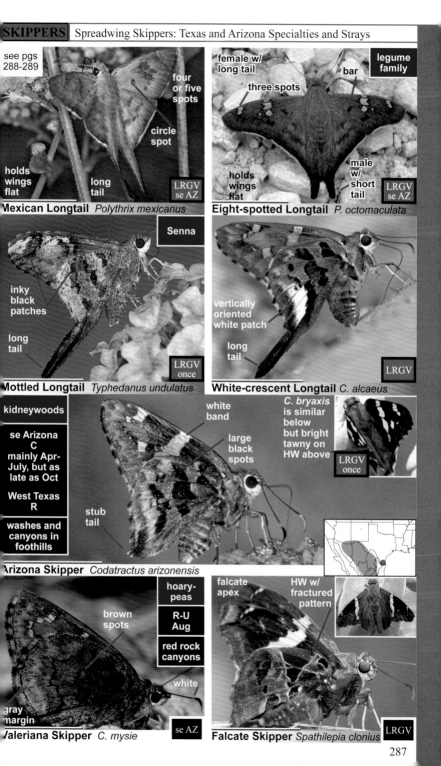

Eight-spotted Longtail *P. octomaculata*

Senna
inky black patches
long tail
LRGV once

Mottled Longtail *Typhedanus undulatus*

vertically oriented white patch
long tail
LRGV

White-crescent Longtail *C. alcaeus*

kidneywoods

se Arizona C mainly Apr-July, but as late as Oct

West Texas R

washes and canyons in foothills

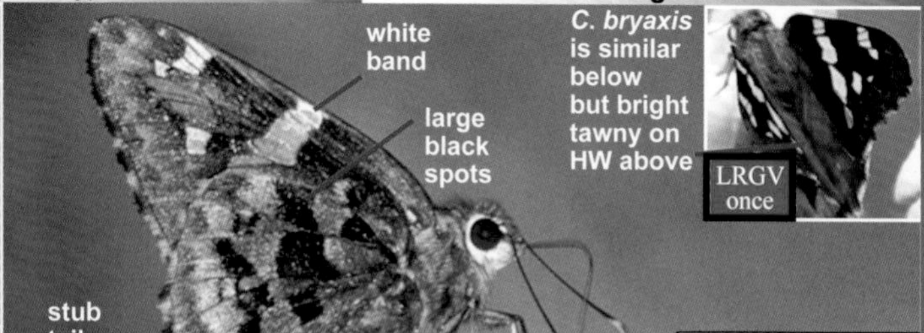
white band
large black spots
stub tail
C. bryaxis is similar below but bright tawny on HW above
LRGV once

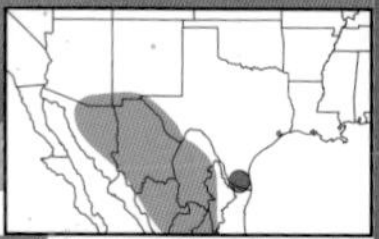

Arizona Skipper *Codatractus arizonensis*

Valeriana Skipper *C. mysie*

falcate apex
HW w/ fractured pattern
LRGV

Falcate Skipper *Spathilepia clonius*

legumes

U-C
LRGV and
south Florida
U-C
all year

decreasing
immigrant
northward

open woods,
thorn-scrub,
gardens

colonized the Florida Keys in late 1960s and is still moving north

when fresh, often with a lilac sheen below

sm band
interrupted
broad and large
pale median
spotband
long
tail

Dorantes Longtail *Urbanus dorantes*

grasses

LRGV
C

elsewhere
RS

open woods,
thorn-scrub,
gardens

often chase one another flying close to the ground, but routinely perch on grasses, bushes, etc., about 3 to 4 feet above ground

this is the commonest longtail in the LRGV

male
males
w/ few,
if any,
spots

females
often w/
median
spot-
band

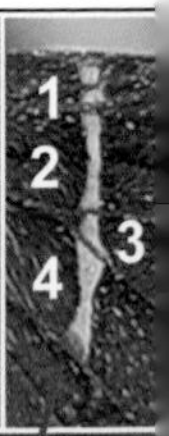
1
2
3
4
usually w/ 4
white spots,
if present,
the fifth spot
is usually
displaced
outwardly

two
dark
spots
not white
long
tail

Brown Longtail *Urbanus procne*

grasses

almost all reports of this species from the LRGV are of misidentified Brown Longtails

over thirty-five years of butterflying the LRGV I have personally seen only two Teleus Longtails and photos of about six others

almost always w/ 5 white spots, the fifth spot aligned
often w/o dark spots here
narrow, pale median spotband
white
bands of reflective black
long tail

LRGV

Teleus Longtail *Urbanus teleus*

median band connects to top spot
long tail

faint median band w/ etched appearance

LRGV once

Plain Longtail *Urbanus simplicius*

legume family

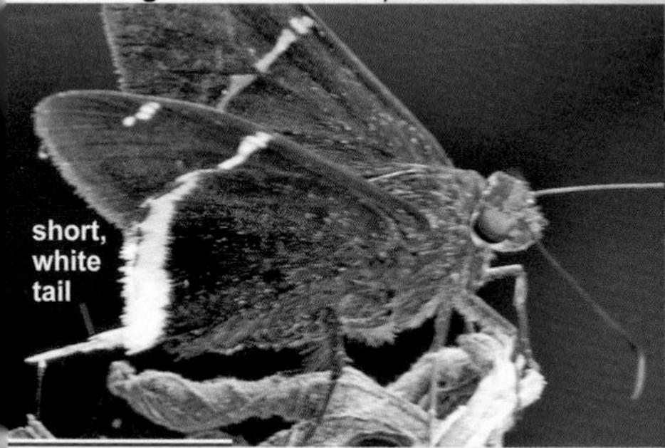
short, white tail

short, white tail

LRGV

White-tailed Longtail *Urbanus doryssus*

legumes

Southeast C-A

LRGV U

northward and in Arizona R immigrant

woods edges, open fields, gardens

a minor agricultural pest on beans

the long tails of longtailed skippers, frequently are damaged by wear —broken or missing

sm band continuous

usually w/ a spot here
blue-green

usually w/ a spot here
pale area broad and continuous from trailing edge to apex
long tail
not white

Long-tailed Skipper *Urbanus proteus*

legumes

first reported from the United States in December 2003 from the National Butterfly Center in Mission, Texas, this species was seen in January 2004 at Santa Ana NWR and again at the National Butterfly Center in 2010 and 2011

turquoise

usually dark here
pale area stops here
constricted pm band

LRGV

Turquoise Longtail *Urbanus evona*

legumes

one hasn't been seen in the LRGV for at least 50 years — you're not looking hard enough!

blue
into
tails

outer spot much
smaller than inner spot
usually w/
a spot here
pale
area
stops
here
white

Esmeralda Longtail *Urbanus esmeraldus* LRGV once

aster
family
gold-yellow
iridescence
turquoise

aster
family
cobalt blue

median band
connects to spots
the one report from the
LRGV was probably of a
misidentified Cobalt Longtail

Double-striped Longtail *U. belli* not yet LRGV

median band
connects to spots

Cobalt Longtail *U. viterboana* LRGV twice

multiple plant families, but mostly, if not exclusively, Coyotillo in the LRGV

LRGV
U-C

elsewhere
RS

tropical woods, thorn-scrub, gardens

recent data suggests that this species may actually be a complex of many species; however, the actual taxonomic status remains controversial

blue-green costa
white spots
white lead

brilliant iridescent blue
two white "bars"

Two-barred Flasher *Astraptes fulgerator*

legumes

similar to Two-barred Flashers, but without the two white bars on the FW

Frosted Flashers (next page), even rarer than Gilbert's Flashers, have more restricted blue above and a wide frosted white HW border below

white costa
white lead
black spots

brilliant iridescent blue
no white

LRGV

Gilbert's Flasher *Astraptes gilberti*

erythrinas
wide
frosted
border
LRGV

Frosted Flasher *Astraptes alardus*

legumes
no white
blue-
green
hairs
white
white spots
variable, often
small or absent
LRGV

Small-spotted Flasher *Astraptes egregius*

legumes
extensive
green
iridescence
LRGV
once

Green Flasher *Astraptes talus*

legumes
yellow
patch
median
and pm
dark bands
short yellow
tail
LRGV

Yellow-tipped Flasher *Astraptes anaphus*

American Hog Peanut in the East, a variety of legumes in the West

East
LR

West
U-C

Apr-June, July-Sept where two brooded; mostly June-July where single brooded

wooded ravines, canyons and gulches with streams

has declined over much of the East

pm
and m
bands
solid
black
broad
golden
band

not
white
broad
golden
band
bottom spot
usually
displaced
outwardly
checked
fringe

Golden Banded-Skipper *Autochton cellus*

legumes

R
Mar-Aug
Big Bend National Park, especially in Green Gulch

perhaps not present every year

montane oak woods

narrow
yellow
band
white
fringe
narrow
yellow
band
white
fringe

Chisos Banded-Skipper *Autochton cincta*

legumes

hasn't been seen in southeastern Arizona for more than 70 years, but, because it is still common in nearby Sonora, it could show up again

montane oak woods

white patch before antennal club

below, HW median band spots are outlined in black, not solid spots

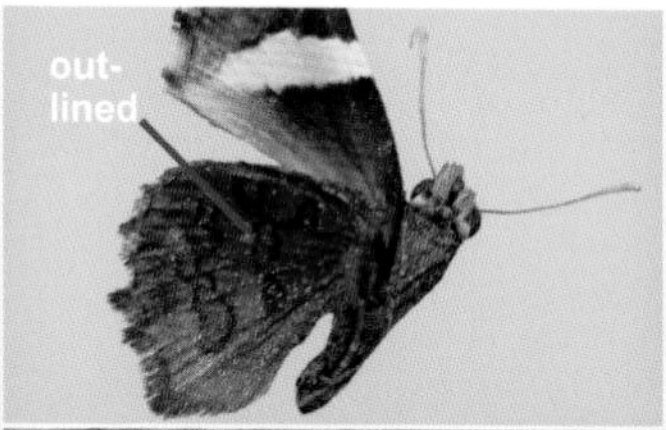

white
broad golden band
bottom spot not much displaced outwardly

Sonoran Banded-Skipper *Autochton pseudocellus*

se AZ

privas

R-U all year, but mostly Oct-Dec

open woods, gardens

potrillo means colt in Spanish, so it makes sense that it has a saddle-shaped spot

saddle spot
gray base

blue-green head and thorax
spot shaped like a saddle, w/ a horn

Potrillo Skipper *Cabares potrillo*

ticktrefoils

U-C

two-brood areas mostly May-June, July-Sept

one brood areas June-July

open woods and nearby open areas

unlike Silver-spotted Skippers, Hoary Edges aren't commonly found in suburbia and gardens

golden band
encloses
brown

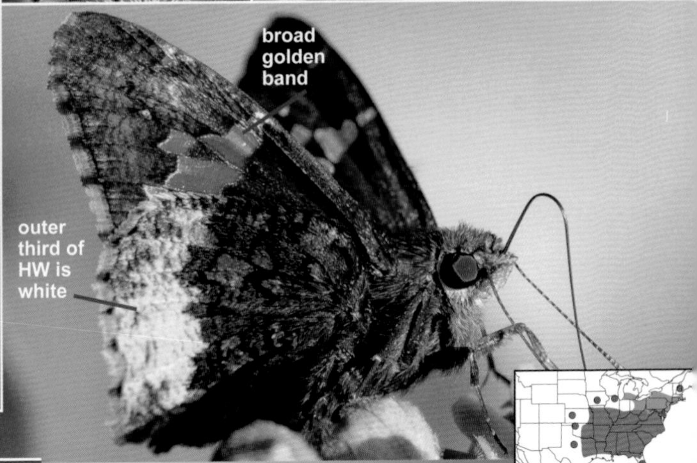
broad
golden
band
outer
third of
HW is
white

Hoary Edge *Achalarus lyciades*

ticktrefoils and other legumes

R-U Apr-Sept mostly May and Aug

foothill and mountain canyons and washes, especially in areas with steep rock walls

see Gold-costa Skipper, page 303

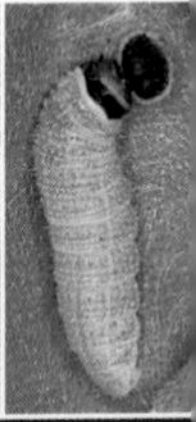

caterpillar

white
spots
outer
quarter
of HW is
white

Desert Cloudywing *Achalarus casica*

R-U
all year

occasionally becomes a common immigrant north of the LRGV

open woods, thorn-scrub

males w/ a
costal fold
white
fringe

pale
tracings

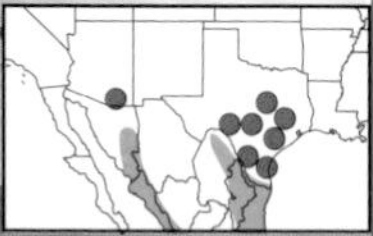

Coyote Cloudywing *Achalarus toxeus*

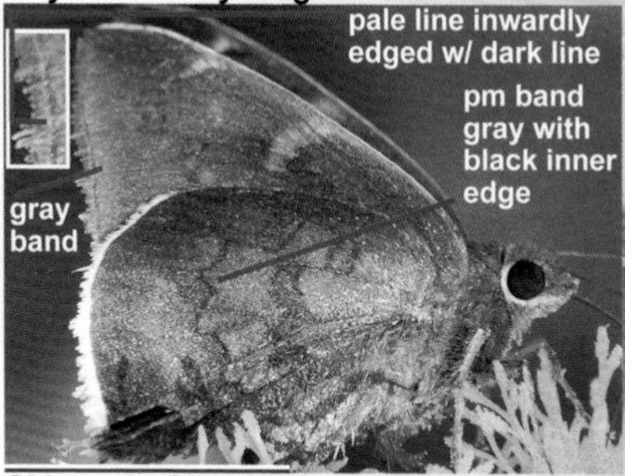
pale line inwardly
edged w/ dark line
pm band
gray with
black inner
edge
gray
band

males w/o a
costal fold

LRGV

Skinner's Cloudywing *Achalarus albociliatus*

stub
tail

pale
tracings
white
fringe
stub tail

LRGV

Jalapus Cloudywing *Achalarus jalapus*

gray marginal band
white
spots
black
wing
base
outer
quarter
of HW
is
white

LRGV
once

Dark Cloudywing *Achalarus tehuacana*

ticktrefoils, clovers, and other legumes

two brood areas C Mar-Oct mostly Apr-May and Aug; one brood areas May-July

widespread in open, usually dry, habitats

this species is the most common and widespread cloudywing; almost anywhere in the United States, if you see a cloudywing and call it a Northern, you'll most likely be right!

unlike duskywings, which are usually quite mottled, cloudywings have their topside ground color an even brown

in se Arizona, some individuals have white faces

Northern, Southern and Confused Cloudywings are all very variable; some individuals defy identification

Kern Co., CA

Travis Co., TX

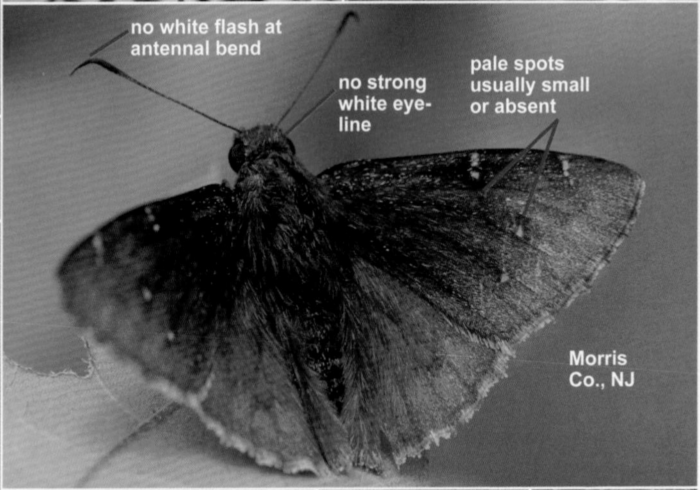
no white flash at antennal bend
no strong white eye-line
pale spots usually small or absent
Morris Co., NJ

Cochise Co., AZ

Morris Co., NJ

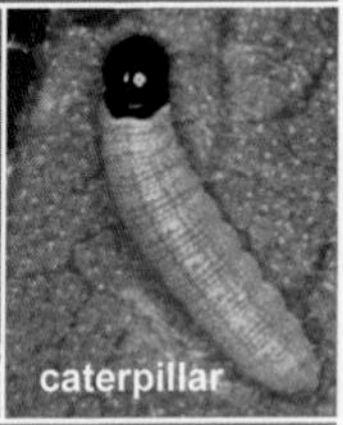
caterpillar

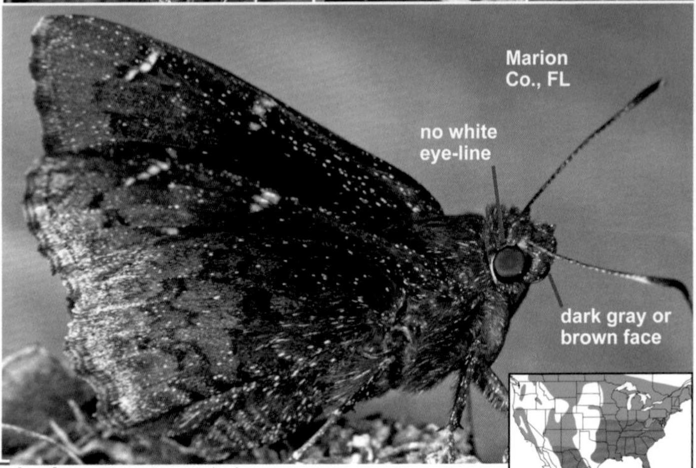
Marion Co., FL
no white eye-line
dark gray or brown face

Northern Cloudywing *Thorybes pylades*

ticktrefoils, clovers, and other legumes

two brood areas LU-C Mar-Oct, mostly Apr-May and Aug-Sept

one brood areas June-July

widespread in open, usually dry, habitats

will form localized colonies

males are often highly territorial

white
face

white flash at antennal bend
pale spots usually large
top spot overlaps bottom spot

Southern Cloudywing *Thorybes bathyllus*

legumes

R-U Mar-May July-Sept

dry, open areas

at some locations, one can find Northern, Southern and Confused Cloudywings flying together

individuals can resemble either Northern (see top right inset) or Southern Cloudywings (main photo)

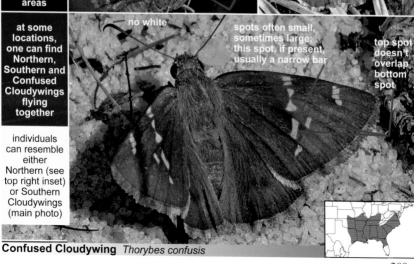

strong white eye-line
white face

no white
spots often small, sometimes large; this spot, if present, usually a narrow bar
top spot doesn't overlap bottom spot

Confused Cloudywing *Thorybes confusis*

unknown

R-U
Apr-Sept

pine-oak woods

these white-fringed populations might warrant treatment as a full species

little information about the population genetics of this group is available

white fringe
broad frosting
fringe w/ obvious checks
white fringe

Northern Cloudywing *Thorybes pylades albosuffusa*

cologanias and probably other legumes

R-U
July-Aug

grassy openings in oak woods

above, usually w/ fewer white spots than on white-fringed subspecies of Northern Cloudywing

below, little if any HW frosting

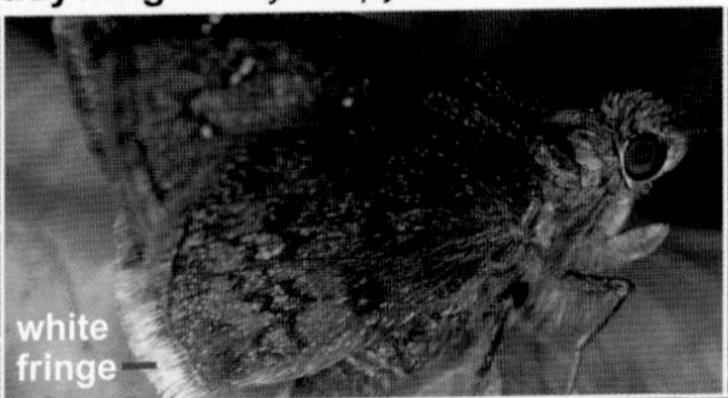
white fringe

pale spots greatly reduced
fringe black (or tan) w/ weak checks
white fringe

Drusius Cloudywing *Thorybes drusius*

clovers and probably other legumes

C
May-Aug, about one month at any particular location

open areas in montane conifer woods

hilltops

smaller than Northern Cloudywings, page 298

some with very reduced spots (see top right inset)

frosted (or pale) outer third of HW

some with pale spots w/ darker outlines
fringe tan w/ only partial checks

Mexican Cloudywing *Thorybes mexicanus*

legumes

R-LU
June-July

open areas in moist conifer woods

this is one of the most range restricted species in North America

smaller than Northern Cloudywings, page 298

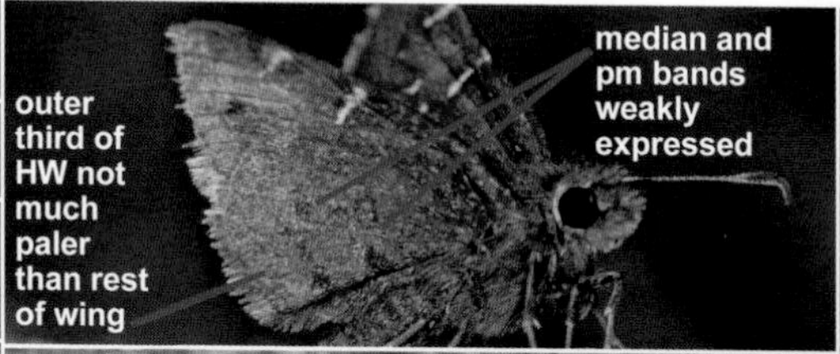
outer third of HW not much paler than rest of wing
median and pm bands weakly expressed

fringe tan w/ checks

Western Cloudywing *Thorybes diversus*

acacias

U-LC
Apr-Sept

dry grassland and rocky canyons

rarely opens wings while landed

usually with a faint lilac sheen when fresh

pyramid-skippers (genus *Cogia*) have divergent subapical and median bands, that create the appearance of steps up a pyramid

caterpillar

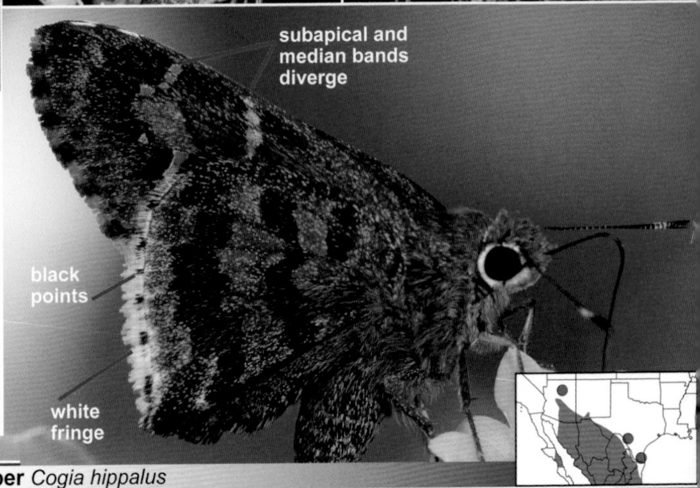
subapical and
median bands
diverge
black
points
white
fringe

Acacia Skipper *Cogia hippalus*

Puerto Rico Sensitive-Briar (a mimosa) and probably other mimosas

R-LC
all year
present in the LRGV most, possibly every, year, but numbers fluctuate

mostly seasonally flooded areas

flight is usually close to the ground and individuals often land on the ground

white streaks

subapical and
median bands
diverge
median and pm gray

LRGV

Mimosa Skipper *Cogia calchas*

Prairie Acacia and probably other acacias

U
Mar-May, July-Sept

rocky canyons

although they will come to flowers, they usually land on rocks or on the ground

males take up territories on canyon bottoms and other depressions

gold
costa

food
plant

subapical and
median bands
diverge
gold
costa

Gold-costa Skipper *Cogia caicus*

acacias

R-U
Apr-May, late June-Aug

acacia prairies, rocky hillsides and open woods

low butterfly population density along with low population density of people inhabiting the butterfly's territory, makes this a rarely seen species

smaller than Northern Cloudywings

white streaks
white
white face
gray

Outis Skipper *Cogia outis*

unknown

R
probably present in the LRGV most years, most frequent Oct-Dec

open woods, thorn-scrub

holds its wings flat when landed

yellow neck line
usually, but not always, w/ subapical white spots
pm band of angular dark spots
two large dark spots

Hermit Skipper *Grais stigmatica*

Wild Crapemyrtle and others in the Barbados Cherry family

R
probably present in the LRGV most years, most frequent Oct-Dec

open woods, thorn-scrub

holds wings flat when landed

pale vertical bar
spot band
solid dark bands
copper-brown ground

Brown-banded Skipper *Timochares ruptifasciatus*

multiple plant families

R
probably present in the LRGV most years, most frequent Oct-Dec

open woods, thorn-scrub

holds wings flat when landed

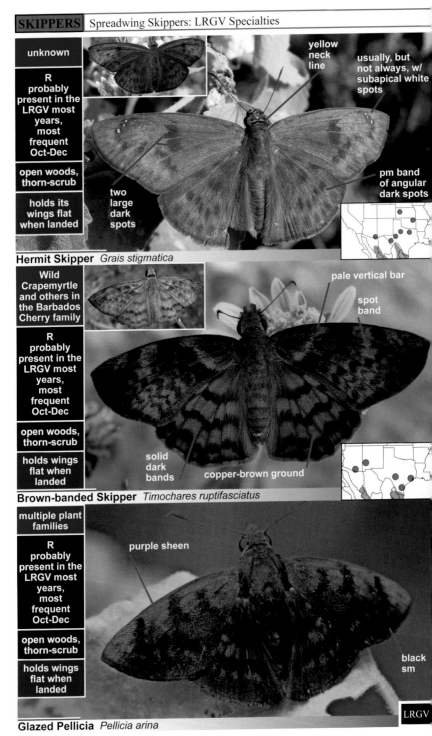

purple sheen
black sm

LRGV

Glazed Pellicia *Pellicia arina*

acanthus family
dark gray palps
brown head
pale spot
fringe checked
LRGV se AZ

Fritzgaertner's Flat *C. fritzgaertneri*

water-willows
pale gray palps
blue-gray head
dark spot
fringe unchecked
LRGV

Stallings' Flat *Celaenorrhinus stallingsi*

crotons
black sky w/ white star
LRGV

Starred Skipper *Arteurotia tractipennis*

multiple plant families
gray oval
red spots
falcate
LRGV once

Red-studded Skipper *Noctuana stator*

Barbados Cherry family
pale vertical bar
black spot
LRGV once

Common Bentwing *Ebrietas anacreon*

Barbados Cherry family
grainy gray
LRGV

Variegated Skipper *Gorgythion begga*

morning glory family
no purple sheen
pale sm
LRGV once?

Morning Glory Pellicia *Pellicia dimidiata*

morning glory family
band is xtra dark
dark band forms a Y
three white spots
lobed HW
LRGV

Purplish-black Sk. *Nisoniades rubescens*

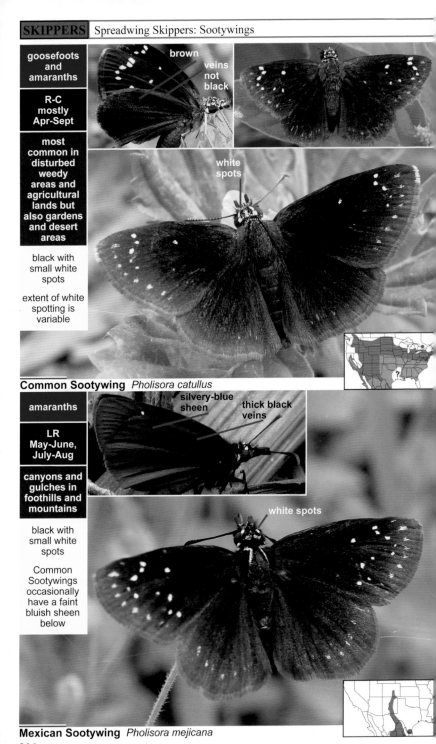

goosefoots and amaranths

R-C mostly Apr-Sept

most common in disturbed weedy areas and agricultural lands but also gardens and desert areas

black with small white spots

extent of white spotting is variable

brown
veins not black
white spots

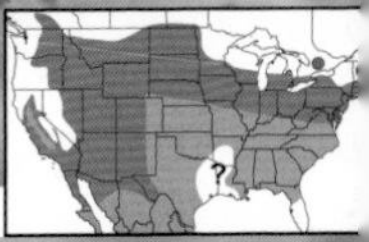

Common Sootywing *Pholisora catullus*

amaranths

LR May-June, July-Aug

canyons and gulches in foothills and mountains

black with small white spots

Common Sootywings occasionally have a faint bluish sheen below

silvery-blue sheen
thick black veins
white spots

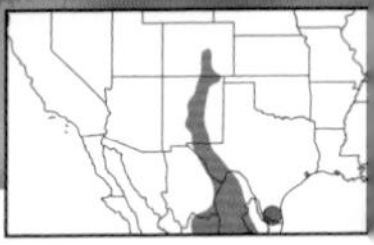

Mexican Sootywing *Pholisora mejicana*

saltbushes

R-U
two broods May-Sept;
one brood Apr-July

desert riveredges, washes and sagebrush w/ extensive saltbush

some treat the subspecies *gracilae*, found along Colorado River from Nevada south, and shown in main photo, as a full species

Cameron Co., TX
thin white bar

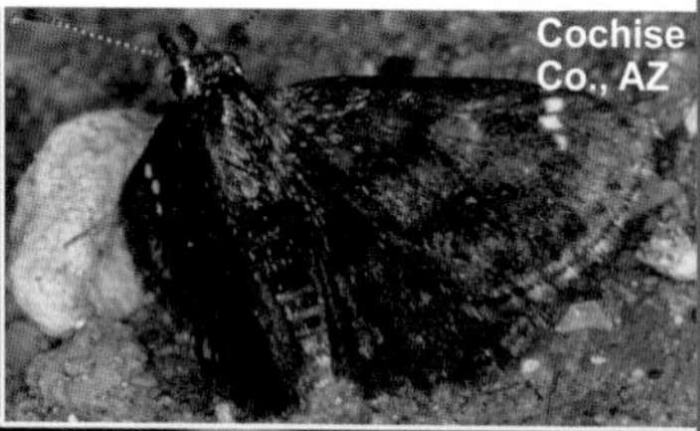
Cochise Co., AZ

Yuma Co., AZ
pale cell-end bar
mottled dark brown

Saltbush Sootywing *Hesperopsis alpheus*

saltbushes

R-U
two broods Mar-Oct;
one brood June-Aug

desert areas w/ extensive saltbush

HW underside is tan with white spots; in most of range resembling the individuals shown in insets; from central Utah northeastward, white is usually reduced to a cell-end bar and faint marginal spots

white spots
San Diego Co., CA

White Pine Co., NV
black disk

no white spots
Pima Co., AZ
ground color even dark brown

Mojave Sootywing *Hesperopsis libya*

goosefoots

R-U mostly Apr-June, July-Sept

disturbed areas, gardens, moist open woods

many not separable from Mazans Scallpwing in the field; those with very strong and distinctly checked fringes can be assumed to be this species

Common Sootywings with white head spots

female

male

female
gold or silver flecks
scalloped wing

Hayhurst's Scallopwing *Staphylus hayhurstii*

goosefoots and amaranths

U mostly Mar-Nov

open woods and nearby open areas

prefers shaded situations

scallopwings and bollas rarely close their wings while landed

see Hayhurst's Scallopwing, this page, and Common Sootywing, page 306

male

male

female
gold or silver flecks
scalloped wing

Mazans Scallopwing *Staphylus mazans*

goosefoots

AZ to w TX
U-C
all year

LRGV
R mostly
Feb-May

moist areas in arid regions

black with two or three subapical FW spots usually with white fringe at the FW apex (see inset photos)

some females and worn males have only a few gold scales on the head

female

male

golden head
gold or silver flecks
male

Golden-headed Scallopwing *Staphylus ceos*

unknown

larger than scallopwings with a less irregular HW

broad, diffuse median band
usually w/ two white subapical spots
females usually w/ a spot here that males lack
often w/ an olive reflection here
female

Mottled Bolla *Bolla clytius*

LRGV

unknown

dark oval
rounded HW

Obscure Bolla *Bolla brennus*

LRGV

Lime Pricklyash and others in the rue family

LRGV
U-C
all year

decreasing immigrant northward

open woods and thorn-scrub

flight is generally slow as they work up and around shrubs

most males resemble the individual shown in the main photo

male

pale wedge
sicklewing
blue-puple sheen
male

pale wedge
female
sicklewing

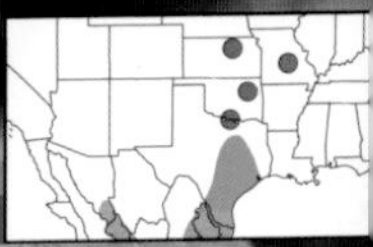

Sickle-winged Skipper *Achlyodes thraso*

rue family

large

washed out look

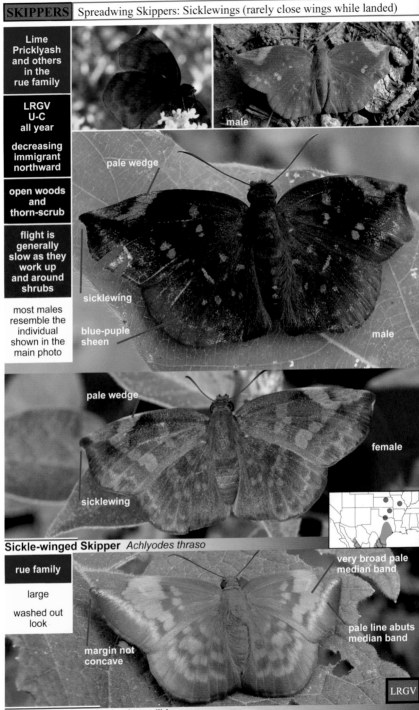

very broad pale median band
pale line abuts median band
margin not concave
LRGV

Pale Sicklewing *Achlyodes pallida*

unknown
zigzag black line edged w/ tan
purple sheen
se AZ once

Slaty Skipper *Chiomara mithrax*

Barbados Cherry family
blue spotting
LRGV

Blue-studded Skipper *Sostrata bifasciata*

Gua-zuma
soft, blue-gray ground
spurred wing
male
gray bands on brown ground
female
spurred wing
LRGV once

Dusted Spurwing *Antigonus erosus*

mallow family
large translucent spots
LRGV

Glassy-winged Sk. *Xenophanes tryxus*

mallow family
hoary below
gray-brown ground
pale median area
LRGV

Hoary Skipper *Carrhenes canescens*

multiple families
pale blue vent
purple sheen
wide pm band
LRGV

Common Bluevent *Anastrus sempiternus*

Coastal Indigo and probably other indigos and other plants in the legume family

central Texas coast
U-C
Mar-Nov

LRGV
R

coastal scrub, open fields, disturbed areas

there's nothing false about this butterfly

flies low

wedge-shaped median band
gray sm band

False Duskywing *Gesta gesta*

Long Key Locustberry

R-U
all year with a peak Mar-May

pine rockland

as are almost all of south Florida's butterflies, this species' populations are seriously declining

dark, with a "basket" of white spots on the FW

males are very dark with smaller white spots FW

females with a purple sheen

male

"basket" of white spots
female

Florida Duskywing *Ephyriades brunneus*

shrubby oaks

most of East
U-C

Florida
C-A

Rockies
C

California
LR-U

early spring

openings in oak woods

mainly in dry areas and barrens but also in some rich woods

without white spots

mid-sized

restricted gray
female

short palps
well-defined pm gray band edged w/ black
gray at "wrist" more restricted (except in CA)
male
usually w/o pale rings

Sleepy Duskywing *Erynnis brizo*

willows and poplars

East
U-C

West
mostly R-U

late spring

open moist woods

without white spots

small

flies later than Sleepy Duskywing

female

long palps
well-defined pm gray band edged w/ black
gray at "wrist" more extensive
gray rings
male

Dreamy Duskywing *Erynnis icelus*

oaks

C-A early/mid spring

oak woods

a large, spring-flying eastern duskywing

males with much FW gray overscaling

females similar but more patterned

males of most duskywing species have a costal fold that females lack

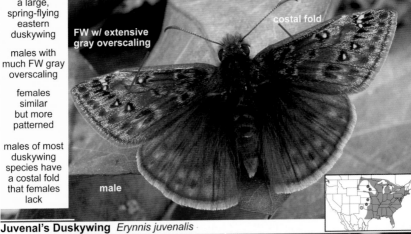

usually w/
pale apical
spots

female

costal fold
FW w/ extensive
gray overscaling
male

Juvenal's Duskywing *Erynnis juvenalis*

oaks

U-C spring-early fall

oak woods, especially on poor soil

males more evenly brown than Juvenal's

females more boldly patterned than Juvenal's

uncommon in spring when Juvenal's are common

similar female Wild Indigos have small, distinct pale spots on HW margin below

usually w/o, or w/
faint, pale apical
spots

female

FW w/o extensive
gray overscaling
male
large dark marginal spots

Horace's Duskywing *Erynnis horatius*

Gambel and other oaks

LC
Mar-July
mostly
May-June

oak woods

a large, spring-flying western duskywing

males with much FW gray overscaling

females similar but more patterned

Propertius and Meridian Duskywings lack the prickly gray thorax hairs

usually w/
pale apical
spots

female

FW w/ extensive
gray overscaling
prickly gray hairs on
thorax (when fresh)
male

Rocky Mountain Duskywing *Erynnis telemachus*

legumes

C
throughout
warm
weather

dry, sandy areas

a mid-sized, all-season, southeastern duskywing

extensive black above

tan patch below FW "wrist"

males similar to male Horace's Duskywings

females similar to female Wild Indigos

usually w/ "eye"
spot here
female

usually w/ three top
spots aligned and
bottom spot jutting
out
tan patch
FW cell
all black
black
coalesced
into a band
male

Zarucco Duskywing *Erynnis zarucco*

oaks

C-A
Mar-July
mostly
May-June

oak woods

a large, spring-flying Pacific Coast duskywing

males with much FW gray overscaling

females similar but more patterned

other large duskywings in its range have white fringes

usually w/
pale apical
spots

female

long gray hairs
dark fringe
male

Propertius Duskywing *Erynnis propertius*

oaks

U-C
Mar-Sept

oak woods

hilltops

a large, spring and late-summer/ early fall flying Southwestern duskywing

lacks bright gray thorax hairs of Rocky Mountain Duskywing

often with white-tipped fringe

usually w/o pale apical spots below

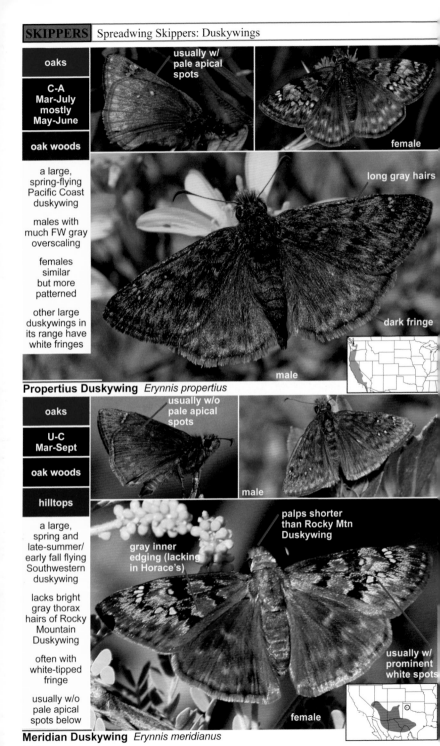

usually w/o
pale apical
spots

male

palps shorter
than Rocky Mtn
Duskywing
gray inner
edging (lacking
in Horace's)
usually w/
prominent
white spots
female

Meridian Duskywing *Erynnis meridianus*

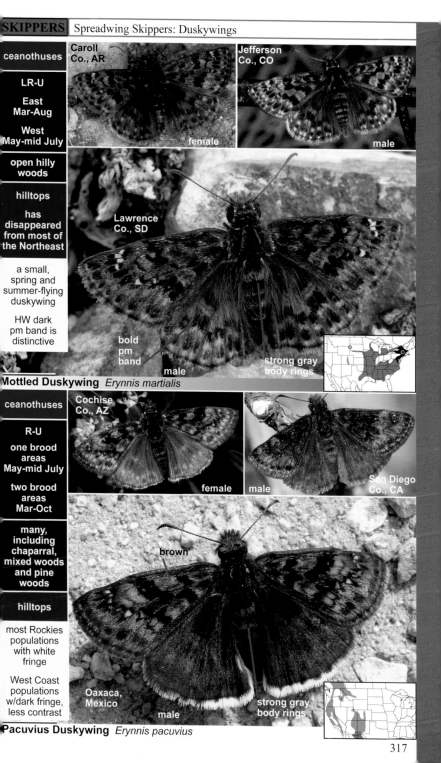

ceanothuses

LR-U

East
Mar-Aug

West
May-mid July

open hilly woods

hilltops

has disappeared from most of the Northeast

a small, spring and summer-flying duskywing

HW dark pm band is distinctive

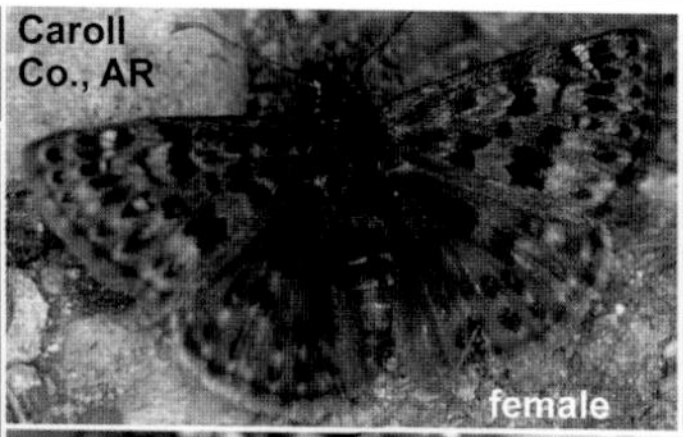
Caroll
Co., AR
female

Jefferson
Co., CO
male

Lawrence
Co., SD
bold
pm
band
male
strong gray
body rings

Mottled Duskywing *Erynnis martialis*

ceanothuses

R-U

one brood areas
May-mid July

two brood areas
Mar-Oct

many, including chaparral, mixed woods and pine woods

hilltops

most Rockies populations with white fringe

West Coast populations w/dark fringe, less contrast

Cochise
Co., AZ
female

male
San Diego
Co., CA

brown
Oaxaca,
Mexico
male
strong gray
body rings

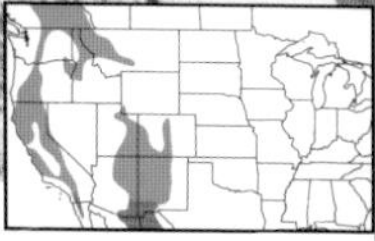

Pacuvius Duskywing *Erynnis pacuvius*

wild indigos, Crown Vetch

U-C mostly Apr-Oct

roadsides, meadows and other open areas

the recent switch to non-native Crown Vetch has caused a surge in population, range and flight period — all still on the increase

a mid-sized, all-season, eastern duskywing

small,
defined
pale
spots

FW base often "oily" black
female

cell is mainly black
black "fingers" usually prominent
male

Wild Indigo Duskywing *Erynnis baptisiae*

Red Columbine and other columbines

United States LR

Ontario C

Apr/May-July-Aug

limestone barrens, open woods with columbines

a small, spring and summer, northeastern duskywing

look for small size and close association with columbines

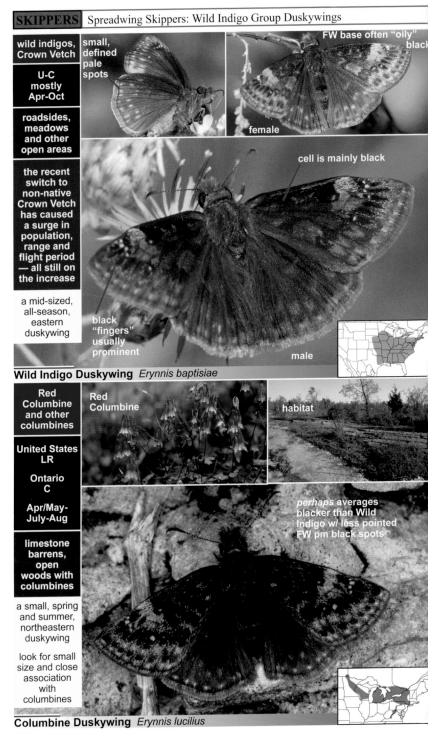

Red
Columbine

habitat

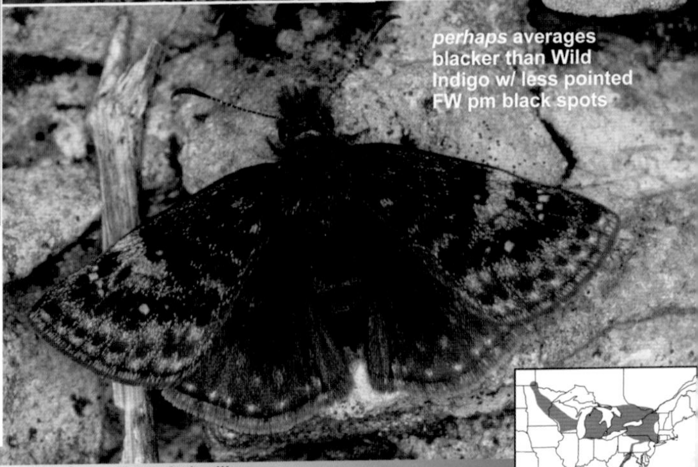
perhaps averages blacker than Wild Indigo w/ less pointed FW pm black spots

Columbine Duskywing *Erynnis lucilius*

lupines, golden-banners and other legumes

East: LR

WI: C

West: U-C

mostly May-June

East: barrens

West: mostly montane meadows

hilltops

small/mid-sized

males especially, w/ gray hairs on FW creating blurred look

prominent
pale spots

male

extensive gray
hairs on FW
female

Persius Duskywing *Erynnis persius*

legumes

U-C Mar/Apr-Aug/Sept

many open habitats

males patrol gullies

a small/mid-sized, all-season, western duskywing

males usually with more faded, blurrier HW spots than Persius

where range overlaps, females perhaps not separable from Persius

female
male

Afranius Duskywing *Erynnis afranius*

oaks

se Arizona-w Texas
C
elsewhere
R-U
Mar-Oct

oak woods

hilltops

a large southwestern duskywing

FW topside is mottled brown

HW below with vertical white marginal spots (faint in California)

Hidalgo
Co., TX

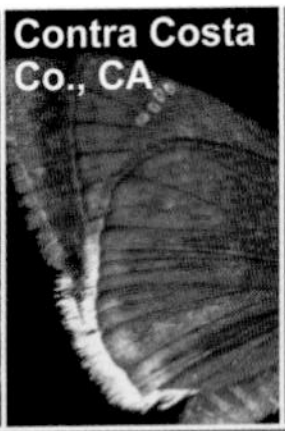
Contra Costa
Co., CA

female

vertical
white
spots
male

Mournful Duskywing *Erynnis tristis*

legumes

southward
U-C
most of the year
northward
R-U
May-Sept

open areas, especially hot and dry

range increasing northward and eastward

a large duskywing

FW topside is black overall with a paler pm area — the blackest duskywing

pale
spots
absent or
horizontal

San Diego
Co., CA
male

FW cell is almost
all black
pale
area
female
Hidalgo
Co., TX

Funereal Duskywing *Erynnis funeralis*

female

extensive gray overscaling
male

oaks

R-U
Mar-Aug
mostly
pr-May and
July-Aug

montane
voods with
oaks

nay best be
considered
as a full
species

a mid/
large-sized
outheastern
Arizona
duskywing

nale topside
W with much
gray

nderside HW
vithout white
arginal spots

rizona' Juvenal's Duskywing *Erynnis juvenalis clitus*

male
white fringe w/ some dark checks

oaks

R-U
Apr-Sept
nostly May

voods with
aks, above
6000 ft

hilltops

small

unlike
Iournful, HW
inge usually
with some
lark checks

underside
W often with
ale marginal
oots, but less
ntense than
Mournful

ee Pacuvius
Duskywing,
page 317

cudder's Duskywing *Erynnis scudderi*

C
three brood areas most of the year
two brood areas May-Oct

median and pm
bands are similar

female

a wide variety of open situations, including disturbed and agricultural areas

Common Checkered-Skippers are by far the commonest and most widespread of the checkered-skippers

faint or no
spot here
usually w/o
spot here
male
black checks
evenly spaced

Common Checkered-Skipper *Pyrgus communis*

C
most of the year

a wide variety of open situations

Common and White Checkered-Skippers are not separable in the field and may actually be one species

females with less gray-blue above than males, with head and shoulders more olive-colored

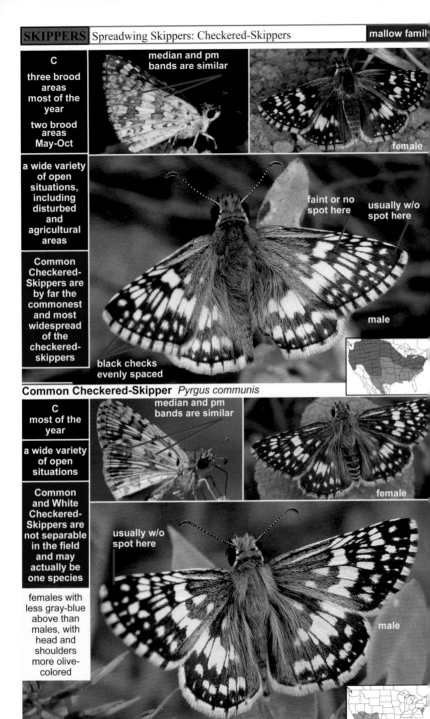

median and pm
bands are similar

female

usually w/o
spot here
male

White Checkered-Skipper *Pyrgus albescens*

C-A

south Texas and south Florida all year

Houston - north Florida Apr-Oct

a wide variety of open situations

other than the contrasting black HW border, field marks for the separation of females from White/Common and Desert Checkered-Skippers are the same as for males

leading edge
w/ dark spots

female

usually tanner than Common/
White Checkered-skippers
strong
white spot
white
spot
black
checks
usually
coalesce
usually w/ black border more
contrasted w/ rest of HW
male

Tropical Checkered-Skipper *Pyrgus oileus*

R-U all year

thorn-scrub, desert

more frequently encountered at flowers than are Common/White or Tropical Checkered-Skippers

two
small
dark
spots
HW even
tan-gray

female

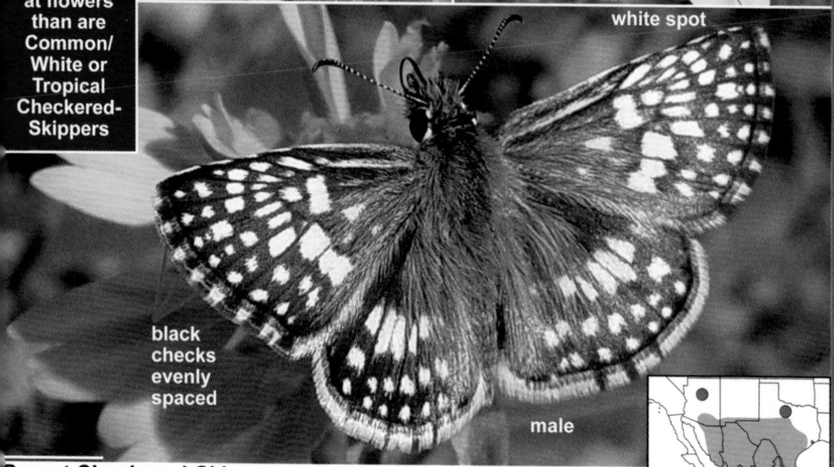
white spot
black
checks
evenly
spaced
male

Desert Checkered-Skipper *Pyrgus philetas*

strawberries and cinquefoils

LR-U

East
Apr-May

West
June-early Aug

VA/NC montane grassy hilltops and meadows

Michigan openings in oak-pine barrens

West alpine meadows

has greatly decreased in eastern U.S.

Park
Co., CO

missing
white spot
Rockbridge
Co., VA

Grizzled Skipper *Pyrgus centaureae*

cinquefoils and horkelias

northern California and Northwest
C
Apr-Aug

Rockies
R-U
June-July

San Diego Co (endangered 'Laguna Mountains' subspecies)
LR
Apr-May

montane meadows, conifer woods openings, down to sea level on Pacific Coast

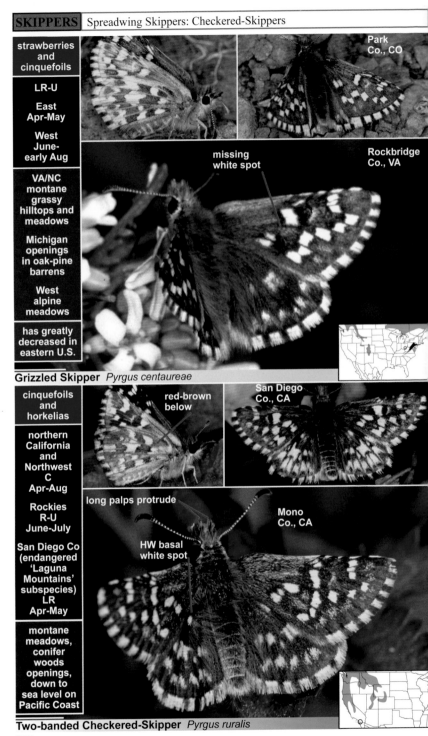

red-brown
below

San Diego
Co., CA

long palps protrude
Mono
Co., CA
HW basal
white spot

Two-banded Checkered-Skipper *Pyrgus ruralis*

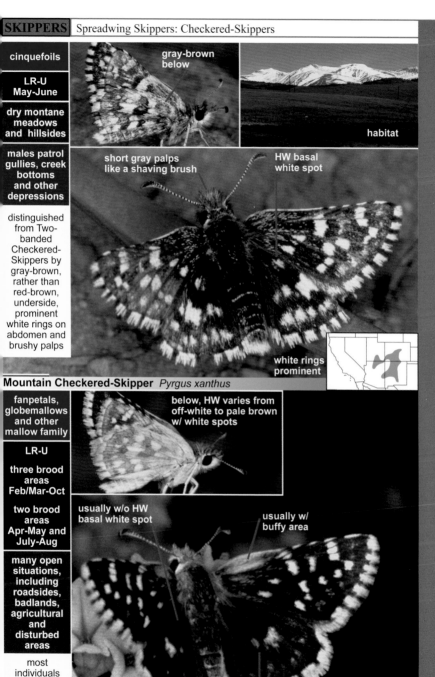

cinquefoils

LR-U
May-June

dry montane meadows and hillsides

males patrol gullies, creek bottoms and other depressions

distinguished from Two-banded Checkered-Skippers by gray-brown, rather than red-brown, underside, prominent white rings on abdomen and brushy palps

gray-brown
below

habitat

short gray palps
like a shaving brush
HW basal
white spot
white rings
prominent

Mountain Checkered-Skipper *Pyrgus xanthus*

fanpetals, globemallows and other mallow family

LR-U

three brood areas
Feb/Mar-Oct

two brood areas
Apr-May and July-Aug

many open situations, including roadsides, badlands, agricultural and disturbed areas

most individuals with only half-checks on the HW fringe

below, HW varies from
off-white to pale brown
w/ white spots

usually w/o HW
basal white spot
usually w/
buffy area
black check
stops halfway
usually w/
reduced spots

Small Checkered-Skipper *Pyrgus scriptura*

mallow family

LRGV
C-A
all year

elsewhere
R immigrant

tropical woods, thorn-scrub and nearby areas

larger than other white-skippers in its range

as with other white-skippers, females have more extensive black borders than do males

female

male

dark band slants in
dark band slants in
dark bands form a Y

Laviana White-Skipper *Heliopetes laviana*

mallow family

U-C
all year

tropical woods, thorn-scrub and nearby areas

probably because of behavioral differences, as with Laviana White-Skippers, one sees more males than females

often can be distinguished from Laviana White-Skipper on the wing, due to smaller average size

female
white ray to margin

male
white ray to margin

dark band slants in
wide strong brown border
dark band slants out

Turk's-cap White-Skipper *Heliopetes macaira*

mallow family

R-U all year

thorn-scrub and desert

prefers drier habitats than Laviana and Turk's-cap White-Skippers

Northern White-Skipper, page 324, has less extensive black borders on both FWs and HWs, has marginal black chevrons and lacks the dark area near the base of the FW below

narrow
white
band

dark band
constricted
dark area
dark band
slants out

Erichson's White-Skipper *Heliopetes domicella*

mallow family

rare stray to the LRGV, one record from Corpus Christi

first seen in the U.S. in Oct 2004

thorn-scrub and desert

as does Erichson's White-Skipper, East-Mexican White-Skipper has broad black and white HW borders

above with wider white bands than on Erichson's White-Skipper

two white
"fingers"
wide
white
band

dark band fairly
evenly wide
dark band
slants out

East-Mexican White-Skipper *Heliopetes sublinea*

southern California and southern Nevada
C

elsewhere
R-U

mostly Apr-June, Aug-Oct

dry canyon and chaparral

the only white-skipper in most of its range

Erichson's White-Skipper, page 327, has more extensive black and white HW borders and a dark spot on the FW below

male

female

pale brown patch

Northern White-Skipper *Heliopetes ericetorum*

no dark patch
black veins
orange
no black patch

thin
black
band
female
male

LRGV

Veined White-Skipper *Heliopetes arsalte*

black veins
black patch

thick
black
band

LRGV once

Alana White-Skipper *Heliopetes alana*

Wild Crapemyrtle

three brood areas
U
all year

one brood areas
R
immigrant/ temporary colonist

thorn-scrub, open woods, gardens

although with white HW patches, this species is closely related to the duskywings

mottled gray-brown and white

female

male
large white median patch
wide gray rings

White-patched Skipper *Chiomara asychis*

unknown

HW w/ spur
narrow gray rings
se Az
sw NM

White Spurwing *Antigonus emorsus*

multiple plant families

oval
falcate
white hairs
not yet LRGV

White-haired Skipper *Noctuana lactifera*

Indian Almond family

dingy gray-brown overall
seAZ
once

Pale Mylon *Mylon pelopidas*

Barbados Cherry family

black veins
not yet LRGV

Black-veined Mylon *M. maimon*

mallow family

three brood areas
U
most of year

two brood areas
R-U
immigrant, mostly July-Nov

thorn-scrub, open woods, gardens

pale underside is prominent during rather weak flight

inner edge of band is straight
soft "powdered" look
scalloped HW

Texas Powdered-Skipper *Systasea pulverulenta*

mallow family

U
all year
mostly spring and fall

desert canyons

pale underside is prominent during rather weak flight

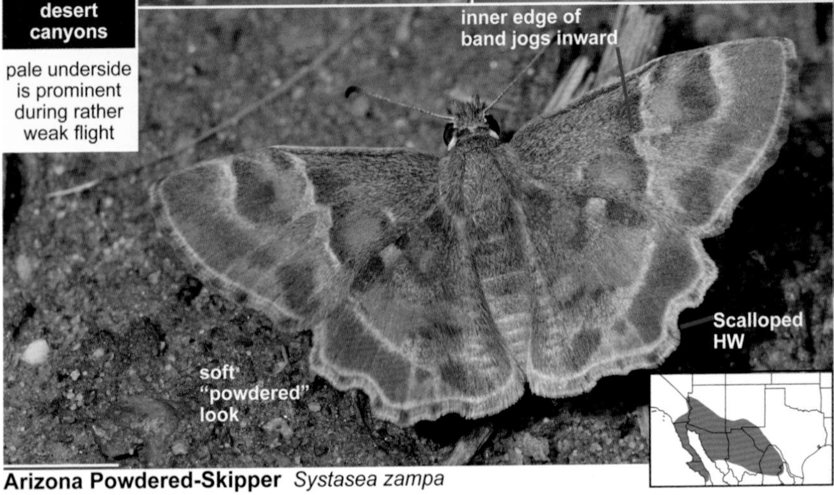
inner edge of band jogs inward
Scalloped HW
soft "powdered" look

Arizona Powdered-Skipper *Systasea zampa*

mallow family

U-C
Mar-Sept
mostly
Mar-May
in LRGV

thorn-scrub, open woods, gardens

the unusual pleated appearance of streaky-skippers is distinctive

Common Streaky-Skipper *Celotes nessus*

mallow family

R-U
Mar-Sept

montane gullies and streamsides

it is not currently known how to definitively distinguish Common and Scarce Streaky-Skippers in the field; identification of the individual shown at right is only highly probable

Scarce Streaky-Skipper *Celotes limpia*

grasses

LR-LC
late spring/
early summer

grassy openings in moist conifer or mixed woods

a circumpolar gem that is called chequered skipper in the U.K.

this, and all the skipperlings, have a strong proclivity for nectaring at geraniums

Jackson
Co., OR

very large white
spots on yellow-
brown ground
Berkshire
Co., MA

Arctic Skipper *Carterocephalus palaemon*

grasses

LU-LC
mostly
June-July

moist, grassy edges of creeks and streams

nectaring at a geranium in the photo at right and top right inset photo

small and reddish-brown with an unmarked HW, except for a narrow, faint cell-end bar

black disk

unmarked HW

Russet Skipperling *Piruna pirus*

LC
July-Aug

wet, grassy areas in montane woods

exact spot pattern on topside is variable

red-brown
ground
four white spots

tan fringe

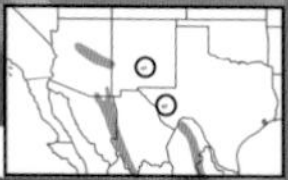

Four-spotted Skipperling *Piruna polingi*

LU-LA
Aug

mid-elevation grassy gullies and other depressions in oak woods

topside is similar to Four-spotted but with whiter fringe

spots not aligned
no white streak
elongated spot
off-white
fringe

white
fringe

Many-spotted Skipperling *Piruna cingo*

very rare stray

mid-elevation oak woods

resident in the Sierra Picachos, just 45 miles south of the border in Nuevo Leon, Mexico

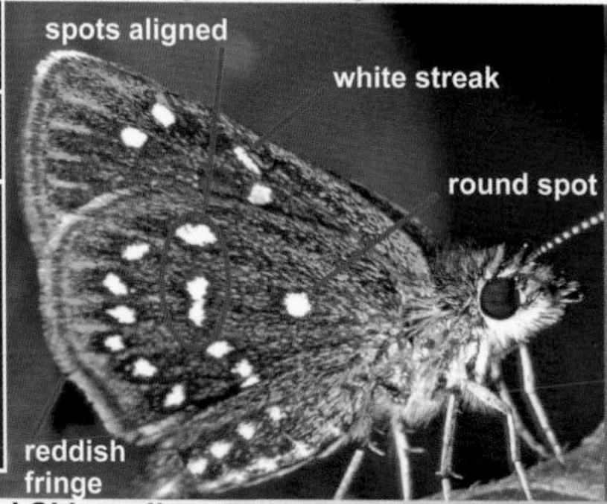
spots aligned
white streak
round spot
reddish
fringe

Small-spotted Skipperling *Piruna microstictus* LRGV

R
Mar-Sept

montane pine-oak

hope for it in Green Gulch, in Big Bend National Park, Brewster Co., Texas

HW w/ dark
inverted
patch
violet-
gray

no HW spots

Chisos Skipperling *Piruna haferniki* Big Bend

U-C throughout warm weather

open moist, but not wet, grassy areas, including fields, roadsides, gardens

small but snappy!

tiny and bright orange, with very narrow wings

usually opens its wings only as wide as shown in top right inset

little, or no, orange on leading edge

veins darker than ground
gray-white ray

Southern Skipperling *Copaeodes minimus*

C throughout warm weather

many habitats in dry regions, especially canyons and gardens

the arid region counterpart of Southern Skipperling

slightly larger than Southern Skipperling, with the same narrow wings but without the gray-white HW ray

usually w/ orange on leading edge

veins paler than ground
pale fringe

Orange Skipperling *Copaeodes aurantiacus*

C-A
sometimes with thousands

three broods
May-Oct

two broods
June-Aug

one brood
July

wet grassy areas, including marshes, meadows, and roadside ditches

small

usually with much black visible on the topside during the slow and low to the ground flight

Least Skipper *Ancyloxypha numitor*

LR-LU
Feb-Oct

grassy water edges

narrow dark border
wide dark border
faint pale ray
black points

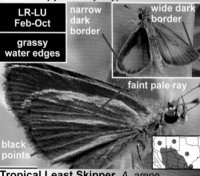

Tropical Least Skipper *A. arene*

LR
June-Sept

grassy desert seeps

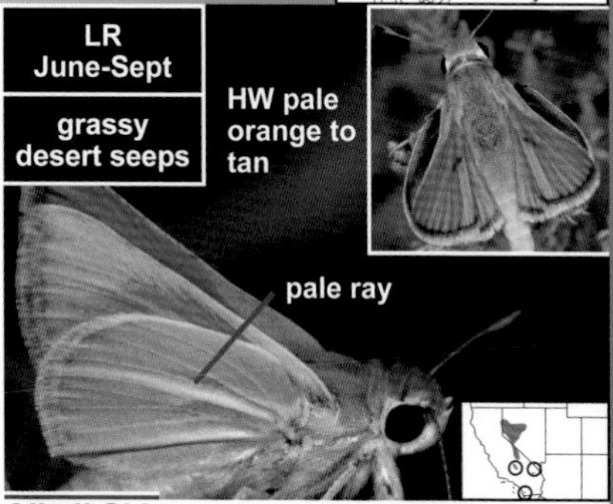
HW pale orange to tan
pale ray

Alkali Skipper *Pseudocopaeodes eunus*

LR
May-Oct

cienegas at about 5000 ft

pale yellow ray
shadow

se AZ
w TX

Sunrise Skipper *Adopaeoides prittwitzi*

LR
all year

scrub

sharp pale ray
red-brown ground
white trailing edge

LRGV

Pale-rayed Skipper *Vidius perigenes*

Timothy and other grasses

LC-A
May-Aug

dry fields and roadsides with tall grasses

a European species that first appeared in Ontario in 1910; now one of the most common skippers in the Northeast, its range is still expanding, especially in the West

flight is weak

gray-white overscalling
female

veins w/ black
female

short, narrow stigma
male

wings relatively short and broad
short antennas
male

European Skipper *Thymelicus lineola*

grasses

C
June-mid Aug

prairies and montane grasslands

by far the most common and widespread of the three species of *Oarisma* in the United States and Canada

flies slowly as it weaves through grasses

black overscaling

orange FW disk
white veins

Garita Skipperling *Oarisma garita*

Elliptic Spikerush

LR
late June-July

undisturbed tall-grass prairie

usually lands below tops of grasses

to see this butterfly, you better go fast, because it may be extinct in the near future

dark topside contrasting w/ pale underside is apparent during the slow, and awkward-looking, flight

black

black FW disk
white veins

Poweshiek Skipperling *Oarisma poweshiek*

Deergrass and perhaps other grasses

U-C
late May-mid Aug

se AZ and sw NM, mostly July-early Aug

northward mostly June-July

montane open grassy areas, most frequently in pine-oak from 5000 to 8000 ft

larger than Orange Skipperling with a slower flight

clear orange

orange FW disk
wings relatively long and narrow
veins not white

Edwards' Skipperling *Oarisma edwardsii*

Little Bluestem

LU-LC

mostly May-Sept but in Deep South Mar-Oct

areas with low vegetation and bluestem grasses

usually with a yellowish cast below but, especially when worn, can appear brown

usually with no FW spots, but some with largish, diffuse spots

Hunterdon
Co., NJ

pale spots
absent or
diffuse
no
subapical spot

Okeechobee
Co., FL
usually w/
paler veins

Swarthy Skipper *Nastra lherminier*

bluestem grasses

LU-C

almost all year most common Aug-Oct

areas with low vegetation and bluestem grasses

usually browner than Swarthy Skipper, with veins the same color as the ground, and with a faint pm band

above, pale spots are small but distinct

FW w/
small and
distinct
pale spots
one or
more
subapical
spots

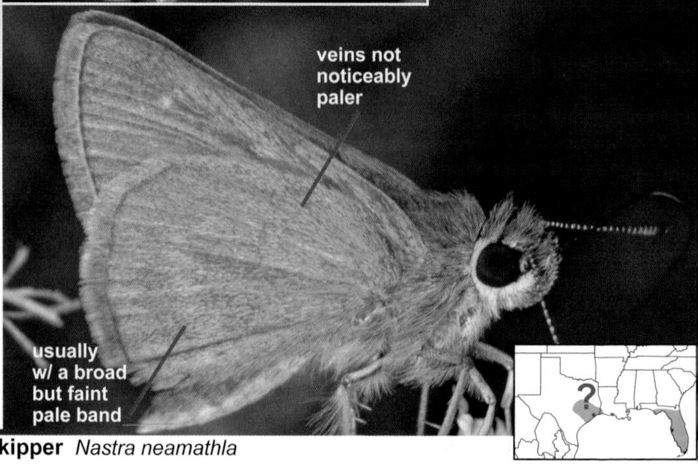
veins not
noticeably
paler
usually
w/ a broad
but faint
pale band
?

Neamathla Skipper *Nastra neamathla*

Texas
C
most of year

California-Arizona
LR
Aug-Oct

open grassy areas

often with a faint, pale, angular HW pm spot-band (see left inset)

some with gray overscaling along HW trail and outer margin

Eufala Skipper, page 340, is grayer

no bright patch
tawny center w/ black veins
ground color variable — but usually w/ a yellow or gold cast
pale belly

Julia's Skipper *Nastra julia*

bright patch
tawny to margin, w/o black veins
dark belly
LRGV

Redundant Skipper *Corticea corticea*

crescent spot
hidden ray
white patch
LRGV

Hidden-ray Skipper *Conga chydaea*

often with double dot
LRGV

Double-dotted Skipper *Decinea percosius*

often w/ separated and narrow pm spots
orange brow
olive cast
LRGV once

Greenish Brown-Sk. *Mnasilus allubita*

grasses

U-C

three broods almost all year

two broods mostly June-Oct

widespread in open habitats

gray-brown ground with a vague paler HW pm band

after landing, often claps its wings together twice

usually w/ one or two cell spots

vague pm band, usually like a 3
short antennas
gray-brown ground

Eufala Skipper *Lerodea eufala*

grasses

LU
all year

open grassy woods and nearby areas

antennas longer than Eufala, with white before the clubs

browner ground color than Eufala, usually with a more well-marked pm band

long antennas

tawny costa

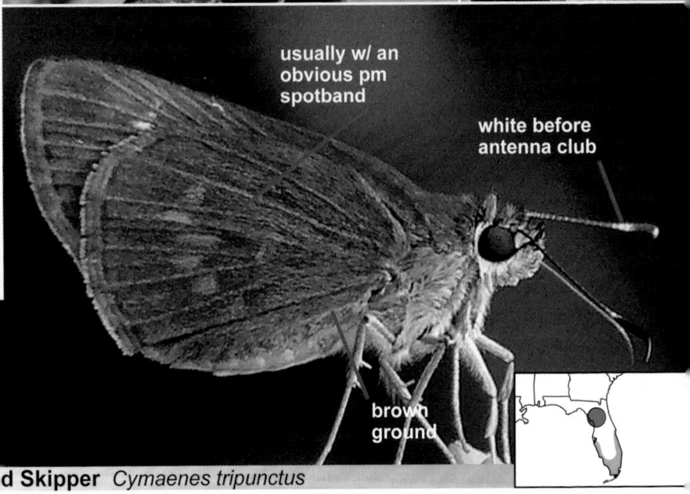
usually w/ an obvious pm spotband
white before antenna club
brown ground

Three-spotted Skipper *Cymaenes tripunctus*

grasses

prefers shaded situations

large

bottom spot
displaced outward
central white spot
three small
white spots

large white
spots

LRGV

Osca Skipper *Rhinthon osca*

grasses

R
all year, but mostly Oct-Nov

thorn-scrub, gardens

with a violet sheen when fresh

large, for a grass-skipper
dark spot

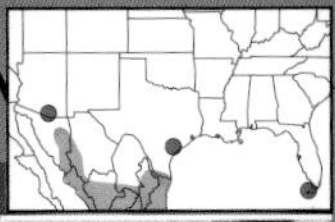

Violet-banded Skipper *Nyctelius nyctelius*

grasses

R
all year, but mostly Oct-Dec

open woods, gardens

this & Violet-clouded may be one species

usually w/o strong
pale spot here
dark central patch

LRGV

Olive-clouded Skipper *Lerodea dysaules*

grasses

LU
all year, mostly early spring and late fall

thorn-scrub,

gullies

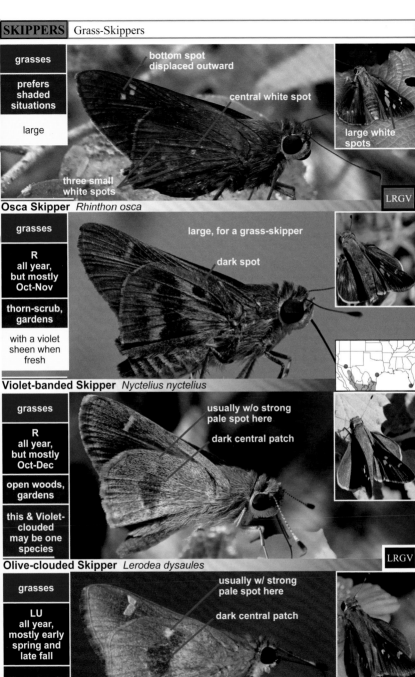

usually w/ strong
pale spot here
dark central patch

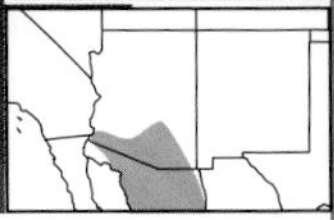

Violet-clouded Skipper *Lerodea arabus*

three broods
C-A
all year

decreasing
immigrant
northward

many habitats, but most common in open grassy woods

an early riser, often seen early in the morning, basking in the sunshine and playing butterfly tag

one of the most common dark, grass-skippers of the southeast

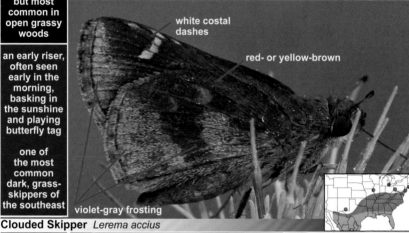

female

male

white costal
dashes
red- or yellow-brown
violet-gray frosting

Clouded Skipper *Lerema accius*

U-C
all year

open woods

as are most skippers, this species is fond of blue and/ or purple flowers

shade loving

smaller and less robust than Clouded Skipper

no white costal
dashes
paler square

Fawn-spotted Skipper *Cymaenes odilia*

no white costal dashes
yellow-brown ground
no frosting
LRGV

Liris Skipper *Lerema liris*

small
gray reaches lead
LRGV

Violet-patched Skipper *Monca tyrtaeus*

faceted, dark area
striated ground
LRGV

Malicious Skipper *Synapte malitiosa*

gray patch from apex to base
flocked ground
LRGV

Salenus Skipper *Synapte salenus*

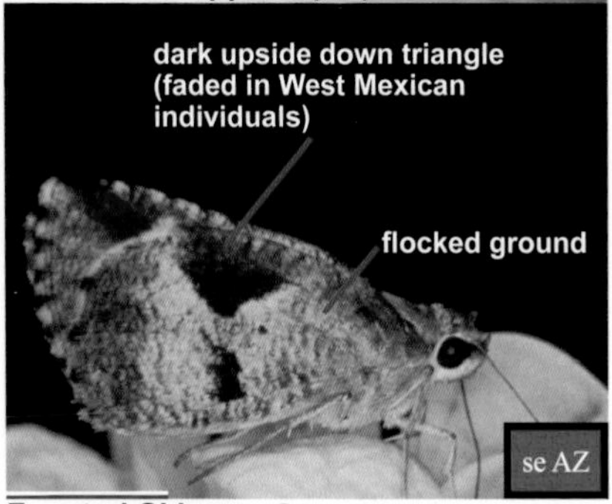
dark upside down triangle (faded in West Mexican individuals)
flocked ground
se AZ

Faceted Skipper *Synapte syraces*

off-white w/ dark veins and two dark patches
LRGV

Fantastic Skipper *Vettius fantasos*

large
chestnut markings
white stripe
LRGV

Chestnut-marked Skipper
Thespieus macareus

large
ruby eye
dark pyramid
LRGV

Green-backed Ruby-eye
Perichares philetes

Bermuda Grass

three broods C-A almost all year

two broods U-C summer-fall

one brood irregular fall immigrant

lawns, roadsides, open fields

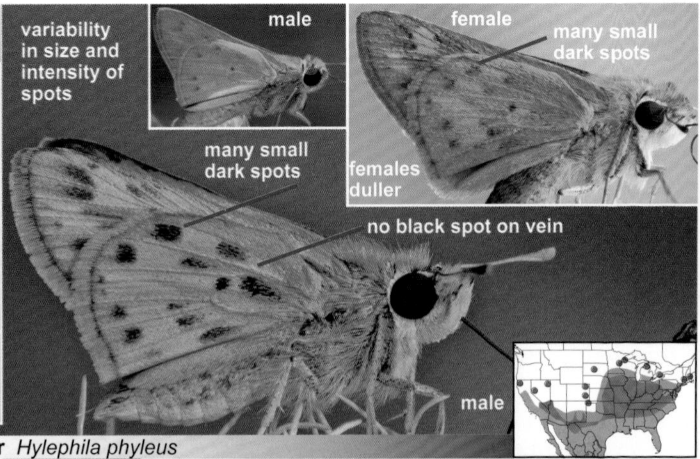
variability in size and intensity of spots
male
female
many small dark spots
females duller
many small dark spots
no black spot on vein
male

Fiery Skipper *Hylephila phyleus*

three broods C almost all year

two broods U-C May-Oct

barren fields, roadsides, woods edges

very jumpy, with whirling flight

south Texas females with olive cast

rarely, almost unmarked
male
female
Hidalgo Co., TX
usually w/ large dark spots
black spot on vein
Taylor Co., FL
female
male

Whirlabout *Polites vibex*

three broods C-A almost all year

two broods R-C summer-fall

open fields, roadsides, disturbed areas

some males are almost unmarked

male
female
pale chevron w/ central spot narrow and jutting out
worn female
dark area
male

Sachem *Atalopedes campestris*

out-
wardly
pointing
arrow
female
border
jagged

male
veins
not
dark
border
jagged
border
jagged

Fiery Skipper *Hylephila phyleus*

female
w/o bright
orange above

male
border
jagged
veins
dark
border
smoother

Whirlabout *Polites vibex*

female
black
triangle
large
glassy
spots
female

male
black patches
well-separated
large gray/
black patch

Sachem *Atalopedes campestris*

R-U
Mar-June
mostly
Apr-May

open
pine woods

hilltops

strong HW
basal spike

see Sonoran
Skipper,
page 355

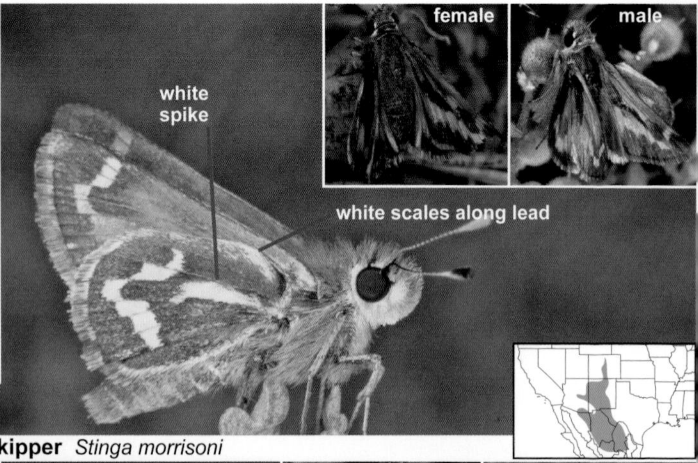
female
male
white
spike
white scales along lead

Morrison's Skipper *Stinga morrisoni*

LU-LC
mid Sept-Oct

open
montane pine
or pine-oak
woods

limited range
and fall flight
time

antennas are
blacker than
other Hesperia
skippers, with
white just
before the
clubs

dark
brown, or
green-
brown,
ground
white
female
male
white

Apache Skipper *Hesperia woodgatei*

mostly U

two broods
Apr-July,
Aug-Oct

one brood
mostly
June-July

canyons and
gullies at
low to mid
elevations

may not be
separable in
the field from
some female
Pahaskas

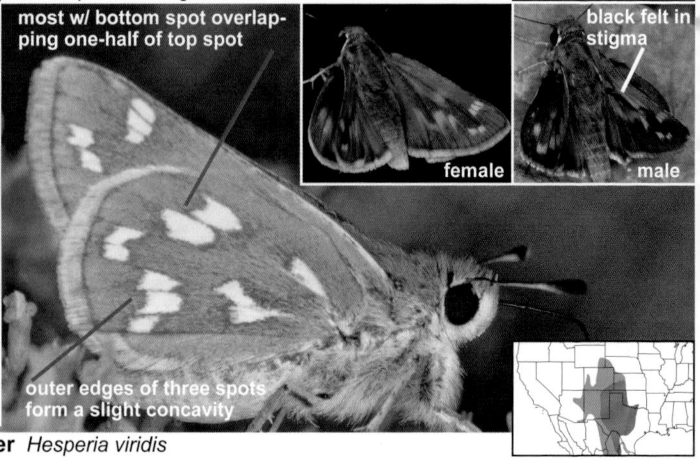
most w/ bottom spot overlap-
ping one-half of top spot
female
black felt in
stigma
male
outer edges of three spots
form a slight concavity

Green Skipper *Hesperia viridis*

mostly U-C

two broods Mar-Oct

one brood May-July

open pine woods to grasslands

hilltops

males have yellow "felt" in stigma

spot pattern below is quite variable

see female Sachem, page 344

Pima Co., AZ
female
yellow felt in stigma
male
Custer Co., SD
bottom spot not overlapping one-half of top spot
Arapahoe Co., CO

Pahaska Skipper *Hesperia pahaska*

mostly U

May-early Sept, but much shorter flight period at any given locality

high mountain meadows and grasslands, northern prairie

hilltops

topside with ill-defined FW borders

see Common Branded Skipper, page 348

Alpine Co., CA
female
usually w/ spots edged w/ black
Park Co., CO
usually w/ a green tint when fresh
strong basal "C"
bottom spot displaced inward, often barely touching adjacent spot

Nevada Skipper *Hesperia nevada*

mostly C-A

most frequent July-Aug but as early as May in southern California and as late as Nov at some locations

many, from prairies to sagebrush, to open conifer woods, to above treeline

hilltops

some treat eastern + northwestern (south to Clallam Co, WA), western, and northern plains (in U.S., mainly in MT and ND) populations as three species

most individuals in most populations with a prominent "C" at the base of the HW below; however some individuals in some populations, e.g. in Del Norte Co., California, can be almost unmarked

in Northeast, also see Leonard's Skipper, page 351

White Pine
Co., NV

female

male

spots usually
squarish
Mono
Co., CA
fringe
unchecked

Flathead
Co., MT

Clallam
Co., WA

Essex
Co., VT

Common Branded Skipper *Hesperia comma*

LR-LU

southward mostly late Mar-May and Sept-Oct

northward mostly late May-June and Sept

chaparral, oak woods

hilltops

upper portion of HW pm chevron is missing or incomplete

ground color varies from pale to dark

Siskiyou
Co., CA

male

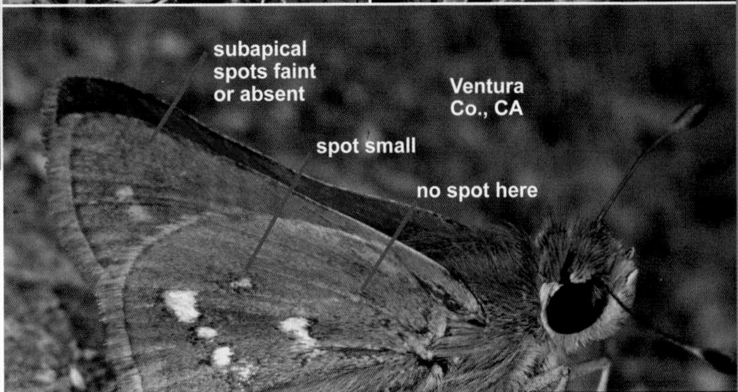
subapical spots faint or absent
Ventura Co., CA
spot small
no spot here

Columbian Skipper *Hesperia columbia*

LR July-Aug

mountain tops above treeline in Sierra Nevada and White Mountains

hilltops

spots usually long and narrow
white overscaling
dark brown ground
fringe often semi-checked

male

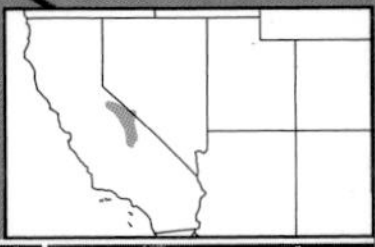

Sierra Skipper *Hesperia miriamae*

southward LR-U

northward U-C

mostly mid May-early July

foothill chaparral and open oak woods

cream spots, not white (males)
long vein extensions
indistinct FW borders

female

male

Lindsey's Skipper *Hesperia lindseyi*

mostly Blue Grama

LR-U

two broods May-June July-Sept

one brood mostly June-July

short-grass prairie and alkaline grasslands

hilltops

populations in Mono County California and in Minnesota have reduced white veining

see Rhesus Skipper page 358

White Pine
Co., NV

most females
w/ prominent
white
female

male

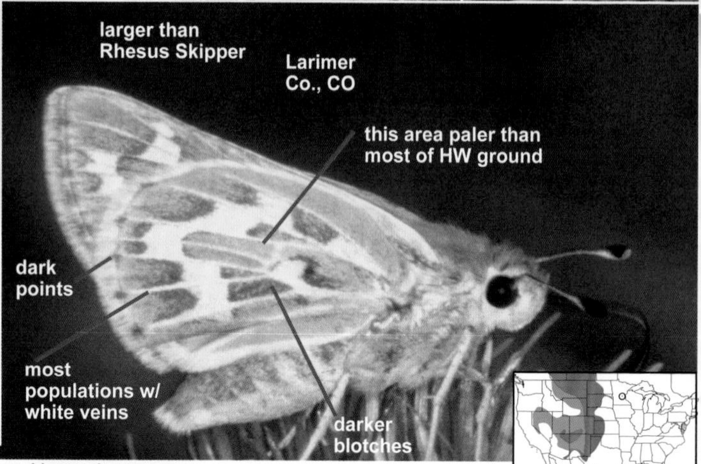
larger than
Rhesus Skipper
Larimer
Co., CO
this area paler than
most of HW ground
dark
points
most
populations w/
white veins
darker
blotches

Uncas Skipper *Hesperia uncas*

Jefferson
Co., CO

female

male

mostly C

late Mar/Apr-June, late Aug-Sept/Oct

montane meadows and sagebrush

gullies

jagged, well-
defined border
San Diego
Co., CA
spot displaced
inwardly
mushroom-
shaped spot

Juba Skipper *Hesperia juba*

LR-LC late March (TX, NC) -early June

dry fields, barrens, power-line cuts

flight is low

females are darker brown both above and below

Texas and Oklahoma individuals are often weakly marked below

female Sachems, page 344, are larger without white veining

female
Ocean Co., NJ

female
Cherokee Co., OK

female

Morris Co., NJ
male
white costa
white chevron

male

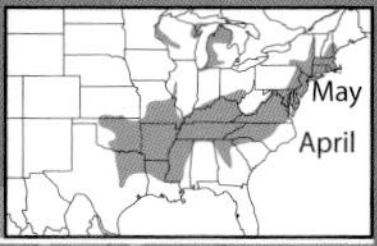

Cobweb Skipper *Hesperia metea*

LR-U mostly late Aug-Sept as early as late July northward and as late as mid Oct southward

open areas with extensive bluestem and a profusion of fall-blooming purple flowers

large

eastward, reddish with bold spots

westward, orange or yellow with spots small, faint or absent

Boulder Co., CO

female

male

Westchester Co., NY
reddish ground (eastward)
usually w/ white spot here

Boulder Co., CO

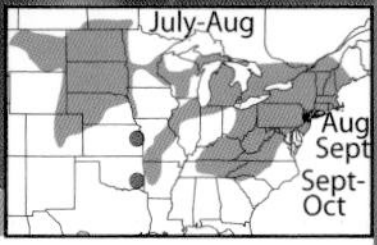

Leonard's Skipper *Hesperia leonardus*

LR-LU
mid June-early Aug

mixed- and tall-grass prairie

seriously declining

large

dull yellow-orange to straw yellow with no or very faint pm band

flies earlier in the year than Leonard's Skippers page 351

Dakota Skippers are smaller with a more pronounced spot-band

Jefferson Co., CO

some females w/ a dark spot-band
Crawford Co., WI

female

Custer Co., SD
pm band faint or absent

male

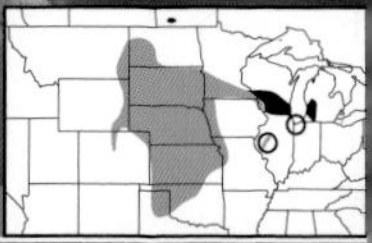

Ottoe Skipper *Hesperia ottoe*

LR
mid June-mid July

high quality calcareous prairie, usually around glacial lakes

less than one percent of our prairies remain, thus prairie butterflies are in trouble; this species and Poweshiek Skipperling are especially endangered

males are dull yellow-brown, females darker gray-brown with stronger spots

female
usually w/ spot here

female

male

usually w/ a faint, but obvious, spot-band
male

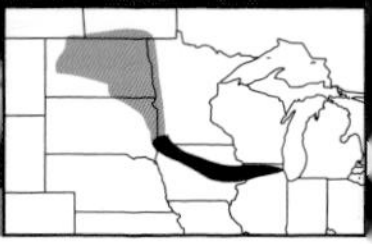

Dakota Skipper *Hesperia dacotae*

Little Bluestem and other grasses

LR-LC
May-June, Sept-Oct

dry open longleaf pine woods

the distinctive Big Pine Key subspecies may now be extinct

below, bright orange to orange-brown

pm spot-band absent to moderate

above, FW black border is wide and well-defined

male
double-spot
female
male
complete pm band

pm spot-band varies from prominent to faint to absent
female

Meske's Skipper *Hesperia meskei*

LR-LU

two broods March-June, July-Oct

one brood July-early Aug

East sandy open pine barrens

MidWest short-grass prairie

large

below, ground color and intensity and size of spots is variable

see Crossline Skipper page 356

Ocean Co., NJ
well-defined dot-band
female
male

one or two subapical spots (Crossline Skipper has none)
white dots often well-defined (but not on this individual)
no spot here
Liberty Co., FL
July
May-Sept
June, Aug-Sept
Mar-May, July-Oct,

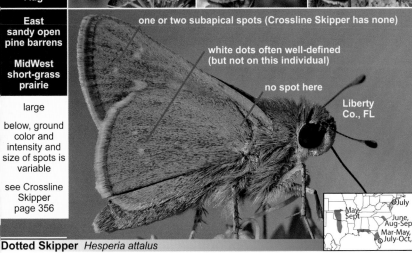

Dotted Skipper *Hesperia attalus*

U-C
May-July

dry brushy fields, grassy openings in and near woods, including powerline cuts

generally paler than Long Dash, with narrower post-median spots

HW spot-band is less pronounced than on Long Dash and the spots are more concave outwardly

some males are almost unmarked below

male

female

thin stigma
male

third and fourth spots displaced outwardly, compared to spots below them
spot-band moderate to faint
female
spots concave outwardly
June-July
May-June

Indian Skipper *Hesperia sassacus*

mostly LU-C
late May-July

mostly high and dry montane meadows

common in the White Mountains of Arizona, where it is sometimes abundant

skippers in the genus *Hesperia* don't have jagged, double-pointed central chevron spots

Sandhill Skippers, page 359, have white veining

female

male

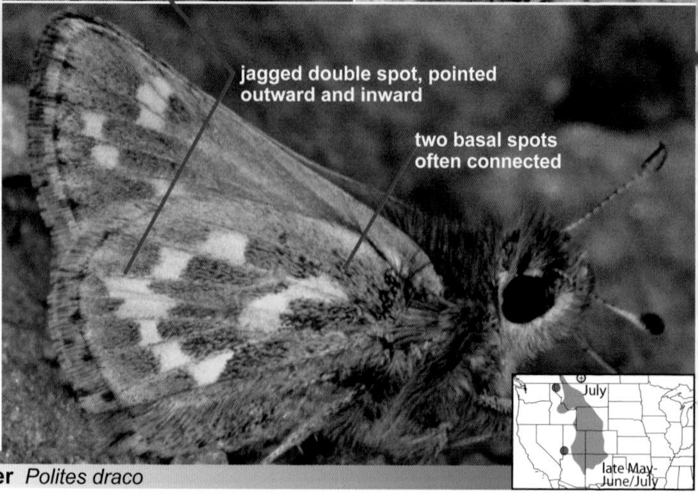
jagged double spot, pointed outward and inward
two basal spots often connected
July
late May-June/July

Draco Skipper *Polites draco*

mostly U-C

mostly June-July

moist meadows

may be spreading in parts of the West as it adapts to suburbia

below, HW pm spot-band is strong with wide spots

Peck's Skipper, page 356, has middle spots of HW pm chevron jutting outward

Lawrence Co., SD
male

female

male

third and fourth spots not displaced outwardly, compared to spots below them
basal spots
Morris Co., NJ
wide pm spots
female

Long Dash *Polites mystic*

mostly U-C

late May-Aug

wet meadows

presumably named for Sonora, California, this species isn't found in the dry Sonoran life zone

ground color below mostly is yellow-brown but red-brown along the Pacific

pm spots below are usually whiter than on Long Dash

Sublette Co., WY

female

Sublette Co., WY
male

no subapical spots
Jackson Co., OR
basal "spike"
narrow pm spots

Jackson Co., OR
male

Sonoran Skipper *Polites sonora*

Purpletop Tridens, Big Bluestem and other grasses

U-C

two broods May-Sept

one brood mid June-early Aug

dry open grassy areas

averages larger than Tawny-edged

ground usually not as dark as Tawny-edged

HW pm spots of variable intensity

dull orange
female
male
yellow spot
often w/ a brassy cast
usually w/o strong contrast between FW costa and HW
usually w/ pm spots

Crossline Skipper *Polites origenes*

mostly C-A but LU in some of the West

two broods May-Oct

one brood June-Aug

eastward: widespread in grassy areas, including suburbia

westward: moist meadows

in much of the Northeast, a frequent garden butterfly

female
male
central spot is rectangular and juts outward
very wide basal and pm bands

Peck's Skipper *Polites peckius*

U-A, mostly C

three broods Apr-Oct

two broods May-June, Aug-Sept

one brood mostly June-July

widespread in open, grassy areas

HW dull, usually without pm spots; if present pm spots usually more curved than on Crossline Skipper

bright orange
female
jet-black stigma
male
no yellow spot
usually w/ strong contrast between FW costa and HW
usually w/o pm spots

Tawny-edged Skipper *Polites themistocles*

R-LU Florida almost all year

short grass open areas, including lawns

small

HW pm band sometimes absent

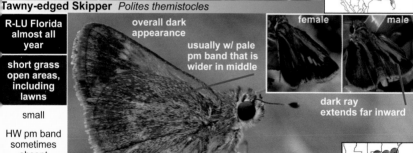

overall dark appearance
usually w/ pale pm band that is wider in middle
female
male
dark ray extends far inward

Baracoa Skipper *Polites baracoa*

LR Northwest mid May-July

low grassy slopes; foggy rhodo-dendron forest

Woodland Skipper, page 366, w/ orange end of abdomen

wide pm band
spot
male
female
female
male
inside edge of spot angled out

Mardon Skipper *Polites mardon*

Blue Grama grass

R-LC
May-July, mainly mid May-mid June

short-grass prairie, usually at high elevation

as I said in BTB:West, the dark spots are Rhesus pieces

resembles a small Uncas Skipper with more extensive dark patches below and no orange above

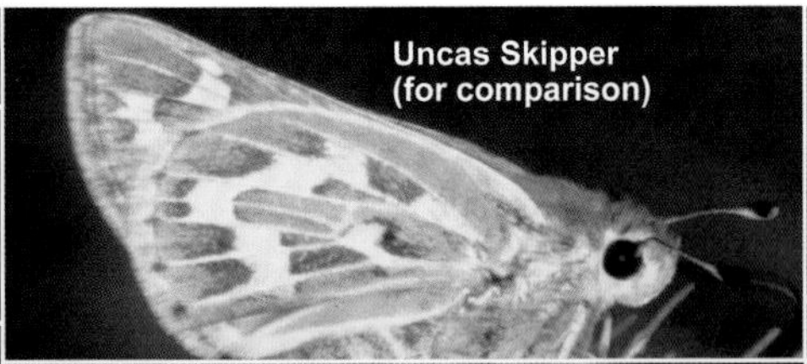
Uncas Skipper
(for comparison)

female

strong white chevron
chocolate patch extends over two veins
white shoulders
male

Rhesus Skipper *Polites rhesus*

R-U
Mar-May, July-Sept

males often perch just below hilltops or at the edges of gullies

dry grassland, usually with oaks

pattern is similar to Rhesus and Sandhill Skippers, but without dark areas

topside is similar to Rhesus Skipper

pm white band
ground varies from gray-brown to yellow-brown
basal white band
gray fringe

Carus Skipper *Polites carus*

Saguache
Co., CO

Tulare
Co., CA

Tulare
Co., CA
female

Saltgrass, Bermuda Grass, et al.

U

three broods
Apr-Sept

two broods
May-Sept

one brood
June-Sept

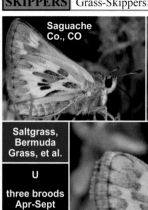

many habitats, including sand dunes, lawns, high elevation dry meadows

Los Angeles
Co., CA
dark patch bounded by thick and curved pale area

Kern
Co., CA
male

White Pine
Co., NV

White Pine
Co., NV
female

Mono
Co., CA
female

variable, with many named subspecies

lowland populations (see Los Angeles County photo) are usually paler with a less distinct pattern than are high-elevation populations (see Mono County photos)

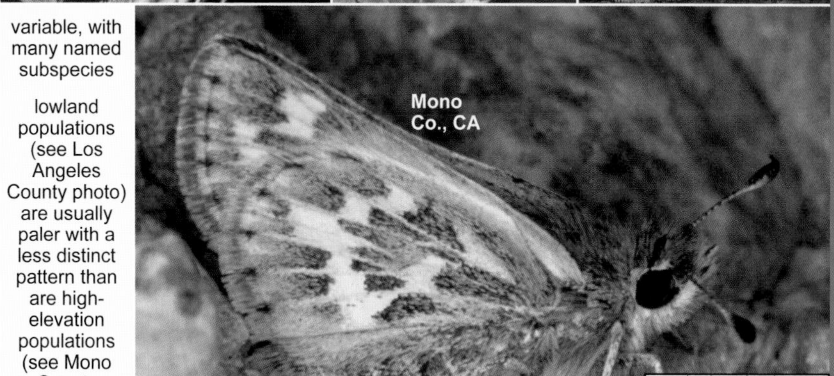
Mono
Co., CA

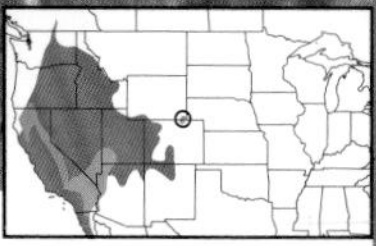

Sandhill Skipper *Polites sabuleti*

panicgrasses

U-LA

two broods Apr-Oct southward, mid June-Sept northward

one brood late June-early Aug

grassy fields and meadows, including disturbed areas

underside often with purplish sheen (see inset)

see more photos, page 362

dull orange costal margin
female
male
rectangular spot at end of two-part stigma
wide, pale pm band, often shaped like a 3
yellow-brown ground

Northern Broken-Dash *Wallengrenia egeremet*

south Florida south Texas C all year

north to NC and east Texas C mostly May-June, Aug-Sept

northward R-U

moist, but not wet, grassy areas, including woods edges and gardens

brighter and redder than Northern Broken-Dash

see more photos, page 362

Hidalgo Co., TX
bright orange costal margin
female
male
rectangular spot at end of stigma
wide, pale pm band, often shaped like a 3
reddish ground
Monroe Co., FL

Southern Broken-Dash *Wallengrenia otho*

Purpletop
Tridens

U-C

two broods
May-mid
June, mid
July-Sept

one brood
mid June-
July

moist,
grassy areas,
usually near
woods

Jane Scott
claims that
they're called
witches
because
no one can
tell which is
which

see more
photos,
page 362

small spot
square spot
female
rectangular spot
male
pm band, if present, narrow and w/ distinct spots
white just before antennal club

Little Glassywing *Pompeius verna*

sedges

U-A

two broods
southward
Mar-Sept,
northward
June-Sept

one brood
June-Aug

moist,
grassy areas,
usually near
woods

on females
above, lowest
white spot
is usually
characteristically
crescent-shaped

see more
photos,
page 362

often w/ golden head
small white spots
female
normally spotless above
male
dark brown, ground, often w/ purplish sheen
usually w/o, or w/ weak pm band (but see inset)

Dun Skipper *Euphyes vestris*

Southern Broken-Dash *Wallengrenia otho* (page 360)

Northern Broken-Dash *Wallengrenia egeremet* (page 360)

white

Little Glassywing *Pompeius verna* (page 361)

Little Glassywing *P. verna* (page 361)

not white

Dun Skipper *Euphyes vestris* (page 361)

Travis
Co., TX

Jefferson
Co., CO

Dun Skipper *Euphyes vestris* (page 361)

female

male

female

grasses

U
all year

open thorn-scrub, woods edges, gardens

females usually darker with well-developed pm spots

see Southern Broken-Dash, page 360 and 362

pm spots faint to well-developed, coming to a point
ground color smooth yellow brown, often tinged w/ pink
female

male

LRGV

Common Mellana *Quasimellana eulogius*

HW w/ yellowish ground and orange veins

Glowing Skipper *Anatrytone mazai*

not yet LRGV

grasses and sedges

U-C

two broods mid May-mid July, late July-Sept

one brood late June-Aug

wet prairies, open, moist grassy meadows and savannas, powerline cuts, etc.

no HW pm band below

also see European Skipper, page 336

Larimer Co., CO

black basal area
female

cell-end bar
black veins
narrow border
male

bright yellow-orange ground
Taylor Co., FL
orange fringe

Delaware Skipper *Anatrytone logan*

bluestem grasses and others

Midwest: U

Eastward: LR

two broods Apr/May-June/early July, Aug-Sept/Oct

one brood June-July

high quality prairie, open grassland and grassy barrens

much rarer than very similar Delaware Skippers; best to see the upperside to be sure

Pontotoc Co., OK

black "needle"
female

no cell-end bar
wide border
male

pale/white veins
dark overscaling
Morris Co., NJ
gray/white fringe

Arogos Skipper *Atrytone arogos*

Big Cordgrass in NJ, wildrice and Giant Cutgrass southward

LR-LU

two broods June-Aug

one brood July

brackish, tallgrass tidal marsh near the mouths of large rivers

larger than Delaware Skipper

wider black margins above

limited range and habitat

female
white body rings

male
wide border

bright yellow-orange ground

Rare Skipper *Problema bulenta*

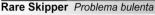

Barry Co., MO
male

Taylor Co., FL
female

Taylor Co., FL
female

LR-LC

two broods May-Oct

one brood June-July

East: wetland edges

Midwest: tall-grass prairie

usually with a wide, pale HW pm band & pale veins, but a few with uniform color

male
Barry Co., MO
usually w/ pale veins
wide pale area
male
Bibb Co., AL

Byssus Skipper *Problema byssus*

C-A
June-Oct
mostly
Aug-Sept

widespread

due to its abundance and late-season flight time, at times it is the most common butterfly flying

below, HW pale chevron varies from prominent to indistinct

ground color usually red-brown but can be yellow or brown

dark
rectangle
female

fringe
variable,
but
usually not
unmarked
gray
usually
w/ bright
orange
abdominal
tip
uneven black
border

male

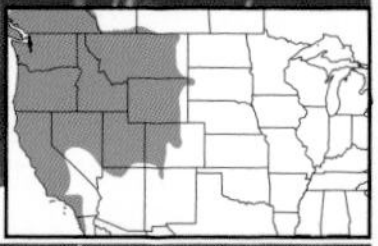

Woodland Skipper *Ochlodes sylvanoides*

U-C
May-July

woods openings and edges; riparian areas

not normally at high elevations

small

often with a dark area in the middle of the HW below, this area often with a pink sheen on females

male

female

male

female
dark area
fringe usually
unmarked gray
usually w/
bright orange
abdominal tip

Rural Skipper *Ochlodes agricola*

Common Reed

LR
two broods
June-July
Aug-Sept

one brood
July-Aug

wet spots with Common Reed

may have many individuals in its limited colonies

large

eastern populations are often darker with some pm pale spots below

female

male

usually unmarked
orange-yellow below

Yuma Skipper *Ochlodes yuma*

LR-U
July-Sept

openings in high elevation pine woods

mid-sized

chestnut ground color

HW with small, pale postmedian spots

rapid flight

hourglass
spot
female

male

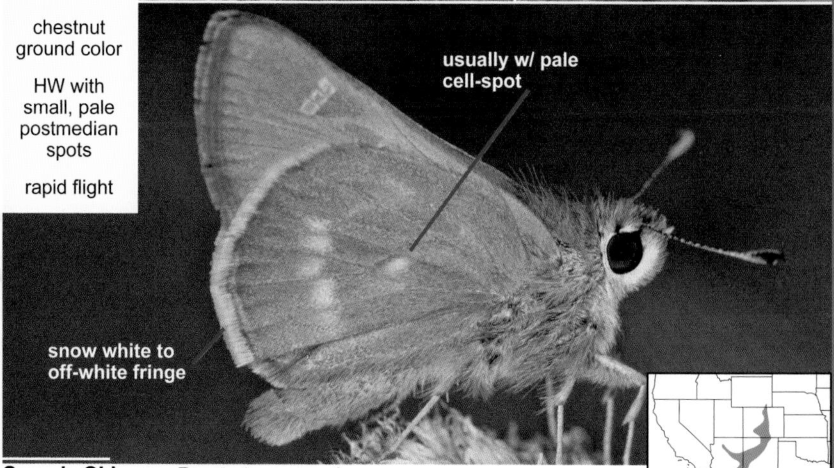
usually w/ pale
cell-spot
snow white to
off-white fringe

Snow's Skipper *Paratrytone snowi*

two strong white spots
prominent white apex
female

female

veins not black
male

U-C spring-fall; mostly May-June, late July-early Sept

openings and edges of woods; suburbia

flies higher than other grass-skippers

males perch on tree/shrub leaves, twigs and rocks

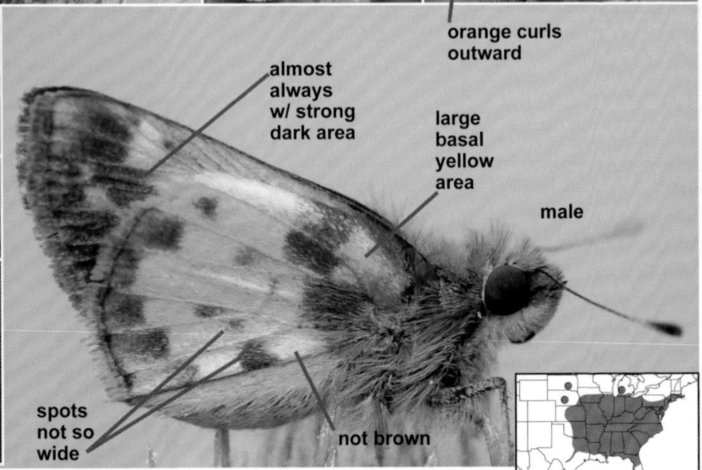
orange curls outward
almost always w/ strong dark area
large basal yellow area
male
spots not so wide
not brown

Zabulon Skipper *Poanes zabulon*

form pocahontas
female

form pocahontas
female

veins black
male

East C-A

West U

mostly late May-early July

openings and edges of woods

most males and females are similar, both above and below, but some females are darkened (see two left insets)

orange does not curl outward
female
small, if any, basal yellow area
wide brown border w/ gray frosting
basal brown reaches midwing

Hobomok Skipper *Poanes hobomok*

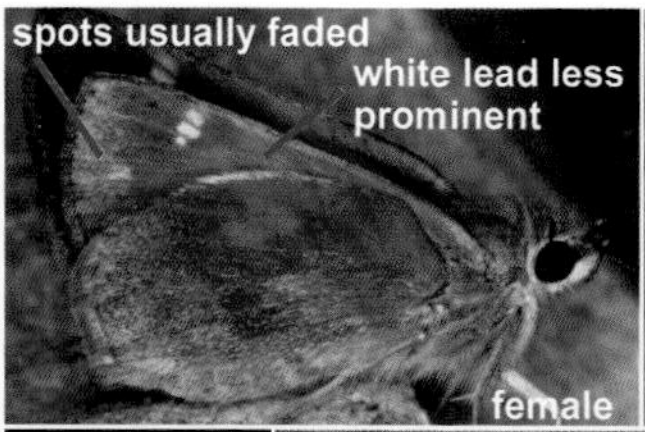
spots usually faded
white lead less prominent
female

female

male

C-A
mostly
June-Aug

openings and edges of woods

very similar to more eastern Zabulon Skippers but males have more rectangular brown spots below, and white on females lead is forward of the apex

usually w/o strong dark area
basal yellow area
two stacked lozenges
male

Taxiles Skipper *Poanes taxiles*

female

Santa Clara Co., CA
female

Los Angeles Co., CA
male

California U-C

elsewhere R

Mar-Oct

open woods and scrub

females are similar to males but, above, have whiter spots

quite similar to Hobomok below, but ranges don't overlap

male

Umber Skipper *Poanes melane*

sedges

LU-LC
mid June-early Aug, mostly July

freshwater wetlands

wings above black with a mulberry-like purple sheen — hence the name

often found with Black Dash, page 375

flight is relatively weak (airplane is missing its tail)

female
male

large yellow patch that resembles an airplane
red-brown ground color

Mulberry Wing *Poanes massasoit*

grasses

LR-LU
mostly Apr-June, Aug-Sept

marshes, both salt and fresh water; drainage ditches

pale HW ray of variable width and length, sometimes reaching margin, usually not

male above, stigma is thin and pale gray, not black

female
male

usually w/ no, or small, subapical spots
w/o large pale spots flanking central ray
paler ray (usually blends into ground near margin)
dull brown ground color of variable darkness

Aaron's Skipper *Poanes aaroni*

presumably grasses

LR-U
May-Oct
mostly June and Sept

openings and edges of swampy woods and adjacent areas

smaller than Broad-winged and usually darker/redder

zero to four (usually three) HW spots that are faint to well-defined

see Twin-spot Skipper, page 390

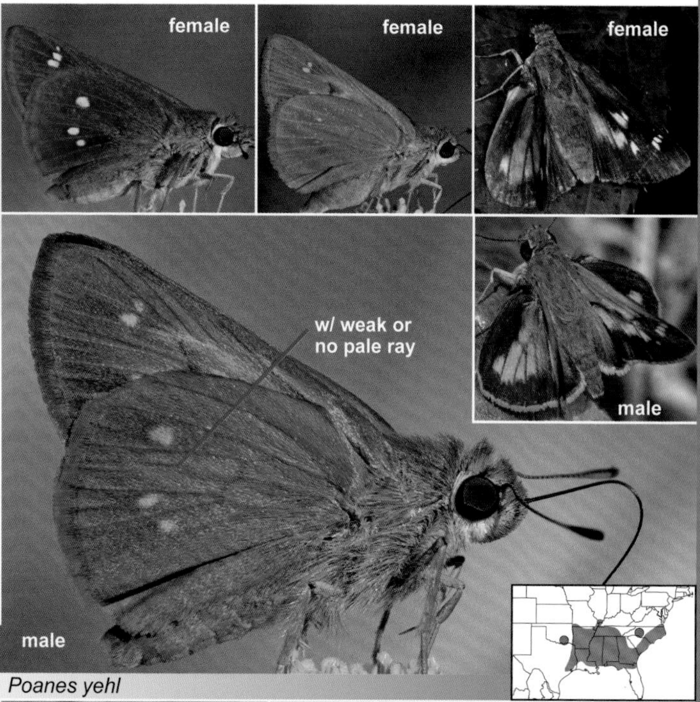
female
female
female
w/ weak or no pale ray
male
male

Yehl Skipper *Poanes yehl*

Common Reed and Annual Wildrice

mostly C-LA

Gulf Coast LR-LU

two broods Apr-Oct

one brood July-Aug

tidal and freshwater marshes

expanding range

very large

often lands with head up, oriented vertically

female
male
usually w/ distinct subapical spots
Variable: HW ray can be more intense than shown or almost absent (see inset)
usually w/ large pale spots flanking central ray

Broad-winged Skipper *Poanes viator*

sedges

LR-LU

two broods May-June, July-Aug

one brood mid June-early July

freshwater marshes, bogs and wet meadows

boots required

very active and quite wary

mid-sized

range doesn't overlap Palmetto Skipper

most w/ brighter
orange at base
of HW

female

male

usually w/ pale veins
yellow orange ground
golden head
white
fringe
wide white trail

Two-spotted Skipper *Euphyes bimacula*

Saw Palmetto

R-U
Mar-May
July-Oct
mostly Sept

prairies, sandhills, flatwoods

foodplant is abundant but the butterfly is rare; perhaps it is limited by nectar plant availability

very skittish and hard to approach

Florida Keys race is probably extinct

large

female

male

yellow orange ground
golden head
white
fringe
narrow white trail

Palmetto Skipper *Euphyes arpa*

Jamaica Swamp Sawgrass

LU-LC May-July, Aug-Oct

marshes (esp brackish), pine rockland (Florida Keys)

often nectars well outside of sawgrass habitat, where nectar is scarce

Florida Keys race is endangered

very large

see Monk Skipper, page 391

some w/ a faint, pale pm patch

Big Pine Key
Monroe Co., FL

female

Taylor Co., FL
cinnamon brown ground
wide double stigma
jagged border
male

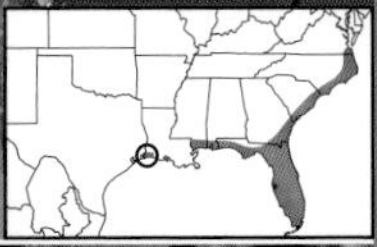

Palatka Skipper *Euphyes pilatka*

probably sedges

LR

mostly Mar-May, Aug-Oct

freshwater wetland edges

one of the least seen Eastern butterflies

mid-sized

ground color varies from rich orange-brown to cinnamon

see Dion Skipper, page 374 and Byssus Skipper, page 365

female

male

pale veins
no pm pale patch
no ray
off-white to buffy fringe

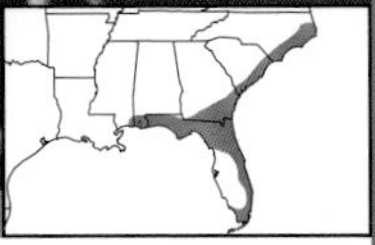

Berry's Skipper *Euphyes berryi*

LR-U

two broods May-July, Aug-Sept

one brood mostly July

edges of open wetlands

ground color varies from bright orange-brown to dull brown

HW trailing ray sometimes faint or absent

Morris
Co., NJ

female

male

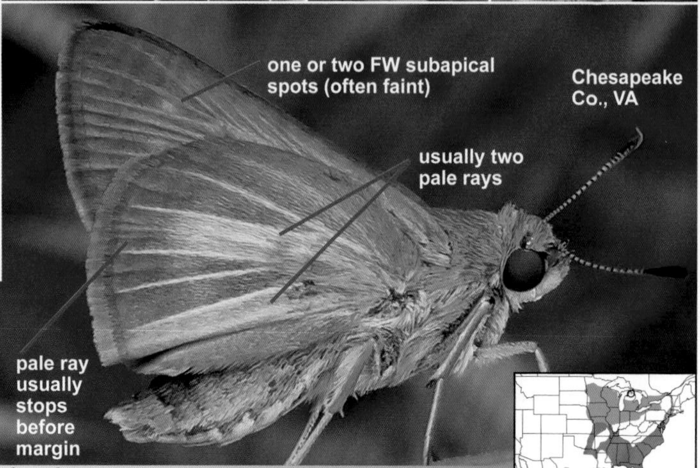
one or two FW subapical spots (often faint)
Chesapeake Co., VA
usually two pale rays
pale ray usually stops before margin

Dion Skipper, *Euphyes dion*

female

male

LR-LU

May-July, Aug-Oct

brackish coastal marsh

Bay Skipper is almost identical to Dion, and is possibly conspecific with it

best identified by habitat and location

Bay Skipper, *Euphyes bayensis*

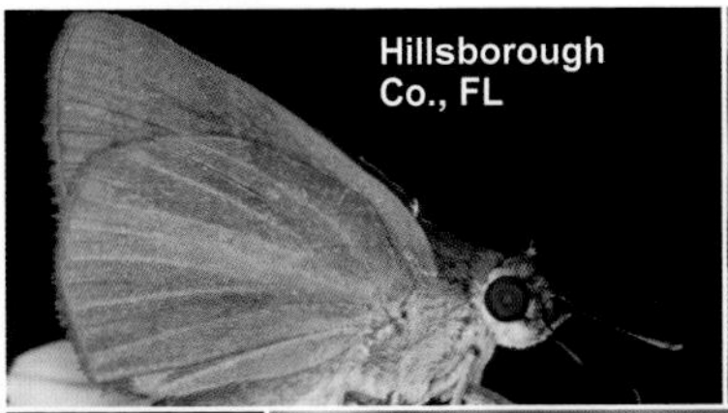
Hillsborough
Co., FL

female

male

LR-LU

two broods mostly May-June, Aug-Sept

one brood mostly July

very wet woods and edges

ground color varies from bright orange-brown to dull brown

mostly black above

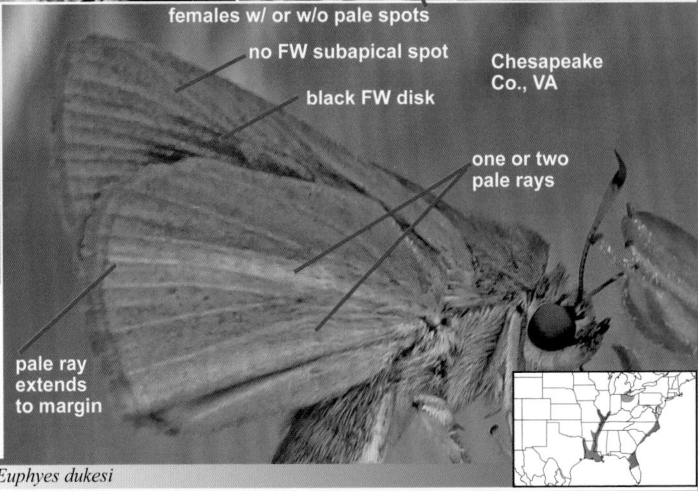
females w/ or w/o pale spots
no FW subapical spot
black FW disk
Chesapeake
Co., VA
one or two
pale rays
pale ray
extends
to margin

Dukes' Skipper, *Euphyes dukesi*

female

male

LR-LC June/July-early Aug

wet meadows, freshwater marsh edges

this species and Mulberry Wing, page 370, are often found together, along with Swamp Milkweed

ground color varies from bright red-brown to dark red-brown

pm pale patch
wider in the middle

Black Dash, *Euphyes conspicua*

bluestem grasses

LR-LC

two broods mostly Mar-Apr, Aug-Oct

one brood late Apr-mid June

open, dry grassy fields and prairies, grassy openings in oak-pine woods, barrens

black bar in front of eye creates a masked appearance

usually flies low to the ground

Custer
Co., CO

female

male

usually w/ a white basal spot
Morris Co., NJ
strong white over eye
wide black bar in front of eye
frosting

over most of range, mostly as shown in top panel main photo; in most of Florida, mostly as shown in main photo in bottom panel

some treat the southeastern double-brooded, usually strongly spotted, populations as a separate species, *A. loammi*, however there are little published data to support this treatment

Barry
Co., MO

Osceola
Co., FL

Osceola
Co., FL
in Florida and along southeast Coast, mostly w/ strong white basal and pm spots

Dusted Skipper *Atrytonopsis hianna*

unknown, probably grasses

U-C mostly May-June

canyons and washes in oak-juniper-pinyon woods

spots here vary from almost absent to prominent
hourglass spot
w/o strong black bar in front of eye
gray fringe
m and pm bars

Viereck's Skipper *Atrytonopsis vierecki*

unknown, probably grasses

LC-LA late Apr-early July mostly May-June

mid elevation oak woods

often found with Python Skipper, page 378

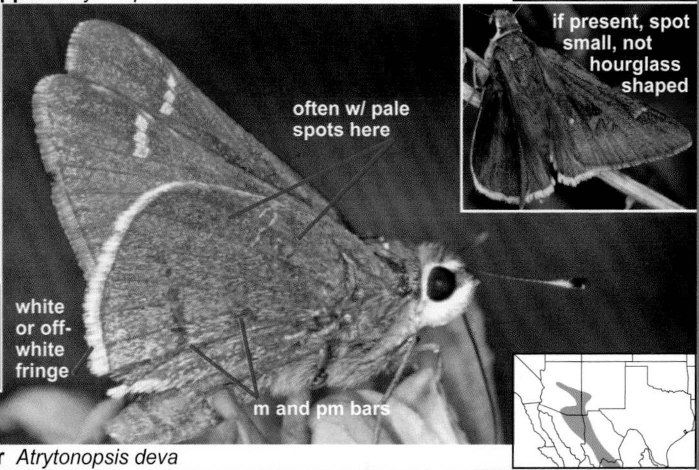
often w/ pale spots here
if present, spot small, not hourglass shaped
white or off-white fringe
m and pm bars

Deva Skipper *Atrytonopsis deva*

Bullgrass

LU July-Aug

mid elevation oak-juniper woods

exhibits thistlemania

broad white HW fringe evokes a crescent moon

Deva Skipper flies earlier in year

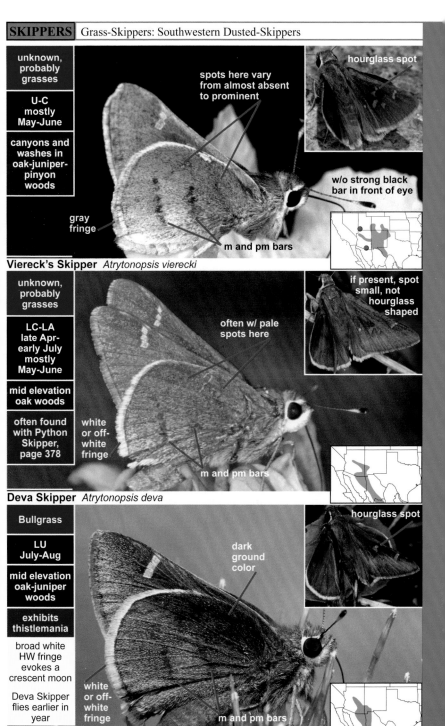

dark ground color
hourglass spot
white or off-white fringe
m and pm bars

Moon-marked Skipper *Atrytonopsis lunus*

unknown

U-C
Mar-May
with a partial second brood in Sept-Oct

grassy oak woods at mid elevations

often found at mudpuddles, sometimes on hilltops

lighting and viewing angle affect apparent prominence of the HW white bar

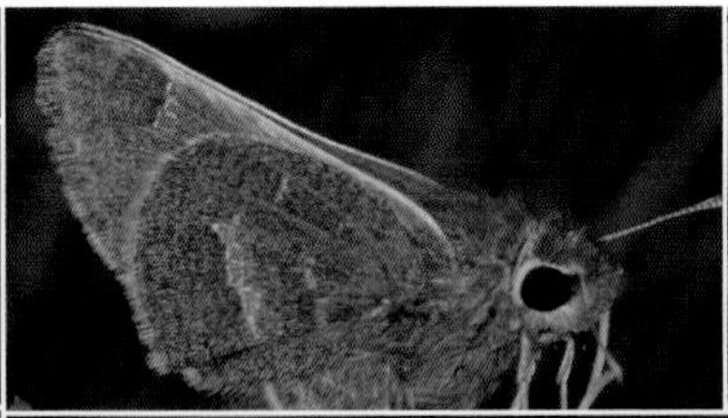

band
straight

not
white
fringe
unchecked
translucent
white bar

White-barred Skipper *Atrytonopsis pittacus*

unknown

R-U
May-early July

mid to high elevation open oak woods

often found with Deva Skipper, page 377

white patch below antennal club separates Python from Cestus, as does yellow spotting above

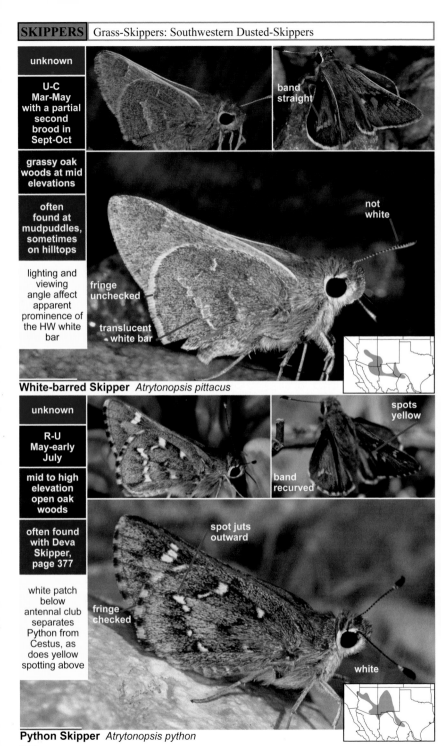

spots
yellow
band
recurved

spot juts
outward
fringe
checked
white

Python Skipper *Atrytonopsis python*

Bamboo Muhly

LR
mid Apr-May, mid Aug-early Oct

deep canyons with ample populations of its foodplant

males spend most of the day on steep rock faces, waiting for females and investigating any small dark flying objects by flying high-speed sorties

boldly patterned

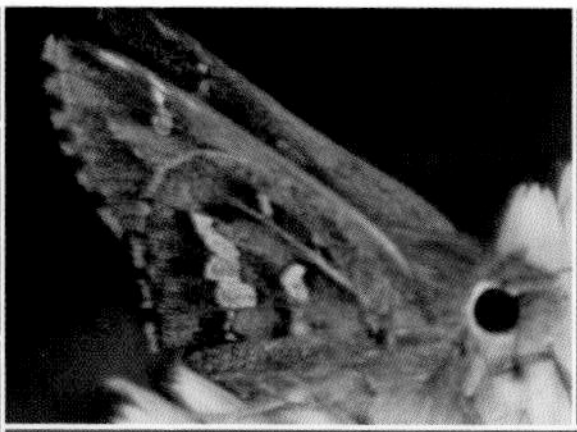

male w/ light-ening bolt; female w/ hour glass
male w/ strong spot; female w/ weak spot
male

wide pm white spots
fringe checked
not white

Cestus Skipper *Atrytonopsis cestus*

Sideoats Grama

U

Apr-June, Aug-Oct

mostly May and Aug

canyons and gulches in low to mid elevation oak grassland

occasionally at flowers but usually seen perching on rocks

large

extent of HW spotting is variable

Nuevo Leon Mexico

spots off-white
band recurved

FW more rounded than other dusted-skippers
grizzled gray ground
fringe checked
Pima Co., AZ

Sheep Skipper *Atrytonopsis edwardsii*

Giant Cane

U-LC
Apr-June,
July-Sept

wet woods, usually deciduous, with Giant Cane

this distinctive and attractive butterfly is the most common cane-feeding roadside-skipper

HW below with white, or off-white, cobweb pattern

Suffolk
Co., VA

Taylor
Co., FL
white veins
dark brown/
black ground
white m and
pm bands

Lace-winged Roadside-Skipper *Amblyscirtes aesculapius*

Giant Cane

LR-U
Mar/Apr-May,
June-July,
Aug-Sept

wet woods, usually deciduous, with Giant Cane

many individuals appear as mainly yellow with darker chestnut brown spots

see female Fiery Skipper, page 344

Carroll
Co., AR

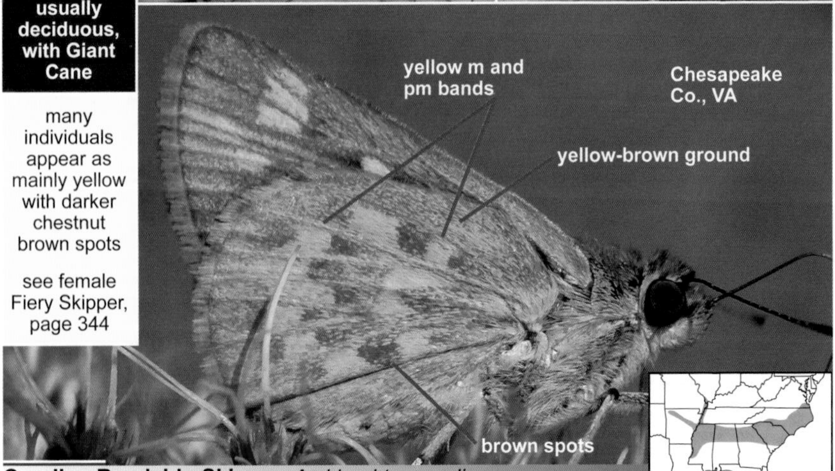
yellow m and
pm bands
Chesapeake
Co., VA
yellow-brown ground
brown spots

Carolina Roadside-Skipper *Amblyscirtes carolina*

Giant Cane

LR-U
Apr-Sept

wet woods, usually pine woods, with Giant Cane

although in Francis Marion National Forest in South Carolina this species may be abundant, in general it is more local and rare than is Carolina Roadside-Skipper

yellow m and pm bands
dark red-brown ground
?

Reversed Roadside-Skipper *Amblyscirtes reversa*

grasses

LR-U
Mar/Apr-May, Aug-Sept

mostly flatwoods, but also sandhills and prairies

very small

dark

very few markings

Common and Bell's Roadside-Skippers (next two pages), have antennal clubs with tapered extensions

blunt clubs, w/o tapered extension
dusted w/ blue-gray scales
?

Dusky Roadside-Skipper *Amblyscirtes alternata*

R-LC
Mar-Sept

two broods mostly Apr-May, July-Aug

one brood mostly June

roadsides and other woods/ grassland interfaces

barrens

second brood is partial

dark, usually without strong HW markings below

see Zabulon Skipper, page 368

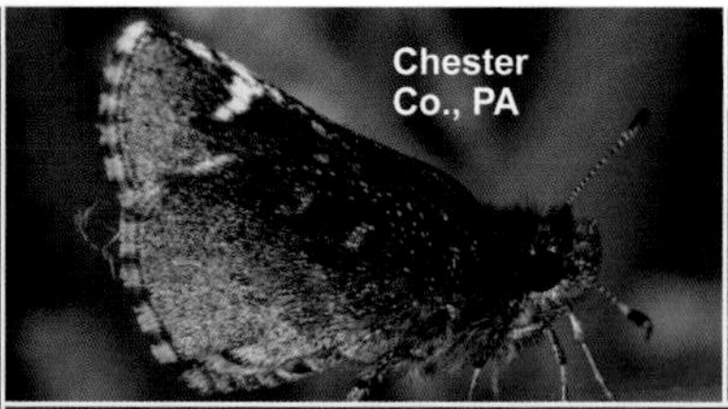
Chester
Co., PA

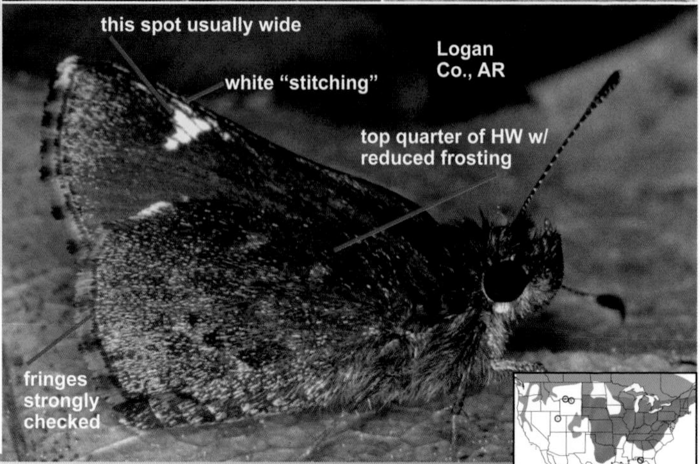
this spot usually wide
white “stitching”
Logan
Co., AR
top quarter of HW w/
reduced frosting
fringes
strongly
checked

Common Roadside-Skipper *Amblyscirtes vialis*

LR-U

two broods, second is partial Apr-May, July-Aug

one brood mostly May-June

open woods and edges

ground color usually green-gray, sometimes pink/purple-gray

pm usually more prominent than on other eastern roadside-skippers

females usually tan
Sussex
Co., NJ

FW spots
strongly
expressed

Logan
Co., AR
male
males usually green tinged
strong pm band

Pepper and Salt Skipper *Amblyscirtes hegon*

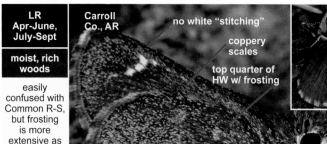

LR
Apr-June, July-Sept

moist, rich woods

easily confused with Common R-S, but frosting is more extensive as are coppery FW scales

see Bronze R-S, page 384

Carroll Co., AR
no white "stitching"
coppery scales
top quarter of HW w/ frosting

coppery scales

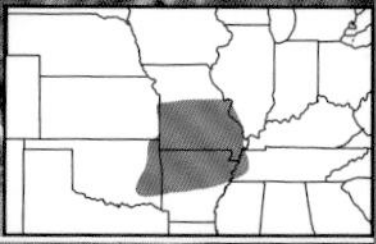

Linda's Roadside-Skipper *Amblyscirtes linda*

LR-LU
Apr-June, July-Sept

moist, rich woods

when fresh, Bell's Roadside-Skipper is usually darker than is Celia's Roadside-Skipper, especially above

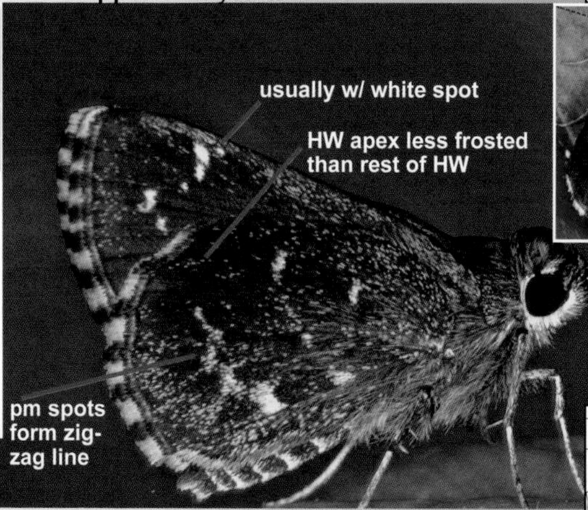
usually w/ white spot
HW apex less frosted than rest of HW
pm spots form zig-zag line

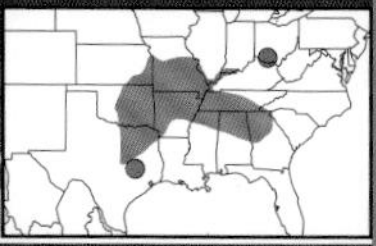

Bell's Roadside-Skipper *Amblyscirtes belli*

U-C

LRGV all year

northward Apr-Sept

open, moist, grassy woods

gardens

partial to shady situations

w/o white spot
HW apex frosted similarly to rest of HW

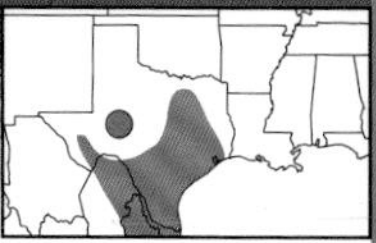

Celia's Roadside-Skipper *Amblyscirtes celia*

grasses

U-C

two broods (first partial) Apr-June July-Sept

one brood Apr-June

rocky canyon bottoms, open woods and prairies

HW below variable, as shown

some coppery scales on FW, both above and below

Cassus R-S has more orange both below and above

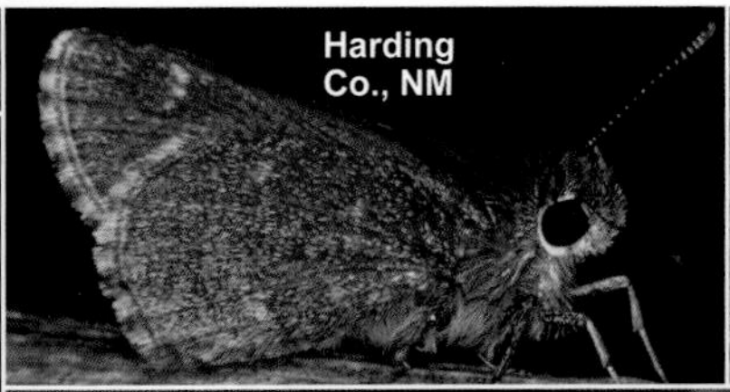
Harding
Co., NM

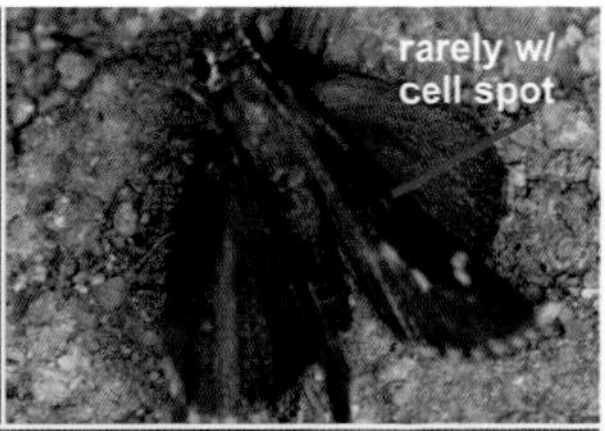
rarely w/
cell spot

coppery
scales
Cochise
Co., AZ

Bronze Roadside-Skipper *Amblyscirtes aenus*

Bulb Panicgrass

R-U

May-Sept

low elevation rocky canyons and washes

males perch in gullies and canyons bottoms

HW below usually with indistinct pattern

FW cell spot, both above and below

Bronze R-S with more copper-coloring, both below and above

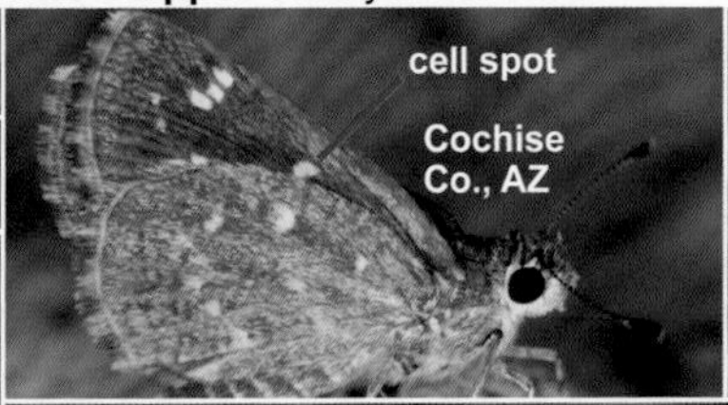
cell spot
Cochise
Co., AZ

cell spot

dull gray
ground
color
Dona Ana
Co., NM
?
?

Texas Roadside-Skipper *Amblyscirtes texanae*

grasses

C
June-Aug

mid to high elevation oak-pine woods

bright orange on FW, both above and below

HW pm band below usually wider and straighter than on similar roadside-skippers

Cassus Roadside-Skipper *Amblyscirtes cassus*

Cane Bluestem

R-U
July-Aug

mid elevation oak-juniper woods

yellow-brown ground color is distinctive

spots in HW pm band below usually well developed and because ground color is more uniform than on other roadside-skippers, is more prominent

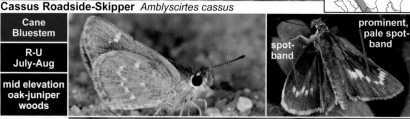

Slaty Roadside-Skipper *Amblyscirtes nereus*

Bullgrass

se AZ
C

northward
R-U

June-Aug

oak-juniper and oak-pine woods

HW below pm spots are pointed outwardly

large (compared to other roadside-skippers)

gray overscaling below quickly wears to flat brown

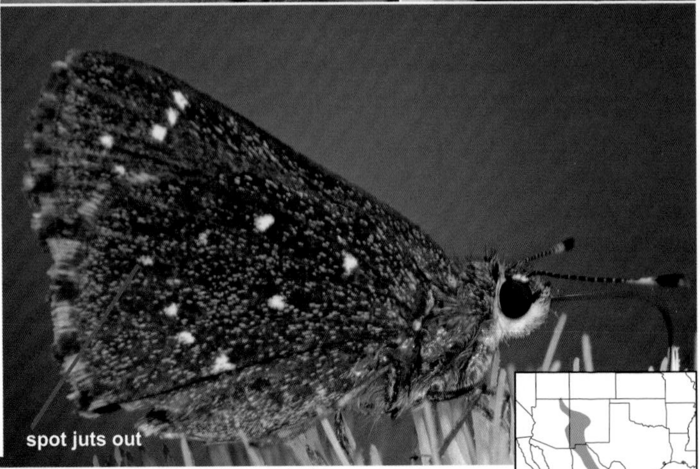

Large Roadside-Skipper *Amblyscirtes exoteria*

Vine Mesquite

R-U

Mar-Sept
mostly Apr, July-Aug

open oak woods, usually at low elevations

when fresh, bold white spots are dark edged and the ground color has a brassy sheen

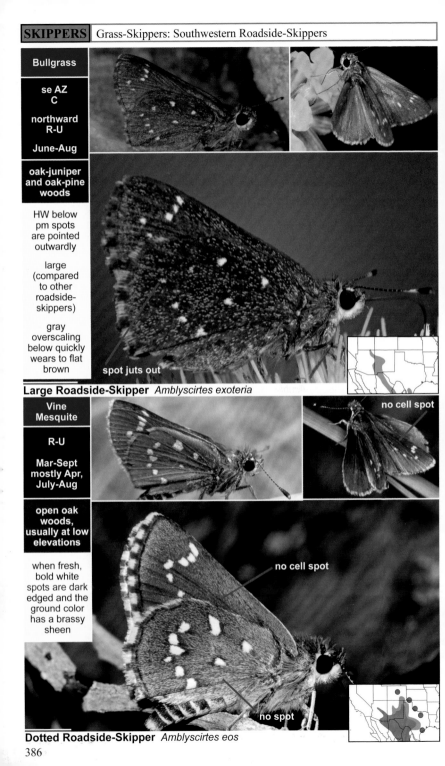

Dotted Roadside-Skipper *Amblyscirtes eos*

grasses

LR
May-Sept

mid to low elevation canyons and washes

as are many of the southwestern roadside-skippers, this species is most active early in the morning

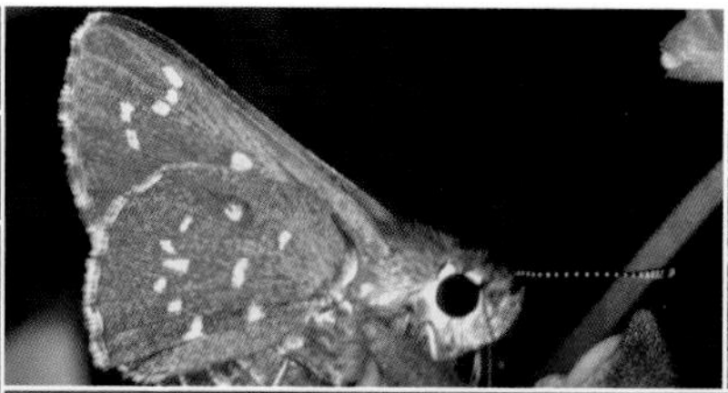

cell spot(s)
spot

cell spot
this spot vertically elongated
spot

Toltec Roadside-Skipper *Amblyscirtes tolteca*

Sideoats Grama

LR
mid July-mid Aug

oak-mesquite juniper woods

as are many of the roadside-skippers, this species is most active early in the morning; by 10 am individuals are resting in the shade

barely enters the United States in southeastern Arizona

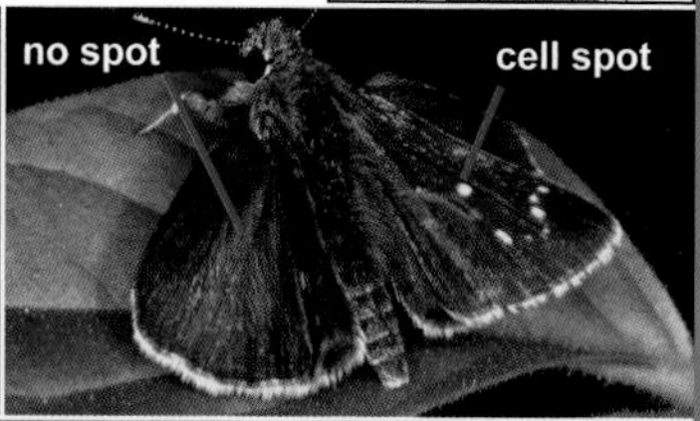
no spot
cell spot

cell spot
this spot round
no spot

Elissa Roadside-Skipper *Amblyscirtes elissa*

Sideoats Grama

R-U
May-Sept

northward mostly June

southward mostly July-Aug

canyons and gulches in high prairies and foothills

males patrol gulches and canyon bottoms

unmarked dull orange-brown above

below, gray overscaling obscures median band

dull orange-brown
no spots

orange
gray fringe
w/o strong median band

Oslar's Roadside-Skipper *Amblyscirtes oslari*

Blue Grama

R-U
May-Aug

northward mostly June

southward mostly Aug

short-grass prairie

hilltops

often just below the summit of grassland knolls

topside varies from almost black to extensively orange, and everything in between

female

male
yellow spots

pale fringe
strong median band

Simius Skipper *Notamblyscirtes simius*

grasses

R-U
Mar-Oct
mostly
Mar-Apr,
July-Sept

thorn-scrub, canyons, gardens

males patrol trails and gully bottoms in the morning

HW below with a distinctive mottled pattern

scattered dark markings

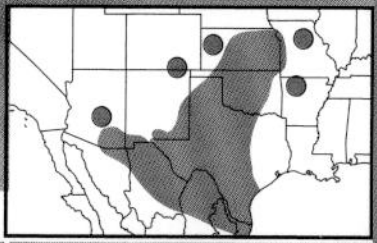

Nysa Roadside-Skipper *Amblyscirtes nysa*

Big Bluestem

R-U
mostly
June-July

canyons and gulches in high elevation prairie or sparse woods

blue sheen
orange head
white fringe

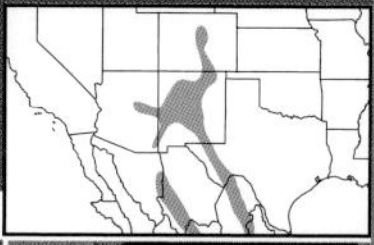

Orange-headed Roadside-Skipper *Amblyscirtes phylace*

grasses

LC
May-Aug
mostly June-July

montane pine woods

blue sheen
orange head
orange fringe

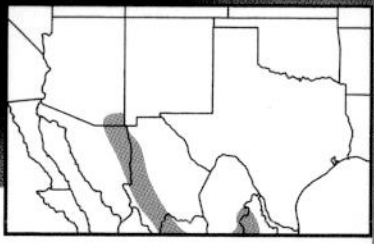

Orange-edged Roadside-Skipper *Amblyscirtes fimbriata*

bluestem grasses

U-LC

south Floida all year

northward mostly Apr-June, Aug-Sept

wetlands and pine woods

as do most grass-skippers, prefers nectaring at purple flowers

mostly as in main photo; rarely as in inset; sometimes w/ spots much reduced

older sibling
twins

Twin-spot Skipper *Oligoria maculata*

Canna

R-U

south Florida, south Texas all year

northward decreasing immigrant as the season progresses

wetlands, gardens

somewhat crepuscular

if you live northward, plant cannas and hope

translucent caterpillar

very large

very large spots
caterpillar
elongated FW
four translucent spots in a row

Brazilian Skipper *Calpodes ethlius*

palms

U
all year

woods edges, gardens

some view this skipper as severely ascetic; others see it as a very jazzy skipper; still others see it as compusive and filled w/ phobias

colonized Florida from Cuba in 1947

very large

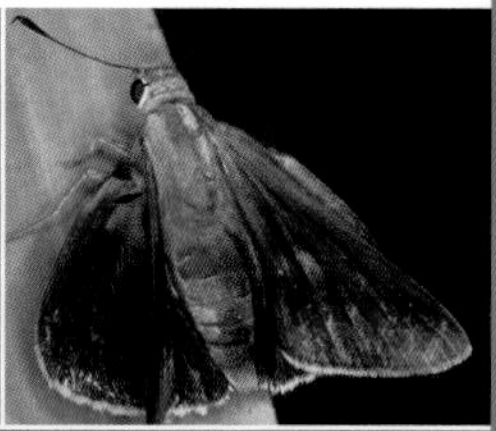

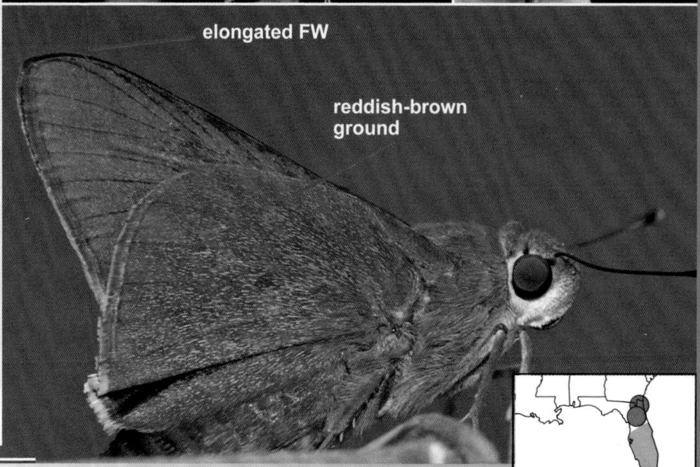
elongated FW
reddish-brown ground

Monk Skipper *Asbolis capucinus*

bamboo

first U.S. record, Apr 2016 at Bentsen-Rio Grande Valley SP

postmedian pale band
olive-brown ground
semi-hyaline spots

LRGV once

Olive Nicon *Niconiades nikko*

Costus

first U.S. record, Nov 2016 at Estero Llano Grande SP

very large (for a grass-skipper)

long cell spot
off-white HW base
HW outer half dark purplish

LRGV once

Perching Saliana *Saliana esperi*

Saltgrass

U-A

southward Mar-Oct

northward June, Aug-Sept

most common late summer/fall

salt marsh and nearby areas

long, horizontal pale spot

Salt Marsh Skipper *Panoquina panoquin*

Saltgrass

LR-LU July-Sept

salt marsh

apparently becoming scarcer

pale yellow pm spots
yellow veins

Wandering Skipper *Panoquina errans*

Saltgrass

U-C all year

salt marsh and nearby areas

Twin-spot Skipper, page 390, doesn't have yellow veins or elongated FW

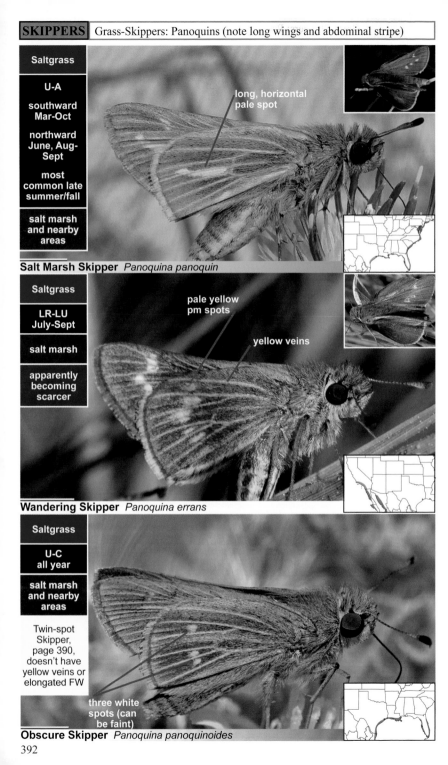

three white spots (can be faint)

Obscure Skipper *Panoquina panoquinoides*

grasses

three broods
C
all year

two broods
C immigrant
summer/fall

one brood
R-U
immigrant
late summer/
fall

open areas

usually w/o
cell spot
usually w/ two spots
outer 1/4
of HW
darkened

Ocola Skipper *Panoquina ocola*

grasses

U-C
all year
most
common in
fall

thorn-scrub,
gardens

Ocola Skippers sometimes have purple sheens and white spots, look for white cell spot and very long FW

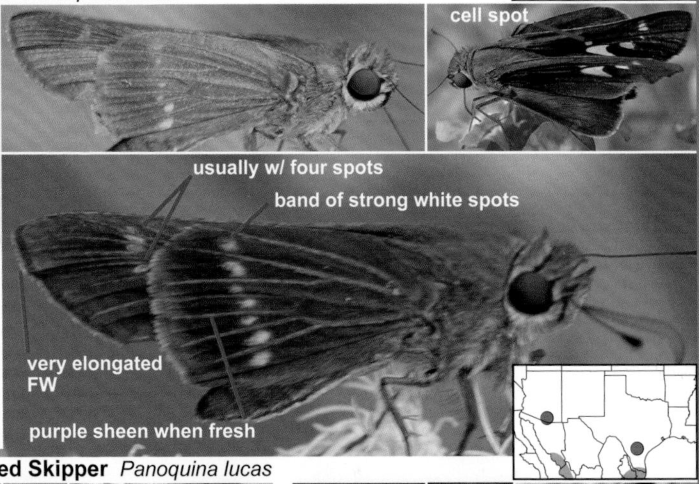
cell spot
usually w/ four spots
band of strong white spots
very elongated
FW
purple sheen when fresh

Purple-washed Skipper *Panoquina lucas*

grasses
cell spot
distinctly yellow
ground color
darkened outer portion of
HW less sharply defined
LRGV

Hecebolus Skipper *P. hecebola*

grasses
blue or purple
sheen when fresh
large
wide white
band
LRGV

Evans' Skipper *Panoquina fusina*

yuccas

R-U
Feb-June
mostly
Mar-Apr

areas with extensive stands of yuccas, including coastal dunes, grasslands, pine woods and semi-deserts

in most areas, more rarely seen than its actual occurrence

habitat
yucca

large white spot
ground color very dark
fringe narrow and weakly checked
no white spot

Yucca Giant-Skipper *Megathymus yuccae*

yuccas

R

two broods
Mar-Apr,
Sept-Oct

one brood
July-Aug

coastal dunes and pine woods with extensive stands of yuccas

as you can see by the size of the butterflies on these two pages, giant-skippers deserve their name!

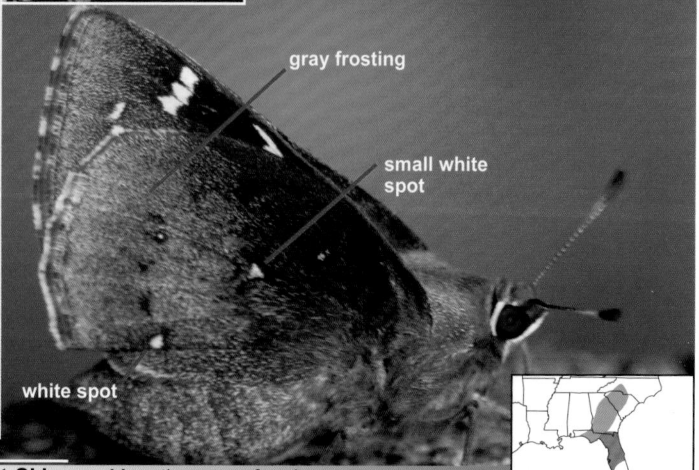
gray frosting
small white spot
white spot

Cofaqui Giant-Skipper *Megathymus cofaqui*

yuccas

R-LC

mostly mid May-early July

south-central Texas Mar-Apr

rolling grassland w/ extensive stands of yuccas

recent sightings in Louisiana suggest that it may be overlooked in east Texas

s-c Texas population often w/ outer angle white spot faint

habitat
yuccas

ground color not very dark
usually w/ broad white, unchecked fringe (except around Four Corners)
usually w/ white spot

Strecker's Giant-Skipper *Megathymus streckeri*

yuccas

R

mostly July-Aug

Big Bend area June-July

dry grassland with yuccas, especially where it meets oak woods

when fresh, bluish-white frosting covers most of the outer HW

extremely large

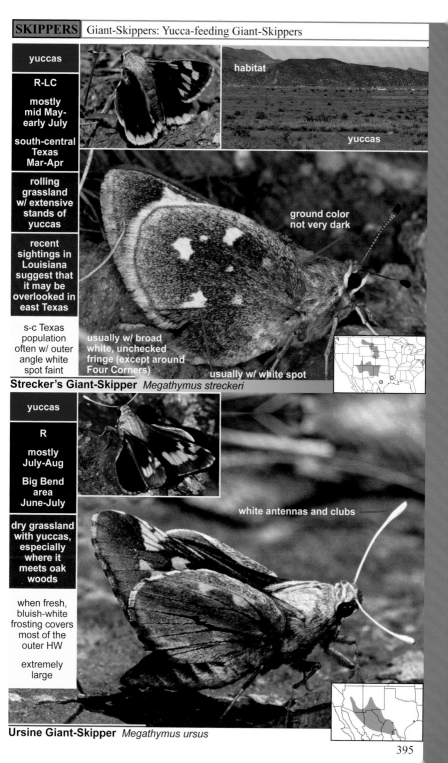

white antennas and clubs

Ursine Giant-Skipper *Megathymus ursus*

agaves

R
Aug-Oct, mostly mid to late Sept

dry grassland

agave-feeding giant-skippers usually keep their wings closed while landed, but they will rarely bask with open wings

although most often marked as shown, some individuals are more heavily spotted

extensive orange above
fringe checked buff and black

Orange Giant-Skipper *Agathymus neumoegeni*

Palmer's Century Plant and other agaves

U-C
Sept-Oct

dry grassland; sparse woods with agaves

mudpuddles

some treat populations from central Arizona west as a separate species, Bauer's Giant-Skipper — these are often more well-marked

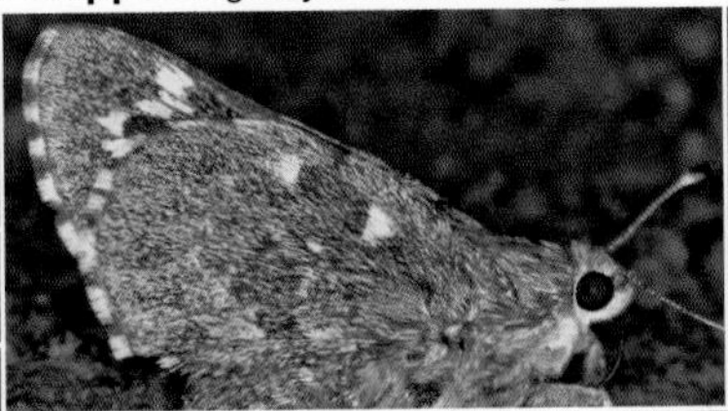

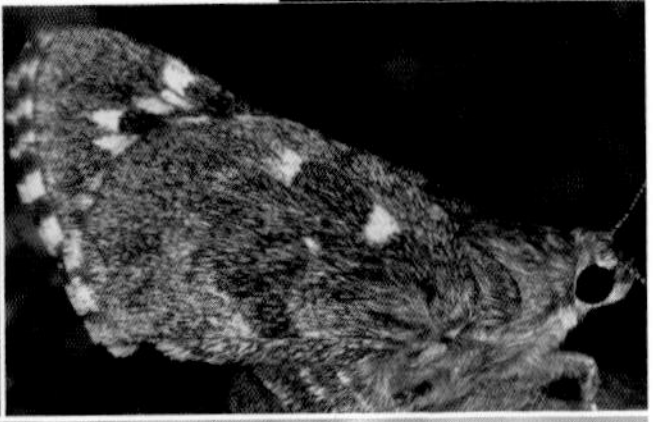

fringe checked white and black

Arizona Giant-Skipper *Agathymus aryxna*

Parry's Agave

C
limited to Huachuca Mountains and vicinity
mid Aug-mid Nov, mostly Sept

high elevation open pine-oak woods

mudpuddles

very similar to Arizona Giant-Skipper; best identified by association with the host plant

host
plant

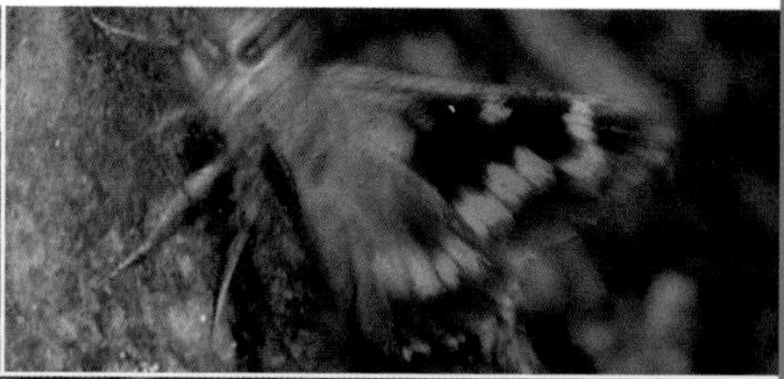

Huachuca Giant-Skipper *Agathymus evansi*

Utah Agave

LR-LU
Sept-Nov
mostly late Sept-Oct

sparse pinyon-juniper woods on rocky limestone slopes

mudpuddles

very similar to Arizona Giant-Skipper; but then again, what agave-feeding giant-skipper isn't?

host
plant

habitat

spots are buffy, not white
fringe weakly checked

Mojave Giant-Skipper *Agathymus alliae*

Schott's Century Plant

LU-LC
Oct

dry, rocky slopes covered with Schott's Century Plant

the host plant is also known as shindaggers, and you'll probably cut your ankles on them, trying to see this oxymoronic relatively shrimpy giant-skipper

small

habitat specific

habitat w/
host plant

Poling's Giant-Skipper *Agathymus polingi*

Desert Agave

U
Sept-Oct

desert hillsides and canyons

unlike other giant-skippers, usually lands with its head up

the only agave-feeding giant-skipper in its range

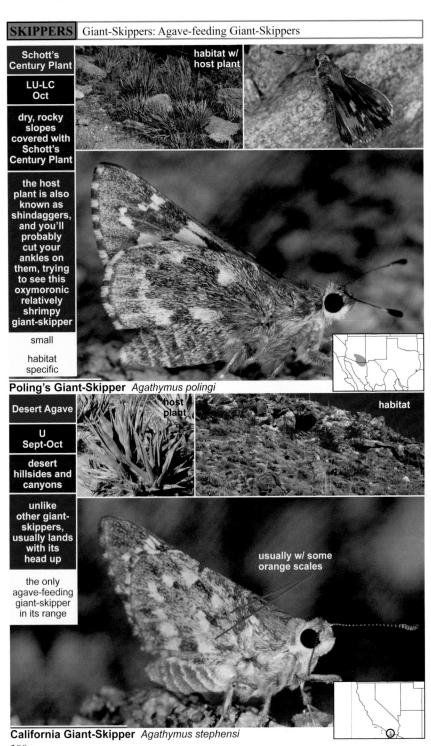

host
plant

habitat

usually w/ some
orange scales

California Giant-Skipper *Agathymus stephensi*

Lechuguilla

R-U
Sept-Nov
mostly Oct

rocky desert with extensive stands of Lechuguilla

usually with a silvery reflection

habitat w/
host plant

Mary's Giant-Skipper *Agathymus mariae*

Lechuguilla

LR
Aug-Nov
mostly Sept-Oct

rocky desert with extensive stands of Lechuguilla

some treat A. estellae as a separate species and place these populations with it

sharply pointed spot
museum
specimens
sharply
pointed
spots

Coahuila Giant-Skipper *Agathymus remingtoni*

tuberoses (*Manfreda*)

LR
Apr-May, Sept

open thorn-scrub

possibly extirpated in U.S., last reliably reported in the U.S. in 1980

host plant
host
plant

white stitching
museum
specimens
dark ground color

Manfreda Giant-Skipper *Stallingsia maculosa*

Waimea pipturus

U
all year

areas with native vegetation

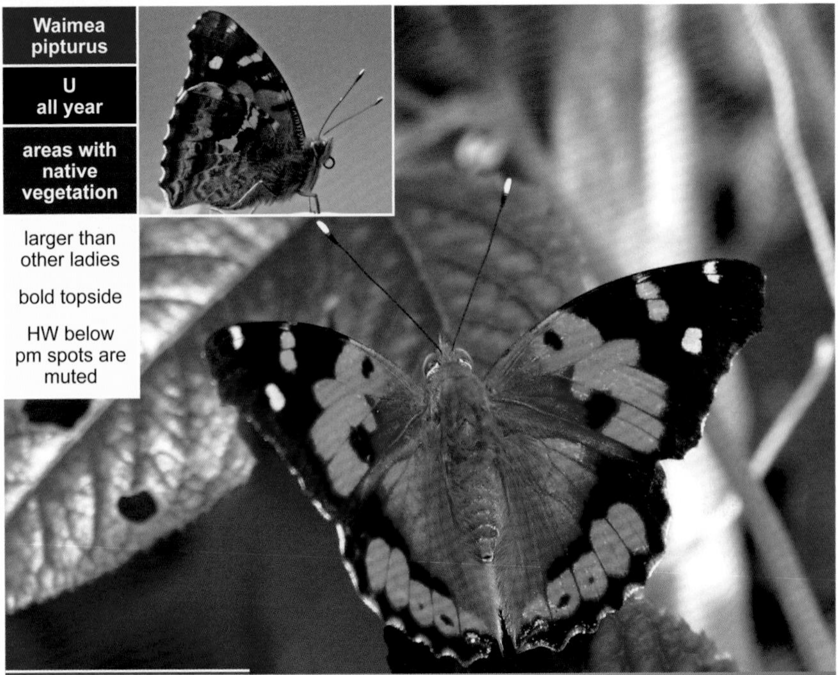

larger than other ladies

bold topside

HW below pm spots are muted

Kamehameha Lady *Vanessa tamenamea*

Koa

U
all year

areas with native vegetation

16 non-native species are now established in Hawaii: Cabbage White, Large Orange Sulphur, Sleepy Orange, Lantana Scrub-Hairstreak, Red-spotted Hairstreak, Western Pygmy-Blue, Gulf Fritillary, Painted lady, American Lady, Red Admiral, Monarch, and Fiery Skipper, plus species on page 401.

Hawaiian Blue *Vaga blackburni*

HAWAII — Non-native Species Now Established on the Hawaiian Islands

citrus

U-C
all year

gardens

the only swallowtail in Hawaii

Chinese Swallowtail *Papilio xuthus*

legumes

LC
all year

grassy areas

a recent arrival, first seen in 2008

Lesser Grass-Blue *Zizina otis*

legumes

C
all year

widespread

Pea Blue *Lampides boeticus*

bananas

U
all year

gardens

crepuscular

Banana Skipper *Erionota thrax*

Photo Credits

Photos are designated by page and photo number. 20:4,5 Jane Ruffin means that on page 20, the fourth photo (main photo of a Pink-spotted Swallowtail) and the fifth photo (inset photo of the underside of a Pink-spotted Swallowtail) were taken by Jane Ruffin. Photos are numbered from top panel to bottom panel, with the main (large photo) in each panel coming first and then the insets (smaller photos with white borders) in each panel numbered clockwise, starting at the top left of the panel. If there are two or three main photos in a panel, they are numbered clockwise, starting at the top left of the panel. For example, on page 62, the photo of a Southen Dogface caterpillar is photo 60:5 while the main photo of a Cal. Dogface is photo 60:6 and the photo of a Cal. Dogface in flight is photo 60:8; All photographs, even small "detail" insets, count in the photo numbering scheme. All photographs not attributed to a photographer listed below were taken by Jeffrey Glassberg.

16:1 **Anaxibia**; 19:4 **Julio Álvarez**; 20:4,5 **Jane Ruffin**; 21:4 **Gill Carter**; 21:6 **Alana Edwards**; 21:7 **Robert Grosek**; 23:1,2 **Rick Ballard**; 25:4 **Rob Santry**; 25:5 **Nicky Davis**; 26:3 **Timothy Kadlecek**; 30:1 **Rob Santry**; 30:4 **Gill Carter**; 33:1 **Holly Salvato**; 33:2 **Dean Jue**; 33:4,5 **Paula Cannon**; 33:6: **Cape Verde Wave**; 34:3 **Gil Quintanilla**; 36:2 **Rob Santry**; 40:8 **Kaldari**; 41:3 **Dennis Holmes**; 41:7 **Bob Janules**; 41:8 **Mike Reese**; 43:4 **Gil Quintanilla**; 44:5 **David J. Powell**; 48:1,2 **Kenelm W. Philip**; 48:4 **Aaron Lang**; 53:3 **Bob Janules**; 54:4,5 **Dennis Holmes**; 55:3 **Brett Badeaux**; 56:3 **Bob Janules**; 59:3 **Matt Rowlings**; 60:5-12 **Canadian National Collection:J. Gill**; 61:5 **Kenelm W. Philip**; 62:6,8 **Dennis Holmes**; 63:7 **Berry Nall**; 66:4 **Berry Nall**; 66:5 **Stephen Baig**; 66:6 **E.J. Haas**; 69:3 **Berry Nall**; 69:6 **Dan Jones**; 70:8 **Berry Nall**; 71:4 **Martin Reid**; 75:6 **Brett Badeaux**; 78:1 **Bart Jones**; 78:4 **Timothy Kadlecek**; 80:1 **Mike Reese**; 81:8 **Bob Janules**; 84:3 **Cory Maylett**; 88:4 **Kathy Malone**; 94:5 **Pat Sutton**; 94:6 **Jeffrey S. Pippen**; 95:2 **Ken Kertell**; 97:1 **Robert Pemberton**; 97:2 **Berry Nall**; 98:4,5 **Dennis Holmes**; 99:1 **Christian Nunes**; 99:3 **David G. James**; 99:4 **Ken Kertell**; 101:1,3 **Kathy Malone**; 102:6 **Ken Wilson**; 107:7 **Mary Ann Friedman**; 109:1 **Rob Santry**; 109:2 **James Miskelly**; 109:7 **Stan Shebs**; 111:2, 3 **Nick Grishin**; 111:4 **Mike Rickard**; 112:7 **Holly Salvato**; 119:2 **Bob Beatson**; 121:9 **Veronica Prida**; 125:8 **Jane Ruffin**; 126:7 **Stan Shebs**; 129:7 **Meneerke Bloem**; 130:4 **Stan Shebs**; 132:5 **Jane Shelby Richardson**; 132:7 **USFS**; 132:8 **Dennis Holmes**; 134:4 **Kathy Malone**; 134:6 **Tom Murray**; 134:7 **Abbey Paulson**; 135:6,9 **Alice Abela**; 139:3 **Mike Reese**; 143:6 **Stan Shebs**; 145:7 **Martin Reid**; 147:1 **Ken Wilson**; 148:7 **Thomas D. Lewis**; 157:1 **Arlene Ripley**; 157:3 **David J. Powell**; 162:1,3 **Fred Habegger**; 162:4 **Dave Hanson**; 162:6 **Eric Valentine**; 163:3 **Thomas D. Lewis**; 163:4 **Jim Thayer**; 170:6,7 **Steve Cary**; 173:5 **Rob Santry**; 175:2 **Jack Levy**; 176:5 **Lucie Bruce**; 176:7 **Ken Kertell**; 176:8 **Rob Santry**; 179:6,7 **Ken Hickman**; 182:5 **Rob Santry**; 183:1,3 **Mike Reese**; 183:2 **Jim Springer**; 187:3 **David Pavlik**; 187:5 **David Pavlik**; 188:1 **Thomas J. Simonsen**; 188:2 **Martin Reid**; 188:4 **David Pavlik**; 189:1 **Kenelm W. Philip**; 189:2 **Kim Hanson**; 189:3 **J.T. Troubridge**; 189:4,5 **Sharon Wander**; 189:6 **Jerry Friedman**; 190:3 **Stan Shebs**; 192:7 **Dave Hanson**; 193:4,5 **Linda Cooper**; 214:1,2 **Rob Santry**; 215:5,6 **Bart Jones**; 222: 2,5 **Erik Nielsen**; 230:7 **Laura Gooch**; 231:7 **Paula Cannon**; 231:8 **Mark Salvato**; 238:4 **John Young**; 243:5 **Jan Dauphin**; 243:8 **Martin Reid**; 245:1,2 **Paula Cannon**; 247:7 **Gill Carter**; 248:5,8 **Berry Nall**; 249:2 **Terry Fuller**; 255:1 **Bart Jones**; 255:4 **Jeff Trahan**; 256:6 **Henry Kindervatter**; 259:5 **Vitaly Charny**; 261:1 **Ray Bruun**; 261:4 **Alida Madero Farias**; 261:5 **Ro Wauer**; 262:5 **Kathy Malone**; 266:1 **Tom Murray**; 267:3 **Urs Geiser**; 268:5 **Aaron Lang**; 269:1 **Dave Hanson**; 272:4 **Bill Bouton**; 274:4 **Rob Santry**; 274:5 **Larry de March**; 276:4 **Jeff Ingraham**; 276:5,6 **Kenelm W. Philip**; 277:7,8 **Dave Hanson**; 281:6 **Jason Hollinger**; 283:4 **Dave Hanson**; 284:6 **Dave Hanson**; 287:4 **John Dicus**; 287:6 **Jane Ruffin**; 287:7 **Ken Kertell**; 293:5,6 **Andrew Neild**; 299:4 **Bill Berthet**; 301:2 **Ken Kertell**; 303:3 **USGS**; 303:4 **Cat Traylor**; 309:2,3 **Cat Traylor**; 316:4 **David J. Powell**; 316:5,6 **Ken Kertell**; 328:1 **Ken Wilson**; 329:4 **David J. Powell**; 331:2 **Ken Kertell**; 331:4 **Bill Bouton**; 337:4 **Matt Brown**; 337:6 **Stan Shebs**; 339:10,11 **Dave Hanson**; 340:4 **Linda Cooper**; 343:13 **Rob Gill**; 349:4,7 **Jack Levy**; 351:3 **Jim Thayer**; 351:7,10 **Christian Nunes**; 352:3 **Mike Reese**; 353:1,2 **Linda Cooper**; 353:4 **Parker Backstrom**; 358:5 **Bart Jones**; 358:7 **Matt Brown**; 367:1 **Dave McElveen**; 369:5 **Ray Bruun**; 371:5 **Jeff Trahan**; 373:7 **Rick Cech**; 376:5 **Linda Cooper**; 376:7 **Bill Berthet**; 386:4 **Ken Kertell**; 387:1 **Bart Jones**; 389:4,5 **Jane Ruffin**; 391:1 **Jim Springer**; 392:3 **Bill Bouton**; 393:6 **Jan Dauphin**; 394:4; **Bill Berthet**; 394:5 **Mary Ann Friedman**; 395:4,5 **Greg Lasley**; 396:1 **David J. Powell**; 397:2 **Stan Shebs**; 397:5 **USDA-NRCS**; 398:5 **Noah Elhardt**; 400:1,2,3 **Jim Snyder**; 401:3,4,7 **Jim Snyder**

Selected Bibliography

The following short bibliography mainly includes selected fairly recent publications (since 2000) whose authors take a modern approach to butterflying.

Allen, T.J., J. P. Brock and J. Glassberg. 2005. Caterpillars in the Field and Garden: A Field Guide. Oxford University Press.

Belth, J.E. Butterflies of Indiana, a field guide. 2013. Indiana University Press.

Butterflies of Toronto Working Group. 2011. Butterflies of Toronto. City of Toronto.

Cary, S.J. 2009. Butterfly Landscapes of New Mexico. New Mexico Magazine.

Cech, R and G. Tudor. 2005. Butterflies of the East Coast. Princeton University Press.

Dole, J.M., W. Gerard and J.M. Nelson. Butterflies of Oklahoma, Kansas and North Texas. University of Oklahoma Press.

Glassberg, J. 2001. Butterflies through Binoculars: The West. Oxford University Press.

Glassberg, J. 2007. A Swift Guide to the Butterflies of Mexico and Central America. Sunstreak.

Glassberg, J. 2011. Butterflies of North America. Sterling.

Glassberg, J. M.C. Minno and J.V. Calhoun. 2000. Butterflies through Binoculars: Florida. Oxford University Press.

Heath. F. 2004. An Introduction to Southern California Butterflies. Mountain Press Publishing Co.

James, D.G. and D. Nunnallee. 2011. Life Histories of Cascadia Butterflies. Oregon State University Press.

Ogard, P.H. 2010. Butterflies of Alabama. University of Alabama Press.

Pyle, R.M. 2002. The Butterflies of Cascadia. Seattle Audubon Society.

Shapiro, A. and Manolis, T.D. 2007. A Field Guide to Butterflies of the San Francisco Bay and Sacramento Valley Regions. University of California Press.

Stewart, B., P. Brodkin and H. Brodkin. 2001. Butterflies of Arizona. West Coast Lady Press.

Sutton, P. and C. Sutton. 1999. How to Spot a Butterfly. Houghton-Mifflin

Venable, R. 2014. Butterflies of Tennessee. Maywood Press.

Wauer, R. 2004 Butterflies of the Lower Rio Grande Valley. Johnson Books.

Wauer, R. 2006. Finding Butterflies in Texas. Johnson Books.

Selected Websites

North American Butterfly Association (and its more than 20 chapters): www.naba.org. The many pages of this website offer information about recent sightings throughout the country, information about butterfly gardening throughout the country, latest news from the National Butterfly Center, from NABA chapters and from the NABA Butterfly Count Program, including the 4th of July Counts. Many of the chapters have detailed information about local butterflies, including a selection of localities for butterflying.

Massachusetts: www.butterfliesofmassachusetts.net. Presents extensive and detailed information about Massachusetts butterflies.

North Carolina: http://149.168.1.196/nbnc/. Presents extensive and detailed information about North Carolina butterflies.

Sunstreak Tours: www.sunstreaktours.com. Offering butterflying tours both in the United States and abroad since 1993.

WeButterfly: www.webutterfly.org. NABA's database of butterfly sightings + maps, photos and species information. Allows anyone to enter their own sightings and photos into the database.

Wisconsin: http://wisconsinbutterflies.org/. Presents extensive and detailed informaion about Wisconsin butterflies.

Caterpillar Foodplant Index

Caterpillar Foodplant Index, Continued

Butterfly Species Index

Visual Index

pg 16-17 | pg 18 | pg 19 | pg 22-25 | pg 26-27

pg 28-30 | pg 31 | pg 32-35 | pg 36-37 | pg 38-39

pg 40-41 | pg 42-45 | pg 46-49 | pg 49-51 | pg 52-61

pg 62 | pg 64-67 | pg 68-73 | pg 74-83 | pg 76-83

pg 85 | pg 86 | pg 87 | pg 88-91 | pg 92-93

pg 94-95 | pg 96-101 | pg 102-103 | pg 104-105 | pg 106-109

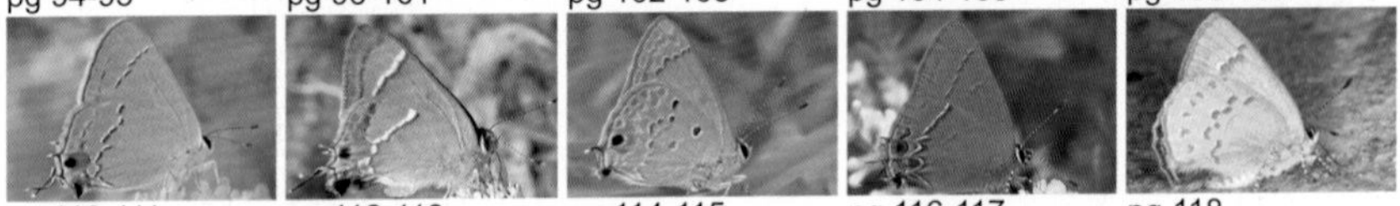

pg 110-111 | pg 112-113 | pg 114-115 | pg 116-117 | pg 118

pg 119 | pg 122 | pg 123 | pg 124-125 | pg 126

pg 127 | pg 128-129 | pg 130-135 | pg 136-137 | pg 138-143

pg 140-145 | pg 146 | pg 147 | pg 148-151 | pg 154-157

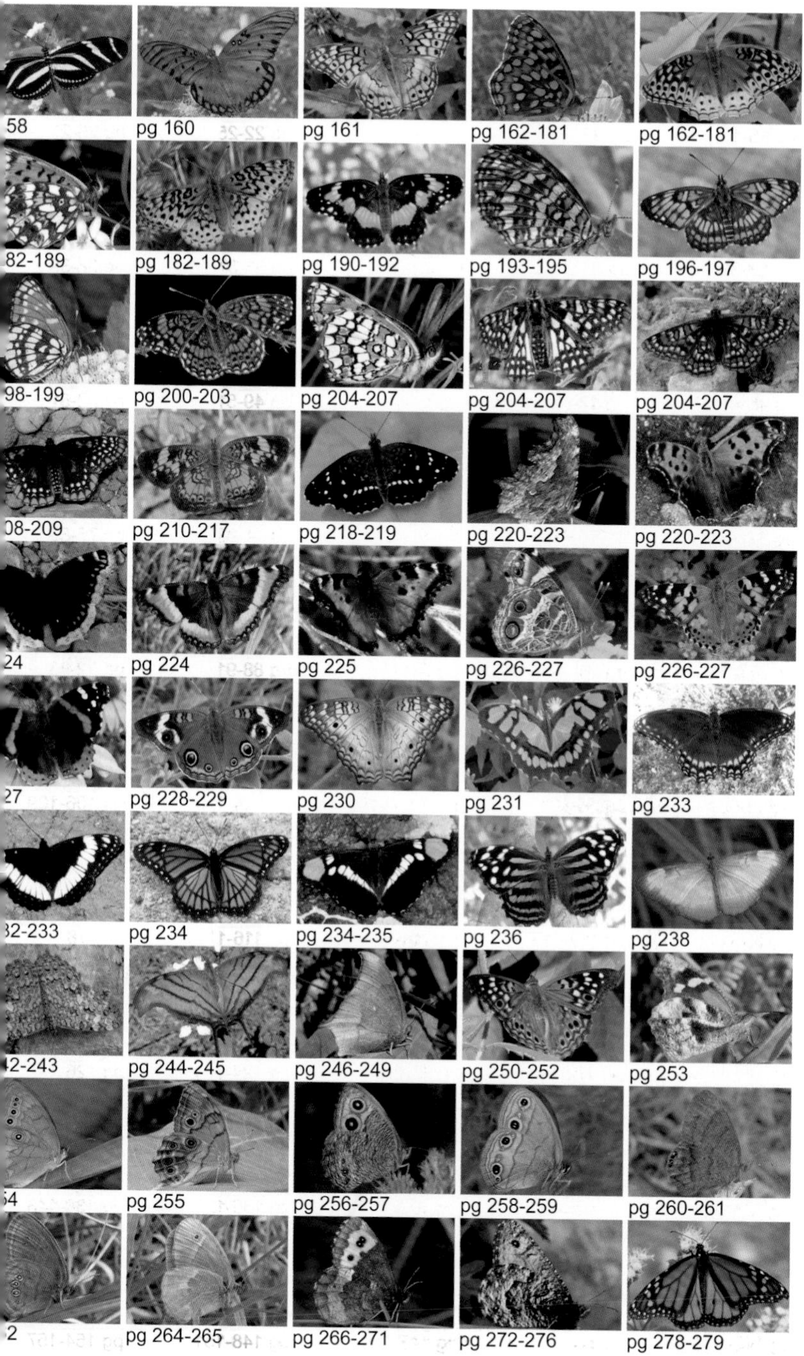
58 pg 160 pg 161 pg 162-181 pg 162-181
82-189 pg 182-189 pg 190-192 pg 193-195 pg 196-197
98-199 pg 200-203 pg 204-207 pg 204-207 pg 204-207
08-209 pg 210-217 pg 218-219 pg 220-223 pg 220-223
24 pg 224 pg 225 pg 226-227 pg 226-227
27 pg 228-229 pg 230 pg 231 pg 233
32-233 pg 234 pg 234-235 pg 236 pg 238
42-243 pg 244-245 pg 246-249 pg 250-252 pg 253
54 pg 255 pg 256-257 pg 258-259 pg 260-261
2 pg 264-265 pg 266-271 pg 272-276 pg 278-279

Visual Index

pg 280-281 pg 282-283 pg 284 pg 285 pg 286

pg 288-289 pg 290-291 pg 292-293 pg 294-295 pg 296-297

pg 298-301 pg 302-303 pg 306-309 pg 310-311 pg 312-321

pg 322-325 pg 326-329 pg 330 pg 331 pg 332-333

pg 332-333 pg 334-337 pg 338-339 pg 340-341 pg 342-343

pg 344-345 pg 344-354 pg 351, 358-359 pg 352-353 pg 354-355

pg 356 pg 356-357 pg 360 pg 361-362 pg 364-365

pg 366-367 pg 367 pg 368-369 pg 368-369 pg 370

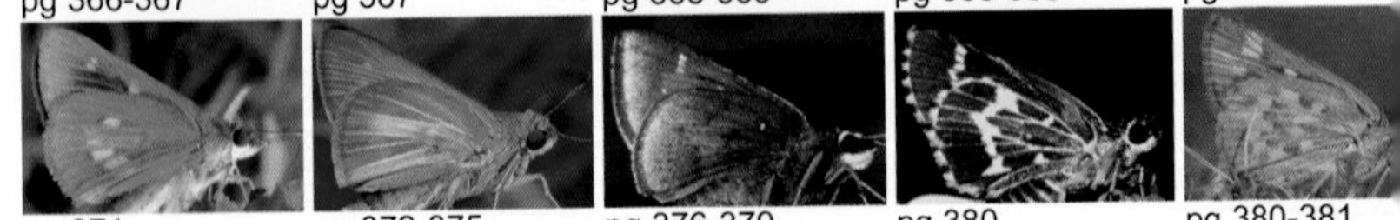

pg 371 pg 372-375 pg 376-379 pg 380 pg 380-381

pg 382-383 pg 384-388 pg 392-393 pg 394-395 pg 397-399